Literary Rebels

Literary Rebels

A History of Creative Writers in Anglo-American Universities

LISE JAILLANT

Great Clarendon Street, Oxford, OX2 6DP,
United Kingdom

Oxford University Press is a department of the University of Oxford.
It furthers the University's objective of excellence in research, scholarship,
and education by publishing worldwide. Oxford is a registered trade mark of
Oxford University Press in the UK and in certain other countries

© Lise Jaillant 2022

The moral rights of the author have been asserted

Impression: 1

All rights reserved. No part of this publication may be reproduced, stored in
a retrieval system, or transmitted, in any form or by any means, without the
prior permission in writing of Oxford University Press, or as expressly permitted
by law, by licence or under terms agreed with the appropriate reprographics
rights organization. Enquiries concerning reproduction outside the scope of the
above should be sent to the Rights Department, Oxford University Press, at the
address above

You must not circulate this work in any other form
and you must impose this same condition on any acquirer

Published in the United States of America by Oxford University Press
198 Madison Avenue, New York, NY 10016, United States of America

British Library Cataloguing in Publication Data

Data available

Library of Congress Control Number: 2021951803

ISBN 978–0–19–285530–5

DOI: 10.1093/oso/9780192855305.001.0001

Printed and bound by
CPI Group (UK) Ltd, Croydon, CR0 4YY

Links to third party websites are provided by Oxford in good faith and
for information only. Oxford disclaims any responsibility for the materials
contained in any third party website referenced in this work.

For my husband, Marc-Aurèle

Preface and Acknowledgements

I once had hopes of becoming a published novelist. Being French, I had absolutely no idea that there was such a thing as 'creative writing programmes'. If someone had tried to explain the term to me, I would probably have dismissed it as too *American*—like getting a Cordon Bleu degree to show that you can cook, instead of doing an apprenticeship at a Michelin-starred restaurant. It is only in my early twenties, when I moved from Paris to London, that I encountered the discipline for the first time. Even then, 'creative writing' seemed a foreign concept: I was writing in French and joining an English workshop would have been useless. In less than one year, I had finished a novel. Literary agents are rare in France, and usually deal with bestselling writers. So, I mailed my manuscript to publishers, spending a fortune on stamps. What followed was predictable: I received dozens of letters of rejection.

I then opened a blog in 2005, which—in the early days of Web 2.0—became a popular community for would-be writers. I asked famous and emerging authors for interviews and posted the videos online. In all cases, it seemed, these writers had known their publishers personally before getting published or had obtained an introduction. Their manuscript had been read, while mine (I was convinced) had simply been returned without being opened. I then decided to test my hypothesis that publishers did not read manuscripts by unknown writers. I copied Michel Houellebecq's novel *Les Particules Elémentaires* (translated in English as *Atomized*), I changed the names of the main characters, and sent the manuscript to Gallimard and other publishers under a penname. A couple of weeks later, I received the now familiar form rejection letters.

If publishers do not read unrecommended manuscripts, why do they still present themselves as discoverers of new talents? As Pierre Bourdieu pointed out:

> The 'discoverer' never discovers anything that is not already discovered, at least by a few—painters, already known to a small number of painters or connoisseurs, authors, 'introduced' by other authors (it is well-known, for example, that the manuscripts that will be published hardly ever arrive directly, but almost always through recognised go-betweens.)
>
> (*The Field of Cultural Production* 77–8)

French publishers continue to promote the myth of the first-novel-discovered-in-the-slush-pile for two main reasons. First, it allows them to build relationships with customers. Before sending their manuscripts, aspiring authors are asked to familiarize themselves with the editorial line of the publisher. Buying a few books is the best way to know what the imprint is looking for. Second, the myth of the publisher-discoverer-of-new-talents supports the idea that only exceptional literary texts are published. The text itself is supposedly the only criteria worth considering when making a publishing decision. The fact that the publisher knew the writer before, or belonged to the same networks, is rarely mentioned.

My experience of the French literary field had convinced me that networking was key. Being based in London, it was difficult for me to go to literary parties and other events that are central to success in Paris. Like any writer based outside the French capital, I was at a geographical disadvantage. Moving back to France was not an option, so I decided to enrol in a Master's degree in creative writing at a London university. The experience was not a success. Eric Bennett writes that at the University of Iowa, he was 'disappointed by the reduced form of intellectual engagement' ('How Iowa Flattened Literature'). This was also my experience in London. Retrospectively, I was asking too much. Having invested all my savings, I expected an academically rigorous training in writing, and an introduction to writers, literary agents, and publishers. No degree can deliver such expectations. After only one semester, I quit the programme, and transferred to an MA in Modern and Contemporary Literature. It was cheaper, and I had more contact time with my instructors. Crucially, I was learning new things, an intellectual development that had seemed totally absent in the creative writing programme.

Is creative writing a scam designed to lure naïve would-be writers? In the decade that followed my MA, I have met many writers who are dedicated to both the Critical and the Creative. The best programmes encourage the development of craft and offer intellectual stimulation. They also provide an introduction to literary agents and publishers through readings and events. This is particularly valuable for writers who lack the social capital essential to literary success. But too often, creative writing is dissociated from literary scholarship. At the University of British Columbia in Vancouver, where I did my PhD, writers and scholars occupy different locations on the large campus. As a newly minted literary scholar, I never saw the creative writers: they never came to our events, and we never went to theirs. I became interested in the history that explains such divisions, which are very frequent in North America.

In Britain, creative writers are generally located within English departments, but tensions with scholars are frequent. In 2016, the UK Quality Assurance Agency for Higher Education (QAA) released a Subject Benchmark Statement for Creative Writing, to define what is 'involved in the design, delivery and review of programmes of study in Creative Writing or related subjects' (1). Whereas creative writing had previously been grouped together with English, it was now treated as a separate discipline with distinct characteristics. Once again, the *separateness* of creative writing was proclaimed.

Literary Rebels: A History of Creative Writers in Anglo-American Universities is the outcome of five years of research—including several months working in a wide range of archives on both sides of the Atlantic. This research has been funded by several grants:

- British Academy/Leverhulme Grant (2017–18). For archival work in the USA (Archives of Ian McEwan and Kazuo Ishiguro at the Harry Ransom Center in Texas; Wallace Stegner archives at Stanford University and the University of Utah).
- Modernist Studies Association Research Travel Grant (2017). For archival work in the Ezra Pound papers at Yale Beinecke Library.
- Loughborough University Start-up Grant (2016). For archival work at the University of Iowa.
- Everett Helm Visiting Fellowship (2014). For archival work in the Malcolm Bradbury archive at the Lilly Library, Indiana University.
- University of East Anglia, Malcolm Bradbury Memorial Trust Fund (2014). To do archival work (Indiana) and conduct oral history interviews.
- Rockefeller Archive Center Grant (2013). For archival work at the RAC in Sleepy Hollow, NY.

I also received a British Academy Rising Star Engagement Award for my project 'After the Digital Revolution: Bringing together archivists and scholars to preserve born-digital records and produce new knowledge'.

Permissions to reproduce pictures have been obtained from: Special Collections, at the J. Willard Marriott Library, University of Utah; Princeton Alumni Weekly; Lilly Library, Indiana University, Bloomington, Indiana; *The Sunday Times*/News Licensing; *Punch*/TopFoto; *Listener*/Immediate Media Co.; Antoine Chereau.

Earlier versions of Chapter 2 and Chapter 6 were published as articles: Jaillant, Lise. '"I'm Afraid I've Got Involved With a Nut": New Faulkner Letters'. *Southern Literary Journal*, vol. 47, no. 1, 2014, pp. 98–114, doi:10.1353/slj.2014.0019. © 2015 by The Southern Literary Journal and the University of North Carolina at Chapel Hill Department of American Studies. Jaillant, Lise. 'Myth Maker: Malcolm Bradbury and the Creation of Creative Writing at UEA'. *New Writing*, vol. 13, no. 3, 2016, pp. 350–67, doi:10.1080/14790726.2016.1192196. © 2016 Informa UK Limited, trading as Taylor & Francis Group.

I am grateful to these institutions and individuals for making this project possible, and to the reviewers who have given me detailed feedback on earlier versions of this book. Some people are born to be writers, the myth goes. If that's the case, I was born to be an academic writer. Thanks very much to all those who have helped me find my way.

Contents

List of Figures — xi
List of Abbreviations — xii

Introduction: Literary Rebels: A History of Creative Writers in Anglo-American Universities — 1

I. USA

1. Think Global, Act Local: Paul Engle and the Modernist Roots of Creative Writing at the University of Iowa — 21

2. 'I'm afraid I've got involved with a nut': William Faulkner, Random House and the Post-war Generation of Aspiring Writers — 41

3. Healing the Breach between Writers and Scholars? Wallace Stegner and the Diffusion of the Creative Writing Gospel — 60

4. Fighting Organization Man: The Rockefeller Foundation and the Re-discovery of the Individual Creative Writer — 84

5. Fame, Fortune, and Freedom: The Rise and Fall of the Famous Writers School — 105

II. UK

6. Myth Maker: Malcolm Bradbury and the Creation of Creative Writing at UEA — 129

7. Lorry-Driver Poets and Student Radicals: Inventing the 'Writer-in-Residence' in Britain — 151

8. Kazuo Ishiguro: 'The First Product of a Creative Writing Course to Win the Nobel' — 175

9. Beyond Academia: From Arvon to the Faber Academy — 197

Epilogue: The Future of Creative Writing Programmes in Continental Europe — 216

Conclusion: Rebel Forever? How to Be a Writer in the
Program Era   228

Afterword by Mark McGurl: Paradoxes of Institutional
Belonging   246

Works Cited   248
Index   262

List of Figures

3.1. Wallace Stegner, undated. Special Collections, J. Willard Marriott Library, The University of Utah. 61
3.2. Edith Mirrielees (right) and Mrs Untermeyer at Bread Loaf Writers' Conference, 1940. 68
3.3. Gender, Stanford Writing Fellows, 1947–48 to 1965–66. 76
4.1. Richard P. Blackmur in the 1940s. 87
5.1. Famous Writers School Tuition Fees and Enrolment, 1961–70. 114
6.1. Graph displayed on Google Books Ngram Viewer, for the phrases 'Malcolm Bradbury, Ian McEwan, Kazuo Ishiguro, David Lodge, Angus Wilson', between 1950 and 2015 from the corpus 'English'. 140
6.2. Kazuo Ishiguro, Interview by Malcolm Bradbury, ICA, London, 17 Mar. 1982, Poster. 145
6.3. Graph representing 'The University of East Anglia mafia' and other literary groups. 148
7.1. E. S. Turner, 'Writers in Residence', *Punch*, 26 Nov. 1975. 173
8.1. Launch of the Faber Fiction Tour, *Listener*, 23 May 1985. 182
9.1. UK-based, non-academic providers of creative writing courses. 204
10.1. Cartoon, *The Happiness of Being an Author*. 224
11.1. How to become a published writer: Three models. 233

List of Abbreviations

AMWLT, UEA:	Archives of Modern Writing and Literary Translation, University of East Anglia, UK.
Benson—Stegner, Stanford:	Jackson J. Benson Research material about Wallace Stegner, M0952, Dept. of Special Collections, Stanford University Libraries, Stanford, Calif.
BP:	Blotner Papers, Brodsky collection, Rare Book Room, Kent Library, Southeast Missouri State University, Cape Girardeau, Missouri.
COX:	Papers of Brian Cox, John Rylands Library, University of Manchester, UK.
CQ:	*Critical Quarterly* archive, John Rylands Library, University of Manchester, UK.
FF:	Ford Foundation Archives, Rockefeller Archive Center, Sleepy Hollow, NY.
HRC:	Harry Ransom Center, U of Texas, Austin, Texas.
Indiana:	Lilly Library, Indiana University, Bloomington.
RF:	Rockefeller Foundation records, Rockefeller Archive Center, Sleepy Hollow, NY.
RH:	Random House records, Columbia Rare Book & Manuscript Library, New York City, NY.
UI:	The University of Iowa Libraries, Iowa City, Iowa.
V&A:	Victoria & Albert Museum, London.
WS CW, Stanford:	Wallace Stegner Creative Writing Program: correspondence and manuscripts M0558, Stanford.
WS misc., Stanford:	Wallace Stegner miscellaneous papers SC1188, Stanford.
WS, Utah:	Wallace Stegner papers Ms0676, U of Utah.

Introduction
Literary Rebels
A History of Creative Writers in Anglo-American Universities

How many times have you heard that creative writing programmes are factories that produce the same kind of writers, isolated from real life? Only by escaping academia can writers be completely free. Universities are profoundly conservative places, designed to favour a certain way of writing—preferably informed by literary theory. Those who reject the creative/critical discourse of academia are the true rebels, condemned to live (or survive) in a tough literary marketplace. Conformity is on the side of academia, the story goes, and rebellion is on the other side.

This book argues against the notion that creative writing programmes are driven by conformity. Instead, it shows that these programmes, in the United States and Britain, were founded and developed by literary outsiders who left an enduring mark on their discipline. To this day, creative writing occupies a marginal position in Anglo-American universities. The multiplication of new programmes, accompanied by rising student enrolments, has done nothing to change that positioning. As a discipline, creative writing thrives on opposition to the mainstream university, while benefiting from what the university has to offer. Historically, this opposition to scholars was so virulent that it often led to the separation of creative writing and literature departments. The Iowa Writers' Workshop, founded in the 1930s, separated from the English department three decades later—and it still occupies a different building on campus, with little communication between writers and scholars. This model of institutional division is less common in Britain, where the discipline formally emerged in the late 1960s/early 1970s. But even when creative writing is located within literature departments, relationships with scholars remain uneasy. Creative writers and scholars are not, and have never been, natural bedfellows. 'The position of writers within university walls has long been a theme for discussion and controversy,' Theodore Morrison wrote in 1940. 'The literary world outside has wondered at the inability or unwillingness of English departments to recognise writers as on any sort of equality with scholars' (1).

At first, I was simply surprised that people who love reading and books so often find themselves on opposite sides. I was also puzzled by the image of creative writing as a conformist discipline, as opposed to the non-academic world presented as a source of freedom and creativity. It was only later that I began to understand the historical roots of these contradictions: as a discipline, creative writing was shaped by men who saw themselves as outsiders. Their success in establishing the discipline—and the subsequent accusations of conformity—changed nothing to this positioning. Creative writing began on the margins of academia, and the discipline continues to be uncomfortable with the university system.

Paul Engle at Iowa, Wallace Stegner at Stanford, and Malcolm Bradbury at the University of East Anglia had one thing in common: they all came from lower middle-class backgrounds, and they were the first in their families to go to university. These men had struggled to get their foot in the literary door. They had no easy access to connections who could put them in contact with publishers and agents. They had learnt the hard way how to succeed in the literary world, and they were driven by a mission: teach the new generations not only *how to write*, but also *how to publish*. They saw themselves as self-made men and as cultural warriors—fighting for professionalism in a literary world dominated by amateurism and nepotism. Once they became successful, they did what many powerful men do: they used their new power to advance the interests of their disciples. Started as a reaction against nepotism, their creative writing programmes paradoxically became a source of nepotism.

Those who benefited from these new networks were overwhelmingly men. To give just one example, in 1947, Wallace Stegner arranged for Richard Scowcroft to help him run the programme at Stanford. Scowcroft had been his student at the University of Utah, before doing graduate work at Harvard (where Stegner also worked before joining Stanford). For the next two and a half decades, the two men alternated teaching the Stanford graduate writing workshop. In a male-dominated institution, women occupied a marginal place for several reasons.

First, married women had to spend parts of their days doing housework, leaving less time for writing. In 1962, the *Writer's Digest* described the routine of a married couple, both of them students at the Iowa Writers' Workshop (Polking 21). Mark and Antonia's day began at 10am when they checked the mail and had breakfast. From 11 to 1, Mark wrote while Antonia did housework. The rest of the day was spent going to classes and socializing with other Workshop students. Antonia later trained as a clinical psychologist, while her husband Mark Strand had a long and successful career as a poet (in the 1990s, he was appointed US poet laureate and won the Pulitzer Prize).

For single women, the problem was not lack of time but social isolation. In February 1973, Marcia Blumenthal wrote a letter to Jack Leggett, the director of the Iowa Writers' Workshop.¹ She had started feeling uncomfortable when another student, Louise, dropped out, and she remained the only woman in a group of men. It was like being 'a tag-along in a hunting pack or a stag party'. She received harsh criticism from the class on her stories, and when she tried to offer feedback to her fellow students, she was always 'up in arms' trying to defend women characters from being stereotyped. The military vocabulary used by Blumenthal reflects the war-like atmosphere of the Workshop, which led her to drop out. Other women managed to graduate, but were left with emotional bruises and an enduring sense of injustice. In the mid-1970s, Suzanne McConnell declared that 'male chauvinism' was a central characteristic of the Workshop. At the first party she went to, she was told that women could not write. The social organization of the Workshop centred around 'a group of young lions, usually married, a little older, who drank together, were friends with some of the writers, a la Hemingway style somehow, like good ol' Southern boys …'² For McConnell, the experience of social exclusion raised her feminist consciousness.

Being a woman in a male-dominated workshop sometimes led to unwanted attention. Suzanne McConnell recalled that, at a party, she started talking to a writer she admired very much. They were both rather drunk, and the man told her he hadn't liked the last story she'd given him. In a very sweet and seductive tone he added: 'That's all right Suzanne, you're a pretty girl, you'll get married anyway.'³ McConnell was shocked: she felt she was not being taken seriously as a writer, and thereafter, she struggled to believe in her own creative abilities.

Nepotism and the marginalization of women also defined the institution of creative writing in Britain. The 1980s saw the rise of a number of talented young men—including Ian McEwan and Kazuo Ishiguro, who had studied at the University of East Anglia (UEA) in Norwich, home of the successful Master's degree in Creative Writing, created by Malcolm Bradbury and Angus Wilson in 1970. Women associated with UEA received less attention. In 1984, Angela Carter told an interviewer: 'It's amazing what the Old Boys' club does for itself' (Gordon, *The Invention of Angela Carter* 321–2). Carter had spent several years teaching creative writing at UEA, but she did not feel that Bradbury's influence was helping her career.

By the early 1990s, Malcolm Bradbury had become one of the most powerful men in the UK literary world. 'In reviews and anthologies,' declared *The Sunday Times* in 1992, 'Bradbury has promoted several of his most promising pupils and friends, helping to turn them into literary stars' (Palmer). A graph gave more details about this UEA mafia, with Bradbury at the centre of a network that included

---

[1] Blumenthal to Leggett, 8 Feb. 1973, Series III, Box 9, John Leggett Papers, UI.
[2] McConnell to Stephen Wilbers, *c.* 1976, Iowa Writers' Workshop RG 06.12.08, Series XI, Box 2, UI.
[3] Ibid.

his ex-colleague David Lodge and his former students. In these pre-digital days, *The Sunday Times* had a circulation of around 1.4 million readers (double its current circulation).[4] That so many people found an interest in the cosy little world of literary fiction is surprising, but what is even more intriguing is the radical transformation of Bradbury's position—from literary outsider to mafia boss based in the unfashionable city of Norwich.

Thirty-six years before, the young Bradbury had published an article on 'The Rise of the Provincials' in *The Antioch Review*, a literary magazine based in Ohio. Bradbury, who had recently returned to England after studying at Indiana University, declared his admiration for F. R. Leavis and the Cambridge academics affiliated with the literary quarterly *Scrutiny*. He presented this admiration in class terms. Like himself, the *Scrutiny* people had been brought up in lower middle-class households, a group that had only recently obtained access to university education. 'To people of this background,' wrote Bradbury, 'dilettantism and the "amused superiority" of the sophisticated may very well be repugnant' ('The Rise of the Provincials' 471). Virginia Woolf, E. M. Forster, and others in the Bloomsbury group exemplified the amateurism that Bradbury despised. 'The people who tend to regard the practice of criticism, literature or literary scholarship as a dilettante activity' were on the decline—a trend that Bradbury welcomed ('The Rise of the Provincials' 476).

Bradbury became a literary insider precisely by touting his status as outsider. Think of the number of ex-losers who have positioned themselves on the margins of literary life, while enjoying the perks of success (a recent example would be Michel Houellebecq, who is regularly presented as a 'French literary rebel' [AFP]). But Bradbury was different in at least one respect: he created a structure, the first MA in creative writing in Britain that targeted would-be writers and gave them the keys to become literary winners. Fighting dilettantism with professionalism, he led the fight against the London-based literary establishment from his provincial base in Norwich.

By the early 1990s, it was obvious that Bradbury yielded an enormous amount of power in the literary world. But like Houellebecq and other literary rebels, Bradbury still refused to see himself as an insider. In 1995, he declared on the BBC Late Show: 'I've always believed that there was a mafia, and it wasn't me. It was Oxbridge, it was the London literary establishment and so on. I think we have a fair bit of crossfire from the London press and the Oxbridge press because of building this particular nest of singing birds in flat, sometimes wind-blown, dark East Anglia' (O'Toole). Paradoxically, Bradbury combined this anti-establishment positioning with a conservative worldview and a profound dislike for political extremes. As in the United States, creative writing courses in Britain became a success story—led from the geographical margins by a self-proclaimed outsider.

---

[4] Audit Bureau of Circulations (UK).

It is, of course, not a coincidence that creative writing appeared in the new universities that opened in the 1960s: the University of East Anglia but also Lancaster University. In October 1964, the first student intake of 296 undergraduates and thirty-six graduates arrived in Lancaster, a Northern working-class town where higher education was almost unheard of. Unusual academics with very liberal views headed the new university. The founding Vice Chancellor, Charles Carter, had been a conscientious objector during the Second World War, spending three months in Strangeways Prison, Manchester, for refusing to fight. Although Carter was politically on the Left, he found the social aspects of the counterculture threatening. The University's reputation relied on a thoughtful and reasonable academic community, Carter believed, and he was deeply concerned about the multiple scandals involving sex, alcohol, drugs, and water fights in the city centre with students wearing nothing but loincloths (Snape). Academic staff were amongst the 'radicals'—including David Craig, who founded the creative writing programme at Lancaster.

At first sight, Craig was the anti-Malcolm Bradbury. While the latter was politically conservative, Craig included himself amongst the most extreme activists. 'Call us left-wingers, socialists, free-thinkers, whatever,' he wrote in an essay on the history of protest at Lancaster. For Craig, creative writing was a radical tool with which to change an elitist university system. He described the discipline as 'the most democratic of all literary studies since it gives free rein to the talent and experience of students, both as makers of their own works and as critics of their fellows' ('History of Protest at Lancaster'). This emphasis on creative writing as a democratic discipline was shared by Bradbury. Both men wanted to reshape literary studies, a discipline that had traditionally privileged scholarship to the detriment of creativity. It is striking that creative writing at Lancaster—which began in 1969, at approximately the same time as UEA—had attracted so little attention. This is partly due to the difficulty in accessing primary records. The university does not hold an archive related to the Creative Writing programme or to David Craig. Archival records have a direct impact on scholarship, and archives are changing, following the digital revolution.

This book offers a new model of scholarship in paper and born-digital archives. Emails and other born-digital documents are essential primary documents for scholars who work on the contemporary period, and yet, most of these collections are closed due to data protection and technical issues (I was the first scholar to access Ian McEwan's emails at the Harry Ransom Center in Texas).[5] Access to born-digital collections is essential to produce new knowledge. In addition to archival work, I also conducted many oral history interviews in the United States and Britain. In 2014–15, I was based at the University of East Anglia, which gave me access to people associated with the first creative writing programme

---

[5] See Jaillant, 'From Letters to Emails' and 'After the Digital Revolution'.

(including McEwan, Victor Sage, and Jon Cook). These research methods shed light on the contradictions at the heart of creative writing, an academic discipline that had always been uneasy with academia.

0.1 The Rise of Creative Writing Programmes

When was the last time you heard good news about the Humanities? Departments are being closed, the job market is bleak, and the number of PhD students is falling. In this gloomy landscape, creative writing stands as the exception. The Iowa Writers' Workshop was founded in 1936 and by 1975, there were 79 US programmes conferring degrees in creative writing, including undergraduate degrees. This number had jumped to 1,808 in 2016. During the same period, the number of MA/MFA (Master of Arts/Master of Fine Arts) degrees was multiplied by more than eight, to reach 408.[6]

The rise of creative writing programmes has attracted a deluge of criticisms, mostly from journalists and writers convinced that academia has a deadening effect on creativity. Writers' workshops seemed particularly suspicious in a Cold War context that valued the individual over the group. In a 1975 article, the American writer Nelson Algren dismissed the entire enterprise. 'Creativity, by its own essence, is a solitary enterprise: one in which the individual … takes his own chances and wins or loses off by himself' ('On Kreativ Righting'). With its group rituals and institutional setting, the workshop had no place in the Land of the Free. It was both not American enough, and too American—deriving from a tradition of optimism that promised that anyone could achieve anything. In short, creative writing students were cut off from real life, a separation that had disastrous effects on their work.

Fourteen years later, Tom Wolfe pushed this argument further, arguing in *Harper's* magazine that creative writing programmes had nearly destroyed the novel ('Stalking the Billion-Footed Beast'). The insularity of the Ivory Tower had led writers to privilege form over content, turning inwards rather than outwards. He called for a new social novel that would reflect American life. Like Dickens and Zola, the contemporary novelist had to get out and write about the real world. Wolfe's article appealed particularly to disillusioned writers, many of whom had first-hand experience of creative writing programmes. In a 1991 article in the *Los Angeles Times*, Chris Altacruise (not his real name) criticized the stereotypical production of university creative writers. Protected from the market, these 'Stepford Writers' thought in the same way, behaved in the same way, and wrote in the same way.

---

[6] AWP Official Guide to Writing Programs 2016.

Within universities, the growth of creative writing programmes went almost unnoticed. Apart from Stephen Wilbers' *The Iowa Writers' Workshop* (1980) and D. G. Myers' *The Elephants Teach* (1996), the topic attracted little interest, perhaps because it was too embarrassing to analyse in detail. For the past three decades, student enrolments have been decreasing in 'traditional' literary classes and increasing in creative writing. Doctoral programmes have not been isolated from this trend. In 2017, there were 839 doctoral recipients in English and American Language and Literature—a 40 per cent drop compared to the peak in 1973.[7] This downward trend has continued, with only 766 PhDs in this field in 2020.[8] In the meantime, creative writing has continued to thrive. In 2016, fifty programmes conferred a PhD in creative writing—ten times more than in the 1970s.[9] Although the number of doctoral recipients remains modest, there is little doubt that the PhD in creative writing is here to stay. The Master of Fine Arts is no longer seen as the terminal degree for creative writers in academia. In an ultra-competitive job market, having an MFA *and* a PhD can make a difference.

It was not until the late 2000s that literary scholars started to analyse the boom in creative writing and its impact on post-war literature. The turning point was the release of Mark McGurl's *The Program Era* (2009). The book boldly argued that the rise of the creative writing programme stands as 'the most important event in postwar American literary history' (ix). Published by Harvard University Press and authored by a former *New York Times* staffer turned professor, *The Program Era* immediately grasped the attention of the critical establishment. Reviews by famous names—from Fredric Jameson to Louis Menand—appeared on both sides of the Atlantic. Yet, McGurl's call for a dispassionate analysis of the creative writing boom was often ignored. Instead, many articles revived the debate of whether the rise in university creative writing had been good or bad for literature. 'Get a Real Degree' was the title of Elif Batuman's piece in the *London Review of Books*. The same scepticism could be seen in *The New York Times*, with a review by Charles McGrath entitled 'The Ponzi Workshop'. Not everyone agreed with McGurl that it was time to bury the hatchet and accept that university creative writing was here to stay.

The buzz around McGurl's book led other academics to pay more attention to a largely neglected phenomenon. Unsurprisingly, *The Program Era* found an attentive audience at the University of Iowa, the birthplace of creative writing programmes. Loren Glass, a professor of English, published a series of articles on the institutionalization of the discipline. He also edited a collection of essays, *After the Program Era: The Past, Present, and Future of Creative Writing in the University*

---

[7] National Center for Science and Engineering Statistics. *Doctorate recipients by fine field of study, 2008–17*. See also: MLA Office of Research, *Report on the Survey of Earned Doctorates, 2013–14*, Dec. 2016.
[8] *Doctorate recipients by fine field of study, 2010-20.*
[9] AWP Official Guide to Writing Programs 2016.

(University of Iowa Press, 2017). The same imprint published Eric Bennett's *Workshops of Empire: Stegner, Engle, and American Creative Writing During the Cold War*. 'Did the CIA fund creative writing in America?' asked Bennett in a provocative article in the *Chronicle of Higher Education* ('How Iowa Flattened Literature'). The debate was no longer whether creative writing programmes were good or bad for universities, but whether the discipline had been funded by Cold War warriors to spread American ideology. The latest addition to this scholarship—David O. Dowling's *A Delicate Aggression* (2019)—focuses on well-known authors who have participated in the Iowa Writers' Workshop, such as Flannery O'Connor, Dylan Thomas, Kurt Vonnegut, Jane Smiley, Sandra Cisneros, T. C. Boyle, and Marilynne Robinson.

Looking from abroad, this scholarship seems strikingly US-centric. McGurl has called for a vertical development of the field—from the study of elite institutions at Iowa and Stanford, towards non-elite creative writing programmes. Likewise, Glass has focused on the American context, encouraging other scholars to pay more attention to poetry—for example through the figure of Yvor Winters, who taught for many years at Stanford. Within and outside academia, voices have denounced the workshop as a hostile place for women and people of colour and pushed for more diversity (Watkins; Díaz; Nguyen). But these concerns mostly relate to workshops in the United States. With only a few exceptions, creative writing programmes in the rest of the world have been largely ignored.

It is, of course, true that the discipline of creative writing emerged in the US well before it was adopted in other countries. It was not until the 1960s that newly founded universities in England began to experiment with creative writing in undergraduate programmes. As we have seen, the University of East Anglia started assessing creative writing at the MA level in 1970—the only student to choose this option was Ian McEwan. Australia waited longer to institutionalize the discipline. In the late 1980s, Michael Wilding set up the first creative writing course at the University of Sydney. In France, the rise of university creative writing is even more recent. Since 2012, four Master's programmes in 'création littéraire' have emerged—in Toulouse, Le Havre, and the Parisian region at the Universities of Paris 8 and Cergy-Pontoise (Houdart-Merot). In Asia, creative writing has also become part of the academic landscape, a phenomenon that has attracted increasing interest (see the work of Fan Dai and Richard Jean So, for example).

This book does not attempt to cover every country where the discipline has developed. Instead, it uses a transatlantic perspective, focusing on British creative writers in relation to their American counterparts. It comes at a moment of canonization of the first generation of British writers who studied creative writing in the 1970s and early 1980s (including Kazuo Ishiguro, who was awarded the Nobel Prize for Literature in 2017). According to the National Association of Writers in Education, there are over eighty-three Higher Education Institutions in the UK that offer undergraduate courses in creative writing. A similar number offer MA courses, with almost 200 to choose from. More than fifty universities offer Creative Writing PhDs.[10]

Half a century after the discipline appeared in British universities, we still know too little about this history. The works of Graeme Harper and Michelene Wandor shed light on certain aspects but are far from exhaustive. Existing scholarship has focused mostly on the United States, and it has also privileged a literary-sociological approach rather than a historical perspective. Major archives have been neglected, and new ones—such as the archives of Ian McEwan and Kazuo Ishiguro in Texas—have never been examined for the purpose of writing a cultural history of creative writers on both sides of the Atlantic.

My approach is influenced by book history 'from below'. Rather than a macrohistory of creative writing programmes, this monograph seeks to recover the voices of writers associated with these programmes: those who became famous, but also the more obscure ones. The first category included a majority of men (hence my focus on Wallace Stegner, Ian McEwan, Kazuo Ishiguro, and others), although there were a few exceptions (for example, Flannery O'Connor, discussed in Chapters 2 and 4). Women writers were less likely to study creative writing at university, but they enthusiastically enrolled in courses outside academia (such as the Famous Writers School, discussed in Chapter 5). At the annual conference of the Society for the History of Authorship, Reading, and Publishing in 2010, Jonathan Rose asked the audience to think of an important aspect of book history that might still be unexplored: when we are doing 'book history from below', what are we missing? In response to Rose's question, my own suggestion is to start paying more attention to would-be writers, including those who failed to get into print for lack of connections and (sometimes) talent. At Iowa, Paul Engle repeated over and over again that his mission was twofold: find promising writers and get funding to allow them to join the programme. If these writers worked hard enough and had the toughness necessary to endure a speculative career, their future was assured. Transforming would-be writers into published authors, that was Engle's mission. As a self-proclaimed outsider in Iowa, he saw himself as defender of the underdogs who, like himself, did not come from well-connected families. These writers needed all the help they could get, and the programme was there to serve them.

At first sight, a 'book history from below' approach seems at odds with my focus on elite creative writing programmes at Iowa, Stanford, and the University of East Anglia. But no matter their success, the founders of these programmes continued to present themselves as outsiders, far from the traditional literary centres. This position on the margins was at the core of their own identity, and of their programme's image. In turn, these programmes (that of Iowa, in particular) have shaped a model that has been extremely influential at the international level. As a

---

[10] 'Writing Courses', *National Association of Writers in Education*, https://www.nawe.co.uk/writing-in-education/writing-at-university/writing-courses.html. Accessed 30 Apr. 2021.

discipline, creative writing continues to see itself as different from traditional academic pursuits—hence the still-unresolved debates about its institutional location: does it fit in Literature Departments? In Arts Schools? Or should it be on its own?

To understand the oddity of this situation, consider the discipline of music in academia. Music practitioners do not spend time agonizing over their place in the university system: they belong in music departments. They do not see themselves in opposition to theorists of music. Take the example of the Faculty of Music at the University of Cambridge. It hosts the Cambridge Centre for Musical Performance Studies, which supports the work of a performance community and provides a platform for practice-based research into musical performance. Students can use period instruments and even a Javanese Gamelan (a traditional large percussion ensemble consisting of a large number of bronze gongs, metal xylophones, drums, a zither, and a flute.) If you think that Cambridge creative writers are in the same situation as music practitioners, think again. For all the talk about creative writing as practice-based research, the discipline is not located within the Faculty of English. The Centre for Creative Writing is based within the Institute of Continuing Education, located at Madingley Hall, just outside Cambridge. At the University of Oxford, creative writing occupies a similar institutional location, within Continuing Education and separate from the Faculty of English. Far from being a mainstream academic discipline, creative writing remains on the fringe of the university system.

0.2 Creative Writers versus Literary Scholars

Anyone who has spent time in a literature department knows that creative writers and literary scholars are not natural allies. Writing in the *Times Higher Education*, Nicholas Royle provocatively declared that many English scholars 'would not be willing to teach a course with any creative writing component and, secretly, quite possibly wish their creative writing colleagues would die horrible deaths'. The hostility is two-sided: many scholars regret the growth of creative writing programmes to the detriment of their own discipline, but writers also criticize the narrow-mindedness of traditional literary scholarship. Until recently, the US Association of Writers & Writing Programs stated on its website that it has 'rescued literature from the exhumations of philologists to elevate literature's status as a living art' (Fenza).

This claim had been made earlier by the New Critics, many of them poet-critics, whose formalist theories of the text revolutionized the pedagogy of English in the post-war period. The influence of New Criticism on the institutionalization of modernist studies is well known. In *Modernism, Mass Culture, and Professionalism*, Thomas Strychacz notes that the New Critics' endorsement of difficult modernist writings 'functioned as a means of institutionalizing an elite readership capable of using new interpretive modes and promoting a situation in which reader, author, and text maintain hegemony over a wide range of cultural matters' (34).[11] Although the New Critics worked in universities and deployed the discourse and practice of professionalism, they remained deeply ambiguous towards academia in general, and literary scholarship in particular. For John Crowe Ransom, Allen Tate, Robert Penn Warren, and Cleanth Brooks, English departments had for too long been dominated by philologists and scholars more interested in biographical, social, and historical facts than in literature. Universities were guilty of favouring this kind of pseudo-scientific scholarship, to the detriment of the true appreciation of literary texts. This distrust was largely influenced by their readings of T. S. Eliot and Ezra Pound, who often attacked the academic system. Few scholars have noted that the relationship between New Criticism and literary modernism cannot be dissociated from the then-new institution of creative writing. Because the New Critics were the first generation of creative writers in American universities, they have left a long legacy of ambivalence towards academia.

To start exploring the modernist roots of creative writing as an institution, let's take the example of the poet-critic Allen Tate. When Tate first read T. S. Eliot's *The Sacred Wood* in the early 1920s, he was an undergraduate student at Vanderbilt University in Nashville, Tennessee. The model of the poet-critic hostile to the university system was already taking shape in Eliot's short book: 'It is to be expected that the critic and the creative artist should frequently be the same person' (14). Eliot also criticized the 'historical' and the 'philosophical' critics who 'had better be called historians and philosophers quite simply' (14). For Eliot, it was regrettable that 'the culture of ideas has only been able to survive in America in the unfavourable atmosphere of the university' (39). Eliot had first-hand experience of the academic system, having earned Bachelor's and Master's degrees at Harvard, and completed a doctoral dissertation (which was never examined). Like Ezra Pound, Eliot feared the deadening life that seemed to await him in the university system. When he was completing his dissertation, he wrote in the *New Statesman* that the labour of preparing a doctoral thesis was 'fatal to the development of intellectual powers. It crushes originality, it kills style' ('Mr Leacock Serious'). For Eliot, as Gail McDonald argues, 'the creation of poetry seemed to be generative of insights not available through the academic disciplines of philology and philosophy' (44).

Eliot's work had a profound influence on Allen Tate, who was increasing annoyed by the English classes he was taking. One of his professors and head of the English department, Edwin Mims, became a symbol of all that was wrong with the teaching of literature. Every year, Mims required the entire class to recite the end of Tennyson's *Ulysses* from memory and in unison (Underwood 34). Mims's

---

[11] For more on the links between New Criticism and modernism, see Graff 145–61 and Diepeveen 226.

appeal to emotion was particularly exasperating to Tate and to his mentor, John Crowe Ransom, then a young professor at Vanderbilt. Ransom would later talk about the traditional ways of teaching literature:

> 'Open your books to page 50,' the professor would say. The professor, unnamed by Mr Ransom but clearly Dr Mims, would read through the poem, gaze out the window for a silent moment, then say, 'Isn't that beautiful? Now turn to page 52.'
> (Sullivan 30)

Tate and Ransom rejected Mims's emotionalism in favour of Eliot's appeal to detachment and impersonality. 'Poetry is not a turning loose of emotion, but an escape from emotion,' wrote Eliot in *The Sacred Wood*. 'It is not the expression of personality, but an escape from personality' (52–3). For Tate and Ransom, Mims was guilty not only of injecting emotion into poetry, but also of promoting a perverted faith in industrial civilization. Mims had once been to the Chicago World's Fair, and the scientific marvels he observed there strengthened his belief in material progress (Sullivan 19). Tate and Ransom's opposition to the industrialization of the South, expressed in the Agrarian manifesto 'I'll Take My Stand', was entirely at odds with Mims's worldview.

To the end of his life, Tate held Mims responsible for his failure to go to graduate school. Tate received his Bachelor's degree in 1923, and he applied for a graduate fellowship at Yale. Tate believed that the application was rejected because Mims sent an unsolicited letter to the selection committee (Underwood 95). According to another story, Tate obtained the fellowship, but Mims used his considerable power in academic circles to have it revoked (Sullivan 19). In any case, it is clear that Tate deeply resented the influence of Mims and his allies at Vanderbilt. The university seemed a hostile environment for a young poet with little interest in traditional scholarship and institutional politics.

Despite his opposition to professors, Tate became one himself in 1934, when he was appointed lecturer in English literature at Southwestern College in Memphis (the position had been left vacant by the departure of Tate's friend and fellow Agrarian, Robert 'Red' Penn Warren). According to his biographer, Tate 'took his teaching very seriously, spent hours preparing for each of his courses, and was consequently unable to do any of his own writing' (Underwood 222). Although Tate's academic position was far from ideal, it allowed him to participate in discussions with fellow poets and writers-in-residence. Ford Madox Ford came to see the Tates in April, before going to the writers' conference at Louisiana State University, where Red Warren and Cleanth Brooks were also teaching (Mizener 426–7). Neither Warren, nor Brooks had PhDs, and their successful textbooks *Understanding Poetry* and *Understanding Fiction* revealed their ambition to change the teaching of English literature. At the time when the discipline of creative writing was being institutionalized, Tate found himself at the centre of a new generation of poet-critics opposed to traditional literary scholarship.

In the late 1930s, Tate taught at the Olivet conference in Michigan. Olivet College, a small liberal arts school, pioneered the model of the writers' conference, bringing to campus well-known writers such as Katherine Ann Porter, Sinclair Lewis, Sherwood Anderson, Carl Sandburg, Ford Madox Ford, W. H. Auden, and Gertrude Stein. The Olivet conference became a site where writers could exchange ideas and strengthen friendships. In summer 1937, Porter, who had been invited by the Tates to the conference, then drove with them to their home in Clarksville, Tennessee. They were joined by Cleanth Brooks and his wife, as well as a young poet, Robert Lowell, and Albert Erskine, an MA candidate who later became editor at Random House (Givner 304). This kind of literary community was different from the bohemia that Tate had experienced earlier in New York, London, and Paris. It was no longer necessary to go to metropolitan centres to meet famous and aspiring writers. Institutions such as the writers' conferences at Olivet and Louisiana State University, as well as the Iowa Writers' Workshop revealed the importance of regionalism in the identity of writing programmes (McGurl 148–54).

For Tate and the former Fugitives-Agrarians, who had long promoted their Southern identity, the late 1930s was an exciting time. Southern literary journals such as the *Kenyon Review* and the *Sewanee Review* were starting to gain enormous prestige at the national level. In 1939, Allen Tate left the Woman's College of North Carolina, where he had been teaching for one year, to become Resident Fellow in Creative Writing at Princeton University. His position had been made possible by a grant from the Carnegie Foundation to establish a Creative Arts Program that would bring writers to the Princeton Faculty—'another case of the unity of interest, in this period, of criticism and creative writing' (Graff 158). In short, Tate and his fellow New Critics were becoming established members of an academic system that had once seemed hostile to them.

In 1940, Allen Tate launched a strong attack against literary scholars in his essay 'Miss Emily and the Bibliographer'. The title comes from William Faulkner's famous story, 'A Rose for Emily', in which a woman conceals the dead body of her lover in an upstairs bedroom until concealment is no longer possible. Unlike Miss Emily, who treats a corpse as a living thing, the bibliographers see a living thing (literature) as a dead body. They pretend that their work is 'to lay the foundations of literary criticism', while in fact dismissing criticism as mere 'impressionism' (39). These scholars, Tate argued, discourage young would-be critics in their graduate seminars by telling them that anybody can write criticism. For Tate, literary criticism had to start in the classroom, where all literature should be taught as 'the literature of the present' (47).

This new pedagogy had an important influence on many students who took Tate's classes. In Autumn 1979, shortly after Tate's death, a former student wrote an article to celebrate his legacy as a teacher and a poet. Michael True was in graduate school at the University of Minnesota in the 1950s when he met Tate. 'He had a genius for making highly complex poems such as *The Waste Land* or Crane's "Voyages" understandable simply by reading them aloud,' declared True ('Allen Tate' 325). A professor of English himself when he wrote this article, Michael True openly admitted his debt to his former teacher. His bookshelf still held works recommended by Tate, for example (325). In an essay published in the *English Journal*, True also prescribed that 'poems must be read aloud' in the classroom ('Teaching Poetry' 42). Tate's most important legacy on the next generation of English teachers was perhaps his insistence that literature was not the dead thing studied by bibliographers and philologists. Michael True thus remembered that when Tate was discussing the work of Keats, Shelley, Yeats, and Faulkner, 'students felt as if they had happened upon a conversation among these writers, about their work' ('Allen Tate' 325).

The ambivalence towards literary scholarship and the academic system, at the core of both criticism and creative writing, had long-term consequences. It largely explains the separation between English departments and writing workshops that became increasingly common in America in the 1960s. It also explains why the Association of Writers & Writing Programs has referred to philologists as antagonists who treat literature as a dead body. The discipline of creative writing is therefore a good example of the 'mobilization and deployment of hostility' central to key movements in English studies. As Ben Knights puts it, the disciplinary discourse and classroom practice of these movements can be 'visualized as a triangle composed of discredited authority, radical authority, and initiate' (47). In the case of creative writing, the place of the discredited authority is taken by literary scholarship (bibliographical, historical, and sociological studies, and, more recently, critical theory); the radical authority is the creative writer who sees literature as a living thing; and the ensuing dynamic invites the student to reject the discredited authority and align with the radical authority. This model illuminates the ongoing tensions between creative writers and literary scholars, which can be traced to the modernists' simultaneous rejection of, and dependence on, academia.

0.3 Structure

Literary Rebels: A History of Creative Writers in Anglo-American Universities is divided into two parts: USA (five chapters) and UK (four chapters). Through specific case studies, the book sheds light on the marginal position of a discipline founded by self-declared outsiders. Chapter 1 focuses on Paul Engle, who directed the Iowa Writers' Workshop from the 1940s to the mid-1960s. Born and raised in a small Iowan town, Engle spent time studying in Oxford on a Rhodes scholarship, before returning to his home state. He was both a cosmopolitan and a regionalist, an uncomfortable position that he turned into an asset. The duality of Engle's personal brand influenced the positioning of the Workshop—a programme both anchored in the Midwest and opened to the world. Drawing on little-known documents in the University of Iowa archives, I show that Engle transformed creative writing at Iowa by embracing internationalism and reinventing regionalism.

Turning from the Midwest to the South, Chapter 2 focuses on the story of James Culpepper, a young would-be writer who tried to convince William Faulkner to help him succeed in the literary world. While young Southern writers such as Flannery O'Connor launched their careers through the newly created creative writing programmes, Culpepper relied on what I call the *informal mentorship model*. In this model, new writers established informal links with successful authors to gain access to publication. The chapter highlights a key moment in the history of the American literary field: the moment when the *informal mentorship model* was being challenged by the model of university education and affiliation. The new model was designed to help outsiders like Culpepper get their foot on the literary ladder, without having to get sponsorship from a famous writer or move to New York City.

Turning from the South to the West, Chapter 3 focuses on Wallace Stegner, the founder of the creative writing programme at Stanford University. When Stegner took up his position at Stanford, the East Coast establishment nearly forgot about him. 'It was as though I stepped off a pier into the Pacific Ocean without a ripple,' he later said (Jones, 'The Dean of Western Letters'). Like Engle, Stegner saw himself as an outsider who would never really fit amongst the East Coast literary elite. And, like Engle, he presented creative writing as an integral part of a literary training that should also include scholarship and criticism. In the long term, however, neither Engle nor Stegner managed to unite the creative and the critical—a failure that has had enduring consequences on their discipline.

Turning from the West to the East Coast, Chapter 4 shows the central role of the Rockefeller Foundation (RF) in the post-war funding landscape. In the late 1940s and 1950s, the Foundation privileged support for New Critics and their university-based little magazines (including the *Kenyon Review* and the *Sewanee Review*) and awarded fellowships in creative writing to the University of Iowa. But in the late 1950s and 1960s, RF officers started having doubts about this institutional approach. In response to criticisms of the university system as a source of conformity, they decided to fund individual writers independently of academic affiliations. The example of the RF's changing policy illustrates a turning point in the image of creative writing programmes. As these programmes developed across the country, they were increasingly accused of stifling creativity and threatening the autonomy of writers.

The rediscovery of the individual creative writer in the 1960s benefited institutions outside the traditional academic system—including private correspondence schools. Chapter 5 takes the example of the Famous Writers School (FWS), which promised fame, fortune, and freedom to anyone who had the aptitude to become a writer. This marketing pitch addressed the aspirations of many Americans, who yearned for an autonomous life, liberated from daily commutes and household chores. The immense success of the FWS shows the consolidation and appeal of the discourse on freedom as a central characteristic of the writing life outside academia (what I call the model of *radical individualism*).

Chapter 6 addresses the emergence of creative writing programmes in Britain, focusing on Malcolm Bradbury at the University of East Anglia. Throughout his career as writer-scholar, Bradbury cultivated a positioning on the margins of the establishment. Being based in Norwich, at a university deeply influenced by the American academic model, he was able to replicate what Paul Engle had done at Iowa: to create a new literary powerhouse outside traditional centres. The chapter adapts Bourdieu's model of the 'loser wins' (*The Field of Cultural Production* 39) to show that creative writing in Britain was, from the start, positioned as an outsider's discipline—built as a reaction against existing models of literary success. The enduring influence of Bradbury on the discipline is illustrated through the myth of 1970, which is often presented as the founding year in the history of university creative writing in Britain.

American programmes in creative writing offered one model for the rise of the 'writer-in-residence' in Britain. As Chapter 7 shows, a second model was informed by progressive educational ideas, which also led to the expansion of the comprehensive school system. Funded by the Arts Council and other organizations, writers-in-residence advised underprivileged populations: from lorry-driver poets to dry-cleaners-turned-novelists. With the rise of the discourse on creative writing in academia as a source of conformity, all institutions started becoming suspicious—including the Arts Council. The only way to be completely autonomous was to reject funding from institutions and survive in the marketplace, argued the novelist and playwright Jack Trevor Story after a stint as writer-in-residence in Milton Keynes.

Creative writing programmes have continued to position themselves on the margins of the literary field—despite obvious signs that they are now part of the 'system'. In his 2017 Nobel Prize lecture in Stockholm, Kazuo Ishiguro talked about his experience studying creative writing at the University of East Anglia. His tutors Malcolm Bradbury and Angela Carter helped him develop his writing style and offered practical help to launch his literary career. Chapter 8 argues that Ishiguro's Nobel Prize award was a moment of triumph for the Anglo-American model of university creative writing, and a symbolic victory over the European model of literary production, long endorsed by the Nobel Prize committee. But this was a double-edged victory. By consecrating a bestselling writer, the Swedish Academy also gave ammunition to the criticisms of creative writing programmes as factories producing crowd-pleasing products for the mass market.

Chapter 9 examines the development of creative writing courses outside the academic system in Britain—starting in the late 1960s with the creation of Arvon, to the present day and the proliferation of courses sponsored by publishers and literary agents. As in the case of the Famous Writers School in America, aspiring writers are sold the dream of a glamorous writing lifestyle characterized by fame and freedom. Once again, academia is criticized for its blandness and conformity, while the non-academic world is associated with autonomous creativity.

In an ultra-competitive literary world, the global rise of creative writing courses (within and outside academia) has been largely driven by a quest for self-fulfilment and access to publishing networks. More needs to be done to understand the rapid development of these programmes around the world. There is ample scope for a spatial expansion of the field, towards Europe and Asia in particular. This book touches on the expansion of creative writing in Continental Europe in the Epilogue. It then concludes with an overview of the three models of writing careers that have shaped the literary landscape since the early twentieth century, and with an afterword by Mark McGurl.

PART I
USA

1
Think Global, Act Local
Paul Engle and the Modernist Roots of Creative Writing at the University of Iowa

In October 1980, Judith E. Green—the arts editor at the *Daily Iowan*—read an article on the Writers' Workshop and its former director, the seventy-two-year-old Paul Engle. The article followed Engle's own interpretation of his achievements and presented him as the founder of the famous workshop. This seemed ludicrous to Green, who wrote a letter denouncing the 'arrogance' of this narrative. 'The "Iowa atmosphere" existed long before Mr Engle was born,' declared Green. The University started offering creative writing courses in the late nineteenth century and, by the 1920s, the writing programme was well established. The Writers' Workshop itself was not founded by Engle, but by Wilbur Schramm—who then left Iowa, leaving Engle free to put his mark on the programme. For Green, Engle was just one talented administrator amongst many others.[1]

Green was not the only one to think that Engle had received too much credit. In a 1991 obituary, Frank Conroy (who was then Director of the Workshop) said that Engle had 'an enormous ego'. This served him and the Workshop well, Conroy added. 'He was a terrific publicist' who 'could go in and charm the socks of the boards of the John Deere Tractor Co.' (qtd in Svetvilas). This reappraisal of Engle's contribution to the Workshop—from founder to mere fundraiser—led to quasi-oblivion in the 1990s and 2000s. It was not until McGurl's *The Program Era* (2009) and the rise of scholarly interest in American creative writing programmes that Engle staged a comeback. Drawing on Max Weber's sociology, Loren Glass gave an illuminating account of Engle's achievements in a short article. Eric Bennett also included a chapter on 'Paul Engle: The Creative Writing Cold Warrior' in his 2015 monograph *Workshops of Empire*.

This scholarship focuses mainly on the twenty-five years when Engle was Director of the Writers' Workshop, touching only briefly on his earlier and later years. This is problematic because Engle's youthful experiences of studying and travelling in Europe gave him a life-long commitment to an international community

---

[1] '"Arrogance" in Article on Engle, Writers' Workshop', *DMSR*, 5 Oct. 1980, Faculty Vertical Files: Paul Engle, UI.

Literary Rebels. Lise Jaillant, Oxford University Press.
© Lise Jaillant (2022). DOI: 10.1093/oso/9780192855305.003.0002

of writers, a commitment that coloured his vision of the Workshop. In 1937, Engle got his first academic post in Iowa when he was already twenty-nine years old, after several years of an itinerant life on the East Coast and in Europe. He was thirty-three years old when he became Interim Director of the Workshop, and the rest of his career was spent at the University of Iowa. Engle's local roots and patriotic poetry have contributed to his image as a 'middle man'. As Glass puts it, 'Engle prided himself on being of the middle—the Middle West, the middle class, the middlebrow' ('Middle Man' 258).[2] It is certainly true that Engle used his regional credentials to promote the Workshop and attract funding from local business people. He shared their social codes and he understood their interests. He was proud that they trusted him, that they believed in his vision for the Workshop.

But Engle's true talent was in his ability to combine a regional positioning with an international outlook. This dual identity finds its origins in Engle's youth, before he returned to Iowa. Oxford-educated on a Rhodes scholarship, Engle often presented himself as part of a cosmopolitan elite.[3] His letters to contacts on the East Coast are peppered with references to his prestigious education, and to the famous writers he had met during his time in Europe (including the poet Edmund Blunden, who was his tutor at Oxford and became a close friend). His European trip was a pivotal moment for Engle, the moment when he learnt to combine—in Harry Levin's words—'the attitudes of an outgoing cosmopolitan and a homecoming nativist' (42).[4]

Engle felt at ease amongst business people in Iowa and on the East Coast, but he repeatedly presented himself as an outsider in the academic system. In a 1977 interview, he said: 'Universities are made in part of people who couldn't make it in the tough competitive world. They are cautious places.' He saw himself as an exception to the rule. 'I was the kind of eccentric who managed somehow to get along in the academic world, but not really conforming to it. I'm not really the average professor. I've always been an innovator' (Gildner 38). For Engle, the discipline

---

[2] Glass describes Engle's poetry as 'resolutely middlebrow'. When the term appeared in Britain in the 1920s, 'middlebrow' described someone with high intellectual or aesthetic aspirations, but who lacked the cultural capital necessary to understand high art. As I have showed in *Modernism, Middlebrow and the Literary Canon*, the term has evolved differently in Britain and America (5). In the US context, Joan Shelley Rubin and Janice Radway have defined the middlebrow as an autonomous cultural sphere hostile to literary experiments. Engle was not interested in literary experimentation in his own poetry, but he consistently defended modern literature as an important academic topic. As Glass puts it, 'Engle's passionate endorsement of the Workshop is related to his insistence on the academic study of modern literary innovators' ('Middle Man' 260). For more on creative writing programmes as middlebrow institutions, see Chapter 7.

[3] In the past three decades, scholarship on cosmopolitanism has appeared in multiple disciplines. As Janet Lyon puts it, 'this new work has informed and invigorated modernist studies, particularly as the field has sought to address an ever broader range of global cultural production' (388). The term 'cosmopolitan' (etymologically *citizen of the world*) has been used in different ways. In this chapter, it designates, in Lyon's words, 'an individual's attitude or a set of practices in the world: a cultivated stance of detachment from one's culture of origin'. More positively, it points to a stance of active interest in, engagement with, and belonging to 'parts of the world other than one's nation' (Robbins 250).

[4] See also Lutz, *Cosmopolitan Vistas: American Regionalism and Literary Value*.

of creative writing was a force of renewal, pushing narrow-minded professors to take creativity seriously. Having grown up in a lower-middle-class family in Cedar Rapids, without access to the cultural offerings of the big city, Engle wanted to offer opportunities to young people who did not have the social capital needed for a literary career. Creative writing would lead to a shake-up of the university system, but also the publishing industry—a sector that had traditionally selected writers from a small pool of well-connected insiders.

Like the New Critics, Engle tried to combine a university post with a radical criticism of universities. Although he was never interested in formal experimentation for his own poetry, he admired modernist writers and was deeply influenced by the model of the poet-critic who had one foot inside, and one foot outside academia. At the end of his career, he wanted to be remembered for his pioneering role in the teaching of modernism at university level. Responding to Stephen Wilbers' history of the Workshop, Engle insisted that 'he introduced, and himself taught the first course in Contemporary Literature on the campus; the first Poetry Workshop, the first Fiction Workshop; the basic courses in Understanding Poetry and in Understanding Fiction; the first Seminars in such major individual writers as James Joyce, W. B. Yeats, Proust, etc.'[5] Here, Engle highlighted his commitment to modernist literature and New Criticism, to the creative as well as to the critical.

Engle's vision for the Workshop was influenced by the modernist writers' model of expatriation (think of Ernest Hemingway, who had spent long periods in Europe while retaining a strong American identity). International modernism, for Engle, was a lifestyle rather than a literary style. For a young man born and raised in a small Iowan town, this lifestyle entailed frequent travels to meet writers abroad and a push to bring foreign writers to the United States. Drawing on little-known documents in the University of Iowa archives, I show that Engle and Schramm transformed creative writing at Iowa by embracing internationalism. Their desire to 'make it new' should be placed in the historical context of the late 1930s, at the time when an earlier generation of regionalist writers was declining. The men who had done so much to transform Iowa into a regional literary centre—including John T. Frederick and Edwin Ford Piper—were no longer dominant forces. Frederick left Iowa City in 1930 and his influential little magazine *The Midland* was discontinued soon after. Piper was in his sixties, and vulnerable to attacks from younger colleagues. The creation of the Workshop in 1936 and its development in the following years was a revolution rather than a painless evolution from earlier models. And this revolution was informed by the model of the poet-critic developed by modernist writers and their disciples. Unlike the Southern 'Fugitives', however, Engle and Schramm had little interest in resisting industrialization and boosting local self-esteem. Although they kept some ties with the regionalists, their ambition was not to 'encourage the making of literature in the Middle West'

---

[5] Engle to University of Iowa Press Editorial Board, 24 Jan. 1980, Box 4, Papers of Paul Engle, UI.

(as *The Midland* proclaimed).[6] What they wanted was to attract the best students at the national and international level.

After Schramm's departure, Engle was left alone to realize this plan: bringing the world's best writers to Iowa City. Modernism offered an entire imaginary landscape that could be transplanted to the university campus. In Engle's vision, Iowa would replace Paris as the international literary centre, as the place to be for ambitious young writers around the world. Academia would become a new bohemia, home to a community of cosmopolitan writers, united by shared interests rather than common origins.

The first section gives an overview of the literary scene in Iowa in the 1920s and early 1930s, at the time when Paul Engle was still a student. I then turn to Engle's formative experiences in Europe, which broadened his outlook beyond regionalist influences. The final section sheds light on Engle's return to Iowa and the early days of his directorship of the Writers' Workshop. In the late 1930s and early 1940s, Engle pushed for an international agenda for the creative writing programme, an agenda modelled on the cosmopolitan ethos of modernism. Like Ezra Pound and other modernist writers, Engle continued to describe himself as a literary outsider, as a disruptive force in a world dominated by conformity and timidity.

1.1 Iowa's Literary Scene in the 1920s and Early 1930s

What was it like to have literary ambitions in Iowa in the early twentieth century? What kind of trajectory would writers follow to achieve publication and recognition? In a 1973 letter supporting the nomination of John T. Frederick for a Distinguished Service Award, Paul Engle presented the literary world of his youth, a world proud of its regional identity and eager to compete against established literary centres on the East Coast. 'When I began writing poetry in the schools of Cedar Rapids, Iowa,' wrote Engle, 'the most distinguished place one could hope to publish was MIDLAND.' Although his manuscripts were repeatedly rejected, he was grateful for the 'handwritten notes of encouragement, and precise critical comments'. When an acceptance finally came, Engle celebrated the day 'with more fervor than the Fourth of July'. Amongst young people with literary ambitions, having a text accepted for publication in *The Midland* was taken as proof of talent. 'It was proof on the East Coast, as well as in Iowa,' declared Engle.[7]

John T. Frederick began publishing *The Midland* in Iowa City in 1915, while still an undergraduate student. He was encouraged by Clarke Fisher Ansley, head of the English Department. The two men developed a close relationship, and in 1919,

---

[6] Qtd in University of Iowa News Bulletin, Nov. 1932, p. 3. Subject Vertical Files, Writers' Workshop, UI.
[7] Engle to Thomas L. Irwin, 16 Jan. 1973, Faculty Vertical Files: John T. Frederick, UI.

became neighbours when Frederick bought a farm in Michigan. 'Mr Ansley was a man who was not addicted to scholarship in the usual sense,' Frederick later said. He 'thought of himself as a creative figure, and his greatest interest was in students who could show some competence and promise in creative ways, so that I think the atmosphere of the Department at that time was particularly stimulating and helpful for the young person who wanted to write'.[8] Nearly every student interested in writing took the course on the Short Story taught by Perceval Hunt. Far from being dismissed as a hobby, creative writing counted towards the final degree.

Frederick joined the University of Iowa faculty in 1921, leaving one year later for a new position at the University of Pittsburgh. In 1923, Iowa lured him back with a higher salary and ample time to edit *The Midland*, which the Head of Department Professor Craig described as 'a stimulation to literary activity in the university'.[9] During his negotiations with Craig, Frederick pushed for graduate work in creative writing to be recognized as credit-bearing. 'I shall welcome developments in the direction you suggest,' wrote Craig before suggesting that he teach two courses in the Short Story: 'One our usual undergraduate course and the other of distinctly higher and more selective quality, for which graduate credit may be given.'[10] In the early 1920s, then, Iowa was already developing a model of creative writing courses at the graduate level.

Craig also confirmed that Carl Seashore, dean of the Graduate College, had approved the hiring of a female assistant, who would spend twenty-four hours a week helping Frederick with his various activities. The woman they had selected was 'satisfactory in every way'. But Craig, displaying casual misogyny, warned Frederick: 'I hope you are not ... too sensitive on the question of looks.'[11] Women occupied a marginalized place in Iowa's Department of English, a department dominated by male professors on one side or another of the creative/scholarly divide.[12]

Amongst those engaged in creative work was Edwin Ford Piper, who had taught at Iowa since 1905. Born and raised in western Nebraska, Piper's poetry reflected his experience of pioneer life on the prairies. As the University of Iowa News Bulletin put it, 'his poems tell of the desolation of drought, the terror of prairie fire ... the claim jumpers and cattle rustlers. The convincing truth of hard experience is the backbone of these poems.'[13] Although Piper's regional poems were only

---

[8] Frederick, Interview by Jean Wylder, 20 Oct. 1972, Faculty Vertical Files: John T. Frederick, UI.
[9] Hardin Craig to Frederick, 5 Jan. 1923, Box 6, Papers of John T. Frederick, UI.
[10] Craig to Frederick, 23 May 1923, Box 6, Papers of John T. Frederick, UI.
[11] Craig to Frederick, 23 May 1923, Box 6, Papers of John T. Frederick, UI.
[12] On the division between scholars and writers, see Frederick's interview: 'The Department of English was always divided, and at times rather consciously and sharply between would-be writers and would-be scholars. And the graduate student who entered the Department of English was usually put to it pretty well to decide whether he wanted to be a scholar or a writer. He couldn't be both. That was the impression he got from us, I'm afraid.' Frederick, Interview by Jean Wylder, 20 Oct. 1972, Faculty Vertical Files: John T. Frederick, UI.
[13] University of Iowa News Bulletin, Jan. 1929, qtd in 'UI Press Renames Poetry Award for Edwin Ford Piper', Press Release, 16 Apr. 1990, Faculty Vertical Files: Edwin Ford Piper, UI.

'moderately famous', he was an influential teacher.[14] Frederick, who had once been his student, kept a vivid memory of these courses. Sitting on a stiff classroom chair, the young man would listen to Piper's reading of English ballads. 'I carry away from the classroom not only the music and feeling of the ballad itself,' wrote Frederick, 'but some sense of contact with the people who first made and sang it' (Andrews 15). Other sources confirm that Piper was greatly skilled at reading poetry, his own as well as that of others. Alice Weitz, who attended one of his readings in Des Moines in the 1910s, said she would 'never forget the occasion'. 'The modesty in his manner, the pathos in his voice, the warmth of love in his tone, the strength of his phrases teeming with artfully suppressed emotion, the measure of tribute which was in his soul to pay to the memory of those who had made from the plastic frontier so great a civilization—all these gave to his ardent listeners an unforgettable introduction to the heroic pioneers of the sixties' (39). Confronted with the rapid change of their environment, Midwestern audiences looked back at pioneer life with nostalgia. Although Piper's poetry might seem sentimental to us today, it resonated with readers at the time.

Frederick also remembered the informal classes that took place in Piper's basement office. Students would sit in nooks between bookcases or even share a table with piles of papers and magazines. Attendance was optional, but few students would fail to come to these stimulating sessions, during which they read texts they had written for the comments of one another and their instructor (Andrews 15). These reminiscences, written more than two decades later, convey the excitement of an earlier form of the creative writing workshop. Following Piper's example, younger men like Frederick turned towards regional literature. They wanted to write about the Midwest, but they also wanted to be taken seriously outside their own region. '*The Midland* is a national literary magazine published monthly at Iowa City, Iowa,' declared a 1922 circular. 'It is *of* the Middle West, and *for* all the world.'[15] For Frederick, regionalism was not an end in itself. 'A good regional writer is a good writer who uses regional materials,' he later wrote. 'His regionalism is an incident and condition, not a purpose or motive' (xv). Anchored in the author's personal experience, good writing could reach a broad audience.

Frederick achieved this national ambition remarkably quickly for someone with so little experience. Edward J. O'Brien, editor of the annual *Best Short Stories*, lauded the magazine in its first year, writing that it was the 'one new periodical' that 'claim[s] unique attention this year' (9). Only five years after the creation of *The Midland*, H. L. Mencken, perhaps the most influential figure in American writing at the time, told Frederick that *The Midland* was full of 'excellent stuff'. In 1923, he

---

[14] Paul Engle to Marvin Bell, 9 Oct. 1963, Faculty Vertical Files: Paul Engle, UI.
[15] *The Midland*, Circular, 1922, Milton Monroe Reigelman: Collection on *The Midland*, UI.

wrote in the *Smart Set* that *The Midland* was 'probably the most influential literary periodical ever set up in America'.[16]

Frederick's little magazine was often associated with the Chicago renaissance. O'Brien credited it for preparing the way for Carl Sandburg, Sherwood Anderson, Ben Hecht, Vachel Lindsay, and Edgar Lee Masters.[17] *The Midland* was also favourably compared to the little magazines edited in Chicago, *The Dial* and *Poetry*. In a 1924 letter, Jay Sigmund, the Vice-President of Cedar Rapids Life Insurance Company, thanked Frederick for encouraging him: 'I have had to be a rather isolated figure due principally to the fact that I was a business man and writing about things that were not finding special favor among the clicks, which edit the Poetry Magazine.'[18] As an aspiring poet, Sigmund was grateful for Frederick's feedback on his writing. For some local writers, *The Midland* seemed a less cliquey, more approachable option than the Chicago little magazines. But the audience for Frederick's magazine remained very limited.[19] One librarian in Des Moines wrote: 'It has surprised me many times to find *The Midland* better known in literary circles in the East than it seems to be here.' He wanted the magazine to be 'on the shelves of every public library as well as on the library table of every home in which there is an interest in modern American literature.'[20] Although Frederick's magazine had an established reputation at the national level, finding a sustainable readership was a constant struggle.

Following the 1929 economic crash, financial difficulties forced Frederick to move the magazine from Iowa City to Chicago. Once again, *The Midland* was compared to *The Dial*. In May, O'Brien told Frederick: '*The Dial* was not sufficiently representative of American writing, it did not interpret our American generation as it might have done, and it did not appreciate the value of good honest clean American wood.' And he added: 'I want to see a magazine appearing in America like yours which I can show in Europe as an expression of American life.'[21] One month later, O'Brien reported that he had talked to the British writer Edward Garnett about *The Midland* during a recent visit in England.[22] Following the death of *The Dial*, O'Brien hoped that *The Midland* would carry the voice of American literature abroad. Although the move to Chicago led to a rise in circulation figures, the magazine continued to experience financial difficulties, and publication ceased in 1933.

---

[16] *The Midland*, Circular, 1922, Milton Monroe Reigelman: Collection on *The Midland*, UI; *Smart Set* July 1923: 141.
[17] John C. Gerber to Thomas L. Irwin, 12 Jan. 1973, Faculty Vertical Files: John T. Frederick, UI.
[18] Jay G. Sigmund to Frederick, 23 Oct. 1924, Box 6, Papers of John T. Frederick, UI.
[19] 'Circulation ranged from 200–500 until the move to Chicago, when the subscription list swelled to 1200 and as many as 2000 copies were printed. The price was $1.50/year, raised to $2 in 1920, $3 in 1924' (Lutz, 'The Cosmopolitan Midland' 84n3).
[20] Forrest B. Spaulding to Frederick, 19 Mar. 1930, Box 6, Papers of John T. Frederick, UI.
[21] Edward O'Brien to Frederick, 21 May 1930, Box 6, Papers of John T. Frederick, UI.
[22] O'Brien to Frederick, 20 June 1930, Box 6, Papers of John T. Frederick, UI.

The Midland was, in many ways, a pure product of the 1920s—a time that saw the emergence of American literature as a subject taught at university level. This growing academic interest was paralleled with the opening of new markets for American literary fiction, at the national and international level. The annual anthology of short stories edited by O'Brien showed that American fiction could compete with the best fiction in Europe and elsewhere. For ambitious writers outside the traditional literary centres of the East Coast, *The Midland* and other little magazines offered the opportunity to write what they knew, without being confined to local audiences.

Frederick played the role of a middleman, who helped would-be writers get into print and attract the attention of influential tastemakers such as Mencken and O'Brien. In 1924, he wrote *A Handbook of Short Story Writing* (published by Alfred Knopf in New York). The book gave advice on the form and content of an efficient short story, but also on possible markets. Jay Sigmund, the businessman from Cedar Rapids, found this aspect of the handbook particularly useful: 'A writer might strive to write such material as *The Midland*, *The Reviewer*, etc. are publishing and if he kept sending his stories to such magazines as TELLING TALES, they would keep coming back to him forever and he would never quite know just what was the matter.'[23] It was therefore essential for writers to research the market before sending their work to little magazines or more popular outlets. The commercial tone of Frederick's handbook responded to a growing demand from would-be writers, who wanted to know how to make it into print.

In *The Culture and Commerce of the American Short Story*, Andrew Levy noted the continuity between what he calls the 'handbook era' and the 'current workshop era' (103). The key principles of creative writing as an academic discipline—including the emphasis on suggestion (Show, Not Tell)—find their roots in the handbooks that Frederick and others were writing at the beginning of the twentieth century. The first generation of creative writers had no problem seeking commercial opportunities for their writing, and encouraging others to do the same. It is, of course, true that *The Midland* did not compete with mass-market periodicals. Frederick's scorn for 'the tyranny of the market' and his focus on high-quality, literary works have led scholars to present his periodical as non-commercial—a 'regional magazine publishing Midwestern art for art's sake', in Jeffrey Swenson's words (564). In fact, Frederick worked as an entrepreneur eager to identify demand and offer creative solutions. When he realized that literary writers struggled to find relevant advice, he thought of setting up a new enterprise to give 'professional guidance and criticism' for a fee.[24] Frederick was teaching courses on the short story at the University of Iowa, but he was also actively seeking new opportunities (from handbooks to writing consultancies). His career

---

[23] Jay G. Sigmund to Frederick, 22 Sept. 1924, Box 6, Papers of John T. Frederick, UI.
[24] Millikin University (Illinois) to Frederick, 3 May 1930, Box 6, Papers of John T. Frederick, UI.

sheds light on the close relationship between the discipline of creative writing and the network of commercial enterprises that promised to guide would-be writers towards publication and success.

After Frederick's departure in 1930, the teaching of creative writing was in the hands of three men: Piper, Frank Luther Mott, and Norman Foerster. Mott was born in Keokuk County, Iowa. His father published the *What Cheer Patriot*, a weekly newspaper, and it was there that Mott got his start in the newspaper business. He attended Simpson College at Indianola, Iowa, before transferring in his senior year to the University of Chicago where he received a Bachelor's degree in 1907. After ten years working as newspaper editor, he went to Columbia University in New York for graduate study. Like John T. Frederick, Mott was brought to the University of Iowa by Professor Craig to teach English and to co-edit *The Midland*. In 1927, he was named professor of journalism and director of the School of Journalism at Iowa.[25]

Mott worked hard to strengthen the discipline of creative writing. The course on the Short Story, which he taught every year in the 1930s, required high standards: 'not usually open to students whose grade in English 1 (2) is mediocre' declared the University Catalogue for 1930–31. He also built relationships with local writers' groups, such as Iowa Authors Club, and he planned a state-wide Literary Caucus to bring together Iowans interested in literary work.[26] When Norman Foerster proposed a doctoral degree in creative writing in 1930, Mott supported the idea, writing to the president of the University: 'I am sure that if it is put into effect it will attract very wide attention as a milestone in graduate work.'[27]

Foerster's proposal was indeed a milestone. In 1930, aged forty-three, he had just started a new position as Director of the School of Letters at Iowa. Foerster's work was shaped by New Humanism: turning away from historical scholarship and philology, he wanted to establish a tradition of rigorous criticism. His attempt to engage students in a dialogue with the great thinkers of the Antiquity was not always successful. 'I never bought Foerster's ideas,' said Wilbur Schramm, who had taken the Literary Criticism course in the early 1930s. Although the course gave students 'a chance to live with the men who lived with ideas—Plato, Aristotle, Acquinas, and the like', Schramm felt that Foerster had 'a certain rigidity of mind and character' that prevented a productive exchange of ideas.[28] This absence of flexibility was perhaps Foerster's greatest strength. At Iowa, he was determined to impose his vision of a twentieth-century literary department, and he had, as he later confessed, the 'friendship and hearty support of President Jessup'.[29] Foerster's plan

---

[25] See Obituaries—Frank Luther Mott, 1964, Box 7, Papers of John T. Frederick, UI.
[26] Mott to President E. A. Gilmore, 22 Nov. 1934, Box 1, Papers of Frank Luther Mott; Mott to Karlton and William E. Kelm, 25 Mar. 1935, Box 2, Karlton and William Kelm Papers, UI.
[27] Mott to President W. A. Jessup, 7 Nov. 1930, Box 1, Papers of Frank Luther Mott, UI.
[28] Wilbur Schramm to Stephen Wilbers, 10 Mar. 1977, Records of the Iowa Writers' Workshop, Series XI, Box 2, UI.
[29] Foerster to 'Roy', 10 Aug. 1944, Papers of Norman Foerster, UI.

was simple: he wanted to bring scholarship, creative literature, and criticism into a fruitful relation. This would require 'PhD training for creative writing'.[30]

Foerster's proposal for doctoral work in creative writing found fertile ground at Iowa. In 1922, Dean Seashore had announced that the University would accept creative work as theses for advanced degrees. Although Seashore was primarily interested in music, he defined 'creative work' broadly to include writing and the arts. But it was Foerster who gave impetus to this statement by first urging the acceptance of creative writing for all degrees. Paul Engle later said: 'it was under his motivation that I came here as a graduate student from Coe College in Cedar Rapids and took the MA with a volume of poems.'[31]

Not everyone was convinced by Foerster's ideas. Baldwin Maxwell, a scholar who had chaired the Department of English since 1926, later said: 'I suffered a great deal of ridicule by my other colleagues at other Big Ten universities because of our granting the doctorate for creative writing.'[32] However, Maxwell was not hostile to creative writing (Engle described him as 'always considerate, always sympathetic toward an effort which must have seemed a curious one to him').[33] Scholars at Iowa did not feel particularly threatened, because Foerster never advocated the replacement of scholarship by criticism and creative writing. In his 1929 essay *The American Scholar*, he described the ideal training for MA students, who would benefit from 'practice in writing, some of it historical, some of it critical, and some of it creative (to assist an inner comprehension of art)'. What he wanted was to bring these disciplines together, to create a dialogue that would benefit both scholars and the 'lamentably uneducated' creative writers (60). As D. G. Myers put it, 'creative writers would do scholarship; scholars would creatively write' (136).

More problematic was the attitude of Piper and other regionalist writers, a group that had once dominated the Department of English. Schramm presented Piper as increasingly isolated. 'Midwestern regionalism was a movement of the 20s rather than the 30s,' he wrote:

> [A]ll the currents were headed elsewhere. Foerster was leading a parade of students back to Plato and Aristotle and across the channel to Saint Beuve and French explication. The Department of Art was bringing in visiting artists even during Grant Wood's time who represented a vastly different concept of painting from Grant's. It seems reasonable to me, then, that Mr Piper must have felt a bit out of the main stream. He had been member of a very orthodox English department; he found those patterns being torn up and the department broadening out. He must have felt ... the impatience and ambition of vigorous young fellows like Paul

---

[30] Foerster, Plan for the School of Letters, 27 Oct. 1930, Papers of Norman Foerster, UI.
[31] Engle to Marvin Bell, 9 Oct. 1963, Faculty Vertical Files: Paul Engle, UI.
[32] Baldwin Maxwell, Interview by James Beilman, 19 Oct. 1976, Oral History Interviews—University of Iowa 1976–1977, UI.
[33] Engle, 'General Remarks on the Engle Workshop', undated, Faculty Vertical Files: Paul Engle, UI.

[Engle] and Wally Stegner and me, whose eyes were mostly on new writers, new art, and new ways.

Here, Schramm describes a conflict of generation, with the older regionalists on the one side and the new writers and artists on the other. Grant Wood had been Paul Engle's art teacher in Cedar Rapids and, like Piper, he suffered from attacks from 'vigorous young fellows'. In Schramm's narrative, Piper and Wood could do nothing to prevent their marginalization. Even if Piper had lived longer (he died of a heart attack in 1939), he would have been a poor leader for the creative writing programme. 'I doubt,' wrote Schramm, 'that he wanted to build up the kind of program that would bring in young talented writers from all over the country, or start a journal, or offer a doctorate that, under suitable conditions, might be earned with a creative dissertation.'[34]

What Schramm describes is not a peaceful transition: it is a brutal takeover by the new generation, one that inflicted pain and resentment. Writing at the end of his life, Schramm regretted a behaviour that he now saw as ruthless: 'I wish I had realized at that time some of the things I myself might have done to show how fond we were of [Piper] and to keep him from being hurt.' This revolution against the regionalists was inspired by the Make It New motto of international modernism. 'The poets our young writers would be likely to read would not be [John] Neihardt,' said Schramm, 'but rather Eliot, Auden and Rilke and later lesser known people who were far from the regionalists of the 20s.'[35] In this context, Paul Engle's return to Iowa as an instructor in 1937 might seem surprising. Why would a Department that had increasingly turned its back from regionalism hire a young poet who wrote mainly about Iowa? Why did Foerster—born in Philadelphia, educated at Harvard—think that Engle would be a worthy addition to the creative writing programme?

1.2 Paul Engle, a Cosmopolitan Regionalist

In the five years between his graduation and his first academic position at Iowa, Engle acquired an image as a cosmopolitan regionalist who could bridge the gap between the old and the new guard.[36] In 1932, Engle completed the requirements for his Master's degree at the University of Iowa. His thesis consisted of an original book of poems, *Worn Earth*, which won the Yale Series of Younger Poets prize that year. It was then published on both sides of the Atlantic by Yale University

---

[34] Wilbur Schramm to Stephen Wilbers, 15 Apr. 1977, Records of the Iowa Writers' Workshop, Series XI, Box 2, UI.
[35] Schramm to Wilbers, 15 Apr. 1977, Records of the Iowa Writers' Workshop, Series XI, Box 2, UI.
[36] For a discussion on cosmopolitanism in relation to regionalism, see Lutz, *Cosmopolitan Vistas: American Regionalism and Literary Value*.

Press and the London branch of Oxford University Press. This was one of the first books of poems to be submitted for a graduate degree in the United States. After a year at Columbia University in New York City, studying English and anthropology towards a PhD, Engle was awarded a Rhodes scholarship (1933–36) at Merton College, University of Oxford. At the end of his career, Engle described these two 'profound moves' as life-changing. The first move to New York led to artistic discoveries for the young Iowan. 'I had never before heard an opera!' he said (Gildner 37). The second move to Europe offered opportunities to network with British writers. The twenty-five-year-old Engle already had an emerging reputation: the year before, *The Times Literary Supplement* had praised the 'stark, elemental and alien beauty' of *Worn Earth*.[37] A naturally gregarious individual, Engle built a close relationship with his Oxford tutor. In a collection of poems published thirty years later, Engle remembered his anxiety before their first meeting, but Blunden put the young man immediately at ease by talking about cricket rather than academic work (*A Woman Unashamed* 27). Engle's memories of Oxford take the form of a coming-of-age narrative: under Blunden's guidance, he learnt how to be a better poet and a better man (xii, 25). He quickly mastered the codes that governed the lives of Oxford men, transforming himself into a cricket-playing gentleman. Long after his student days, Engle would proudly remember his athletic accomplishments: not only did he play on the College cricket team, he also rowed in the College First Eight, and went on to row in the International Regattas at Marlow and Henley on the river Thames. His schedule left him plenty of free time, and he travelled extensively around England and on the Continent, including in Germany where he perfected his knowledge of the German language and witnessed life under the Nazi regime. Engle's activities at that time—writing poetry, playing competitive sport, travelling widely—show a determination to fit in with the cosmopolitan elite he encountered at Oxford. No longer an 'uneasy Iowan', he was now a citizen of the world—an image that seemed to clash with his previous positioning as a regional writer.

In 1934, Engle's collection of poems *American Song* was published by Doubleday in the United States. The book attracted a great deal of attention, appearing on the front page of *The New York Times Book Review* (Adams). Jonathan Cape, who published the volume in England then used an extract from this review in his advertisements, presenting Engle as 'a poet to be watched, a writer who will play his part in the resurgence of creative force that will mark this decade in our literary history'.[38] However, reviewers in Britain were far from enthusiastic. They frowned upon Engle's description of Europe as a derelict continent, exhausted by the Great War and unable to compete against the New World. Writing for *The Times Literary Supplement*, Hugh l'Anson Fausset mocked the 'naive excesses' of Engle's poetry.

---

[37] Review of *Worn Earth*, by Paul Engle, *The Times Literary Supplement*, 8 Dec. 1932, p. 940.
[38] Advertisement for Jonathan Cape, *The Times Literary Supplement*, 24 Jan. 1935, p. 39.

Adopting a patronizing tone, Fausset declared that 'Old Mother Europe' can 'afford to smile at such an ascription to her of extreme decrepitude, and even welcome it as an index of the defiant vitality of this young American poet' (240).

Paradoxically, this kind of review comforted Engle's image as the new voice of US poetry. Engle was now seen as an American expert, qualified to speak on anything related to his country. He participated in a national radio broadcast with the poet Cecil Day-Lewis, to discuss American versus British poetry. He was also invited to compare Oxford with the US education system (Cooke, 'Education on Two Sides of the Atlantic'). Far from being a sign of immaturity, his youth was used as part of a marketing strategy.[39] For readers of poetry, Engle was now 'in the front rank among the youngest American writers'.[40] *The Listener* even created a Question-and-Answer game, asking readers to guess who was the youngest American poet: T. S. Eliot? Archibald MacLeish? Shirley Temple? Or Paul Engle? The latter was twenty years older than Temple, the famous child actress, but still younger than the rest (Cooke, 'American Game').

In the radio broadcast on 'Modern Poetry', Engle presented himself as a Marinetti of the Corn Belt, eager to destroy the past and build something entirely new. 'Ever since the War we have been trying to break down the rigid forms of nineteenth-century verse,' he said (852). He went on to celebrate the Machine age as a source of inspiration for poets (853). For Engle, the modernity of US poetry (both in terms of form and subject matter) was inseparable from national pride. 'There is a strong national feeling in American poetry today,' he said. 'It's no wild-eyed patriotism—it's the discovery that America is a permanent place in which one lives—not a moving succession of frontiers' (854). Many Europeans still looked down on American poetry, a fact that seemed incomprehensible to the young Engle. Reviewing an anthology published in the Oxford World's Classics series, he strongly criticized the selection of twentieth-century poems. 'The inadequacy of the book is painful to one who has read modern American poetry,' he wrote. 'This is not the verse of America, but of nineteenth-century anthologies' ('American Poetry').

How can we explain Engle's juxtaposition of patriotism and cosmopolitanism? On the one hand, Engle was not interested in joining the ranks of the previous generation of American expatriate writers who had settled permanently in Europe. Unlike T. S. Eliot, he did not marry an English woman but a former neighbour from Cedar Rapids, Mary Nomine Nissen. He did not attempt to speak with an English accent, or convert to Anglicanism. But on the other hand, Engle did not want to be pigeonholed as a regionalist writer unable to relate to other cultures. He

---

[39] In an article on novelists in Britain in the 1920s, Marius Hentea writes: 'youth ... was its own publicity' (174).
[40] *The Times Literary Supplement*, 27 Dec. 1934, p. 920.

had no intention of emulating John T. Frederick—who never went to England.[41] The young Iowan was a deeply competitive individual, and he wanted to master the codes of the intellectual elite before going his own way. To be able to speak on equal terms with the Oxford-educated Cecil Day-Lewis and others, Engle needed to boost his credentials as a celebrated poet, Rhodes scholar, and distinguished athlete.

For Engle, then, it was perfectly possible to combine an emerging reputation as a regional writer with the cultural prestige of a well-travelled intellectual. In Summer 1934, he told *The New York Times* that he was spending some time in the Bavarian Alps:

> A spell of Oxford … always makes me feel how grand it would be to get back to rounding up cows and shoveling horse dirt and spading garden again. I'm off to the Rhine and Heidelberg and the Black Forest and Munich, to settle down in the Bavarian Alps for two months, swimming and writing very hard on my horse novel which I hope to finish this Summer. Later Greece, Hungary or the Mediterranean.[42]

Did Engle really miss 'shoveling horse dirt' while spending an idyllic summer in the Swartzwald? My guess is that he genuinely felt nostalgic for the Iowan lifestyle: his father had been in the horse business, and he often spoke fondly of those who worked in contact with horses. But Engle also wanted *New York Times* readers to know that he enjoyed the leisure and cultural opportunities that his Rhodes scholarship offered him. He had become a regionalist cosmopolite—a unique positioning that he nourished until the end of his life.

1.3 Pushing for an International Agenda at Iowa

In 1935, when Engle was still in Europe, Grant Wood's essay 'Revolt Against the City' was published as a pamphlet edited and independently published in Iowa City by Frank Luther Mott. 'Sweeping changes have come over American culture in the last few years,' wrote Wood. 'The Great Depression has taught us many things, and not the least of them is self-reliance.' For Wood, American artists no longer looked towards Paris and other European cities for inspiration. 'Painting has declared its independence from Europe, and is retreating from the cities to the more American village and country life.' Wood described this sweeping change in geographical terms: from Europe to America, and from the city to the countryside. The model of expatriation was not entirely dead, but it belonged to a previous era:

---

[41] Frederick to Reigelman, 18 Mar. 1971, Milton Monroe Reigelman: Collection on *The Midland*, UI.
[42] 'Books and Authors', *The New York Times*, 12 Aug. 1934, p. BR15.

We will send scholars to Oxford, but it is significant that Paul Engle produced on his scholarship time one of the most American volumes of recent verse. Europe has lost much of its magic. Gertrude Stein comes to us from Paris and is only a seven days' wonder. Ezra Pound's new volume seems all compounded of echoes from a lost world. The expatriates do not fit in with the newer America, so greatly changed from the old.

(231)

Interestingly, Wood mentioned Engle alongside modernist expatriates: Gertrude Stein and Ezra Pound. The European model had long attracted American artists—including Wood, who spent long periods of time in Paris when he was in his thirties. In 1923, he took a life study class at the Académie Julien and, three years later, he exhibited his impressionist-like paintings in the Galerie Carmine. While in Germany in Autumn 1928, he studied fifteenth- and sixteenth-century artists, such as Albrecht Dürer, Hans Holbein, and Hans Memling. In the 1930s, however, Wood loudly rejected the European influence.

At the beginning of his career, Engle was often presented as a disciple of the painter, who was seventeen years older and much more established. 'Do you know who my art teacher was in the eighth grade?' Engle once asked an interviewer. 'Grant Wood. I was his worst student. I was simply shocking. I could not draw or paint' (Gildner 35). Despite his lack of artistic abilities, Engle stayed in touch with his former instructor. There were many common points between the two men, including their deep attachment to the Cedar Rapids community. Wood was supported by several patrons in this small town—including David Turner, the owner of a funeral parlour, who let the artist live in an apartment above the mortuary's garage. Like Wood, Engle eagerly courted local business people. He had personal reasons not to disdain the world of commerce. When he was a child, the insurance salesman Jay Sigmund—who lived across the street from the Engle family—had given him translations of French poetry by Charles Baudelaire and Arthur Rimbaud. 'For a young kid growing up in Cedar Rapids that was strong meat,' Engle later said (Gildner 35). As we have seen, Sigmund wrote poems and was in contact with John T. Frederick at *The Midland*. The young Engle also benefited from the help of Art Clark, the owner of the drugstore where he worked as a teenager. Clark would order little magazines such as *transition* especially for his employee, even though they were unlikely to sell. While many modernist artists rejected the narrow-minded consumerism of small towns, both Engle and Wood praised local businessmen who had believed in them, providing financial support or simply encouragement.

At first sight, Engle's return to Iowa in the late 1930s seemed to confirm this break with the previous generation of modernist expatriates. Like Wood, Engle embraced his regional, and national identity. Following the publication of *American Song*, he wrote several collections of poems—including *Corn*, published in

1939 by Doubleday. That same year, *Life* magazine published a photo-reportage entitled 'The Flowering of the Valley, Iowa Trains Creative Artists'. The article started with an overview of Wood's work at Iowa: 'He is there primarily to paint, serving as sort of a working model and inspiration to students, but he also conducts classes.'[43] In addition to painting, Iowa trained students in creative writing, drama, and music. 'Iowa's creative writing division runs on the same principle as its graphic arts division,' declared *Life*. 'It has a resident poet, Paul Engle, whose career was very like Grant Wood's—birth in Iowa, a stay abroad (where he mixed with the effete Oxford poets), then a return to Iowa and overalls.'[44] A photo showed Engle, his wife, and Wood's secretary having a picnic. With his dungarees, Engle looks more like an Iowan farmer than a professor—a down-to-earth appearance that Wood himself favoured.

In his correspondence, Engle explicitly compared his academic position with that of Grant Wood. In 1937, he wrote to Edmund Blunden:

> My arrangement is pleasant, as I am here with the understanding that I am to spend most of my time writing, with only two mornings a week of teaching. The university is very friendly to the idea, as they also have a painter, Grant Wood, under the same scheme, though he is a much better artist than I. The idea is that a university should be a center of all culture, not just of scholarship, and that students who wish to be helped with painting or writing or music can have someone to go to who is practicing the art in which they are interested. I wish you could have a job with so much free time, away from the distraction of daily tutorials. But you must come to America for that![45]

There are several interesting things here: first, Engle presented the University of Iowa as a major artistic centre, a centre that attracted not only writers but also well-known painters such as Wood. Second, he described his own working conditions as more attractive than what Oxford offered to a well-established poet such as Blunden. His light teaching load left him plenty of time to write and compared favourably to Blunden's daily tutorials. Engle's confident tone is particularly striking: he would spend the rest of his career comparing Iowa to leading intellectual centres (Paris, Oxford, and even Classical Athens).

However, Engle was ferociously ambitious and his satisfaction with his job did not last long. There were two main issues. First, he found his salary too low. 'I was the lowest paid member of the University faculty,' he later said, 'although I had published four books and had two American and two Oxford degrees, at $2,400 for nine months, $225 for summer.' Looking back on his career, Engle attributed this unfavourable treatment to the fact that many scholars 'loathed Creative Writing

---

[43] 'The Flowering of the Valley, Iowa Trains Creative Artists', *Life*, 5 June 1939, p. 55.
[44] 'The Flowering of the Valley' 56.
[45] Engle to Edmund Blunden, 20 Nov. 1937, Paul Engle Papers, Coe College, Iowa.

and opposed its establishment as a natural part of the Department'. And, he added: 'It was jungle warfare.'[46] A 1941 memo confirms that Engle was not given pay and rank on the same basis as other faculty members. Although the University claimed that they had 'no desire to consider his income from his writing or his lecturing as a basis for keeping his salary low', this additional income seemed to have been on everyone's mind.[47] Foerster thus objected to a salary increase, citing Engle's outside activities. However, Engle was promised that he could eventually achieve full academic rank.

Grant Wood offered a precedent: having taught at the University since 1934, he became University Professor of Fine Arts in Autumn 1941. N. Elizabeth Schlatter has described this position as 'token', a way to isolate Wood whose rigid teaching methods had attracted controversy. Regionalism was on the decline, and Wood's position was far weaker than it had been a few years before. The fact remains that Wood had reached the top of the academic ladder, shortly before dying of cancer. The University of Iowa was one of the few institutions that offered a clear career path for artists, an aspect that probably convinced Engle to stay.

But there was another problem that troubled Engle: the University's management showed little interest in international activities, such as inviting writers from abroad. Funding was not the only issue. Iowa had long defined itself as a centre for regional art, and Engle struggled to change this image. In 1946, for example, he tried to convince Dean Earl McGrath to invite Edmund Blunden, a writer who embodied 'all the aspects of literature, the historical, the critical, the creative'.[48] Engle enlisted the help of his Head of Department Baldwin Maxwell, who also wrote to McGrath, reminding him of the long history of the department:

> Much has been said, as you know, about the hostility between those who teach the literature of the past and those who write the literature of the present. It was in the belief that such hostility was injurious to both that the University of Iowa a few years ago inaugurated graduate work for advanced degrees in creative writing. The interest which this unique program has evoked is so great that now approximately fifty percent of our graduate students in English are seeking degrees in creative writing.[49]

For Maxwell, the University could attract quality students because it offered them the opportunity to write their own creative work and meet contemporary writers. But Blunden never came to Iowa, apparently because the senior management

---

[46] Engle to University of Iowa Press Editorial Board, 24 Jan. 1980, Box 4, Papers of Paul Engle, UI.
[47] H. K. Newburn, 'Conference with Mr Paul Engle', 16 Dec. 1941, Faculty Vertical Files: Paul Engle, UI.
[48] Engle to Earl McGrath, 24 May 1946, Faculty Vertical Files: Paul Engle, UI.
[49] Baldwin Maxwell to McGrath, 23 May 1946, Faculty Vertical Files: Paul Engle, UI.

rejected the proposal. Engle would never forget his frustration—and he redoubled his efforts to get funding to invite the best international writers to Iowa.

When it came to the identity of the Writers' Workshop, Engle argued against regionalism. He worked hard to bring writers from every State and from foreign countries. And he made sure that the press was aware that the Workshop's ambitions extended well beyond Iowa. In 1946, for example, the *Cedar Rapids Gazette* published a photo of Engle with two of his students: Eric Sjogren of Sweden and Edilberto Tiempo of the Philippines.[50] 'The workshop is a cosmopolitan group of men and women who find its sessions informal and stimulating,' declared the newspaper. These workshop writers now benefited from the support of a New York publisher. Indeed, Rinehart had just announced it would award two fellowships of $750 each to the most promising manuscripts. After revising their work, authors would receive another $750 at the stage of publication. By the mid-1940s, then, the key elements of the Workshop's 'brand story' were already in place: its internationalism, its close links with the New York publishing industry and its ability to open the doors of publication for previously unknown writers.

Towards the end of his career, Engle contrasted his own juxtaposition of regionalism and cosmopolitanism with Wood's positioning. 'I have the warmest feeling for the Midwest and have written much about it,' he said, 'but the Workshop had to strive for excellence, not localism. I always felt that Grant Wood was too assertively "Iowan," especially since he learned his stylizing technique not here but in Munich and especially the Pieter Bruegel the Elder paintings in the Alte Pinakothek, and in Paris studios.'[51] Instead of acknowledging the influence of Europe on his own work, Wood had claimed to find inspiration only in regional topics and art. But Engle chose a different path, for his own writing and for the Workshop. He looked both inwards and outwards. He refused to choose between Iowa and the wider world. Yet, Engle never completely dissociated himself from Grant Wood—twenty years after the *Life* article, he posed for the *Des Moines Sunday* with his own copy of Wood's famous painting *American Gothic*.[52]

Engle's literary horizon remained influenced by international modernism. In 1969, he said: 'In English we've lost our greatest writers—Faulkner, Hemingway, Stevens, Joyce, Yeats ... There's no one that good today' (Daien). The international community he had discovered as a student at Oxford left an enduring mark on his *Weltanschauung*. He once explained to the editor of *The New York Times* his early vision for the Writers' Workshop: 'Not only was this the first such Program in this country for young American writers, I also believed deeply that, affected by the Rhodes example and having lived three years at Oxford in a genuinely international University, we should not make nationalistic distinctions between people

---

[50] International Students at the Iowa Writers' Workshop, *Cedar Rapids Gazette*, 24 Nov. 1946.
[51] Engle, 'General Remarks on the Engle Workshop', undated, Faculty Vertical Files: Paul Engle, UI.
[52] Paul Engle and his copy of Grant Wood's American Gothic, *Des Moines Sunday Register*, 2 Aug. 1959.

(also depressed by the howling nationalisms of Europe) of talent, or even without talent.'[53] For Engle, the Workshop had to welcome American and non-American writers, without distinction.

Engle's fierce determination to transform the Workshop into a magnet for talented international writers contributed to the worldwide diffusion of creative writing programmes. Thirty years after the *Cedar Rapids Gazette* published the article on the Workshop's 'cosmopolitan atmosphere', Edilberto Tiempo wrote in support of Engle's nomination for the Nobel Peace Prize. The Filipino writer fondly remembered his former instructor. The training he had received at Iowa had influenced his entire career: 'In 1961 my wife and I opened the National Writers Workshop at Silliman University, patterned after that in Iowa; this was the first writing program in Asia.' And Tiempo added: 'This spread of international programs in writing is in itself a tribute to Paul Engle, the man and teacher.'[54]

Engle was especially proud of this international legacy. In 1967, after resigning his directorship of the Workshop amidst tensions with literary scholars over funding and hiring practices, he went on to fund the International Writing Program (IWP) to bring foreign writers to Iowa. The rest of his career was spent in this international community, and he repeatedly criticized the Writers' Workshop for its 'provincialism'. He was particularly infuriated by the Workshop's refusal to let IWP writers register for its sessions. 'This seems to me provincial, narrow, blind,' he said in 1974.[55] And three years later, the same accusation appears in his letter to Richard Lloyd-Jones, the Chair of the Department of English. 'All foreign writers coming here say that they miss close association with American writers,' Engle wrote. 'The Writers' Workshop, in its provincialism, refuses to have anything to do with our members.'[56]

To this day, the IWP and the Writers' Workshop have few links. When I visited the University of Iowa in August 2016, nearly everyone I met—from literary scholars to IWP writers—mentioned the insularity of the Writers' Workshop. Those who are not affiliated with the Workshop often find it hard to engage with those who are. One academic (who is also a published poet) told me he tried to reach out when he first arrived in Iowa City, but the Workshop people completely ignored him. You need rare diplomatic skills to communicate with these people, he added. Another professor told me about the complete separation between the Workshop and the Department of English—even though the latter had just launched an undergraduate programme in creative writing. It is, of course, impossible to generalize, but after repeatedly hearing these kinds of stories, I got the impression that the Writers' Workshop was not particularly interested in engaging with the

---

[53] Engle to Ed Klein, 20 Feb. 1978, Box 4, Papers of Paul Engle, UI.
[54] Edilberto Tiempo to Nobel Institute, 25 Aug. 1976, Records of the Iowa Writers' Workshop, Series XI, Box 2, UI.
[55] Engle to John Gerber, 27 Oct. 1974, Faculty Vertical Files: Paul Engle, UI.
[56] Engle to Richard Lloyd-Jones, 31 Jan. 1977, Faculty Vertical Files: Paul Engle, UI.

outside world (or even with University of Iowa colleagues). At the other end of the spectrum, the IWP continues to embody Engle's vision of outward-looking cosmopolitanism rooted in regional pride. When I visited Shambaugh House, the IWP's home, I was not surprised to see a large portrait of Engle hung in the main hall. As a self-proclaimed literary outsider, Engle was proud to be a role model for cosmopolitan writers living in Iowa City, far from their country of origin.

2
'I'm afraid I've got involved with a nut'

William Faulkner, Random House and the Post-war Generation of Aspiring Writers

After the Second World War, the centre of the literary world moved from Paris and New York to the Midwest—or so it seemed to Paul Engle and his colleagues at the Iowa Writers' Workshop. They insisted that creative writing was not indulgent self-expression, but a demanding discipline similar to other professional endeavours.[1] At the same time, they also positioned themselves as outsiders, hostile to the conventions and narrow-mindedness of academia. Unlike traditional scholars, creative writers could not expect a pre-determined career path. Being a writer would remain a speculative career. 'It takes a rare combination of talent, will power and discipline to make a writer,' declared Engle in 1962. According to one faculty member at Iowa, less than one-fifth of fiction students had all the qualities necessary to establish a literary career (Polking 22). A creative writing degree would give students the professional tools necessary to a writing career but could not guarantee success for everyone.

At the time when university creative writing was becoming increasingly popular, what kind of choices did young writers make to launch their career? The post-war generation had different opportunities than the previous one—those who, like William Faulkner and Ernest Hemingway, had started to publish in the 1920s. Although this generational transition was noted by many observers after the Second World War,[2] it has received little attention in literary scholarship. This chapter explores the chaotic transition from the dream of bohemian communities and friendship between older and younger writers, to the ambiguous professionalization of the writing career in the university system. I show that the two models coexisted in the period immediately after the Second World War.

Take the example of James Culpepper, a young aspiring writer who attempted to secure William Faulkner's patronage in order to sell his writings to Random

---

[1] See McGurl 129.
[2] See, for example, Wallace Stegner's 1949 article titled 'The Anxious Generation': 'The young writer who in the twenties headed for Greenwich Village and who in the thirties took out by boxcar to bum his way through a hundred odd jobs to fame now heads for some graduate school of English to study with some professional writer' (2).

House. Culpepper had a very high opinion of his own work and was determined to become a literary star. However, he was well aware that the rise to fame would not be easy: not only did he live in Atlanta, Georgia, far from the literary centres of the East Coast, but he was also unemployed and under pressure from his wife and family to start making a living. In several of his letters, Culpepper reminded Faulkner that fame does not happen magically: when Faulkner was himself a young writer, he had been helped by the more experienced Sherwood Anderson. Culpepper stopped at nothing to make sure that Faulkner got his message: he went to Faulkner's home unannounced and posed as a journalist, and he repeatedly threatened to visit again if Faulkner failed to help him; he also wrote to Estelle Faulkner to ask for assistance. At this point, Faulkner started to worry for the safety of his wife and daughter, and he reluctantly agreed to help Culpepper with the publication of his novel. In a letter to the publisher Robert Haas, however, Faulkner explained that he was being blackmailed and discouraged Random House from publishing the manuscript. A form rejection letter was subsequently sent to Culpepper, who reacted angrily. On 8 March 1949, he wrote: 'If I were the wife of some great writer, or his sister, or his drinking companion, or if I drank champagne in New Yirk [sic] with the literary crowd in some Fifth Avenue apartment—it would be different: anyone down here knows that.'[3]

I discovered the correspondence of Faulkner and Culpepper when I was working in the Random House archives at Columbia Rare Book & Manuscript Library in New York. These letters can be found in a box labelled 'General Correspondence; Col-Daz', amongst rejection letters sent by Random House to aspiring writers. This box is part of the uncatalogued collection stored off-site, while Faulkner's known letters are stored on-site. The correspondence between Faulkner, Haas, and Culpepper in the Random House archives is completed by a small cache of letters held in the Brodsky collection at Southeast Missouri State University. I have been able to identify a total of twenty-six letters, dated from 6 January 1949 to 24 September 1949.[4]

It is difficult to evaluate Culpepper's claim to literary talent. His manuscript is not in the archive (Random House returned it to the author). There is evidence that the publisher never ordered a reader's report. The only thing that we do know about Culpepper's first novel is its title: *Jack Shall Have Jill* (a line from Shakespeare's *Midsummer Night's Dream*). Culpepper eventually decided to write a second novel. In September, he told Haas that he was going to stay for some time in Oxford, Mississippi (where Faulkner lived).[5] With this letter, all traces of Culpepper disappear from our view.

---

[3] James Culpepper to Random House, 8 Mar. 1949, Box 249, RH.
[4] The remaining correspondence between Faulkner, Culpepper, and Haas consists of twenty-two letters in Box 249, Folder Cu-Cz, RH; and four letters in Box 9, Folder 5 (1949), BP.
[5] Culpepper to Robert Haas, 24 Sept. 1949, Box 249, RH.

Culpepper was very good at drawing attention to himself; he was less good at being taken seriously as a writer. No established writer was willing to 'consecrate' him, in Pierre Bourdieu's term, and he felt increasingly alienated from the literary world. Culpepper's failure to break into print exemplifies the centrality of networks, friendship, and patronage within the field of cultural production. While young Southern writers like Flannery O'Connor launched their careers through the newly created creative writing programmes, James Culpepper relied on the *informal mentorship model.* He was convinced that the only way to get published was to attract the attention of a well-known writer, as the young Faulkner had done with his own mentor, Sherwood Anderson.

In his correspondence with James Culpepper, Faulkner celebrated individualism and hard work, encouraging the younger writer to rely on himself instead of seeking help and mentorship. Faulkner thus refused to repeat the behaviour of Sherwood Anderson. While Anderson had used his fame to help younger writers get published and noticed, Faulkner told Culpepper to find a job and stop bothering him with requests. Faulkner's dealing with Culpepper is coherent with his post-war image as a self-made writer who kept away from literary groups. In his study of the Faulkner revival of the late 1940s, Lawrence Schwartz rightly suggests that Faulkner's rise to canonical status was not inevitable: 'in almost all the American literary histories of the period up to World War II, Faulkner was judged a talented, but limited secondary writer—hard to read, often macabre, and too involved with style' (3). For Schwartz, Faulkner's rise to fame should be read in the context of the cultural Cold War, at the time when American values were defined and promoted. Faulkner's individualistic themes and difficult style 'served an ideological cause' and were thus used 'as a cultural weapon' (210).

While most scholars will be interested in Faulkner's responses to Culpepper, I believe it is equally important to pay attention to Culpepper's responses to Faulkner. Indeed, there are surprisingly few studies of aspiring writers. This gap in scholarship is all the more striking that the whole field of book history developed out of an interest in the 'sociology of texts', in D. F. McKenzie's words. Scholars who work in book history and print culture pay attention not only to the material aspect of the book, but also to its production, circulation, and distribution. Their point of departure is that literary agents, publishers, printers, booksellers, and other book trade workers are as important as writers to understand the appearance of a book. This approach based on the book trade and its actors has so far excluded aspiring writers who, by definition, are not yet published and accepted as professionals. Yet, recent studies have shed light on marginal figures: working-class readers, non-canonical writers, little-known publishers, and the like (Rose; Cross; Howsam). In Digital Humanities, Franco Moretti has famously criticized close reading, a methodology that relies on 'an extremely small canon'. For Moretti, it is clear that 'you invest so much in individual texts *only* if you think that very few of them really matter'. Instead, Moretti has pushed for an opening up of the canon, using 'distant reading' (48). Similarly, it is time to pay more attention to would-be writers, including those who failed to get published because they lacked talent and/or connections in the literary world.

This chapter is organized into two sections. In the first section, I show that to realize his dream of literary success, Culpepper followed a path rigidly modelled on Faulkner's relationship with Sherwood Anderson. At the time when Random House was becoming increasingly interested in creative writing programmes, Culpepper failed to understand that universities offered a new model to launch a writing career. In the second section, I examine Faulkner's refusal to acknowledge that friendship and patronage mattered enormously in a literary career. Faulkner's discourse on the virtues of individualism, hard work, and perseverance is coherent with his image as a self-made genius who embodied American values in the Cold War context.

James Culpepper's attempts to secure a mentor and attract the attention of a major publishing house exemplify the struggle between the 'have' and 'have-nots' in the literary field of the mid-twentieth century. While Culpepper was an unknown twenty-two-year-old young man in 1949, Faulkner was a critically respected and commercially successful writer. The publication of *The Portable Faulkner* (1946) triggered a renewal of critical interest in his writings. Moreover, the paperback revolution enabled Faulkner to reach the mass-market: by the beginning of 1949, the New American Library had reprinted three of his titles (*Sanctuary*, *The Wild Palms*, and *The Old Man*) under its Signet imprint.[6] Culpepper knew that Faulkner was one of the most important Random House writers, and that a word from him could put a manuscript out of the slush pile and into the hands of an editor.

In February 1949, Faulkner explained to his editor the circumstances of his first encounter with James Culpepper:

> I'm afraid I've got involved with a nut, and that Random H. may get a repercussion
> ...
> Some time ago, maybe two years, I dont [sic] remember, I got a letter from someone I did not remember ever hearing of before, saying something like this:
> 'Dear Mr Faulkner, my destiny lies between Oxford and Cambridge and I have chosen Cambridge. When you write, address me there. James Culpepper.'[7]

In Faulkner's narration, Culpepper immediately appears as a deranged correspondent afflicted with pathological grandiosity. At first, Faulkner assumed that his correspondent was referring to Oxford and Cambridge in England. But in Autumn 1948, Faulkner received another letter, coming from Cambridge, Maryland. Culpepper announced that once his novel was finished, he would come to

---

[6] For more on Faulkner and the paperback market, see Earle 195–207.
[7] Faulkner to Haas, [Feb. 1949], Box 249, RH.

Oxford, Mississippi and stay at Faulkner's house. He expected Faulkner to act as a friend and mentor—somebody who would not only offer him accommodation, but would also help him revise his novel and get it published. Culpepper repeatedly compared himself to the younger Faulkner who had benefited from Sherwood Anderson's hospitality and help. In a letter posted in Atlanta, Georgia, on 22 February 1949, Culpepper wrote:

> You must— as you phrase it—disabuse your mind of any idea that Random House will not publish my novel. If they reject it, I will come down there and stand on your front porch and holler until the neighbors come around and force you to take me in, and I will stay there until we get it published—just as Sherwood Anderson helped you ... I aim to get that novel published through Random House; only a plain fool would write for nothing, and, Mr. Faulkner, I am not that big of a fool ... I repeat, we will get it published.[8]

Culpepper's behaviour seems at first sight entirely irrational: why would Faulkner help him, a total stranger, to find a publisher? Why would an established writer welcome a newcomer into his home and offer him help and encouragement? And why use a threatening tone to convince Faulkner to welcome him as a disciple? In fact, Culpepper's sense of entitlement came from his rigid understanding of a successful literary career, based on the Anderson/Faulkner example. The fact that Anderson had helped the young Faulkner to get published was widely known. For example, in its 1939 issue with Faulkner on the cover, *TIME* magazine declared:

> When Miss Prall, who had recently married Sherwood Anderson, came to New Orleans, Faulkner visited her, became Anderson's close friend. He turned to novels, under Anderson's influence, wrote *Soldiers' Pay*. Mrs. Anderson volunteered to get Sherwood to read the book, to recommend it to Publisher Horace Liveright if he liked it. Next day she brought it back, saying. 'Sherwood says if he isn't required to read this, he'll try to get Liveright to publish it.' Liveright accepted it, gave Faulkner advances of $200 apiece on the next two.
>
> (Cantwell)

Here, Elizabeth Anderson is presented as a mediator between her husband and her former employee, the twenty-seven-year-old Faulkner. She appears generous and sympathetic towards the impoverished young man, who had just resigned from his position as a postmaster. Biographers later confirmed this narrative. For Joseph Blotner, Elizabeth Anderson was a 'considerate hostess' who offered a spare room, 'coffee in the morning', and 'a meal now and then' to the struggling writer (128). The time that Faulkner spent with the Andersons in New Orleans was a turning

---

[8] Culpepper to Faulkner, 22 Feb. 1949, Box 249, RH.

point in his career. Faulkner later said that any young writer feels 'to be with people that have the same problems and the same interests as him, that won't laugh at what he is trying to do, won't laugh at what he says no matter how foolish it might sound to the Philistine'.[9] Not only did Faulkner find comradeship in New Orleans, but he also progressed as a writer. In early 1925, he 'began writing his early sketches for the *Times-Picayune*, found the writing of prose more suitable for him than poetry, and planned his first novel with the working title *Mayday* (published title *Soldier's Pay*)' (Rideout 571). Sherwood Anderson had just accepted an offer of publication from Horace Liveright, and he recommended Faulkner to his new publisher. According to Walter Rideout, it was at a luncheon in April 1925 that Anderson told Liveright about Faulkner, 'a writer to watch and sign up': 'he had read a chapter of his *Mayday*, thought it "good stuff," and hoped to persuade Liveright to give Faulkner an advance on the unfinished novel' (576). However, the letters preserved at Newberry Library show that it was only in June 1925 that Anderson wrote his publisher on Faulkner's behalf. On 5 June, Liveright responded to Anderson: 'I want to let you know that I got your letter of June 1st and that, of course, I would be interested in considering Bill Falkner's [sic] novel'.[10] Contrary to the story that Faulkner often told, it seems that Anderson did read the novel, or at least part of it, before recommending it (Richardson 304). James Culpepper knew that without the Andersons' mediation, it would have been much more difficult for Faulkner to attract the attention of a New York-based publisher such as Liveright.

Culpepper expected Estelle Faulkner and her husband to play the roles of Elizabeth and Sherwood Anderson. Since William Faulkner showed no intention of becoming his mentor, Culpepper contacted Estelle Faulkner, hoping she would welcome him into her home and create the conditions that would launch his literary career. In his two-page handwritten letter to Faulkner's wife, Culpepper adopted a flattering tone: 'Now, Mrs. Faulkner, I know that you must be a very unusual and fine woman to have gotten Mr. Faulkner where he is, and I wonder if you would mind reading over this novel I am working on when it is completed.' Appealing to empathy, a quality traditionally gendered female, Culpepper mentioned his family's anxiety to see him publish his novel: 'At the present time I am living in Cambridge with my wife's family. I am sure that she will be just as pleased as I would be if you promised the assistance you can give.'[11] Culpepper, who had no job and lived with his in-laws, viewed his personal situation in the light of Faulkner's trajectory. Far from being irrational, Culpepper's entire behaviour can be explained by his close following of the *informal mentorship model* exemplified by Anderson and Faulkner.

---

[9] Graduate Course in American Fiction, 21 Feb. 1958 (Gwynn and Blotner 231).
[10] Horace Liveright to Sherwood Anderson, 5 June 1925, Box 23, Sherwood Anderson Papers, Newberry Library. The letter that Anderson wrote to Liveright on 1 June is not extant (Bosha 26).
[11] Culpepper to Estelle Faulkner, 6 Jan. 1949, Box 249, RH.

In the late 1940s, when Culpepper was looking for a publisher, the *informal mentorship model* was no longer the only way to break into print. With the rise of creative writing programmes, the model of professional affiliation with the university was becoming an increasingly common path towards a writing career. This model involved formal mentorship between older and younger writers, within an institution. It was not based on friendship, but on a professional relationship between professor and student. The new model could have been very appealing to James Culpepper, who was isolated from the literary centres of the East Coast and had very few opportunities to meet established authors. Although he repeatedly claimed that he was a writer, he lacked the recognition of his peers. For young writers like him, creative writing programmes housed in universities offered an opportunity to work with their professional elders. For example, the 1948 Bread Loaf Writers' Conference, held at Middlebury College in Vermont, featured a list of well-known poets (Robert Frost, Louis Untermeyer, John Ciardi) and fiction writers (Bernard DeVoto, A. B. Guthrie, Jr.).[12] Conference participants could submit a manuscript for criticism, as well as attend talks on writing techniques, contemporary literature, and publishing. While Bread Loaf took place for a few weeks every summer, other programmes such as the Iowa Writers' Workshop ran through the regular school year. Faulkner's rising reputation in academia in the late 1940s had a direct impact on these programmes. McGurl notes that both Faulkner and Hemingway 'spent little time in the classroom but have been "teachers"' to many students of creative writing (321). Because Faulkner's and Hemingway's works were so widely read at Iowa and elsewhere, they deeply influenced the new generation of writers.

Faulkner's strong association with the South contributed to his influence, since regionalism was crucial to the emergence of university-based writing. In the immediate post-war period, the most prestigious literary journals—the *Kenyon Review*, *Sewanee Review*, and *Southern Review*—were edited by former Agrarians at small Southern schools. No young writer who aspired to publish poetry or literary fiction could ignore names such as John Crowe Ransom, Robert Penn Warren, and Allen Tate. These men invented a new model of writer—the Southern poet who taught writing and criticism at universities. Far from being confined to academia and to small literary circles, 'Southern literature' was successfully sold to the mass-market in paperback editions. The New American Library printed 1,103,424 copies of Faulkner's *Sanctuary* from April 1947 to May 1951,[13] 2,185,830 copies of Erskine Caldwell's *Tobacco Road* from March 1947 to December 1949, and an astonishing 5,324,184 copies of Caldwell's *God's Little Acre* from March 1946 to January 1950.[14] Like paperback publishers, the Book-of-the-Month Club

---

[12] Advertisement for the Bread Loaf Writer's Conference, *Harper's* magazine, Apr. 1948, n.p.
[13] New American Library, Memo, 14 May 1951, Box 18, RH.
[14] Victor Weybright to Bennett Cerf, 19 Jan. 1950, Box 287, RH.

regularly published books by Southern authors. In 1949, the Club sent to its 520,325 members[15] a novel by Frances Gaither, *Double Muscadine*—part of a trilogy on slavery.

Culpepper knew that 'Southern literature' was used as a marketing category, and he was convinced that to succeed, he needed to write about the South (ironically, 'write what you know' was becoming the first commandment of creative writing programmes). In a letter to Robert Haas in late March 1949, Culpepper declared: 'I am writing another novel concerning the poor negroes and whites of Georgia. This is a salable subject: witness Erskine Caldwell's success, Lillian Smith's, etc.'[16] Citing bestselling writers with roots in Georgia, Culpepper positioned himself within the most controversial and successful kind of Southern fiction. Faulkner, Caldwell, and Lillian Smith (the author of the 1944 bestseller *Strange Fruit*) wrote frankly about sex and racial tensions in the South. Culpepper was not the only young writer to realize that the race issue was a highly salable subject. When Paul Engle sent the novel of one of his students to Random House, the editor Harry Maule commented: 'I don't know how many novels about the negro question the public wants.'[17] Engle responded haughtily: 'If you don't take this novel, some one else will.'[18] Random House eventually published the novel, and Engle's student, R. V. Cassill, went on to lead a long and productive career as a writer and a teacher of creative writing.

Like Cassill, James Culpepper was a young writer—at the time when creative writing programmes presented the youth of their students as a sign of stylistic freshness and narrative renewal. This was a logical consequence of the growing impact of youth culture in the publishing business.[19] In his letter to Robert Haas, Culpepper wrote: 'Now, I am just twenty-two years old, and that in itself is salable. Someday I will no longer be that age and that will lessen that possibility of selling: you nor I nor anyone else would be able to exploit my age any longer.'[20] Likewise, Paul Engle was well aware that youth was its own publicity. In the late 1940s, he tried to convince Random House to offer a Fiction Fellowship to students in the Iowa Writers' Workshop. He described the workshop as a site where youth, professionalism, and innovation were closely intertwined, as opposed to more traditional writing courses: 'The program at Iowa differs from the usual "Writing Course" at such a place as Columbia University in that at the latter the course is not a part of the regular work of the student, but is done in the "Extension" part of the University, attracting special, usually *much older people* who are not engaged

---

[15] See United States Congress Senate Committee on Post Office and Civil Service 807. For more on the Book-of-the-Month Club, see Radway.
[16] Culpepper to Haas, [late Mar. 1949], Box 9, Folder 5, BP.
[17] Harry Maule to Paul Engle, 22 Apr. 1949, Box 252, RH.
[18] Engle to Maule, 16 May 1949, Box 252, RH.
[19] Marius Hentea argues that British and American publishers began to target and advertise youth in the 1920s (182).
[20] Culpepper to Haas, [late Mar. 1949], Box 9, Folder 5, BP.

in any other university work but are usually doing this in spare time from jobs' (emphasis added).²¹ When he wrote about his own programme, Engle rarely used the term 'student', preferring 'young writer'. For Engle, the rise of creative writing programmes was inseparable from a change of generations.

In his correspondence with Random House, Engle repeatedly stressed the new spatial characteristics of the writing career chosen by his students. Whereas the older generation had viewed Paris and, to a lesser extent, New York as centres of creativity, younger American writers favoured the Midwest and the South. For Engle, 'the university is the answer to the problem of having some cultural centers in the great area between New York and Hollywood ... Before New York or Paris, the centers of the twenties, the young writer goes on toward graduate work at a university which honors writing, so that universities are his centers of the forties.'²² Engle's oft-repeated argument was surprising for two reasons. First, Engle could hardly ignore that Midwestern and Southern cities like Chicago and New Orleans had attracted Anderson, Faulkner, and other major writers long before the rise of creative writing programmes. Second, it was difficult to present New York as a city past its prime in the 1940s. Not only had the New York art scene established its dominance with abstract expressionism, but the literary scene was also booming (think of the New York School of poets, for example). Engle's dismissal of New York was not due to ignorance: he was published by Random House and made regular trips to the city to see his editor; he also had close links with the poet Allen Tate, who was then teaching at New York University (NYU). In fact, Engle pushed his point on the decay of New York (and Paris) to highlight the emergence of new literary centres in the Midwest and the South. He presented the rise of creative writing programmes as a response to the geographical and organizational problems of the traditional path to a successful writing career (what I have called the *informal mentorship model*).

For Engle, the university system offered a nurturing environment to young American writers, many of whom had served during the war:

> Unlike the Twenties, the bulk of the good young writers of the moment are to be found in Universities. This is partly due to the GI Bill and partly to the greatly increased interest in Universities for writing, with courses offered and a chance for the writer to get some early and friendly criticism.²³

The GI Bill brought a massive influx of students to higher education: from 1944 to 1951, 2,232,000 veterans used the Bill to attend colleges or universities (Gutek 283). As McGurl notes, 'many of the students who were arriving in Iowa City in

---

[21] Engle, Proposal for Random House—University of Iowa Fiction Fellowship [1949], Box 252, RH.
[22] Ibid.
[23] Engle, Memo to Cerf (Notes on a Proposed Random House—Iowa Fiction Fellowship), 30 Mar. 1948, Box 9, RH.

the early years of Engle's tenure were returning soldiers supported by the GI Bill' (175–6). Creative writing programmes promised to these non-traditional students a different approach to writing and literary studies, far from the philological and historical methodologies of literary scholars. This new pedagogy, Engle believed, would address the challenges faced by the new generation of young writers.

There are many similarities between Engle's and Culpepper's discourses on the writing career. Like Engle, Culpepper saw New York as a decrepit literary centre. For Culpepper, cronyism, laziness, and overindulgence had replaced talent and hard work. The 'literary crowd' spent time drinking champagne 'in some Fifth Avenue apartment' while aspiring writers waited too long for a publication decision.[24] Approximately one month after sending his manuscript, Culpepper wrote to Random House:

> It may seem hard for you to believe, but the whole novel could be read in a period of two hours at the most, with a similar period of time necessary for decision. And, too, the whole novel could be written—yes, written—in the time it's lain on your desks in New York: not in the weeks and weeks it's taking you gentlemen to read it.
>
> Now you may have money to burn there in New York, but down here we don't find it and time growing on trees.[25]

The dichotomies between 'New York' (repeated twice) and 'here' (meaning Atlanta) highlight Culpepper's sense of superiority. Convinced that he was much more talented and hard-working than the average New York writer, Culpepper threatened to contact Faulkner if Random House did not offer him an advance of $1,000—approximately $10,500 in today's dollars. Although Engle had none of Culpepper's grandiosity and sense of entitlement, he too wanted Random House to invest more in young writers. In his proposal for a Random House–Iowa fellowship, Engle reminded the publisher Bennett Cerf that Random House had much to gain from this investment:

> I'd like to add that I by no means feel that I'm coming to you begging. After all, I have a Fellowship to offer with Rinehart, and have their support, as well as one student working on a Rinehart Fellowship now. I feel that we have as much to offer you as you have to offer us.[26]

Indeed, Engle had negotiated with the editor John Selby at Rinehart for two fellowships to be offered each year to the best students in the Iowa Writers' Workshop. Convinced that his programme was nurturing the most talented young writers,

---

[24] Culpepper to Random House, 8 Mar. 1949, Box 249, RH.
[25] Culpepper to Random House, 17 Mar. 1949, Box 249, RH.
[26] Engle to Cerf, 30 Mar. 1948, Box 9, RH.

Engle wanted to negotiate on an equal basis with Random House, and he suggested a fellowship of $1,500 'offered twice a year or two offered once a year'.²⁷ Engle's confident tone exemplifies an important turn in the history of literary fiction: with the rise of creative writing programmes, some young writers no longer had to court publishers. Instead, publishers sent their editors to Iowa and other universities to try to 'discover' the future literary stars.

The competition to sign new writers was becoming so fierce that the Random House partners decided to pay a commission to Paul Engle for sending them the best manuscripts, rather than adopt his proposed fiction fellowship. Harry Maule gave two main reasons for dropping the fellowship project. First, very few first novels became bestsellers: most of them sold around 3,500 copies, a figure too low to justify the investment in a fellowship scheme. Second, the multiplication of these schemes meant that 'they no longer have any publicity value and rarely rate more than a line in some obscure literary note'. But if these fellowships were not advantageous to publishers, why did so many of them appear after the war? For Maule, 'the reason publishers are willing to enter such schemes is that they are gambling on getting a best-seller book club choice or motion picture sale'.²⁸ In other words, the Random House management feared that the interest in creative writing programmes had created an investment bubble, where publishers paid too much for manuscripts with a limited audience. Unlike other literary publishing houses such as Rinehart & Company, Random House was prepared to take only limited risks in the competition for the best literary writers. It seemed safer to help established writers like Faulkner relaunch their careers than to invest in budding writers.

James Culpepper failed to understand Random House's careful positioning. Probably influenced by advertisements that promised aspiring authors success in the marketplace, Culpepper saw the publishing field as a space of opportunities for the most aggressively competitive young authors. A study of *Harper's* magazine from January 1947 to September 1949 highlights the ubiquity of these advertisements for correspondence writing courses. The Newspaper Institute of America was the most frequent advertiser, followed by the Magazine Institute, the Palmer Institute of Authorship, the Storycrafters' Guild and the Supervised Story Writing School. The ads published in *Harper's* often featured rags-to-riches stories of struggling writers who managed to get published thanks to writing courses. 'Enter ... BEGINNER' and 'Exit ... SELLING WRITER' ... 'One of our graduate students is the author of THE BIG SKY, current best seller,' declared one ad for the Supervised Story Writing School.²⁹ 'A Magazine Institute Student who is working as a waiter recently signed a contract for his first novel, with an advance of over $1,000—after

---

²⁷ Ibid.
²⁸ Maule to Engle, 20 Oct. 1949, Box 252, RH.
²⁹ Advertisement for the Supervised Story Writing School, *Harper's* magazine, Feb. 1948, n.p.

completing only half the assignments of the course,' announced another ad.[30] It is likely that Culpepper's demand for an advance of $1,000 finds its origins in his reading of similar success stories. Writing to Robert Haas, Faulkner paraphrased a letter in which Culpepper described his financial objectives: 'Hemingway got 125,000 $ for a short story and if I thought he was going to burn up mss. or write for nickles [sic] I was crazy, that if Random H. would give him only $1,000.00 advance he would make out on that while writing another novel.'[31] Culpepper's correspondence shows an impulsive young man, more attracted to the figure of the Great American Writer than to the writing itself. Long before finishing his first novel, Culpepper was already asking Faulkner for help. His aim was to find a publisher and rapidly obtain money, fame, and literary standing.

Culpepper's failure to get published cannot be attributed, at least not entirely, to a lack of literary talent. Indeed, it is likely that his manuscript was rejected without having been read. Culpepper sent his novel to Random House on 19 February 1949, and, because the package was not addressed to Robert Haas, it did not reach the editor until the beginning of March. On 28 February, Haas, who was still waiting for the manuscript, wrote to an anxious Faulkner:

> When you say that you're afraid you've become involved with a nut, I consider that the year's understatement. Mr. Culpepper's correspondence, and indeed all his actions as you relate them, seem to me to be positively unique. I can only hope that for your sake he won't really show up in Oxford, and I should like to express the same pious wish so far as I am concerned with regard to 457 Madison Avenue.
>
> His book has not arrived here, but I will keep an eye open for it and will have the special-delivery postage for its return all ready on my desk.[32]

Because Culpepper did not behave like a typical would-be writer, Haas showed no intention to give him a chance. Only one week later, the editor told Faulkner that Culpepper's newly received manuscript 'has now been read and the report indicates that it is an impossible and confusing job'. Yet, there is no such document in the archives. Random House rarely commissioned reader's reports for unknown aspiring authors, and, considering Haas's explicit intention to return the manuscript immediately, it is likely that there never was any report. 'Here's hoping we can get rid of this lad without more ado!' wrote Haas in the conclusion of his letter.[33]

Although Culpepper presented himself as a victim of champagne-drinking New York publishers, his failure is largely due to his inability to understand the functioning of the publishing business, and the changing patterns in writing careers

---

[30] Advertisement for the Magazine Institute, Inc., *Harper's* magazine, Apr. 1948, n.p.
[31] Faulkner to Haas, [Feb. 1949], Box 249, RH.
[32] Haas to Faulkner, 28 Feb. 1949, Box 249, RH.
[33] Haas to Faulkner, 7 Mar. 1949, Box 249, RH.

(from *informal mentorship model*, to professionalization in creative writing programmes). Consider the case of Flannery O'Connor, who was only one or two years older than Culpepper and, like him, a Southerner from Georgia. O'Connor won a scholarship to go to the University of Iowa in 1945. She was admitted in Paul Engle's Writers' Workshop and graduated with a Master of Fine Arts in 1947. As Melvin J. Friedman puts it, O'Connor's apprenticeship at Iowa 'determined the contours of the remainder of her life'. The contacts she made there certainly helped launch her career as a short story writer. Unlike O'Connor, Culpepper clung to an older career pattern, favouring individual over institutional patronage. Although he was unemployed and impoverished, he could have applied for a scholarship to study creative writing—as O'Connor had done. So why did he fail to recognize the importance of creative writing programmes? His letters show that he came from a family that viewed writing as a frivolous activity (especially for a married young man, who had to provide a living for his wife). Culpepper had to prove that he could make money right away with his novel; he could not afford to waste years practising his craft in writing workshops. This does not mean that he came from a working-class background: his address in Atlanta is in a residential neighbourhood with large houses, built between the First and Second World Wars. But it seems that Culpepper's father was sceptical of his writing aspirations. Two weeks after sending his manuscript, Culpepper wrote to Random House: 'I and my family received a letter from my father tonight, who said that the chances were that you would not buy my novel—of course, anyone knows the setup there.'[34] Even before his son received a rejection slip, the elder Culpepper believed that Random House would not be interested in the manuscript. James Culpepper shared his father's view and sabotaged himself by sending frequent angry letters to Random House and to Faulkner. 'I have absolutely no expectations from my mss,' he wrote to Random House, 'I've been conditioned too long to the way things are there in New York.'[35]

Even if he had envisaged the benefits of enrolling in a programme such as the Iowa Writers' Workshop, it is likely that Culpepper would not have fitted well in an institution that so much valued the writing *community*. Culpepper clearly showed antisocial tendencies (in one letter to Random House, he declared: 'Please do not think that I am trying to annoy you. It makes me mad when someone tries to annoy me.')[36] For Faulkner, Culpepper was a maniac with alternate episodes of aggression and depression: 'high-and-mighty' letters were followed by 'whining' attempts to explain his miserable personal situation.[37] Whether Culpepper was mentally ill, or simply irascible and impatient to get published, it is difficult to picture him in a writing workshop, calmly accepting criticism on his work. As McGurl has shown,

---

[34] Culpepper to Random House, 8 Mar. 1949, Box 249, RH.
[35] Culpepper to Random House, 7 Mar. 1949, Box 249, RH.
[36] Culpepper to Random House, 8 Mar. 1949, Box 249, RH.
[37] Faulkner to Haas, [Feb. 1949], Box 249, RH.

the creative writing programme 'was after all a thing born … in the thirties, with the founding of the Iowa Writers' Workshop in 1936, and the "group-ness" of that decade could easily be detected in its rituals' (5). It is likely that Culpepper viewed Faulkner as a convincing role model not only because of their common Southern roots, but also because of Faulkner's fierce independence and rejection of literary groups.

In his correspondence with Culpepper, Faulkner presented the successful writer as a self-made man, and refused to acknowledge the role of friendship and patronage in a writing career. Despite Culpepper's insistence that it was time for Faulkner to emulate Anderson's generosity towards younger writers, Faulkner was reluctant to help somebody he saw as a dangerous madman. Fearing for the security of his family, Faulkner wrote to Haas:

> If he turns up here, I may have to have the cops take him up. At this rate, he'll scare my wife and daughter out of their shoes. I dont [sic] want to meet him at my front door with an axe-handle, or anything else that will make publicity, though actually I am being blackmailed.[38]

Faulkner's comment on the axe-handle highlights the power struggle between the two men. As an established writer, Faulkner feared the bad publicity that a public encounter with Culpepper could bring. He felt powerless and manipulated by an unknown twenty-two-year-old man. But why exactly did Faulkner believe that Culpepper was blackmailing him? After all, the young man was not particularly threatening. During his first and perhaps only visit to Oxford, Culpepper spoke to Faulkner but did not come into his house. The incident was so insignificant that Faulkner remembered it only when Culpepper described it in his letter to Estelle Faulkner. The only reason why Faulkner felt blackmailed was that the young author threatened to visit him unannounced—which is exactly what Faulkner himself had done with the Andersons. It is probable that Faulkner felt guilty at rejecting a budding writer who was only trying to break into print. Rather than ignoring Culpepper's letters, Faulkner entered into a correspondence and promised to ask his editor to look at the young writer's manuscript. This promise (which he kept) was an attempt to appease Culpepper and keep him away from Oxford. But Faulkner also tried to convince Culpepper that he did not need any help, that the only way to succeed was through hard work and perseverance. Perhaps remembering the difficulty he had in finding a publisher for his third novel, *Flags in the Dust*,[39] Faulkner explained to Culpepper 'that a first book might be refused, but for

---

[38] Faulkner to Haas, [Feb. 1949], Box 249, RH.
[39] Because *Flags in the Dust* had been repeatedly rejected by publishers, Faulkner decided to write *The Sound and the Fury* for himself without thinking of his audience: 'One day I seemed to shut a door between me and all publishers' addresses and book lists. I said to myself, Now I can write.' (1933 introduction to *The Sound and the Fury*, in Meriwether 710).

him to keep on writing until he did a good one'. Faulkner added that if Culpepper were really worried about 'his wife's mental strain', 'he would get a job and go to work'.[40]

There was, of course, a paradox at the heart of Faulkner's discourse. On the one hand, Faulkner had never made a secret of his friendship with Anderson, and the role it had played in his career. But on the other hand, Faulkner was telling a young writer to work hard and expect no help in finding a publisher. Faulkner never offered to read Culpepper's manuscript (thus paralleling the myth of Sherwood Anderson not reading *Soldiers' Pay*), and the letter of recommendation that he sent to his editor was far from enthusiastic:

> A young man, James Culpepper, whom I have seen once when he passed through Oxford some years ago, has written a 210 page novel. I have not read it and know nothing about it except the title, which I understand is JACK SHALL HAVE JILL. So I dont [sic] have any opinion about it, and having seen Culpepper only once and for a vfew [sic] minutes, I dont [sic] know anything about his possibilities either.
>
> Will you look at it? Notify me here, and I will have him send it to you from his home in Atlanta, if you will see it.[41]

Faulkner's coldness is easily explainable, considering Culpepper's aggressive strategy. The young man was arguably no blackmailer, but his sense of entitlement would have irritated many people. However, Faulkner was equally cold with other would-be writers—with a single exception. As Lisa Hickman points out, 'the only writer Faulkner ever mentored' was a young woman he met in the summer of 1949, Joan Williams (167). Faulkner's motives for helping the then twenty-year-old Williams were coloured by erotic intentions. 'What Faulkner felt he needed and wanted with Joan was a redemptive and rejuvenating love affair; what Joan hoped for was a close friendship with an author she greatly admired' (Hickman 11). A few months after the Culpepper incident and the Williams encounter, Faulkner won the Nobel Prize and his growing celebrity led to even more requests from aspiring writers. In 1957 and 1958, when he was writer-in-residence at the University of Virginia, he met with undergraduate and graduate students—some of whom were budding writers. Asked if he was 'besieged with aspiring writers who wish an opinion upon a manuscript or something of that sort', Faulkner said:

> Yes. Nobody can escape that, of course. But I think any writer that brings you a manuscript to read, you can save time by not reading that one because the ones

---

[40] Faulkner to Haas, [Feb. 1949], Box 249, RH.
[41] Faulkner to Haas, 9 Feb. 1949, Box 249, RH.

that write the good ones haven't got time to bring it to you and say, Read this. They don't care whether you read it or not or whether you like it or not.[42]

Faulkner explicitly rejected the *informal mentorship model* that had helped him to get his foot on the publishing ladder. He presented the talented writer as a supreme individualist who worked for himself, without thinking of his audience. Learning to write was a lonely process, not an apprenticeship where the established professional helps the young writer to improve his craft.[43]

Faulkner's discourse on self-reliance should be read in the context of the Cold War, at a time when any kind of groups (including literary groups) had become suspect. In 1957, asked what was necessary to combat communism, Faulkner responded: 'I think the first [point] would be to believe in "me," in "I," rather than "we," to be oneself, to resist the pressure to relinquish individuality. That's the first thing and maybe that's all anyone has to do to combat Communism.'[44] Faulkner's defence of American values during the Cold War is well known. But even before the famous Nobel Prize address about human freedom, Faulkner celebrated self-sufficiency in his correspondence with Culpepper. Faulkner's advice to the young writer was to expect nothing of others, and to concentrate on his own individuality—to believe in 'me', in 'I', rather than 'we'.

Not only did Faulkner reject the *informal mentorship model*, but he also showed distrust of the model of professional affiliation with the university. During his stay at the University of Virginia, he reminded his audience that college education was not for everyone. Conceding that higher education does not 'mak[e] or mar an artist', Faulkner compared the university to a 'warm room': 'to some writers, … the college education might be of great importance, just like some of us couldn't work in a cold room.'[45] In other words, going to university was all about material comfort: young writers with scholarships could expect a room to work in and a regular (if modest) income. For Faulkner, this was important, but not essential. After all, he had never graduated from university, and he had worked a series of odd jobs in his youth (including, he claimed, 'a job passing coal' to pay for new plates for *Sanctuary*).[46] Faulkner's emphasis on odd jobs was characteristic of his generation. In a *New York Times* article celebrating the rise of creative writing programmes, Iowa graduate Wallace Stegner ridiculed this romanticization of manual work ('New Climates for the Writer'). Stegner, who was twelve years younger than Faulkner, felt little sympathy for those who failed to recognize that the university had become a nurturing environment for writers.

[42] Graduate Course in the Novel, 13 May 1957 (Gwynn and Blotner 144–5).
[43] Archival evidence suggests that Anderson spent some time with Faulkner 'during the critical last three weeks that the latter was completing *Soldiers' Pay*' (Bosha 17).
[44] The Jefferson Society, 30 Apr. 1957 (Gwynn and Blotner 100).
[45] Press Conference, 15 Feb. 1957 (Gwynn and Blotner 11–12).
[46] Mary Washington College, 25 Apr. 1957 (Gwynn and Blotner 91).

For the Faulkner of the 1940s and 1950s, there was no such thing as a writing community. There were only individual writers, struggling to make a living, and struggling to get published. He readily acknowledged that, at the beginning of his career, he had received 'plenty of rejection slips': 'I would be frustrated and enraged in the time when I hoped I could get a little money for it, but if I didn't need money at that time it didn't make much difference, I'd send it somewhere else or I was busy still writing another one.' Faulkner told students 'after a while the folks that rejected [his short stories] bought them'.[47] This lesson in hard work and perseverance ended well, with the publication of previously rejected writings. For Faulkner, young writers had to be ready to lead a difficult life, in the hope of later success. But for James Culpepper, this discourse on self-reliance made absolutely no sense. Responding to Faulkner's advice that he should get a job, Culpepper wrote that he had 'no intention of loafing any longer'.[48] He asked Faulkner for work and was stunned to receive no reply. Culpepper became increasingly angry, and in his last remaining letter to Faulkner, he wrote:

> I felt somehow that you would prove unequal to any request involving kindliness, compassion, or generosity, you miserly man. But you'll never replenish your table with a single drop of wine bought with money obtained through selling me your books. I swear before God I'll never buy another of your books, nor read another line written by you as long as I live! But I imagine you are used to getting abusive letters, if you call this such.[49]

What Culpepper saw as a lack of kindness and compassion was in fact the logical outcome of Faulkner's focus on individuality and rejection of literary groups. Faulkner repeatedly claimed that he knew no 'literary people': 'The people I know are other farmers and horse people and hunters, and we talk about horses and dogs and guns and what to do about this hay crop or this cotton crop, not about literature.'[50] For Faulkner, the age of bohemian communities in Paris or New York was over. In a Cold War context, each writer had to work by himself and for himself—and expect nothing of writing groups and writing communities.

The correspondence between Faulkner and Culpepper highlights an important turning point, the moment when a new generation of young writers (including many veterans) tried to negotiate between two different paths to a writing career. Some, like Culpepper, turned to the glorious period when Hemingway and Faulkner had been in their prime and benefited from the help and advice of mentors such as Sherwood Anderson and Gertrude Stein. Others, like Flannery O'Connor, chose to study under the direction of experienced professionals

---

[47] University and Community Public, 5 June 1957 (Gwynn and Blotner 205).
[48] Culpepper to Faulkner, 7 Apr. 1949, Box 9, Folder 5, BP.
[49] Culpepper to Faulkner, June 1949, Box 9, Folder 5, BP.
[50] Undergraduate Course in Contemporary Literature, 13 Mar. 1957 (Gwynn and Blotner 65).

in creative writing programmes. If, as Mark McGurl argues, 'the rise of the creative writing program stands as the most important event in postwar American literary history' (ix), the transition to this new model was certainly not a straightforward process. The *informal mentorship model* remains influential to this day, in the longing for loose associations found in the bohemian communities of early twentieth-century metropolitan centres (Paris, New York, but also Chicago and New Orleans), as opposed to the institutional constraints of the university system.

But in the immediate post-war period, the *informal mentorship model* was no longer the main route to publication. Established writers like Faulkner had no intention of emulating their own mentors by helping young authors get their foot on the publishing ladder. For a militant Cold War individualist like Faulkner, talented artists did not need writing groups or even mentors. And yet, Culpepper and many other aspiring writers longed for role models who could help them get published. Not all of them dreamed of Paris or New York—in fact, Culpepper despised the cronyism of the East Coast literary crowd. What Culpepper wanted, though, was practical advice to break into print. In other words, there was a discrepancy between the demand for, and the supply of, mentors.

Creative writing programmes in universities offered a comprehensive solution to the limitations of the *informal mentorship model*. These programmes included a horizontal and a vertical dimension: young authors received feedback from their peers, and they also interacted with experienced professionals. To find a mentor, budding writers no longer had to come from a prominent family, nor did they need to join artistic coteries. Literary outsiders were no longer condemned to collecting rejection letters from New York publishers. All they had to do was to get accepted in a graduate creative writing programme and build strong relationships with fellow students and faculty members there. This opened up the writing career to numerous young men and women from modest background, who had neither the social capital nor the bohemian pedigree of their elders. It is not a coincidence that the directors of creative writing programmes (including Paul Engle at Iowa and Wallace Stegner at Stanford) kept referring to veterans as representatives of the new generation of young writers. As Mary Stegner recalled, her husband raised money for the Stanford programme by convincing oilman Edward Jones that veterans 'had lots to write, but they were married and some had children … He said they needed a place where they could write and talk, like a coffee house in Europe' (Manuel).

Although James Culpepper may or may not have been a veteran, he was married and had to support his wife. He, too, longed for a place where he could be taken seriously as a writer. In Culpepper's mind, this place was not in Iowa, but in Oxford, Mississippi. Because he failed to see any alternatives to the *informal mentorship model*, Culpepper continued to hope that Faulkner would help him find a publisher. In his last letter to Robert Haas, he announced: 'I am going to Oxford, Mississippi, to stay for a time when I have this present novel completed and I will drop you a short note as to my whereabouts once there so you may take advantage of my previous suggestion. However I must ask you again not to bother me with correspondence unless you feel you will be able to find at least some small place on your publishing lists for my novel.'[51] There is an exclamation mark in pencil next to this last sentence, along with Haas's initials. Dismissed as a 'nut', Culpepper vanished from our view with this last letter.

---

[51] Culpepper to Haas, 24 Sept. 1949, Box 249, RH.

3
Healing the Breach between Writers and Scholars?
Wallace Stegner and the Diffusion of the Creative Writing Gospel

In the late 1940s, Wallace Stegner emerged as a new academic leader, who tirelessly defended the university as a welcoming place for writers. Having grown up in the West, he had long felt like an outsider in a literary world dominated by the East Coast establishment. But he had now found a good home at Stanford University, and he wanted to encourage more writers to enrol in creative writing programmes. Like Paul Engle, he was acutely aware that times had changed, that the young writers of the 1940s did not resemble those of the interwar period. 'Particularly in the Thirties a list of fifteen hard-labor jobs was considered a better diploma for a writer than a degree from Harvard or Yale,' he wrote in *The New York Times* ('New Climates for the Writer'). Three assumptions explained the traditional distrust for universities. One was the feeling that writing could not be taught, that practical experience was better than formal study. Another was the fear that creativity and originality would be crushed in colleges. Finally, writers who became instructors risked losing their energy, their 'creative voltage'.

As the founder of the creative writing programme at Stanford, Stegner was well placed to debunk these assumptions. First, universities were there to provide rigorous education, and writers had to be trained to reach their full potential. 'Like football players, pianists, Renaissance scholars, or typists, writers are the product of original talent plus training,' he claimed. Second, the publishing industry was a much more dangerous place for young writers than universities. Instead of stimulating creativity, commercial publishers set low standards, which led writers to waste their time and talent. In contrast, universities offered an opportunity for experimentation and more challenging writing. Third, teachers of creative writing benefited from improved working conditions. Whereas in the past instructors had heavy teaching loads and few opportunities for advancement, 'promotions are now fairly often made for creative rather than for scholarly accomplishment'.

Fig. 3.1 Wallace Stegner, undated. Special Collections, J. Willard Marriott Library, The University of Utah.
Source: Wallace Stegner Exhibit, U of Utah, https://www.lib.utah.edu/collections/photo-exhibits/stegner-exhibit/exhibit.php. Accessed 30 Apr. 2021.

The New York Times article concluded with an appeal to bridge the gap between writers and scholars. The term Stegner used—'healing of the breach'—gave the impression of a painful division between the critical and the creative. But things were changing. Scholars who frowned upon the living and contemporary literature were in retreat. Journalists and writers who had allowed their standards to fall 'could use some of the scholars' care, some of their restraint, a good deal of their plain learning, and a lot of their taste'. Bringing scholars and writers under the same roof would benefit both sides, as well as the universities themselves ('New Climates for the Writer').

Stegner was uniquely placed to heal the breach between creative writing and literary scholarship. Along with Paul Engle, he had been one of the first to receive a Master's degree at Iowa for a creative thesis. Norman Foerster had then encouraged him to do a PhD in American Literature. 'Those were Depression times,' Stegner later recalled, and a traditional doctorate would be much more useful on the academic job market than a creative writing degree.[1] He did not enjoy all aspects of his doctoral work, but his dissertation on a Western nature writer had a considerable impact on the course of his career. Unlike Engle (who had never finished his PhD), Stegner was an equal amongst scholars. By the late 1940s, he was also the author of several fiction and non-fiction books that had attracted both commercial and critical success.

His conciliatory personality served him well in academic environments. Stegner liked nothing more than feeling part of a community united by strong ties. When his long-time friend Wilbur Schramm offered him a position at the University of Illinois in late 1948, he refused to move from California, a place where he and his family had grown roots. He got along so well with his colleagues—including Richard Foster Jones, the Head of the English Department—that he described his job as 'pure ointment'.[2]

By the end of his life, Stegner no longer believed that scholars and writers could be reconciled. In a 1990 interview, he described the rise of literary theory as a pernicious trend. 'English departments seem to take things apart, and they sometimes breed book-haters,' he said. 'I have known some graduate students who read books in order to despise them, in order to be able to put them down' (Hepworth). The old Stegner had become disillusioned not only with literary scholars, but also with creative writers themselves. When asked why he had left Stanford back in the early 1970s, he always gave the same explanation: he couldn't stand the generation of hippie students who challenged authority, burned books, brought beer in class and refused to listen to their instructors. He was fed up with the 'moral idiocy' of young writers, who seemed to have lost all sense of right and wrong and created monstrous characters in their fiction (Lasden 26). After leaving Stanford, Stegner openly criticized the evolution of the creative writing programme. He described the appointment of Gilbert Sorrentino, an avant-garde novelist, as a huge mistake.

---

[1] Wallace Stegner to Stephen Wilbers, 26 Feb. 1976, Records of the Iowa Writers' Workshop RG 06.12.08, Series XI, Box 2, UI.
[2] Stegner to Wilbur Schramm, 23 Nov. 1948, Box 20, WS, Utah.

'Creative Writing has now been taken over and is being directed by the English Department,' he wrote.³

There are several ways to analyse Stegner's evolution from idealistic young(ish) professor to grumpy old man. Eric Bennett focuses on the social changes of the 1960s and 1970s. Stegner 'never anticipated militant Black Panthers and slutty discos, casual herpes, and ample pot and burnt brassieres,' Bennett claims. 'Austere and hardworking, prudent and steady, modest and prudish, he hated what he saw' (*Workshops of Empire* 139). The new generation had transformed creative writing into a navel-gazing discipline, an evolution that horrified Stegner. Bennett is certainly right to emphasize the generational conflict between Stegner and his students (think of the rebellious Ken Kesey, who went to Stanford before writing *One Flew Over the Cuckoo's Nest*). Although Stegner was openly hostile to counterculture, he was not the stereotypical anti-rebel that Bennett describes. He increasingly felt as an outsider, unable to heal the conflict between writing and scholarship.

Stegner's failure at healing the breach between writers and scholars tells us a lot about the generation that developed creative writing as an academic discipline. Stegner (born 1909) was nearly the same age as Engle (born 1908), both men had studied under the same professors in Iowa and they shared a holistic approach to their discipline. They saw creative writing as an integral part of a literary training that should also include scholarship and criticism. It is certainly true that they wanted to challenge the domination of scholars—particularly historical scholars— over English departments. But the vision of creative writing that they promoted in the 1940s and 1950s was not one of division. 'The University of Iowa has brought scholars and writers together,' Engle told the Rockefeller Foundation in 1952.⁴ Both Engle and Stegner worked hand in hand with the scholars who headed their departments, to get institutional support and funding. Without the help of senior colleagues, their creative writing programmes would have been unlikely to take off. Yet, in the long term, neither Engle nor Stegner managed to unite the creative and the critical—a failure that has had enduring consequences on their discipline.

In this chapter, my objective is to trace the origin and eventual failure of Stegner's plan to unite creative writers and scholars. An outsider at the beginning of his career, he spent several happy years in academia before rejecting the institution. In the 1930s, Stegner moved from one university to the next in the hope of finding a permanent post, and he had first-hand experience of scornful colleagues looking down on creative writers. His experience at Harvard was a turning point. There, he found a welcoming environment where writers were respected and valued. The Harvard job led to an offer for a professorship at Stanford, where Stegner developed the first creative writing programme. From the 1960s, however, he became

---

³ Stegner to John L'Heureux, 24 July 1982, Box 162, WS, Utah.
⁴ Engle to Edward D'Arms, 10 May 1952, RG 1.2, Series 200, Box 448, Folder 3833, RF.

increasingly disenchanted, and he came to see English scholars as book-haters eager to shape creative writing to their own image.

3.1 How to Work with Scholars: Stegner's Itinerant Early Career

In his semi-autobiographical novel *Big Rock Candy Mountain* (1943), Stegner describes the life of the Mason family: Bo and Elsa, and their sons Chester and Bruce. The father is a restless, dissatisfied man who moves his wife and children from one state to another in search of better financial opportunities. A risk-taker by nature, Bo dabbles in bootlegging and gambling. Living on the margins of society takes a toll on his family—Chester turns away from a promising career in baseball and dies of pneumonia. Elsa then dies of cancer. Broke and depressed, the father commits suicide after killing a former mistress. Bruce is left alone to reflect on his dysfunctional family and finds solace in his own studies and future career as a lawyer.

Like his character Bruce, Stegner led an itinerant early life. As a boy, he lived in Grand Forks, North Dakota, then Redmond and Bellingham, Washington, then East End, Saskatchewan, Canada, and then Great Falls, Montana, before settling in Salt Lake City, Utah, in 1921. As a young man, he suffered a series of traumas: the death of his brother and mother, followed by the murder-suicide committed by his father. He yearned for stability and in 1934, he married fellow student Mary Stuart Page. This was a strong, happy relationship which lasted until his death.

On the professional front, however, Stegner struggled to find a permanent academic job. Like his father, he moved his family from one place to another. His son Page attended five schools in his first three grades of school and was, in Stegner's words, 'a somewhat unhappy and maladjusted child'.[5] In 1937, when he was teaching at the University of Utah, Stegner won the Little-Brown novelette prize of $2,500 for *Remembering Laughter*. Despite this success, the department refused to promote him and Stegner decided to move to Wisconsin to take another teaching job.

At the University of Wisconsin, Stegner soon realized that the department was scrabbling for a living, and that cliques competed ferociously against each other. 'There was a lot of backbiting,' he later said. One issue was that the older generation had taken their graduate degrees at Wisconsin before getting a job at the same university. They had never gone anywhere else, and they resented the arrival of younger people who might get promoted before them. Stegner knew that he had to publish scholarship to advance his career. He wrote a couple of chapters in *The Literary History of the United States* and he did his 'chores on this and that,

[5] Stegner to Schramm, 23 Nov. 1948, Box 20, WS, Utah.

articles here and there'. But it wasn't what he most wanted to do. His creative writing earned him little praise from his colleagues. 'There were phrases like "mere journalists" and things like that which scholars had a tendency to use about writers,' he recalled.[6] His mentor Norman Foerster told him that things were changing, and that writers would be more frequently desired in the future.[7]

Bread Loaf, a writers' conference in Vermont, offered a light at the end of the tunnel. Founded in 1926, the conference attracted would-be writers—'mostly female, mostly elderly' in Wilbur Schramm's terms—who came to get criticism on their manuscripts and hear famous authors lecture.[8] It was thanks to his Iowa contacts—Schramm and Foerster—that Stegner was able to join the Bread Loaf faculty. In 1937, Foerster told him that the conference provided 'an excellent chance to meet a number of men prominent in literary affairs in the East'.[9] Schramm then convinced Theodore Morrison, the director of Bread Loaf, to hire Stegner for criticizing manuscripts. 'Your chief occupations will probably be to play tennis in the afternoons,' wrote Schramm, and 'to drink consistently—I hear that the conference is a pretty liquid affair.'[10] Stegner would also get a chance to associate with the regular faculty, including Morrison and the historian and author Bernard DeVoto, and to meet visiting lecturers such as Robert Frost and Louis Untermeyer (Gale).

Teaching at Bread Loaf was the chance of a lifetime, and Stegner eagerly seized it. He liked Vermont so much that he later bought a property there. As an accomplished tennis player, he also enjoyed competing against other Bread Loafers. And, of course, there was the thrill of meeting first-class writers. Bread Loaf 'gave me entrée into a literary community such as I had never seen before,' Stegner said in an interview. 'It was like turpentining a mule; I went straight up in excitement, in emulation' (Etulain and Stegner xxviii). In his biography of DeVoto, he wrote:

> This literary assemblage in greener and tamer mountains produced in [DeVoto] and many others among its participants a kind of frenzy, a heightening of every perception, capacity and emotion. It combined a frantic amount of business with an equally frantic amount of fraternizing, revel, and emotional release ... It was frenziedly, manically literary. It involved daily lectures, workshops, 'clinics,' symposia, conferences, mountains of manuscript.
> (*The Uneasy Chair* 121–2)

Here, the repetitions of 'frenzy' and 'frantic' gives the impression that participants were pushed to their limits. Joseph Conrad famously wrote that that the writer's

---

[6] Stegner, Interview by Benson, 27 Jan. 1988, Box 10, Benson—Stegner, Stanford.
[7] Norman Foerster to Stegner, 22 Apr. 1937, Box 161, WS, Utah.
[8] Schramm to George Mills, 14 Aug. 1945, Box 1, Wilbur Schramm papers RG 99.0118, UI.
[9] Foerster to Stegner, 11 Feb. 1937, Box 161, WS, Utah.
[10] Schramm to Stegner, undated, Box 20, WS, Utah.

task was 'to make you hear, to make you feel—it is, before all, to make you *see*' (14). Bread Loaf offered an opportunity for writers to sharpen their senses, to heighten their perceptions. This emotional aspect was combined with intellectual activities including lectures and the criticism of manuscripts. The writers' conference found its origins in the School of English opened in 1920, and Bread Loafers were encouraged to develop their knowledge of literature. In other words, creative writing could not be dissociated from literary history and criticism.

Bread Loaf led to further career opportunities. Stegner was teaching writing but he was also being mentored by more experienced men. Thanks to Theodore Morrison, he was offered a temporary instructorship at Harvard, where he taught from 1939 to 1944. 'The Bread Loaf connection made the Harvard connection,' he later said.[11] Unlike the University of Wisconsin, Harvard offered a welcoming environment for writers for three main reasons. First, it had a separate writing section from the English Department, and the administration and faculty were receptive. Second, the Harvard Briggs Copeland Instructorship was specifically designed for a practising writer. It was 'an attempt by a university to be hospitable to writers during their critical younger years of development, to make use of their special gifts of teaching and of the stimulation which they can bring to the academic community, and at the same time to provide them with conditions of work which will as little as possible hamper or delay their progress as novelists, poets, or literary critics' (Morrison 4). Stegner had only two classes of freshmen, and plenty of time to devote to his own work. And finally, there was the prestige of working at a top university that brought together many famous names. 'Stegner of Harvard!' wrote Schramm. 'Someday he will be silvery haired and mellow, and will walk around the yard in his bedroom slippers, and students will point him out in the same awed whispers they used to say "Copey" or "Kittredge" or "Palmer."'[12]

Stegner made contacts with established writers but he also networked with funders and publishers on the East Coast. 'Go on to New York to see Mr Moe of the Guggenheim foundation,' wrote Schramm in 1937, 'go on up to Boston and let Little-Brown give you cocktail parties for a week, then go out in the woods and write like hell for the rest of the summer.'[13] Being close to the centres of publishing was a major advantage, as Stegner admitted in an interview for *Harcourt Brace News*.[14] It allowed him to shop around and get the best deals for his novels. In 1943, his new publisher—Duell, Sloan and Pearce—extensively advertised *Big Rock Candy Mountain*. The money that he got from his writing supplemented his meagre teaching salary at Harvard, which amounted to $1,097.26 in 1942—the equivalent of around $18,000 in 2019 dollars.[15]

---

[11] Stegner, Interview by Benson, 4 Nov. 1987, Box 10, Benson—Stegner, Stanford.
[12] Schramm to Stegner, 4 Jan. 1939, Box 161, WS, Utah.
[13] Schramm to Stegner, 8 May 1937, Box 20, WS, Utah.
[14] *Harcourt Brace News*, Jan. 1940, Box 16, Benson—Stegner, Stanford.
[15] Harvard to Stegner, Income tax record, 29 Jan. 1943, Box 160, WS, Utah.

Amongst the original Briggs Copeland instructors were Delmore Schwartz, Mark Schorer, and John Berryman. This was a distinguished cohort. Schwartz was only twenty-five years old when his first collection of poems, *In Dreams Begin Responsibilities* (1938), was published. The book attracted the attention of leading critics, including Allen Tate who wrote in a letter: 'I want to tell you that your poetic style is beyond any doubt the first real innovation that we've had since Eliot and Pound' (Atlas, *Delmore Schwartz* 129). Schwartz was promoted to Assistant Professor in 1947 (Charney), and the following year, Stegner mentioned him in his *New York Times* article amongst the 'good writers' teaching at Harvard. In addition to Schwartz and Theodore Morrison, Stegner also included the poet John Ciardi in his list. Ciardi had joined Harvard in 1946, where he remained until 1953, when he moved to Rutgers University to set up the first creative writing programme.

Harvard acted as a magnet for talented writers, who later spread the creative writing gospel. Although it was badly paid, the Briggs Copeland Instructorship was not a dead-end job: it came with opportunities for promotion and for a prestigious academic career. As Stegner put it, 'a university is a natural place for a writer to be' ('New Climates for the Writer'). Former Harvard writers shared this message, evangelizing their colleagues in other places. By the 1950s, former Briggs Copeland instructors held senior positions across the country. After designing the first creative writing courses at Rutgers, Ciardi became Director of the Bread Loaf Writers' Conference in 1955. The poet John Berryman worked at Princeton, reaching the position of resident fellow before winning the National Institute of Arts and Letters Award (1950), the Levinson prize (1950), and a Guggenheim fellowship (1952).[16]

Harvard attracted experienced writers, but also talented students interested in writing. No wonder that Paul Engle saw the East Coast university as a serious competitor. To differentiate his programme, Engle explained that only the University of Iowa allowed graduate students to do fiction and poetry for their advanced degrees. 'While such places as Harvard and Minnesota offer courses in writing for undergraduates taught by good people, on graduation the young writer has only Iowa to go to,' he told Bennett Cerf in 1948.[17] Iowa's unique positioning in the creative writing field did not last long. By 1950, Stanford was giving a BA and MA for concentration in writing. Wallace Stegner, a product of the Iowa programme, was now competing against Iowa for the best students and instructors.

3.2 Building Stanford's Creative Writing Programme

Stegner's appointment at Stanford finds its origins in the contacts he made at Bread Loaf. In December 1944, the linguist Arthur G. Kennedy approached him.

---

[16] See Athey.
[17] Engle to Cerf, 30 Mar. 1948, Box 9, RH.

Fig. 3.2 Edith Mirrielees (right) and Mrs Untermeyer at Bread Loaf Writers' Conference, 1940.

Source: Middlebury College Special Collections & Archives. https://archive.org/details/mnb_07-1940-04n. Accessed 30 Apr. 2021.

Stanford was looking for someone to take the position vacated by the retirement of Edith Mirrielees (Figure 3.2); he wrote: 'Miss Mirrielees has suggested to us that you might be interested in the possibility of coming to Stanford as a half-time professor to direct our work in narrative writing.'[18] Mirrielees is largely forgotten today, but she was an accomplished professor of writing and literature who taught at Stanford, the Bread Loaf School of English, and the Bread Loaf Writers' Conference.

Her courses on the short story influenced many writers. John Steinbeck, who studied at Stanford in the 1920s, praised her no-nonsense teaching method. The grades he received in her class disappointed him, but also prepared him for the harsh criticism he would later receive from editors. The path of the writer was lonely and desolate, said Steinbeck, and Mirrielees turned unsophisticated students into hard-nosed professionals who could survive in a competitive writing field ('Preface').

Mirrielees did not give them rigid rules on how to write short stories. Irma Hannibal, a former student, recalled: 'She gave us an exercise to test our five senses.

---

[18] Arthur Kennedy to Stegner, 19 Dec. 1944, Box 1, WS misc., Stanford.

She told us to go and find a field where no one else is around. Lie down in it and see how it affects all of your five senses. That's how you learn to write' (Lynch 64). Instead of giving top-down instructions, she helped to form and to disseminate a new kind of Socratic approach in the teaching of creative writing, an approach that influenced Stegner and others. When Stegner started teaching at Stanford, he imported some of the Bread Loaf methods:

> The classes were Socratic to a degree and I guess I got that from Bread Loaf because that was the whole theory of Bread Loaf. You dealt ad hoc with particular manuscripts. And you didn't deal in glittering generalities, and abstract principles because the abstract principles don't fit every case and every personality.[19]

Mirrielees' teaching methods, but also her ability to cross the boundary between scholarship and creative writing, set an inspiring model. In particular, she was at the forefront of what we now call 'modernist studies'. In 1929, she published two companion volumes,[20] the first devoted to the theory and the technique of the modern short story, and the second containing eighteen stories illustrating the principles of the first volume. One reviewer praised her 'excellent discussion of the uses and limitations of the stream-of-consciousness method' (Fulcher 422). He was also impressed by her choice of illustrative stories, by Katherine Mansfield, Virginia Woolf, Ernest Hemingway, E. M. Forster, and others. 'The too well-beaten paths followed by many editors have been avoided without succumbing to the converse danger of eccentricity,' he declared (Fulcher 423). Mirrielees continued to advocate for the new literature. In 1940, she wrote an article on 'Courses in Contemporary Literature' for the newsletter of the College English Association. While she regretted that contemporary writing was seldom taught in academia, she was also careful not to antagonize literary scholars who specialized in older periods. 'Courses in contemporary writing,' she wrote, 'should not be to the exclusion of courses dealing with the magnificences of English literature. The two are not in competition.'

Mirrielees' gentle approach helped to bridge the gap between scholars and writers. Irma Hannibal remembered her warmth and kindness: 'I can still see her serving punch and cookies to us' (Lynch 63). While at Stanford, John Steinbeck described Mirrielees as 'very kind and she hates to hurt feelings'. That did not prevent her from giving honest feedback to students. 'For every bit of favorable criticism, I get four knocks on the head,' Steinbeck added (Benson, *The True Adventures of John Steinbeck* 58). Stegner was also struck by Mirrielees' generosity. 'Years later,' Hannibal recalled, 'I was taking a workshop with Wallace Stegner, and he told us about meeting Miss Mirrielees at a conference and how helpful she had been to

---

[19] Stegner, Interview by Benson, 27 Jan. 1988, Box 10, Benson—Stegner, Stanford.
[20] *Writing the Short Story* and *Significant Contemporary Stories*.

him. It's funny, because she was such a delicate, gentle maiden lady, but inside she was a powerhouse' (Lynch 65). Mirrielees' dainty femininity may have contributed to her disappearance from literary history. Unlike the male founders of creative writing programmes, she did not attract attention to herself. Instead of blowing her own trumpet, she served her university faithfully over decades, and even wrote a history of Stanford (published in 1959).

Replacing Mirrielees at Stanford was an exciting prospect for Stegner, but he was careful not to show too much enthusiasm. After all, there was no guarantee that Kennedy's letter would lead to an actual job offer. Just a few months before, he had learnt that another institution in California, Mills College, had decided not to offer him a position. After reading *Big Rock Candy Mountain*, the hiring committee had concluded that it contained pornographic descriptions. 'They did not want to have seventeen-year-old girls studying with a man who could write such things,' explained the college president, and they had decided to appoint a scholar of American studies instead.[21] Despite the commercial and critical success of his novels, Stegner was still struggling in the academic market. It was not until 1945 that he made his breakthrough and finally obtained his permanent position, jumping to a full professorship at Stanford. The offer came with a generous salary and a part-time contract to allow him to concentrate on his writing.

Soon after, other universities approached him. In 1946, Stegner told Indiana University that only a very good offer would lure him out of California. This included five main conditions. The first was the salary, which had to be high enough to justify the move. Second, the institution should provide 'a ladder of writing courses graduated from rudimentary to the most advanced', so that everyone had a chance to write, but only the most talented could attend the advanced and near-professional class. Third, a good creative writing programme needed funding for prizes and fellowships. While prizes served to motivate student writers, fellowships acted as levers to lift the production of the class above the undergraduate and amateur level. 'It has amazed me, in the past few years, to see how much even a single really good writer can raise the level of a class,' wrote Stegner. Fellowships had to be sufficiently generous to lure that sort of writer into the academic environment, enough to support the fellow for at least one year. The fourth condition was to provide avenues of publication at a professional level, 'well above the usual undergraduate literary-magazine-level'. And finally, the director of the programme should have plenty of free time to concentrate on his own writing.[22]

Money, free time, and ambition: these factors were essential for building a successful creative writing programme outside of traditional literary centres. Having left a position at Harvard to move to California, Stegner was aware that geographic isolation was a major risk. In 1941, Harry Shaw—a writer he had met at the Boulder

---

[21] Lynn White to Stegner, 3 Oct. 1944, Box 16, Benson—Stegner, Stanford.
[22] Stegner to Russell Noyes, 25 Dec. 1946, Box 16, Benson—Stegner, Stanford.

Writers' Conference—recommended him for a course at New York University. 'Much as I dislike certain things about New York City,' Shaw wrote, 'I must confess that it's the center of a helluva lot of opportunities and goings-on.'[23] Moving to Stanford came at a steep price for Stegner. His correspondence with Shaw ceased after 1947, and his contacts with other New York writers became less frequent. The East Coast establishment nearly forgot about him (Jones, 'The Dean of Western Letters').

Determined to build a major creative writing centre at Stanford, Stegner looked for sources of funding. He had the friendliest kind of support from Richard Foster Jones, Head of the English Department and his brother Dr Edward H. Jones, a Texas oilman who generously donated 'the equivalent of a half dozen Guggenheims' to the creative writing programme.[24] This exceptionally generous donation allowed Stegner to set up the Jones fellowships to attract talented writers. Stegner also courted the big foundations. After two failed attempts (in 1939 and 1942), he finally got a Guggenheim fellowship in fiction in 1949—and another one (1952), and another one (1959). Like Engle, Stegner was learning fundraising through persistence and hard work. And like Engle, he attracted the attention of the powerful Rockefeller Foundation.

In 1949, Charles B. Fahs of the RF's Division of Humanities approached Stegner regarding a visit to Asia.[25] He was looking for an American professor in the field of writing who would meet with writers in Japan, India, and the Philippines. In a Cold War context, the main objective was to build and strengthen links with local artists and promote the American cultural model. Since creative writing in universities had first been developed in the United States, the Rockefeller Foundation was eager to export this approach to win the hearts and minds of Asian writers. Stegner gave a few suggestions of people who could do the job, including Theodore Morrison, Paul Engle, and John Crowe Ransom.[26] Eventually, the RF asked Stegner himself to go to Asia, and offered him a $10,000 grant.

Stegner's report, written shortly after returning from this four-month trip, shows that he often had to endorse the role of the scholar to reach out to local communities:

> Though we went primarily to talk with writers, we found ourselves talking to a good many professors of literature and college students as well, and though we went prepared to talk mainly about contemporary American writing, we found ourselves compelled quite often to talk about American literature in general and historical terms—if only to prove that such a thing existed.[27]

---

[23] Harry Shaw to Stegner, 2 Sept. 1941, Box 20, WS, Utah.
[24] Stegner to Schramm, 23 Nov. 1948, Box 20, WS, Utah.
[25] Fahs to Stegner, 3 Oct. 1949, RG 1.2, Series 205, Box 9, Folder 61, RF.
[26] Stegner to Fahs, 23 Oct. 1949, RG 1.2, Series 205, Box 9, Folder 61, RF.
[27] Stegner to Fahs, 3 Apr. 1951, RG 1.2, Series 205, Box 9, Folder 62, RF.

Stegner's scholarly training was useful to convince Asians of the value of American culture. But not everyone was receptive to this message. In India, there was often a Communist minority in audiences, who vocally challenged the speaker.

Another problem was the impossibility of holding seminars in the techniques of writing. Apart from academics and students at the University of the Philippines, few locals had heard of creative writing workshops. Stegner was put in the difficult position of a missionary sent to faraway places to spread the creative writing gospel. He had to use a different language (the language of scholarship) to share ideas that would otherwise have been incomprehensible to local audiences. Once he had convinced the audience of the existence of American literature, he could present creative writing programmes as they had developed in America. Audiences showed 'a great deal of interest in the idea,' he told the Rockefeller Foundation.

Yet, Stegner never shared Paul Engle's passionate zeal for converting foreign writers to the creative writing creed. In 1962, W. McNeil Lowry, the director of the Ford Foundation's Arts and Humanities Program, presented Engle as 'a particular kind of symbol to these foreign writers, in that he is an ambitious, empire-building character who has made his real achievements in building up a big programme in Iowa a substitute for his somewhat dubious creative talent as a writer'. Lowry contrasted Engle with Stegner, 'a somewhat better, if not an important writer, [who] has few illusions about his place in American literary history, and is a somewhat more unassuming and indigenous sort of American symbol'.[28] Stegner was less attention-seeking than Engle, and he never attempted to create an international writing programme comparable to the one established at Iowa in the late 1960s. His ambition was primarily to turn Stanford into a national centre for excellence in writing, a centre that could compete against Iowa.

It would be a mistake, however, to dismiss Stegner as a sort of Engle-lite who simply applied the Iowa model to Stanford. Lowry was probably right to describe Stegner as a better writer. Whereas Engle's poetry has long been forgotten, Stegner's novels are still in print today. Stegner showed that it was possible to build a creative writing programme, to teach writing courses and to continue to produce creative work. He embraced the totality of academic life, excelling at administration, teaching, and practice-based research. Like his friend Wilbur Schramm, he was a workaholic with an extraordinary drive and self-discipline. 'If you regard imaginative writing as "production," wrote Norman Foerster in a 1937 letter of recommendation, 'you should get, in Stegner, a producer.'[29]

The secret of Stegner's productivity was a rigid schedule. Every morning, he forced himself to write for a few hours before doing anything else. The pressures of administration and teaching could become overwhelming, and early on, he negotiated an agreement with Stanford to work at the university six months a year,

---

[28] W. McNeil Lowry to Shepard Stone, 24 Jan. 1962, Ford—Loz Files, Reel L-166 (L62-40), FF.
[29] Norman Foerster to F. W. Roe, 4 May 1937, Box 14, Benson—Stegner, Stanford.

followed by six months of writing. He also arranged for Richard Scowcroft to help him run the creative writing programme.

In 1949, Claude Simpson of Ohio State University asked Stegner if Scowcroft would be suitable for their own writing programme. Stegner replied that he was excellent, a published novelist with a solid PhD. 'He is free from any Artiness, any New Criticism, and any tendency to pour his students into a mold or make them into disciples,' Stegner wrote, before explaining that he wanted to keep Scowcroft at Stanford.[30] The reference to Scowcroft's doctorate is significant. For Stegner, having a PhD was a strong advantage in academia, a way to deal with senior scholars on an equal basis. It was also a sign that the writer did not reject scholarly knowledge. 'I have never understood why American novelists have to pretend to a Neanderthal ignorance,' he wrote in 1950, 'or why professors need to be limited to a kind of eunuch's place in our letters.'[31] To be a teacher-writer was to be part of an academic community, and to accept the rules of that community.

Stegner applied a harsh discipline to all aspects of his life, and he expected the same kind of commitment from his students. Let the literary profession 'be merely another profession', he declared, 'one which, like music, demands a certain native talent and a hard apprenticeship in technique' ('Advice to a Young Writing Man' 3). Stegner imagined the learning process as a *practical* process, a way to build things—a strong narrative structure and lively characters, in the case of fiction. The term 'workshop' was associated with blue-collar apprenticeship, and Stegner fully embraced these connotations. Having grown up in a working-class family, he combined intellectual and physical labour, writing in the morning and cutting wood in the afternoon when he was in Vermont. He saw creative writers as practitioners, who had to remain close to the real world and avoid losing themselves in blue-sky thinking. 'America is a nation of doers, wedded to the practical and material,' he once said, 'our writers have been too persistently dreamers and idealists and carpers' ('Is the Novel Done For?' 83). Writers should join the American family, keep their feet firmly on the ground and embrace hard work.

Of course, Stegner was aware that literary success was not always connected to talent and deliberate practice. 'One of the worst aspects of a career that is speculative and marginal is that so often pure luck decides it,' he noted, 'and talent, devotion, capacity to grow, may go unrewarded for years or for a lifetime, while some sleazy little talent riding a streak of luck may hit the jackpot and gain not merely money but what is much more important: serious consideration and respect' ('What Besides Talent?' 13). In contrast, literary scholarship was a much less speculative career. All scholars had to go through years of labour to earn their PhD, and endure the long and often painful process of peer-review, before publishing their work. Scholarship was a profession, with a rigid trajectory leading to

---

[30] Stegner to Claude Simpson, 20 June 1949, Box 20, WS, Utah.
[31] Stegner to Irita Van Doren (*New York Herald Tribune Books*), c. 1950, Box 134, WS, Utah.

recognition. Stegner did not admire all aspects of this path: when he was a PhD student, he hated studying subjects that had nothing to do with his dissertation. The prospect of having to take Old Norse led him to transfer from the University of California Berkeley back to the University of Iowa. But, at least, scholars rewarded hard work and Stegner was determined to emulate this model when he set up Stanford's creative writing programme.

Stegner often used the imagery of health and cleanliness to describe high-quality courses, as opposed to the dirty tricks of mail-order firms that promised immediate success to naïve would-be writers. In 1941, as a young instructor at Boulder Writers' Conference, he wrote an article to challenge the popular misconceptions about these conferences. Professional writers did not go there to get a nice vacation. They were expected to work until late in the evening, reading manuscripts and meeting with participants. Another misconception was that all attendees were talentless neurotics eager to receive praise. In fact, most participants were conscientious and willing to improve, said Stegner. He gave the example of a middle-aged woman who did physical exercises every morning—'she works hard at them and the dewlaps of fat giggle on her arms'—before turning to her manuscripts with equal seriousness. The fat lady will never be a successful writer, but 'she will leave all the healthier physically and mentally for her stay here'. Would-be writers were lucky to be offered these kinds of opportunities, Stegner said. Alternative options such as vanity presses and correspondence courses were much worse. 'If these people were not in a place like Boulder, in good and friendly and scrupulous hands, they would be in other hands a good deal less clean' ('Writers' Conference in the Rocky Mountains').

Building a clean, healthy programme of learning: Stegner was so attached to this idea that he came back to it more than a decade later in a magazine article. For Stegner, many people (especially foreigners) regarded writers in universities with suspicion, and put them in the same category as quacks who promised literary glory after three easy lessons. The charlatans were rarely writers themselves. They could also teach you the piano without pain or 'transform you into Hercules through a course of simple exercises'.[32] These men, said Stegner, promised something for nothing.

Without hard work and persistence, one could not—or rather *should* not—expect any rewards. Stegner frequently gave the example of his father, who had chased rewards and pleasures without any willingness to work hard and long enough. This was a common trait amongst Americans, Stegner thought. They dreamed of the Big Rock Candy Mountain, with its cigarette trees and lemonade springs described in the 1928 song. Stegner described his father as 'a true believer in the American dream of something for nothing', who 'was marking time between get-rich-quick schemes by running a "blind pig"—an illegal saloon' (*Where*

---

[32] Stegner, 'Everybody Wants to Write', 1953–54, Box 134, WS, Utah.

the Bluebird Sings to the Lemonade Springs 29). Stegner saw his father not as a victim of dishonest schemes, but as a dishonest man himself who imposed his dirty trade on his family. Being associated with this kind of quack was repulsive for Stegner, and he did everything he could to separate writing programmes from the contamination of get-successful-quick schemes.

To detoxify writing programmes, Stegner insisted on the quasi-military discipline that they required. In the mid-1940s, his classes at Stanford were dominated by ex-servicemen, 'students of unprecedented maturity, experience, and seriousness' determined to make up for the lost war years.[33] Many of them were in their late twenties—not much younger than Stegner himself. And many of them showed talent and willingness to learn. When Stegner met his first writing class at Stanford, he read them a manuscript story that he had received from the South Pacific. The story was called 'Night Watch', about a young officer named Mister Roberts. In the back row was a 'round-faced, beaming, enthusiastic Naval lieutenant in wrinkled grays'.[34] His name was Eugene Burdick, and thanks to Stegner's help, he soon became a successful writer.

In 1946, Stegner arranged for Theodore Morrison to give a Bread Loaf fellowship to Burdick and another Stanford student, Jean Byers.[35] Burdick was not particularly impressed by the advice he received at Bread Loaf. He believed that the close analysis and dissection of his writing made him self-conscious. The result was that his work became technically better, but lost some vigour. In a report written shortly after, Burdick made two suggestions to improve college literary instruction. First, 'writing courses should be much more casual, with much more writing and points being made by example rather than by analysis'. Classes should not resemble lectures. Writers did not improve by applying theoretical knowledge, but by discussing their writing informally and trying out new things. Second, students should not think of their instructor's writing style and preferences. Instead, 'the class should feel free to write on anything they like'.[36]

Although Burdick did not find writing classes very useful, he benefited from Stegner's extensive network of contacts in the publishing industry. It was thanks to Stegner that his story 'Rest Camp on Maui' was published in *Harper's* magazine. The Houghton Mifflin fellowship that he later received came out of the sponsorship of Stegner and his wife Mary (Benson, *Wallace Stegner* 163). Burdick was grateful for this sponsorship, and he kept in touch with the Stegners when he was in Oxford on a Rhodes scholarship. 'In a literary sense Oxford is dead,' he wrote before describing English people as malnourished: 'they just don't get enough animal protein and fats and their efforts to make things stretch are pathetic.'[37]

---

[33] Stegner, History Stanford Writing Program, Box 1, WS misc., Stanford.
[34] Stegner, 'Eugene Burdick', undated, Box 153, WS, Utah.
[35] Theodore Morrison to Stegner, 14 May 1946, Box 18, WS, Utah.
[36] Burdick, Report, undated, Box 133, WS, Utah.
[37] Burdick to Stegner, undated (1948), Box 1, WS CW, Stanford.

Burdick's abrasive personality was a far cry from Stegner's reserve. Yet, the two men got along, in part because Stegner admired the model of tough masculinity exemplified by ex-servicemen.

Under Stegner's leadership, the creative writing programme at Stanford developed a male-orientated image that left little place for talented women writers. A 1950 article in the *San Francisco Chronicle* showed a photo of Stegner surrounded by four young men. One student was a former infantry machine-gunner. Another one had served as a fighter pilot during the war. The only woman mentioned in the article is a 'girl reporter from Minneapolis' (Gilliam). In 1947–48 and 1948–49, all the fellowships awarded by the Writing Center went to male writers (Figure 3.3). Although the proportion of women later increased, they constituted only a minority of Stanford writing fellows: 25 per cent on average between 1947 and 1966.[38] This is significant, because the fellowship offered not only financial support, but also status and access to networking opportunities. Many of the former fellows then went on to launch a successful literary career[39]—an opportunity that fewer women writers had.

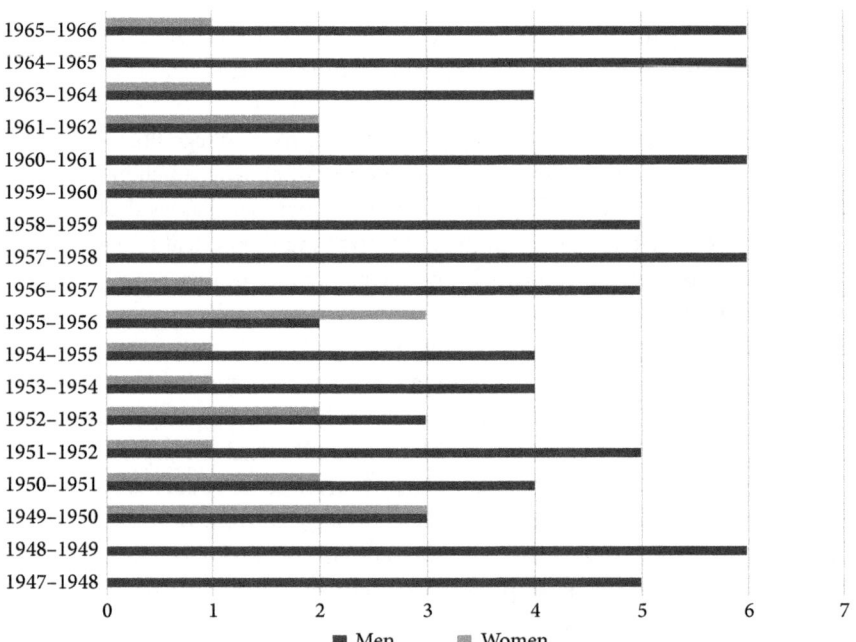

Fig. 3.3 Gender, Stanford Writing Fellows, 1947–48 to 1965–66.
Source: Author's own.

---

[38] Stanford List of Fellowships, Box 1, WS misc., Stanford.
[39] Including Dan Jacobson—see Chapter 7.

Stegner's formative experience at writers' conferences shaped his view of the literary world, a world where women occupied a marginal place. When Schramm arranged for Stegner to teach at Bread Loaf, he wrote that, unfortunately, the role entailed discussions with 'middle-aged school marms who think they are writers'.[40] For men of the generation of Schramm and Stegner, this gendered division between female would-be writers and male faculty members seemed natural. The typical attendee at writers' conferences was 'an oldish and fattish lady,' Stegner noted in 1941 ('Writers' Conference in the Rocky Mountains'). Some of these women were talented but lacked the ability to produce a whole body of work. After attending the Boulder Writers' Conference, Stegner recommended one of the manuscripts to the editor Edward Weeks: 'It is written by an almost-completely naïve woman who could not write anything else, probably, but this one volume of loosely-threaded sketches of small-town life in Michigan fifty years ago is in its way amazingly good.'[41] A key assumption was that a successful writing career required talent, discipline, and a level of commitment that few women had.

At Stanford, Stegner did not always take his women students seriously. In 1955, he wrote a letter of recommendation for a student who had attended his American fiction class and wanted to work in publishing. She showed no sign of extraordinary imagination or inventiveness, Stegner wrote. She was, however, 'an extremely pretty young woman'. 'Without being in any sense a glamour girl, she would certainly adorn any office,' he concluded.[42] Even by the standards of the 1950s, this reference letter seemed condescending to say the least. It encouraged employers to see the young woman not as a prospective candidate with a set of skills, but as an object, pleasant to look at. Stegner probably thought he was helping the student by emphasizing her (physical) qualities.

In a 1953 article, he described some of his women students as talentless and mentally disturbed. And again, he kept coming back to his experience at writers' conferences. 'Every conference I ever heard of has had its strait-jacket cases,' he commented. The first time he taught at Bread Loaf, he sharply criticized the manuscripts of one participant during a two-hour session. The lady was so angry that she left the conference along with her 'captive husband' and 'leashed police dog'. This woman had needed to see a doctor, Stegner wrote, not a creative writing instructor. At Stanford, he refused to admit a woman whose psychiatrist had recommended writing as a cure. The patient was too sick for a creative writing course, Stegner thought. 'She would have sucked me dry of every drop of energy or enthusiasm I possessed,' he added. Only doctors or priests were qualified to deal with such cases. He had often been tempted to hang above his office door a sign that said, 'Why Not Try Jesus?'[43]

---

[40] Schramm to Stegner, undated, Box 20, WS, Utah.
[41] Stegner to Weeks, 3 Sept. 1941, Box 47, Edward Weeks papers, HRC.
[42] Stegner, Reference letter, 11 Apr. 1955, Box 1, WS CW, Stanford.
[43] Stegner, 'Confessions of a Literary Wet Nurse', 1953, Box 134, WS, Utah.

3.3 Disillusion

Unsurprisingly, Stegner showed no enthusiasm for the feminists of the 1960s and 1970s. One review of his 1971 novel *Angle of Repose* is entitled 'No Poet Laureate of Women's Lib' (Maloney). The novel follows the life of Susan Ward, a gifted nineteenth-century writer and illustrator who moves to the West to follow her husband. Her new existence is devoid of intellectual pleasures, but she clings to the veneer of culture and refinement as she endures a series of tragedies. Her story is told by her grandson, who is afflicted with a crippling bone disease. Writing the book allows him to reflect on his own life, and on changing morals and values. In particular, his secretary—a liberated young woman—offers a sharp counterpoint to his grandmother's archaic sexual mores.

Susan shares many common points with Elsa, the mother in *Big Rock Candy Mountain*. Both endure a difficult life on the western frontier, both would have preferred a different existence but accept their fate without complaining. These characters closely resemble Stegner's own mother, whom he described as a saint. In an essay written as he was approaching eighty years of age, he declared: 'saintly and long-suffering women tend to infuriate the current partisans of women's liberation, who look upon them as a masculine invention, the too submissive and too much praised victims of male dominance' (*Where the Bluebird Sings to the Lemonade Springs* 24). Stegner added that his mother was not passive and submissive. She had actively learnt to control her expectations and to suppress her dreams, hopes and desires. Although unselfishness had been partly thrust on her by circumstances, she also chose to be unselfish and focus on the welfare of her boys and irresponsible husband. Stegner later described her as a 'nesting' woman, who 'was born to nest somewhere, and never got a chance to'. A whole body of Western literature dealt with the opposition between 'roaming men' and 'nesting women', he added.[44] Stegner's views on women had an impact on his own writing and on the creative writing programme at Stanford, a programme that offered fewer opportunities (including financial opportunities) to female writers.

As questions of gender and race gained ground in academia, Stegner became increasingly marginalized. During the war, he had worked for *Look* magazine on a series of articles about religious and racial intolerance. He found racism repulsive but could not bring himself to support affirmative action. Race was not a factor that should be considered when awarding prizes and positions, he thought. In 1982, the MacArthur foundation asked him to review the fellowship application of John Steward, a Black writer who had studied at Stanford two decades earlier. In his response to the Prize Fellows Program Committee, Stegner wrote: 'I have essentially the same problem in evaluating John Stewart that I have had in evaluating some

---

[44] Stegner, Interview by Bettina Gray, KQED, undated (1991–92), Box 10, Benson—Stegner, Stanford.

other ethnic or minority candidates for MacArthur fellowships.' Stewart had always been interested in the anthropology of Blacks in America and had published a story on this topic in *Stanford Short Stories* (1962). For Stegner, he was not a distinguished writer of fiction, but an anthropologist with a narrow focus. If the Committee was looking for this kind of work, Stewart would be well placed to get the prize 'especially if the scales are weighted a little in favor of color'.[45] But if the most important factor was the quality of the stories, there were many writers of his age or younger who could write better fiction. Stegner did not envy the position of gatekeepers who attributed prizes and rewards. That was one of the reasons he had left his job at Stanford: he no longer wanted to read stories that he found mediocre.

In particular, Stegner viewed the omnipresence of sex in contemporary fiction as a sign of laziness on the writer's part. When the f-word was scattered across a page, the result was bad writing. 'The sin is not the use of an "obscene" word,' he wrote, 'it is the use of a loaded word in the wrong place or in the wrong quantities.'[46] Stegner was no prude. As we have seen, the sex scenes in *Big Candy Rock Mountain* had once prevented him from getting a job at Mills College. In 1966, he was asked to comment on the Supreme Court's recent decisions on obscenity. In the first decision, the Court condemned Ralph Ginzburg for publishing obscene materials—including *The Housewife's Handbook on Selective Promiscuity*. In a second decision, the Court upheld a sentence to three years in prison given to Edward Mishkin for publishing and selling publications on sadomasochism, fetishism, and homosexuality. In its third decision, the Court found the eighteenth-century novel *Fanny Hill* not obscene. Stegner agreed entirely with the Court's position on the three cases. Ginzburg's and Mishkin's publications had no artistic value—they merely aimed at stimulating and profiting from prurience. In contrast, *Fanny Hill* was an interesting novel, whose main aim was not to titillate readers but to provide an imaginative record of one sort of human experience. No topic should be outside the scope of fiction, Stegner thought. Censorship could apply to pornographic texts, but not to novels that happened to deal with sex.[47]

The increasing polarization of American society forced Stegner to choose his side. He had once been a liberal, who held moderate views on censorship, opposed the Vietnam war and condemned racial discrimination. He became more extreme as he grew older, and repeatedly expressed his disenchantment with social change—ranging from the scrapping of censorship laws, to the activism of women, Blacks, and other minorities. He had no patience for students who cared more about politics than about their writing. And he had even less patience for academics who used their position of authority to indoctrinate students.

---

[45] Stegner to Paul Shullenberger, Reference letter for John Stewart, Box 2, 21 Dec. 1982, WS CW, Stanford.
[46] Stegner, 'Four-letter words', undated, Box 47, Edward Weeks papers, HRC.
[47] Stegner, Interview, 1966, Box 5, WS, Utah.

3.4 Widening of the Gap between Writers and Scholars

Stegner's plan to heal the breach between writers and scholars never materialized. Tensions started appearing in the 1950s, when the poet Yvor Winters insisted on encouraging Stanford writing fellows to do graduate work. Winters explained his reasons in a 1955 letter to Edward H. Jones:

> It is my conviction that a great poet is an intelligent and well-educated adult evaluating serious subjects in a difficult medium for an adult audience. I have therefore endeavored to pick poets who appeared to have minds, and I have encouraged them to educate their minds: in this last respect I am fortunate in being a member of an unusually good department, and I have endeavored to use the department to the utmost. You will observe that most of these people have taken or are taking the PhD.[48]

Unlike Winters, Stegner thought that young writers should learn their art by practice and avoid unnecessary distractions. As we have seen, he had nothing against graduate work per se, but he did not encourage his students to take courses external to the writing programme.

An open conflict erupted in 1963, after Winters complained about the selection of writing fellows. It was a habit of Winters to choose his own students for fellowships, considering criteria such as talent but also financial need. The fellowship committee headed by Stegner wanted more external candidates. Winters wrote an angry letter, expressing his disappointment with the entire writing programme. 'I have not had many good poets,' Winters sneered.[49] In more than thirty years of teaching, he had not had more than a dozen real candidates for greatness. Stegner wrote back: 'If your poems fail to ensure your immortality, your letters should do it.' There were several problems with Winters' attitude, Stegner said. First, Winters had created a coterie around him, and only favoured members of this coterie. Second, he was on a mission to push graduate work on every fellow. And third, he did not understand that writing programmes had nothing to do with greatness. Winters should not expect to get any great poets at all. 'I think it is pretty unlikely that we'll get very many great novelists, too,' Stegner added, 'but I like my system better than yours.'[50]

The conflict between Winters and Stegner sheds light on the ambiguous position of the first generation of creative writers in American universities. Some, like Winters, viewed education as a supreme goal and valued the production of scholarship alongside creative writing. Others, like Stegner, did not put such an emphasis on scholarly work. Writing was a craft, learnt through practice rather than theory. In

---

[48] Winters to Edward H. Jones, 29 Oct. 1955, Box 2, WS CW, Stanford.
[49] Winters to Stegner, 3 Mar. 1963, Box 1, WS misc., Stanford
[50] Stegner to Winters, 7 Mar. 1963, Box 1, WS misc., Stanford.

1968, the newly established National Endowment for the Humanities asked Stegner to sit on a committee to review grant proposals for scholarly projects. Stegner declined: 'by nature and inclination I'm a novelist, not a professor of American literature.' He added that he had not kept abreast of current developments in this field, and he did not go to the meetings of the Modern Language Association.[51]

Winters' and Stegner's positions were, of course, close. Both valued literary scholarship, even though they did not agree on its place in the training of writing fellows. In the 1960s and 1970s, however, radical writers rejected traditional education altogether, embracing behaviours designed to shock academics. In 1973, Tom Mayer—a former student of Stegner—asked for a reference letter for his tenure file at the University of New Mexico. Mayer was worried about his reputation amongst colleagues. 'They don't quite believe I am a real writer,' he wrote before adding, half-jokingly: 'Gregory Corso was here and they think I must be a bit odd, perhaps because I don't shoot heroin in the halls.'[52] Corso, who has been described as the bad boy of the Beat generation, once told an interviewer that he funded his drug use by selling his poetry notebooks to university libraries (Campbell, 'Obituary: Gregory Corso'). His addiction did not prevent him from teaching in universities, setting an example that would have horrified Stegner.

It is easy to dismiss Stegner as a man of the past, whose legacy was wiped out as creative writing programmes became increasingly inclusive. In his final years, Stegner was aware that even his way of writing was technologically obsolete. In one interview, he explained that he didn't need a computer: 'I use an old manual typewriter, and I can work when the power's down.'[53] The University of Utah has preserved three typewriters that he used at various stages of his life, a poignant reminder of the impact of technology on the writing process. Unlike Salman Rushdie who was using a Macintosh Performa, Stegner revised his texts on paper rather than on the screen. He was deliberately looking towards the past, towards a time when one used typewriters, when there was no affirmative action, and when physical attractiveness was a valid reason to recommend a young woman for a job.

His dream of healing the breach between scholars and writers ended in failure, as literary studies drifted towards theory, and creative writing severed links with scholarship. Perhaps Stegner did not believe hard enough that scholars and writers could be reconciled. 'With its built-in tolerance and self-doubt', liberal humanism 'is always vulnerable to those who are convinced they have a monopoly to the truth,' writes David Lodge in his celebration of Malcolm Bradbury's 1975 novel *The History Man*.[54] Like Bradbury who founded the first graduate programme in creative writing in Britain, Stegner believed in liberal humanism. And like Bradbury,

---

[51] Stegner to J. Saunders Redding, 20 Sept. 1968, Box 20, WS, Utah.
[52] Tom Mayer to Stegner, 2 Dec. 1973, Box 2, WS CW, Stanford.
[53] Stegner, Interview by Harold (Hal) Gilliam, 28 May 1992, Box 15, WS, Utah.
[54] Lodge, 'David Lodge on Malcolm Bradbury's *The History Man*'.

he resented what he saw on university campuses in the 1960s and 1970s. Both Stegner and Bradbury were men from modest social backgrounds who had found in the university a haven, an artistic home, and who regarded the values of culture and liberal thought as sacred. These values were under attack, the students were rude, literary professors were celebrating the death of the author, and in America, creative writers were retreating in their own writing centres separated from English departments.

Stegner has left a deep mark on creative writing programmes in the United States. His former students went on to create programmes in other universities, spreading the creative writing gospel and evangelizing their colleagues. Thomas Bontly, a former writing fellow at Stanford, pioneered the creative writing programme at the University of Wisconsin-Milwaukee, where he taught for thirty-five years. Stegner also helped promote university creative writing outside America. In 1965, the publisher Lovat Dickson wrote to Stanford after reading an article on writing schools in *The Times Literary Supplement*. Creative writing was still a new idea in Britain, but the Canadian-born Lovat was already familiar with the discipline. Forty years before, when he was a young instructor at the University of Alberta, he had tried to establish writing seminars. Subsequently, on moving to London, he had again tried to arrange meetings at his home 'for young writers who seemed to have the ability but did not have the experience to express themselves properly, to practice writing with a view to becoming writers'. Lovat was particularly interested in Stanford's creative writing programme, and he asked for further information.[55] Stegner could have asked his staff to send a prospectus, but he instead wrote back a long, personal letter. His attempts to convince British people of the value of creative writing programmes had not always been successful. He had once attended a diner at Magdalen College, Oxford, where he had 'the strong impression that they thought me a rather amiable charlatan'. And he went on to explain the role of creative writing instructors at Stanford: 'to be a critic less loving than a wife, less forgiving than a friend, and more experienced than either.'[56] Love and forgiveness had little place in Stanford's creative writing programme, a programme that emphasized hard work, discipline, and professionalism.

At the commencement address he gave at Stanford in 1972, Stegner asked students to think of the meaning of freedom. For Stegner, routine was paradoxically a way to enable freedom by restricting choice. Instead of spending time and energy on evaluating various opportunities, one could get things done more efficiently by following a strict routine. Stegner also reminded students that their freedom of speech did not imply suppressing discourses that they found appalling. He gave the example of the Nobel Prize physicist William Shockley, a proponent of eugenics. Angry students had disturbed his lectures at Stanford, preventing him from

---

[55] Lovat Dickson to Head of Stanford Writing Center, 13 Apr. 1965, Box 14, WS, Utah.
[56] Stegner to Dickson, May 1965, Box 14, WS, Utah.

speaking. Although Stegner condemned Shockley's ideas, he found the students' methods even more dangerous. 'Laugh at him, debate him, deny him—but let him speak, for if you don't, you open the veins of your own freedom,' Stegner said. 'In times as angry as these, that is a truth that an elder may legitimately remind you of.'[57] This message could well apply to our present time. Stegner's morally severe worldview also carried the seeds of reconciliation and healing, of mutual respect and collaboration. At the time when the counterculture was becoming mainstream, Stegner encouraged students to dare to be different.

---

[57] Stegner, Commencement Speech, June 1972, Box 10, WS, Utah.

4
Fighting Organization Man
The Rockefeller Foundation and the Re-discovery of the Individual Creative Writer

When studying the rise of creative writing programmes one is never far from money. Wallace Stegner's and Paul Engle's achievements cannot be understood without reference to the funding landscape of the post-Second World War, a landscape increasingly shaped by American foundations that had so far shown little interest in the Humanities. In particular, the growing willingness of the Rockefeller Foundation (RF) to fund literary activities led to a fierce competition amongst players in the field. In the late 1940s and 1950s, this competition was at the institutional level. As Mary Ann Quinn puts it, 'the RF had always funded individuals through their institutions, achieving both greater accountability and wider resonance for its actions' (7). The Foundation privileged support for New Critics and their university-based little magazines, and awarded fellowships in creative writing to the University of Iowa.

But in the late 1950s and 1960s, RF officers started questioning the efficiency of this institutional approach. After all, many writers had no affiliation, and continued to see writing as a solitary activity, best practised outside universities and their creative writing workshops. In October 1964, the RF approved an experimental programme in creative writing, subsequently labelled 'Imaginative Writing and Literary Scholarship'. The central idea was to give maximal flexibility in the choice of writers to support—criteria such as age, writing style, or institutional affiliation were not to be taken into account. The programme lasted for five years, and sponsored nearly one hundred writers, including Philip Roth, Cormac McCarthy, Elizabeth Bishop, Thom Gunn, and Louise Glück.

This exceptionally successful programme has attracted almost no scholarly attention, apart from a short article in the 2007 newsletter of the Rockefeller Archive Center (Quinn). Scholars have mainly focused on the Rockefeller Foundation's assistance to New Criticism in the 1940s (Schwartz; Kindley). Likewise, Eric Bennett's chapter on the RF in *Workshops of Empire* looks at the initiatives of the immediate post-war period and does not mention the change of strategy in the 1960s. In his brief presentation of the RF, Bennett tends to oversimplify the

Foundation's origins and objectives. He notes that 'during the Depression and the war, Congress had rewritten the tax code placing an unprecedentedly high tax rate on large businesses' (59). This encouraged Standard Oil to spend the money through its philanthropic arm rather than 'giving it to Washington' (59). The Rockefeller Foundation's main objective was to 'engender a national and international atmosphere conducive to stable markets. World War II was hell on business; World War III would be apocalyptic' (58).

It is, of course, true that high taxes are at the root of the expansion of the Rockefeller Foundation, the Ford Foundation, and the Carnegie Foundation. It is also true that these foundations aimed at promoting the American view of a stable world order. But American foundations did not wait until the Second World War to intervene in the cultural field. Although health and science had dominated the funding priorities of the RF since its creation in 1913, the Foundation created a division of the Humanities in 1928, when it took over the humanistic studies programme from the General Education Board and the International Education Board. The new division was headed by a classicist, Professor Edward Capps. 'In the brief period in which he held the post,' writes Raymond Fosdick, 'the program continued largely along the lines laid down by the other boards, centering to a great extent in archaeological interest, although branching out into some significant work in bibliography' (239). Under the leadership of Director David Stevens (1932–49) and Assistant Director John Marshall (1933–62), the focus of the Humanities programme evolved towards new disciplines (such as communications studies) and new technologies (including microphotography to preserve books and documents and make archival holdings more accessible). From the mid-1940s, the Rockefeller Foundation also increasingly encouraged literary creation through grants to little magazines and programmes of creative and critical writing.

This chapter begins with the literary programmes of the immediate post-war period, which focused on university-based initiatives. It shows that Marshall's long-term interest in modernism deeply influenced the policy of the Humanities division, from his choice of collaborators (including R. P. Blackmur and other New Critics) to his emphasis on little magazines. But as we have seen, modernism had always been marked by a deeply ambiguous attitude towards academia. The poet-critic imagined by T. S. Eliot had one foot inside, and one foot outside the university system. Not only was the institutional position of the poet-critic precarious, the unity of this role was increasingly challenged. At Iowa, Paul Engle pushed for a dissociation of writers and critics—thus endangering the very essence of the New Criticism model. For the Rockefeller Foundation, funding New Criticism and its institutions was no longer an attractive option.

The second section of this chapter examines the RF's experimental scheme Imaginative Writing and Literary Scholarship, conceived as a way to empower writers independently of their institutional affiliations or allegiances to literary groups. The RF was addressing wider concerns about the changing nature of American society expressed in books such as *The Lonely Crowd* or *The Organization Man*. Responding to intellectuals who criticized the conformity, passivity, and deference of post-war society, the Rockefeller Foundation promised to put the individual creator at the centre of its new scheme. The example of the RF's changing policy illustrates a turning point in the image of creative writing programmes. As these programmes developed across the country, they were increasingly accused of stifling creativity and threatening the autonomy of writers.

4.1 Supporting Institutions

4.1.1 The *Kenyon Review*

The Rockefeller Foundation's support to little magazines finds its origins in the early 1940s, at the time when the *Kenyon Review* was under serious financial strain. Founded in 1939 at Kenyon College, the Review was edited by John Crowe Ransom, who had recently written *Understanding Poetry* with Cleanth Brooks. Although the RF would later claim that Ransom himself appealed for emergency funding, it was in fact Richard Blackmur who first told John Marshall about the Review's precarious situation. 'The *Kenyon Review* is nearing the end of the Carnegie grant which has been sustaining it,' wrote Blackmur, 'and unless some foundation steps forward, will expire with the summer number.'[1] Marshall replied that the Rockefeller Foundation could not help magazines and other publishing enterprises.[2] Yet in 1944, three years after Blackmur's initial letter, the RF awarded a $7,500 grant to the *Kenyon Review*, described as 'the only critical journal of first quality under control of a college or university'.[3] So what made the Foundation change its strategy? What convinced Marshall and his colleagues that New Criticism was the new big thing? What triggered a change of policy that led to further grants to little magazines and creative/critical programmes?

To answer these questions, we need to go back to the 1920s, at the time when John Marshall was a student in English at Harvard and met another young man, Richard Palmer Blackmur. From age fourteen to twenty-four, Blackmur clerked in bookstores and Harvard's Widener Library and became a partner in a Cambridge bookstore that failed after a year (Lacey). It is in this bookshop that the two men met and started a friendship based on common literary interests. Neither Marshall, nor Blackmur would ever forget their early fascination for the new art and the new literature, discovered in reviews such as the *Dial* and T. S. Eliot's *Criterion*. Marshall was awarded his MA in 1928, and that same year, Blackmur became

---

[1] Richard Blackmur to John Marshall, 22 Jan. 1941, RG 1.2, Series 200.R, Box 358, Folder 3242, RF.
[2] Marshall to Blackmur, 23 Jan. 1941, RG 1.2, Series 200.R, Box 358, Folder 3242, RF.
[3] Resolutions of the Rockefeller Foundation, RF 43125, 10 Jan. 1944, RG 1.2, Series 200.R, Box 358, Folder 3242, RF.

Fig. 4.1 Richard P. Blackmur in the 1940s.
Source: Princeton Alumni Weekly, 21 May 1943.

editing manager of *Hound & Horn*, one of the most influential little magazines of the time.

In a 1943 memo to his superior David Stevens, Marshall wrote about his excitement reading modernism twenty years before. Although he did not understand all the literary currents reflected in the *Kenyon Review*, he felt that 'the Review must be read by people in those currents with the same keen interest that I used to read the *Dial* in the 20's'. And he added: 'certainly I have the impression that the Review stands for the most advanced literary and critical effort in this country.' However, Marshall was still not convinced that the Rockefeller Foundation should provide assistance to a magazine with a small audience. 'I should prefer to see any help we can give go to the journals with a more popular constituency, e.g., the *Prairie Schooner* or a revived *Frontier and Midland*.' For Marshall, the readership of the *Kenyon Review* was too advanced and specialized to justify assistance from a mainstream philanthropic organization. 'My own feeling,' he wrote, 'is that we should do more for the development of American culture in general if we put in whatever weight we could exert at a slightly less advanced level.'[4]

At the time when Marshall was writing this memo, 'popularity' had become an ugly word amongst the new generation of critics. Consulted before the RF made its first grant to the *Kenyon Review*, Blackmur insisted that the best literary magazines deliberately kept their audiences small and refused to cater to the banal tastes of the masses. In a 1944 report, Blackmur gave the example of the *Atlantic Monthly*, which reached a broad audience only when it 'reduced its standards to those of *Harper's Monthly*'. For Blackmur, the *Dial* remained a model of what a quality little magazine should be. Like Marshall, he fondly remembered his experience as a young man, discovering new literary currents in this little magazine. Indeed, Blackmur insisted on the pedagogical function of the *Dial* for people of his generation:

> This is the class of young men and women who devotedly *went to school* to the *Dial*, never missing an issue and always devouring each in toto, and developing a cross between passion and fury with regard to its chief contents—both in memory and anticipation—as irrational, but also as indubitably grateful as the school spirit to which it is kin. I was myself a member of a group in that class, and from 1920 to 1927 regularly haunted Felix's newsstand in Harvard Square for days before publication date on the chance that the next issue might blessedly be early ... what counted was the sense of belonging to the whole class of readers—whom I felt must be *disciples*—which the *Dial* alternatively challenged and drove. Putting the experience into a lower key, every issue of the *Dial* stretched my sensibility and gave the effect of adding to its stature and intensifying its residual strength. I *learned* the new writing and the new art, and, through the feeling of novelty *mastered*, became a part of them. Judging by those who did not have the privilege of my experience, I was from five to ten years ahead of my otherwise self.[5]

---

[4] Marshall to Stevens, 19 Oct. 1943, RG 1.2, Series 200.R, Box 358, Folder 3242, RF.
[5] Blackmur, 'Literary Magazines Study: Memorandum on American Literary and Critical Magazines', 1944, RG 1.1, Series 200.R, Box 243, Folder 2910, RF. Emphasis added.

Here, the *Dial* is presented as a pedagogical enterprise that not only taught young people about contemporary artistic movements, but also created a community of like-minded readers.

Blackmur's report convinced Marshall that the impact of little magazines on contemporary culture had nothing to do with the size of their audience. It made sense for a mainstream organization like the Rockefeller Foundation to support magazines with a small, active readership, because this small community could shape the future of American culture. Investing the Foundation's money in the fledgling *Kenyon Review* seemed risky at first sight, but the high risks could be met with high rewards. This line of thought was echoed in a 1946 study of little magazines. In this influential book, Frederick Hoffman, Charles Allen, and Carolyn Ulrich presented the small reviews as the 'advance guard' and the commercial publishers as the 'rear guard' (3). They claimed that the little magazines had discovered '80 per cent of our most important post-1912 critics, novelists, poets, and storytellers' (1). In contrast, large-scale publishing enterprises had rarely shown interest in the new literature: 'the commercial publishers are the rear guard because their editors will accept a writer only after the advance guard has proved that he is, or can be, commercially profitable' (3). This sharp opposition between small-scale and large-scale institutions offered academic credibility to Marshall's plan to support little magazines.

As Marshall saw it, the Rockefeller Foundation had a historical chance to transform literary culture, just as the patrons of the *Dial* and other modernist magazines had transformed the culture of their time. This ambitious, quasi-utopian vision met with some resistance. As Lawrence Schwartz notes, the director of the Humanities division 'was far more comfortable with awards granted through universities in the form of academic fellowships to alter the teaching of criticism and the training of younger critics' (113). But Stevens eventually agreed to let Marshall go ahead with his plans to encourage creative writing and criticism.

The Rockefeller Foundation's support to little magazines took two forms. From the late 1940s to the early 1950s, the main focus was on raising rates for contributors. In his report, Blackmur had pointed out that the *Dial*'s rates were 'comparable to the rates paid by the great commercial magazines for inferior and often fraudulent work'. And, he added: 'money was an agent for freedom and for the maintenance of standards in the market of the arts.' Marshall once again looked towards the modernist model when designing the RF's programme of support. He explained to the trustees that increased rates would improve literary quality and ability to attract readers, leading to financial stability.[6] The *Kenyon Review* was awarded $22,500 in 1947 and the *Sewanee Review*, $27,600 in 1948.[7] Despite this

---

[6] Marshall, 'Kenyon Review', 2 Apr. 1947, RG 1.2, Series 200.R, Box 358, Folder 3243, RF.
[7] Resolutions of the Rockefeller Foundation, RF 47037, 2 Apr. 1947, RG 1.2, Series 200.R, Box 358, Folder 3242. Resolutions of the Rockefeller Foundation, RF 48011, 16 Jan. 1948, RG 1.2, Series 200.R, Box 416, Folder 3587, RF.

support, circulation figures remained low (approximately 3,250 for the *Kenyon Review* in 1952) and the Rockefeller Foundation decided to change its strategy. The journals would now distribute the Foundation's money to the most promising younger writers and receive payments for editorial and administrative costs.

The Atlantic Awards in Literature offered a model for this programme of decentralized fellowships administered by an institution. Just after the Second World War, the Rockefeller Foundation had contacted T. S. Eliot, F. R. Leavis, and other well-known literary figures to discuss its plan to help promising British writers whose work had been interrupted by the conflict. The University of Birmingham would administer this three-year programme (1946–48), with a budget of approximately $56,000.[8] The objective was to support individual writers but also to strengthen the Anglo-American relationship at a crucial historical time. 'One totalitarian enemy has been defeated, but the totalitarian temper still thrives and spreads,' announced the university. 'Everything, therefore, which can preserve, elucidate, or give new authority to the threatened values needs to be supported; and the writer, with his special power to represent and interpret every shade of human experience, is one of their chief custodians.'[9] In total, forty-seven writers received an award—forty-five men and two women. By 1950, twenty-eight recipients had at least one new book published or accepted for publication. But the Rockefeller Foundation was not entirely satisfied with the programme. 'Possibly a better scheme would be to strengthen the institutions which encourage literary excellence and which provide media for the publication of new writings,' declared the trustees' bulletin.[10] Two years later, the Foundation decided to give the experiment another try, focusing this time on American writers.

In its 1952 resolution awarding $41,400 to the *Kenyon Review* for this new programme, the Foundation justified its continuing support for a journal with such a small audience. In the *Review* and other little magazines 'often first appears the work of promising writers who later attain wider recognition'—writers such as Hannah Arendt and John Berryman. In contrast, 'magazines of wider appeal' found it 'difficult or impossible' to maintain high literary standards.[11] The Foundation's justification for supporting little magazines had not changed, but the focus of this support was gradually moving towards individual writers. Rather than raising the journals' circulation figures and ensuring financial stability, the main objective of the Foundation's programme was now to substantially improve the material conditions of writers. Of course, raising rates could also help struggling writers. But direct fellowships could have a wider impact, allowing authors to concentrate on their writing for an entire year.

---

[8] 'The Encouragement of Creative Writers', Dec. 1950, RG 3.1, Series 911, Box 1, Folder 5, RF.
[9] U. of Birmingham, 'To the Aid of the Writer, Atlantic Awards in Literature', RG 1.2, Series 401.R, Box 46, Folder 415, RF.
[10] 'The Encouragement of Creative Writers', Dec. 1950, RG 3.1, Series 911, Box 1, Folder 5, RF.
[11] Resolutions of the Rockefeller Foundation, RF 52119, 20 June 1952, RG 1.2, Series 200R, Box 358, Folder 3242, RF.

Flannery O'Connor was one of three writers to receive a Kenyon fellowship in 1952–53 ($2,000, while Edward Watkins and Irving Howe received $3,000 each).[12] This fellowship was renewed in 1953–54. John Marshall was particularly satisfied with these awards. In 1955 (the year O'Connor's first collection of short stories, *A Good Man Is Hard to Find*, was published), he wrote to the young Georgian writer: 'Between ourselves, yours is the most complete success of the three years during which the fellowships have been granted.' Eager to build a friendly relationship with O'Connor, Marshall told her about his student years, when he discovered modernist literature: 'I was a late contemporary at Harvard of Cummings, Cowley, Dos Passos, Hillyer, Damon, et al.'[13] In his personal correspondence with O'Connor, Marshall had two main objectives: he wanted to know more about her career before the Kenyon fellowship, and about the impact of this grant on her writing.

In her replies, O'Connor stressed the importance of her time at the University of Iowa, where she had studied creative writing. Her first story was published in 1946, when she was twenty-one years old and still in graduate school. She gained her MFA the following year and was awarded the Iowa-Rinehart fiction fellowship. After a stay at Yaddo (the artists' colony in upstate New York) and a period living in New York City and in the countryside in Connecticut, she returned to her native Georgia in 1950 due to ill health (Friedman). The two Kenyon fellowships allowed her to avoid money problems. Without the grants, she wrote: 'I doubt if I would have been able to write very well, thinking all the time that I was a financial burden for my family.' The awards gave her peace of mind and creative freedom, as she was able to focus on short stories rather than a more lucrative novel. But this relief from market pressure was only temporary, leading to the need to apply for more grants. 'These things look very good and they save you for a year or two which is wonderful,' she wrote. 'But I have the feeling that to have made the most out of the Kenyon fellowship, I should have invested it in a Coca Cola stock or bought low rental property or set up a shooting gallery. I may have this problem for the next three or four years for the next thirty.'[14] Despite the Rockefeller Foundation's efforts, the condition of literary writers remained precarious, dependent on the renewal of old grants and the awards of new ones.

4.1.2 Iowa

The example of Flannery O'Connor shows that the RF was well familiar with the creative writing programme at Iowa. In 1949, Charles Fahs of the Rockefeller

---

[12] Paul Engle to John Marshall, 5 Sept. 1955, RG 1.2, Series 200.R, Box 448, Folder 3834, RF.
[13] Marshall to Flannery O'Connor, 26 Aug. 1955, RG 1.2, Series 200.R, Box 359, Folder 3246, RF.
[14] O'Connor to Marshall, 12 Sept. 1955, RG 1.2, Series 200.R, Box 359, Folder 3246, RF.

Foundation wrote to Wallace Stegner for advice: the RF wanted to send an American writer on a tour to Asian countries to encourage 'more mature writing in these oriental countries' and build a global community of like-minded writers.[15] In a Cold War context, such a project would boost the image of the United States abroad and foster goodwill amongst intellectual elites. Asked to suggest possible names, Stegner replied: 'There are a good many teachers-writers in American colleges now, but only a handful seem to be thoroughly qualified for a post such as this.' He mentioned prominent New Critics—John Crowe Ransom and Robert Penn Warren—as well as Paul Engle. 'A good deal of experience with the Iowa writing program and considerable success as a poet,' wrote Stegner of Engle before adding: 'A little unpredictable in his personal contacts, but when interested and stimulated, a very good talker.'[16] This description was deemed sufficiently important to be extracted from the letter and preserved in the RF's records. For Fahs and his colleagues, Engle was a man to watch.

Two months later, Engle paid a visit to John Marshall—he wanted to convince the Rockefeller Foundation to fund fellowships for younger writers who struggled to have their books published. A memo summarized Engle's pitch:

> His view is that the marked improvement in the literary environment of some universities due to the influence of critics who are teaching there, makes them, as they never were before, a place where younger writers can achieve their maturity. The critical study of literature such as now has developed in a number of leading universities is so much concerned with the creative process that it provides an environment in which creative work can grow.[17]

This relationship between the critical and the creative was a leitmotiv in Engle's fundraising message. New Critics had challenged the dominance of philologists, bibliographers and historical scholars, opening the door for creative writers. The movement was not limited to universities in the South or the Midwest: the most prestigious universities on the East Coast had also joined the New Criticism wagon, with the hiring of Archibald MacLeish at Harvard and R. P. Blackmur at Princeton. Engle was trying to harness the power of New Criticism and stir the movement in his direction, dissociating the critic from the poet. 'Critic and scholar follow the artist,' he wrote, 'but surely 95% of the help is given them. Wrong way around!'[18]

---

[15] Charles Fahs to Wallace Stegner, 18 Oct. 1949, RG 1.2, Series 205 (California), Box 205, Folder 61, RF.
[16] Stegner to Fahs, 23 Oct. 1949, RG 1.2, Series 205, Box 205, Folder 61, RF.
[17] John Marshall, Interview with Paul Engle, 15 Dec. 1949, RG 1.2, Series 200.R, Box 448, Folder 3833, RF.
[18] Engle to Edward D'Arms, 10 Mar. 1952, RG 1.2, Series 200.R, Box 448, Folder 3833, RF.

Engle situated his proposal in a broad historical context, looking both towards the past and towards the future. 'I've been reading a lot about the Greeks lately,' he told Edward d'Arms of the Rockefeller Foundation in 1952. 'They didn't care much for history, but they did regard music, the composition of verses, the contemporary capacity of a man, very highly. Wouldn't it be pleasant if what I want turned out to be not a grossly new thing but a return to an ancient view of the active mind.'[19] Engle's attempt to anchor creative writing in the classical tradition was a clever idea, considering the RF's reputation as a risk-averse, mainstream foundation. But Engle also stressed the present and future function of creative writing in the fight against communist totalitarianism. 'The program I describe is an original contribution not only to American education but to the world of art, to this nation's cultural future and to the virtue it can offer to a hostile world,' he declared.[20]

For Engle, the discipline of creative writing really mattered, at the national and international level. He explained that if universities had been havens for writers in the early twentieth century, the modernist generation would have been less critical of American society and culture. 'How much less of the Babbitt would [Sinclair] Lewis have found in this country if there had been a university open to him as a young struggling writer?' asked Engle. 'How much finer if not only Lewis, but William Faulkner and T. S. Eliot, had been warmly received and helped by a university at the beginning of their writing careers, instead of having to write their first books in bitter isolation, resentful of a country which seemed uninterested in giving them even so much as sympathy.'[21] Failing to support writers had been an act of self-mutilation that the United States continued to pay with a damaged image amongst international elites. At Iowa and elsewhere, creative writing programmes offered an opportunity to rebuild the country's reputation and to convince the world that America was a land of opportunities for artists.

Engle's vision initially failed to convince the Rockefeller Foundation. The focus of his proposal was on the supply side (the production of new writing), whereas the Foundation was concerned with demand. As d'Arms put it: 'the fact that we have in the United States quite a number of promising and accomplished artists in literature, the fine arts, music and other fields is balanced by the fact that even these artists of recognised ability are having difficulty in maintaining themselves and in reaching a sizable public.' The RF was more interested in raising the circulation figures of the *Kenyon Review* and other journals, than 'simply increasing the number of creative artists'.[22] But in 1952, this strategy was about to change, with the award of Kenyon fellowships to talented writers. And after years of failed attempts, Engle finally enlisted the support of the Rockefeller Foundation.

---

[19] Engle to D'Arms, 19 Feb. 1952, RG 1.2, Series 200.R, Box 448, Folder 3833, RF.
[20] Engle to D'Arms, 10 May 1952, RG 1.2, Series 200.R, Box 448, Folder 3833, RF.
[21] Engle to D'Arms, 10 May 1952, RG 1.2, Series 200.R, Box 448, Folder 3833, RF.
[22] D'Arms to Engle, 5 Mar. 1952, RG 1.2, Series 200.R, Box 448, Folder 3833, RF.

From 1953 to 1956, the University of Iowa received $40,000 from the RF to fund fellowships in creative writing. 'The exclusion of criticism and the inclusion of drama differentiate this proposal from those of Kenyon College and at the University of the South,' declared the RF's announcement.[23] This exclusion is of central importance to understand the positioning of Iowa in the post-war funding landscape. The Rockefeller Foundation—under the influence of Blackmur, Ransom, and others—was already convinced that New Critics had largely replaced traditional literary scholarship. As early as 1943, Ransom had told David Stevens: 'The old line departments of English which still offer little but historical scholarship are losing ground in the competition for able male students.' When the foundation was discussing possible support for a school of criticism, Iowa was mentioned as one of the obvious choices. Norman Foerster, who established creative writing as a graduate discipline at Iowa, was, in Ransom's words, 'most open-minded about the critical project.'[24] Engle could have built on this legacy to compete with the RF-funded Kenyon School of English, as Blackmur did with the Princeton Seminars in Literary Criticism. From a fundraising perspective, criticism was where the money was (at least the RF's money). But Engle was trying to achieve something different. Although he recognized the importance of New Criticism, he was now pushing for the dissociation between the critic and the writer.

Under Engle's influence, the Foundation started questioning the relationship between criticism and creative writing. Repeated grants to Kenyon College (to support the *Kenyon Review* and the School of English) had raised some eyebrows early on. Responding to the 1947 proposal for a school of criticism, d'Arms wrote: 'a further grant of this nature might tend to create the impression among other educational institutions that Kenyon, to the exclusion of other colleges and universities in the literary and critical fields, represented the Foundation's ideal of liberal arts education.'[25] With the rise of the Beat generation, the *Kenyon* and other RF-funded reviews were increasingly seen as the old guard. In 1955, Malcolm Cowley gently criticized John Marshall for being out of touch with the current literary scene, including Beat writers such as Jack Kerouac. 'I think you've been a little misled by what Kenneth Rexroth calls the bow-tie conspiracy,' Cowley wrote. 'Not enough popular writers or off-beat writers or plain drunks and bums. Too many academics.'[26] Marshall admitted that he kept abreast of new writing mainly through the university-based reviews.

---

[23] Resolutions of the Rockefeller Foundation, RF 53005, 16 Jan. 1953, RG 1.2, Series 200.R, Box 448, Folder 3833, RF.

[24] John Crowe Ransom to David Stevens, 27 Aug. 1943, RG 1.2, Series 200.R, Box 358, Folder 3242, RF.

[25] Edward D'Arms, 'Comments on Proposed Grant for School of Criticism, Kenyon College', 23 Oct. 1947, RG 1.2, Series 200.R, Box 359, Folder 3248, RF.

[26] Malcolm Cowley to John Marshall, 28 Aug. 1955, RG 3.1, Series 911, Box 5, Folder 41a, RF.

As the 1950s ended, New Criticism seemed to have lost its momentum, and the Rockefeller Foundation was accused of favouring a tiny coterie. Rexroth told Marshall that all the awards of literary fellowships through the four literary reviews (the *Kenyon*, *Sewanee*, *Hudson*, and *Partisan* reviews) were made within a 'clique'.[27] He believed that that these reviews have completely lost touch with really promising writers and he suggested that the awards should be made through Jay Laughlin's publishing firm, New Directions. Marshall took these criticisms seriously and he wrote to Ransom:

> There has been some comment to the effect that the writers who have received awards represent a fairly homogeneous group; certainly some of the wilder spirits are not included. Perhaps they didn't deserve to be. Perhaps they are not writers to be helped in this way. Perhaps there is no agency technically competent to receive a Foundation grant that is in touch with them![28]

Here, Marshall expressed a dilemma that had long troubled the RF: how can a foundation support individual writers while administering its fellowships through institutions? The answer so far had been to deal with universities. But 'wilder spirits' rejected affiliations with academic institutions, and the RF risked being trapped in the ivory tower, isolated from current literary developments.

Finding a solution to this issue was all the more urgent that the Ford Foundation (the largest foundation in the country) had just announced a new programme of fellowships for writers. Up to ten fellowships were awarded to writers over thirty years old to concentrate on their work for a minimum two-year period. The Ford Foundation contacted around 300 people 'active in the field of creative writing' and asked them to suggest possible candidates.[29] This selection system was designed to maximize literary quality and avoid unnecessary correspondence with writers (who had to wait to be nominated, rather than apply directly). A panel of advisors reviewed first the nominations and then the candidates' applications. In February 1959, eleven American novelists and poets were named recipients of the first Ford Foundation grants to creative individual artists.[30] The list included established authors of the modernist generation (E. E. Cummings and Katherine Anne Porter, who were both in their sixties) but also younger writers, including Flannery O'Connor and Saul Bellow. When awarding the fellowships, the panel had taken into account the current financial situation of candidates. Women generally received smaller grants than men: $8,000 for O'Connor and $13,000 for Porter, versus $15,000 for Cummings and $16,000 for Bellow. This difference is partly due

---

[27] John Marshall, Interview with Kenneth Rexroth, 21 Jan. 1958, RG 1.2, Series 200R, Box 359, Folder 3247, RF.
[28] Marshall to John Crowe Ransom, 18 Mar. 1958, RG 1.2, Series 200R, Box 359, Folder 3247, RF.
[29] Press Release, 7 Apr. 1958, C-638—1958 Writers Program Background, Reel P-1015, FF.
[30] Press Release, 16 Feb. 1959, C-638—1958 Writers Program Background, Reel P-1015, FF.

to the fact that married men received larger amounts to support their families. But even single men received much more than women. The only exception was the Black writer James Arthur Baldwin, who was awarded $12,000 ($1,000 less than Porter).[31]

From the funders' perspective, this scheme had many advantages. It allowed the Ford Foundation to keep total control over the fellowships, rather than outsource its administration to another institution. Since only writers with an established reputation could be nominated, the risk of appointing unworthy candidates was limited. The large pool of nominators also avoided criticisms of favouring a tiny coterie of writers. But the Rockefeller Foundation was not ready to imitate this model and abandon its policy of awarding fellowships through institutions. It took five more years before the RF finally launched an experimental programme that funded writers with or without a university affiliation.

4.2 Supporting Individual Writers

Saul Bellow played a central role in shaping the Rockefeller Foundation's new programme. Back in 1951, Marshall had met with the thirty-six-year-old writer, whom he described as 'one of the most promising of the present group of younger American novelists'. Marshall had been particularly impressed by *The Victim* (Vanguard, 1947), Bellow's second novel that he had read following Blackmur's suggestion. During this meeting, the conversation turned to the economic situation of literary writers (Bellow had just come back from a year in Europe, made possible by a Guggenheim fellowship, and was now teaching at New York University while working on two novels). Marshall frankly told him about the 'perplexities' RF officers faced in considering aid for creative writing, and he asked Bellow to write a report on the responsibility of the novelist in society.[32]

In this five-page report, Bellow wrote about the problem writers faced when trying to create truthful characters: should characters be 'revolutionaries, great natures, born aristocrats' as in the nineteenth-century novel? Or should writers resign themselves to the anti-heroes of Dostoevsky and others? In other words, how could writers combine 'a superior reality with daily fact'? The task of the novelist, Bellow argued, was to rescue 'an original human value' independent of styles, languages, and abstractions. Feeling and vividness brought us to 'conceptions of superior reality'. For Bellow, the novelist had a duty to 'restore value' in a world where 'the value of man has depreciated'. The problem was that few readers were interested in this kind of writing. 'A point of view like mine is not conducive to popular success,' he wrote. 'The commercial organization of society resists it

---

[31] List of 1959 Fellows, C-638—1958 Writers Program Background, Reel P-1015, FF.
[32] John Marshall, Interview with Saul Bellow, 9 Jan. 1951, RG 1.2, Series 200.R, Box 296, Folder 2773, RF.

and, let us face it, there is a widespread disgust, weariness, staleness, resistance, unwillingness to feel the sharp edge of life.'³³ This was a little-veiled appeal for support from the Rockefeller Foundation. But unlike Marshall, Edward d'Arms was not impressed by Bellow. His novels had a focus too narrow to match the writer's proclaimed ambitions, d'Arms thought. In May 1951, Bellow learnt that the RF board could not offer him any financial assistance (Atlas, *Bellow* 168).

By the mid-1960s, however, Bellow had become a successful novelist whose views were echoed amongst high-ranking RF officers. Gerald Freund, who directed the RF's creative writing programme, agreed with Bellow's point on the stature of characters. For Freund, the selection of writers should be based not on style but on the 'highest standards of integrity and decency'. What counted was the 'artistic intention of seeking truths, of ennobling rather than debasing the human individual and society' (qtd in Quinn 8). With its new experimental programme, the RF sought to implement these demanding standards by selecting grantees with the highest distinction or potential.

In Autumn 1964, a series of discussions, between writers (including the poet Robert Lowell) and RF officers, led to an agreement on the practical organization of the experimental programme. As in the case of the Ford Foundation awards, a group of nominators would submit the name of individual writers and the best qualified would then be invited to submit applications. A committee of three literary consultants (Lowell, Bellow, and the poet and critic Stanley Kunitz) would meet monthly and review these applications alongside RF officers. While the Ford Foundation, the Guggenheim Foundation and the National Institute of Arts and Letters favoured established authors, Freund and his colleagues wanted a programme sufficiently flexible to encourage both senior writers and 'younger men and women of some accomplishment and exceptional promise'.³⁴ There were no strings attached to the fellowships, no need to produce a book, no need to reside in a particular place, and, crucially, no need to be affiliated with a university or any other institution.

Freund's task was now to convince the trustees to abandon the RF's longstanding policy of awarding grants through institutions. Boyd Compton (then Assistant Director of the Humanities division) was not impressed. He asked Freund to limit the nominators to those writers with a university connection, and to select a few universities to administer the funds. He also criticized the programme's lack of focus on a particular age group: 'I very much fear that it will appear too amorphous and general in the Trustees' eyes.'³⁵ Freund returned Compton's memo with comments in pencil:

---

³³ Bellow, Report regarding fiction and its development, RG 1.2, Series 200.R, Box 296, Folder 2773, RF.
³⁴ Resolutions of the Rockefeller Foundation, RF 65062, 22 Oct. 1965, RG 3.2, Series 911, Box 5, Folder 27, RF.
³⁵ Boyd Compton, Memo, Writing Project, 8 Oct. 1964, RG 3.2, Series 911, Box 5, Folder 27, RF.

> Bellow argues that English departments are deadly for novelists. He hopes we can encourage writers to have useful experience … interviewing refugees in Jordan, etc! … He is against giving … money simply to sit at Bennington … He hopes we can tailor the grants, have utmost flexibility.

Bellow was not the only one in the committee to support flexible grants, an idea initially suggested by Lowell. But unlike the other literary consultants, he held radical views on university-based writing programmes, programmes that caused creative deaths by limiting the range of experiences. Instead of sitting in a classroom, Bellow argued, writers should travel the world and have full lives. What brought credibility to Bellow's ideas was his extensive experience of the academic system (after Minnesota and NYU, he was then working at the University of Chicago). He had also used his Guggenheim fellowship to travel abroad at a formative time in his career. Bellow was deeply convinced that non-academic experiences produced the best writers, he was tireless at defending his views, and he met with only lukewarm opposition. Nobody in the committee was particularly enthusiastic about creative writing programmes in universities, and Bellow's position prevailed.

How can we explain this lack of enthusiasm for creative writing programmes and creative writers in the university system? Why did the Rockefeller Foundation turn its back on an institution that it had once endowed with money and prestige? Bellow and his colleagues' attitude should be read in a larger intellectual context, characterized by widespread criticism of an American society dominated by passivity, conformity, and deference. As early as 1941, James Burnham's *The Managerial Revolution* predicted that a new ruling class of managers was on the brink of replacing the old capitalist elite. The new ideology favoured order, duty, and discipline and above all, allegiance to the group and the state. The majority of Americans no longer believed in the capitalist ideology that valued '*individualism*; opportunity; "natural rights," especially the rights of property; freedom, especially "freedom of contract"; private enterprise; private initiative; and so on' (158). For Burnham, the America of the mid-twentieth century had little in common with the country that Alexis de Tocqueville had visited in the early nineteenth century. While Tocqueville celebrated Americans' individualism, he also warned that their democracy could degenerate into a tyranny of the majority.

By the 1950s, influential books such as David Riesman's *The Lonely Crowd*, C. Wright Mills' *White Collar*, and William Whyte's *The Organization Man* confirmed Tocqueville's predictions: America had, indeed, become a tyrannical country where the individual was oppressed by rigid social norms and expectations. Riesman's book compared the 'inner-directed man' who relied on himself to achieve greatness, with the new model of the 'other-directed man' who constantly looked towards the group for directions on how to lead his life. 'The other-directed person does not so often think of his life in terms of an individualized career,' wrote

Riesman. 'He seeks not fame, which represents limited transcendence of a particular peer-group or a particular culture, but the respect and, more than the respect, the affection, of an amorphous and shifting ... jury of peers' (137).

Wright was equally pessimistic when describing the new American middle class. He opposed 'the nineteenth century farmer and businessman' who were 'their own men' to the twentieth-century white collar man, who 'is always somebody's man, the corporation's, the government's, the army's'. For Wright, 'the decline of the free entrepreneur and the rise of the dependent employee on the American scene has paralleled the decline of the independent individual and the rise of the little man in the American mind'.

Three years after the publication of *White Collar*, William Whyte would put another name on Wright's 'little man'. Born out of the 'sacrifice of individual accomplishment' (401), the 'organization man' valued 'belongingness' and 'togetherness' (32, 46). Whyte ended his book with a call for action, a call to fight the Organization and rediscover individualism. Whyte was anticipating the sorts of arguments that would be made, very forcedly, in the 1960s. At a time when the 'Organization' was demonized, Bellow and others sought to rescue the individual creative writer from the deadening influence of universities.

Although the RF trustees agreed on an experimental programme without a university tone, the issue continued to be discussed. In May 1965, Gerald Freund was having dinner with the literary consultants and asked them: 'Can foundations promote high-quality writing and literary scholarship through institutional grants?' Bellow replied that the institutional programmes had failed to produce 'quality' amongst either students or faculties. 'The most important thing in my view,' he said, 'is to put the students in touch with writers who can demonstrate that it is possible to be a writer. This is much better than any course in writing.' Lowell was less hostile to university programmes, citing the early success of Kenyon College. All agreed that foundations should award fellowships with the highest degree of flexibility, to target all kinds of writers and offer them total freedom. The RF's earlier support to the 'little magazines' could not be replicated, because there was 'no high-level cultural literary magazine in this country at this time'.[36]

Bellow's repeated opposition to university programmes undoubtedly shaped the RF's policy. During a 1965 meeting, Freund opened the discussion by asking the committee for possible priorities and directions if the Foundation were to extend its literature programme. He mentioned the Buffalo poetry centre and the creative writing programmes at Stanford and Iowa as possible models. Bellow replied that writing centres at universities had not justified themselves. 'The efforts to academize this particular trend have been very dismal,' he declared. 'You cannot try to earn credits or earn degrees.' Lowell and Kunitz thought the picture was more

---

[36] Notes on dinner discussion regarding writing and literary scholarship, 12 May 1965, RG 3.2, Series 911, Box 5, Folder 27, RF.

mixed, with some success stories. But Bellow strongly believed that even the most prestigious writing programmes did not produce the best writers:

> People in the US are drawn to institutions—get neurotics and a low type of life. People are then entirely ignorant of what is going on in the other parts of the college. They build their own world and get into a community like the Village. This type of person won't be productive. The student needs to get into the broader part of the life of the university in order to get a better sense of writing. These students in the English departments don't live.[37]

Bellow was not the first one to describe academia as a system closed to the outside world—think of T. S. Eliot or Ezra Pound's sharp criticisms of the ivory tower. But what is particularly striking is the absolutism of his views. Unlike Eliot and Pound, Bellow had spent most of his life working in universities. Yet, even when the Rockefeller Foundation was ready to put money on the table, even when he could have pushed for a writing centre at his own university, Bellow continued to value the idea of a writer free from any institutional commitments.

Although Bellow's views came to dominate the RF committee, his criticism of creative writing programmes at universities provoked controversy on at least one occasion. In May 1968, he delivered a talk 'What Are Writers Doing in the Universities' at San Francisco State College. Creative writing courses there were fairly informal. One teacher, the crime writer Wallace Markfield, described students arriving 'in beards, crash helmets, paratroops boots and with dogs'. Excuses of non-completion of work included: 'I've been on an LSD trip' and 'I have a hang-up about going to class; do you mind if I don't come?' (Nichols). This kind of environment would have been repulsive to Bellow. As his biographer James Atlas puts it, 'Bellow made no secret of his contempt for student radicals … In the women's movement, the Black Power movement, the student uprisings on campuses, he saw an insurrection against all the things he valued' (*Bellow* 387).

During the question period after his talk, Bellow had a confrontation with Floyd Salas, an ex-boxer and creative writing teacher at San Francisco State. Salas, who had arrived late, thought that Bellow had defended the university as a 'haven from vulgarity for the writer'. Salas asked for clarification and when Bellow refused to answer, the boxer-turned-novelist started insulting him, calling him an old man (Bellow was then fifty-four, Salas was thirty-seven). The episode left Bellow shaken and in October 1968, he wrote to the writer Mark Harris:

> The thing at S. F. State was very bad. I'm not too easy to offend, at my age, and I don't think I was personally affronted—that's not my style. The thing was offensive though. Being denounced by Salas as an old shit to an assembly which seemed

---

[37] Discussion on writing and universities, 1965, RG 3.2, Series 911, Box 6, Folder 29, RF.

to find the whole thing deliciously thrilling ... So I left the platform in defeat. Undefended by the bullied elders of the faculty. While your suck-up-to-the-young colleagues swallowed their joyful saliva. No, it was very poor stuff, I assure you. You don't found universities in order to destroy culture. For that you want a Nazi party.[38]

The interesting thing here is Bellow's defence of a traditional view of the university, as a bastion of civilization and middle-class propriety. In this picture, a rude heckler became a Nazi on a mission to destroy culture.

This episode did not improve Bellow's opinion of university-based creative writers. In May 1969, he wrote a note defending the RF's Imaginative Writing and Literary Scholarship programme, which was now in its fifth year. 'I understand that the future of individual grants is very uncertain,' declared Bellow before adding that 'artists are individuals' and 'foundation support of collective enterprises only would be damaging to the artist and to American culture'.[39] In spite of Bellow's efforts, the programme was not renewed. The RF trustees had never been comfortable with a programme independent of institutions and no other scheme was proposed (in part because Bellow and others had failed to prepare an alternative).

Despite this abrupt ending, Bellow was right to describe the RF's programme of individual fellowships as 'extraordinarily successful'. The list of grantees reads like a Who's Who of major American writers spanning several generations (the youngest was twenty-three years old, the oldest was sixty-nine). In 1966, for example, grant recipients included Philip Roth and Cormac McCarthy (both in their early thirties) as well as older writers such as Elizabeth Bishop and Kenneth Burke.

Considering the Foundation's long history of shunning commercial success in literature, Roth was an unlikely choice. *Goodbye, Columbus*, published by Houghton Mifflin in 1959 when Roth was twenty-six years old, immediately established him as one of the best young writing talents and earned him the National Book Award for Fiction. He then wrote *Letting Go* (Random House, 1962), which was a greater commercial than critical success. From the start of his career, Roth benefited from the support of large publishing firms that helped him reach a wide audience. But in the late 1960s, Roth was going through a difficult period—he told the Rockefeller Foundation that he had $7,000 in debts from medical care and alimony and was struggling to finish his new book.[40] He hoped to use the Rockefeller grant to complement the revenue from his part-time teaching, which he enjoyed and wanted to continue. Roth had extensive experience of teaching creative writing at university level and, like Paul Engle, he believed in harsh pedagogy. 'Part of our

---

[38] Saul Bellow, Letter to Mark Harris, 22 Oct. 1968 (Taylor 283).
[39] Bellow, Memo regarding the Imaginative Writing and Literary Scholarship Program, 28 May 1969, RG 3.2, Series 911, Box 5, Folder 28, RF.
[40] Gerald Freund, Interview with Philip Roth regarding creative writing grants, RG 1.2, Series 200.R, Box 459, Folder 3919, RF.

function,' Roth once said, 'is to discourage those without enough talent. A lot of people come for self-expression or therapy. We try to put a stop to that' (Boroff).

This kind of discourse would have delighted Freund and other RF officers eager to defend the highest standards in the selection of creative writers. It is thus not surprising that Roth was consulted as early as January 1964, at the time when the experimental programme was still being discussed.[41] In April 1965, the RF committee decided to invite him to apply for a fellowship—alongside Cormac McCarthy, Thomas Pynchon, and others. The case of William Burroughs, nominated by Mary McCarthy, was also discussed, but the committee members declined this candidacy ('not quality of others' was the reason recorded in the minutes).[42] Starting in April 1966, Roth was awarded a one-year fellowship of $8,000, which allowed him to complete his third novel.[43] The following year, the RF cited his case as an example of the success of the experimental programme: 'the accomplished novelist Philip Roth was assisted at a critical time with his recently published work *When She Was Good*, which has been acclaimed by leading critics as his best work to date.'[44]

Cormac McCarthy was another success story. His first novel, *The Orchard Keeper* (Random House, 1965), led Ralph Ellison to say that he 'is a writer to be read, to be admired, and—quite honestly—envied.'[45] In his application for an RF fellowship, McCarthy described the aim of his book set in Knoxville, Tennessee, in the early 1950s to be 'an understanding of what life here would mean to a person who was totally aware. In a sense, … these characters are the embodiment of a single soul.' Ellison praised McCarthy's project, judging that 'there is magic even in these bits of characterization and description' (qtd in Quinn 9). The grant from the Rockefeller Foundation allowed McCarthy to write part of his new book, while living in Europe. He also finished the revisions of a shorter novel, *Outer Dark*, published by Random House in 1968. In his report, McCarthy stressed his difficult financial situation: 'I have no trade or profession, and receive next to nothing for my writings, so you can see that assistance must come from somewhere.'[46] The Rockefeller Foundation therefore provided opportunities for less commercially orientated writers, at a time when many publishing houses (such as Random House) were becoming part of large, profit-orientated corporations.

---

[41] At this early stage, the RF was planning to focus not on individual writers, but on 'selected colleges and universities'. Kenneth Thompson, consultations on creative writing grant, RG 3.2, Series 911, Box 5, Folder 27, RF.

[42] Gerald Freund, Literature Discussion Meetings, 14 Apr. 1965, RG 3.2, Series 911, Box 5, Folder 27, RF.

[43] Resolutions of the Rockefeller Foundation, RF 65062, 30 Mar. 1966, RG 1.2, Series 200.R, Box 459, Folder 3919, RF.

[44] Resolutions of the Rockefeller Foundation, RF 67054, 22 Sept. 1967, RG 3.2, Series 911, Box 5, Folder 27, RF.

[45] Resolutions of the Rockefeller Foundation, RF 66055, 24 June 1966, RG 3.2, Series 911, Box 5, Folder 27, RF.

[46] Cormac McCarthy to Gerald Freud, 23 Sept. 1968, RG 1.2, Series 200.R, Box 460, Folder 3928, RF.

Not all writers funded by the programme managed to make progress on their proposed project. Elizabeth Bishop, for example, experienced personal upheaval that hindered the completion of her book about Brazil—a country where she had lived since 1951. Bishop was well familiar with the RF: in 1956, the year she received the Pulitzer Prize for Poetry, she was awarded a *Partisan Review* fellowship funded by the Foundation. In April 1960, she wrote to Robert Lowell: 'Rockefeller has long been interested in South America and I have an idea for getting money to see more of it and finish up a book of stories about Brazil.'[47] But it was not until 1965 that she submitted an application under the Foundation's Imaginative Writing Program. By that time, Bishop's life in Brazil had become difficult: her partner Lota de Macedo Soares was involved in the politics of Rio, and as the political situation worsened, Bishop felt increasingly uncomfortable in her Brazilian home (Colwell). Her grant application arrived after the deadline and Bishop had to reapply the following year, when she held a visiting professorship at the University of Washington in Seattle.[48] With the funding awarded by the RF, she returned to Brazil, hoping to re-establish her life there. It proved impossible: Bishop drank destructively and Soares became increasingly depressed. In a January 1967 letter, Bishop wrote: 'I was going to start off on a trip on a river—for the Rockefeller book—but don't feel up to it yet—in fact I don't know what to do.'[49] Her life took a new chaotic turn when she returned to the United States. Soares joined her in New York on 19 September 1967 and, later that day, committed suicide.

The report that Bishop wrote for the Rockefeller Foundation the next year is marked by a heavily personal tone: 'I sustained a great loss, the prolonged illness and death of my closest friend and the breaking up of my Brazilian home of seventeen years, followed by three illnesses of my own (a broken shoulder; three months later, a broken wrist; three months after that, osteomyelitis of the jaw—all three requiring hospitalization.)' Bishop was well aware that this confessional tone was not what the Rockefeller expected, and that, after two years of financial support, her lack of progress on her proposed book was disappointing. But she concluded on a positive note. 'The Rockefeller grant has been of inestimable value to me,' she wrote, 'it not only helped me through those months financially, but helped me in enabling me to look forward more hopefully to the time when I would be able to devote myself to my work again.'[50] Unaffiliated writers such as Bishop were by definition less accountable than those who relied on an institution to distribute funding. With its Imaginative Writing Program, then, the Rockefeller Foundation took larger risks than with its previous schemes.

The RF's increased emphasis on the individual writer shows that the post-war rise of creative writing programmes did not go unchallenged. With the increased

---

[47] Elizabeth Bishop to Robert Lowell, 22 Apr. 1960 (Giroux and Schwartz 833).
[48] Gerald Freud to Bishop, 3 Feb. 1966, RG 1.1, Series 200.R, Box 297, Folder 2779, RF.
[49] Bishop to Anny Baumann, 20 Jan. 1967 (Giroux and Schwartz 873).
[50] Bishop to Freund, 16 Oct. 1968, RG 1.1, Series 200.R, Box 297, Folder 2779, RF.

popularity of these programmes came accusations of conformity. University-based creative writers were now seen as Organization Men devoid of any originality. Through its Imaginative Writing scheme, the Rockefeller Foundation offered a model based on the writer's rather than the institution's needs. The objective was no longer to help little magazines or academic programmes, but rather to encourage individuals eager to concentrate on their writing. Not all RF-supported writers followed Saul Bellow's advice to go and interview refugees in Jordan, but many used their grant to travel and enrich their work. Yet, the freedom at the centre of the programme made the Rockefeller Foundation uneasy. In his award letter to Cormac McCarthy, Gerald Freund wrote: 'the Foundation prefers in its individual grant program to make awards through qualified universities and colleges which are prepared to administer the grants on behalf of recipients.'[51] Freund went on to suggest that the University of Tennessee would be best placed to administer the grant. This is surprising, considering the fact that McCarthy had left the university seven years before, without even graduating. Despite the RF's eagerness to sponsor writers outside the ivory tower, it found it hard to disentangle writers from universities and to fully embrace the 'wilder spirits'.

---

[51] Gerald Freund to Cormac McCarthy, 2 June 1966, RG 1.2, Series 200.R, Box 460, Folder 3928, RF.

5
Fame, Fortune, and Freedom
The Rise and Fall of the Famous Writers School

Like the Imaginative Writing Program, the Famous Writers School (FWS) was a product of the 1960s, a decade marked by the re-discovery of the individual creative writer. But as we have seen, the Rockefeller Foundation's programme was a very selective affair, aimed at a handful of writers who had already attracted the attention of distinguished referees. These happy few were already part of the literary landscape. In contrast, many would-be writers had no idea how to get started. Some of them were unsure they had enough talent or determination to become published authors. The mere fact of getting published was hard enough—obtaining reviews and endorsements from well-known writers seemed almost impossible. From 1960, the FWS addressed these aspirations and fears through extensive advertising in mass-market and large-circulation periodicals—from *Life* to the *Saturday Review of Literature*, from *The New York Times* to *Commentary*. In 1967 and 1968, over ten million postcard inserts were placed in the paperbacks published by Dell, and the first television advertisements appeared (Byrne 42). The School sold not merely correspondence courses but the dream of the writing lifestyle—promising fame, fortune, and freedom to anyone who had the aptitude to become a writer. The only thing to do was to return a coupon and the FWS would send an 'aptitude test' free of charge. This test was presented as a serious, quasi-scientific tool designed by a 'Guiding Faculty' of famous professionals—including the publisher and TV personality Bennett Cerf.

As a well-liked figure associated with the early days of television, Cerf was instrumental in the success of the Famous Writers School. 'Do you have a restless urge to write?' asked one advertisement, presented as a letter from Cerf to would-be writers. There is something different about people who feel this urge, declared the ad. These people are not content to be only model housewives or good businessmen. 'They yearn for greater freedom, a more meaningful life, through self-expression.'[1] Forty years before, Cerf had assured potential consumers that *reading* would improve their well-being. Inspired by the Harvard Classics and other cheap series of reprints, he advertised the Modern Library as a sophisticated

---

[1] Advertisement for the Famous Writers School, *The New York Times*, 3 Mar. 1968, p. BR33.

series for intellectually curious and socially ambitious readers eager to discover modern classics.[2] Self-improvement was then central to his advertising strategy. Moving the focus from reading to writing, he now endorsed correspondence courses to achieve a fuller life—a life that would bring psychic fulfilment in addition to material success.

This discourse appealed particularly to the growing number of women yearning for more than their roles as wives and mothers. In 1964, Faith Baldwin—a best-selling writer, part of the FWS 'Guiding Faculty'—appeared on advertisements targeting dissatisfied housewives. 'It's very unfortunate that many women with real writing talent bury it under a mountain of dishes,' declared Baldwin. 'For the woman who is tied down to her home, writing provides a wonderful means of emotional release and self-expression, to say nothing of the extra income it can bring.'[3] As the success of Betty Friedan's *The Feminine Mystique* (1963) had shown, many women were no longer content to serve their husbands and children. The Famous Writers School promised not only emotional contentment but also financial autonomy.

In the 1960s, the Famous Writers School was very profitable. In September 1966, Famous Artists Schools (the FWS's parent company) reported that there were 128,788 active students learning art, writing, and photography in the firm's various schools, both in the United States and overseas. New enrolments in the Writers School were up by more than 15 per cent over the previous year.[4] Rising tuition fees also contributed to the profitability of the company, which was listed on the American Stock Exchange.

By the late 1960s, however, Famous Artists Schools were expanding too quickly, acquiring other correspondence businesses and opening international branches. This reckless expansion, combined with the economic crisis and the growing criticism of its methods, led to the company's rapid decline. In 1970, Jessica Mitford published a devastating article in the *Atlantic*, triggering an official investigation in the FWS's advertising practices. The company filed for bankruptcy shortly after.

The immense success of the FWS shows the consolidation and appeal of the discourse on freedom as a central characteristic of the writing life outside academia. This story has never been told. As we have seen in Chapter 2, would-be writers have been largely absent from scholarship—despite the rise of 'book history from below' and related fields. It is easy to dismiss the FWS and other correspondence schools as shams, targeting the gullible masses. Yet, the immense success of these courses sheds light on ordinary Americans and their aspirations in the post-war period. The FWS told these people that there was more to life than material comfort: they could achieve a meaningful existence by sharing their thoughts and experiences

---

[2] See Jaillant, *Modernism, Middlebrow and the Literary Canon* 9.
[3] Advertisement for the Famous Writers School, *The Globe and Mail*, 11 Feb. 1964, p. A3.
[4] 'Famous Artists Schools Shapes Higher Earnings', *Barron's National Business and Financial Weekly*, 5 Dec. 1968, pp. 46, 49.

with a community of readers. The pleasure of self-expression would, in turn, bring material rewards, as publishers were desperate to find good writers. This enticing narrative addressed the aspirations of many Americans, who yearned for a different life—a life without daily commute or household chores, an autonomous life with the pleasures of celebrity and money. The downfall of the Famous Writers School did not destroy these aspirations, even though creative writing courses are no longer sold as an easy way to a lucrative career.

The first section of this chapter examines the market for correspondence schools after the Second World War. With a growing population and expanding economy, the demand for flexible education opened up opportunities for new companies— including Famous Artists Schools. Through extensive advertisements and home visits, the Schools became a profitable enterprise that constantly experimented with new courses—including writing and photography. In the second part, I look at a specific audience targeted by the Famous Writers School: women. Writing courses were presented as a path to self-respect and financial autonomy. With the rise of second-wave feminism, this discourse found an attentive audience amongst many disenchanted women. The third section turns to the criticisms and satires of the FWS, which culminated with Jessica Mitford's *Atlantic* article. The scandal impacted on the career of 'Guiding Faculty' members: Bennett Cerf, but also Paul Engle at Iowa and other well-known literary figures. Following Mitford's investigation, Nelson Algren attacked all 'kreativ righting' workshops as shams. Creativity was by essence a solitary enterprise, said Algren, not a group exercise. The growing demand for education after the war was not limited to universities boosted by the GI Bill. In a country marked by huge distances, many people chose to learn at home. In 1961, more individuals signed up for correspondence courses each year than enrolled in the freshman classes of all US colleges and universities. There were three types of correspondence school: university extension; organizational, such as those sponsored by the Armed Forces and various trade groups; and private. The latter group had seen an explosion of popularity: in the United States alone, 500 private schools with 1.5 million students combined gross revenues of around $100 million in 1960 (Du Bois). Amongst these private schools, Famous Artists Schools—which specialized in painting, commercial art, illustrating, and cartooning—was one of the most successful and innovative.

Founded in 1948, Famous Artists Schools was the brainchild of Albert Dorne, a noted illustrator. Dorne was born in 1904, in a tenement on Manhattan's Lower East Side. He left school after the seventh grade to support his mother, two sisters, and a younger brother. After a stint selling newspapers, he tried other jobs: milkman's helper, salesman, and even professional boxer. At the age of sixteen, he apprenticed himself to an artist during the day, hoping to become an illustrator. Despite working nights as a shipping clerk to support his family, Dorne found the energy to learn the craft and became an established commercial artist. By the time he was twenty-one, he reportedly earned $20,000 a year, and he could travel outside Manhattan. He later said: 'I was delighted to discover that a real cow looked exactly like the cows I had been drawing for some years for the Borden Company.'[5] In the next thirty years, Dorne did most of his illustrations for mass-market magazines—including *Collier's* and the *Saturday Evening Post*. At the height of his career, Dorne went into business with several well-known artists—including his friend Norman Rockwell. The idea was simple: offering art courses by correspondence. Advertisements for Famous Artists Schools promised three main things: a glamorous life, a huge income, and an escape from ordinary routine.

First, the promise of celebrity was central to the Schools' advertising strategy. One student 'had never drawn a thing until she began our training,' declared a 1958 ad. 'Now a swank New York gallery exhibits her paintings for sale.'[6] These students would be guided by a faculty of famous illustrators, who had selflessly taken time off from their careers to design the curriculum. To find men and women with talent worth developing, they had prepared an art talent test, which could be obtained for free simply by returning a coupon. Those who responded to the ads then received the visit of a salesman, who touted the numerous advantages of an artistic career. 'Artists associate with celebrities,' declared one page of the sales book (qtd in Kennedy).

Money was also part of the appeal of Famous Artists Schools. Having escaped poverty, Dorne used his personal story to promote his firm in mass-market magazines, a sector he knew well. A 1957 advertisement in *Life* (circulation 5.7 million at that time)[7] showed photos of him and Rockwell under the title: 'They DREW their way from "Rags to Riches." Now they're helping others do the same.' Like Dorne, Rockwell had left school when he was still a teenager before becoming a well-known, commercially successful artist. Art was the key to upward social mobility, promised the ad. One student, who used to work as a pipe fitter's helper for a gas company, had been transferred to the advertising department 'at a big increase in pay' thanks to his art skills.[8]

In addition to financial rewards, art offered the promise of freedom and escape from a dull life. 'FED UP? ... with your present job? ... your pay? ... your future? ...' asked Dorne in one 1955 ad. 'Here's my success secret. I studied ART at home—SO CAN YOU' (qtd in Kennedy). That same year, Simon & Schuster published Sloan Wilson's *The Man in the Gray Flannel Suit*, a bestselling novel about the difficulty to find contentment in post-war America. Refusing to imitate his workaholic boss, the novel's hero eventually turns down a high-profile job that involves travel and long hours, preferring to spend more time with his family. As Evan Brier has argued, the book suggests that 'one can be rewarded for refusing to conform' (98). The success of Wilson's novel shows that the hectic and

[5] 'Albert Dorne, 61, Illustrator, Dies', *The New York Times*, 16 Dec. 1965, p. 47.
[6] Advertisement for Famous Artists Schools, *The New York Times*, 3 Aug. 1958, p. SM49.
[7] Siff 73.
[8] Advertisement for Famous Artists Schools, *Life*, 5 Aug. 1957, p. 9.

material culture of the 1950s had left many Americans yearning for a different life—a yearning that Famous Artists Schools skilfully exploited.

By 1960, the firm decided to expand by offering four courses in writing (fiction, non-fiction, advertising, and business writing). Announcements for the new Famous Writers School relied on the same formula that had made its parent company so successful: celebrity, money, and escape. In one of the first ads for the FWS, a photo of the twelve famous writers who were part of the 'Guiding Faculty' was followed by a long list of their achievements. Rod Serling was the winner of four Emmys and author of the popular TV series, *The Twilight Zone*; Bruce Catton had won the Pulitzer Prize for *A Stillness at Appomattox*; Faith Baldwin was the author of dozens of bestselling books, novels, and hundreds of short stories; and so on. 'Your training will be supervised' by these illustrious writers, declared the ad. 'They have developed a series of home study textbooks, lessons and writing assignments that present—in a clear and stimulating way—what they have learned in their long, hard climb to the top.' Learning from successful people was the best way to become successful. And there were many opportunities to make money: the demand was particularly great in writing's 'big leagues' (national magazines, newspapers, book publishers, and the like).[9]

Writing could indeed be very lucrative, promised a 1967 advertisement presented as a series of questions and answers with facts and figures. 'Jobs for writers range all the way from $6,000 to $35,000 a year, depending on ability and experience.' Top writers could earn much more. 'Can you have job security?' asked the ad. The answer was yes: writers who worked for magazines, newspapers, and advertising companies, and the staff writers for business firms, enjoyed a good salary, generous benefits, and full security. All the major markets were looking for writers: 'There are 1,100 book publishers turning out 12,000 new titles a year,' declared the ad. 'There are 700 magazines—11,000 newspapers—12,000 trade publications—500 radio and TV stations—2,800 advertising agencies—2,000 publicity firms.'[10] The accumulation of precise numbers strengthened the main point: writing was a good way to make money, lots of money. One year later, another advertisement claimed that Samuel Johnson himself had viewed the writer as a professional, who needed to be paid. 'No man but a blockhead ever wrote except for money,' said Dr Johnson.[11] Like its parent company, the Famous Writers School told prospective applicants that art and profit go hand in hand.

Writers also enjoyed a flexible lifestyle, organizing their schedules as they pleased. In a 1966 advertisement, J. D. Ratcliff—a Guiding Faculty member and 'one of America's highest paid free-lance authors'—explained that he worked only four hours a day, from 8am to noon. With no commuter train to catch and no office

---

[9] Advertisement for the Famous Writers School, *The New York Times*, 11 Sept. 1960, p. 145.
[10] Advertisement for the Famous Writers School, *Commentary*, 1 Jan. 1967, n.p.
[11] Advertisement for the Famous Writers School, *The New York Times*, 5 Jan. 1969, p. SM81.

routine, his life was wonderful. 'I've interviewed a dozen Nobel Prize-winners, including Sir Alexander Fleming who discovered penicillin,' he added. 'I've talked with heads of state, at least one king, scores of leading industrialists.'[12] In the past year, he had covered stories from Bangkok to Buffalo. His life was so amazing that he couldn't understand why more beginners didn't publish in magazines and newspapers. Freedom, celebrity, travel, money: what else could you desire? A photo showed Ratcliff wearing a luxurious, country-gentleman-type jacket and walking his dog (presumably when ordinary people were chained to their office desks).

In *The Road to Character*, David Brooks argues that a profound cultural shift occurred in the 1950s and 1960s—from a 'Little Me culture' to a 'Big Me culture'. Whereas humility had been a central value, self-trust came to define American society. He gives the example of commencement speeches, which rely on the same clichés: 'Follow your passion. Don't accept limits. Chart your own course. You have the responsibility to do great things because you are so great' (7). The ads of the Famous Writers School illustrate this cultural shift towards the model of *radical individualism*, which would soon influence creative writing programmes. Potential applicants were told that self-expression was the key to a good life, a life with money, autonomy, and celebrity. The FWS not only used famous people to sell its product, which would have been nothing new, but it also promised prospective applicants that they too could become famous.

Bennett Cerf, whose career had spanned several media (books, magazines, radio, and television), was the perfect person to endorse the course. From 1951 to 1967, Cerf participated in the TV programme *What's My Line?*, which made him a household name. When the journalist Mike Wallace asked him to explain his long-lasting participation in the programme, Cerf said:

> I'm sort of a ham; I wouldn't be here with you if I wasn't. I like being on television, it's fun for me. Second, it pays very well, helps to take care of that place we have up in Mount Kisco. I wouldn't be able to hobnob with Arlene Francis at Mount Kisco and Josh Logan and Gilbert Kong, unless I had this extra income. You don't get it out of book publishing.

In other words, Cerf was doing the programme for three main reasons: celebrity, money, and a glamourous lifestyle spent entertaining famous people in his second home. But surely, said Wallace, the Cerf family had enough to eat even without the considerable fee of *What's My Line?* Cerf replied: 'I would say that the main reason is that I am a ham, I love to do it, love to lecture.'[13] Several years later, when Jessica

---

[12] Advertisement for the Famous Writers School, *Commentary*, 1 Jan. 1966, n.p.
[13] 'Bennett Cerf: The Mike Wallace Interview', 30 Nov. 1957, *Harry Ransom Center Collections—Digital Collections*, https://hrc.contentdm.oclc.org/digital/collection/p15878coll90/id/36/rec/8. Accessed 30 Apr. 2021.

Mitford asked Cerf why he endorsed the Famous Writers School, he gave a similar response: 'Frankly, if you must know, I'm an awful ham—I love to see my name in the papers!' (48). Cerf exemplifies this shift towards the Big Me culture, a culture that places shallow celebrity above genuine achievements. There is no doubt that Cerf was a talented entrepreneurial publisher. Yet, he did not become famous in 1933, when he won the right to publish James Joyce's *Ulysses* in the United States. He became famous when he appeared on a TV game show, and in turn, he used this celebrity to endorse a wide range of products (including martini, car rental, and the Famous Writers School).

In addition to advertisements in mass-market periodicals, the Famous Writers School relied on a wide network of salesmen. Once the prospective applicant had returned the coupon, they received an aptitude test and the visit of a salesman. When recruiting its staff, the FWS was looking for a very specific profile: sales people had to be men, over 30 or 35 and educated (ideally to degree level). A good appearance and the ability to speak well were essential. They also had to own a late-model car. Job candidates were told that the firm was expanding fast, and that they could earn a generous salary if successful. The company was looking for salesmen in metropolitan centres, including New York City and surrounding areas.[14] The School's job advertisements shed light on the market for its courses: many would-be writers were based not in isolated parts of the country, but in large cities and suburbs; they were educated and aspirational. At a time when relatively few universities offered creative writing programmes, the Famous Writers School opened up new markets for writing courses through extensive advertising and door-to-door visits from salesmen.

In contrast to the sales force, instructors who graded the students' essays were mostly women. Job announcements for teaching staff appeared in the 'Help Wanted—Female' section of *The New York Times*. The School was looking for professional writers of fiction, and for editors of short stories and novels. The job of 'resident instructor' entailed spending 35 hours a week at the School's offices in Westport, Connecticut.[15] While salesmen were expected to travel in a late-model car visiting prospective clients, instructors were chained to the office. In 1971, they complained about the 'productivity-minded company's plan to install a time clock'. The instructors worked a rigid eight-hour schedule in thirty-eight identical soundproofed cubicles, reported *TIME* magazine, and they had to write lengthy comments on six or seven student assignments a day. 'We want to be treated like professionals and less like production-line workers,' said one instructor, a former Radio Free Europe writer.[16] Ironically, the writers employed by the FWS could

---

[14] For examples of job advertisements for salesmen, see *The New York Times*, 4 Feb. 1962, p. 140; 4 Nov. 1962, p. W24; 11 Aug. 1963, p. 417; 14 Nov. 1965, p. W38.
[15] Job advertisement for FWS instructors, *The New York Times*, 15 May 1966, p. W7.
[16] 'Writing Wrongs', *Time*, 20 Sept. 1971, p. 104.

only dream of the autonomous life free from the constraints of the office promised by the School's advertisements.

To speed up the marking process, the School gave instructors a list of autotype paragraphs to attach to the students' essays. For the first assignment, teaching staff had to start with the summary of the course material. Depending on the quality of the essay, they then had a choice between 'good beginning' (three possible paragraphs) and 'fair or weak beginning' (one paragraph). Instructors were encouraged to see most essays as satisfactory, saving them time on comments: 'There's little need to use my blue pencil here.' In the case of an atrociously bad essay, the autotype paragraph still emphasized positive aspects: 'you obviously tried to write an interesting beginning, but I don't think this one wholly succeeds.'[17]

Dissatisfied with these Taylorist conditions, instructors also demanded a greater voice in planning the school curriculum. It is not difficult to see why many were discontent. The FWS textbooks led students on a very slow path from the basics of writing to more advanced elements of storytelling. After giving an overview of the three-year course, Volume 1 told would-be writers: 'Be comfortably dressed when you write, and write in pleasant surroundings.' A picture of a man wearing a straw hat, sunglasses, shorts, and flip flops appeared in the margin with the caption: 'Comfortable dress is a big help' (*Famous Writers Course—Principles of Good Writing*, Vol. 1, 69). The section on grammar is also comically simple. 'A *noun* is the name of a person, place or thing,' explained the textbook on page 80, before moving to adjectives. Examples included: a *good* man, a *bad* man and a *beautiful* automobile.

Why did the School insist so heavily on the basics of grammar? The underlying explanation was that students needed tools to express themselves simply, using plain language to transparently reflect their reality. Publishers were not looking for experimental writing in the style of James Joyce or Gertrude Stein, wrote Bennett Cerf, who had published these difficult writers in the 1930s. 'The young person who writes straight English—clean-cut, straight English—is the writer of the future.'[18] This move away from modernism was not surprising for a School whose parent company had been founded by Albert Dorne, Norman Rockwell, and other artists associated with figuration. Famous Artists Schools did not teach students how to paint like Jackson Pollock and other Abstract Expressionists. Instead, would-be painters were encouraged to view art as a straightforward activity, that could be learnt by following the step-by-step advice of the textbooks. Moving away from the tortured-genius model of Joyce or Pollock, the Famous Writers School and its parent company told students that artists are not *born*, but *made*.

Judging from the index of the multi-volume Famous Writers Course, Bennett Cerf did not contribute much to the curriculum. But he apparently travelled to the

---

[17] 'Autotype Paragraphs for Principles of Good Writing—Section I—Fiction', 30 July 1969, Box 1, Folder 14: 'Dwight Taylor—Famous Writers School', Laurette Taylor Papers, HRC.
[18] *Famous Writers Course—Fiction Writing*, Vol. 4, p. 555.

FWS offices once or twice a year to meet instructors. In 1963, the *Famous Writers Magazine* reported that he and his wife Phyllis had held a seminar in Westport, sharing 'up-to-the-minute news of what's happening in the world of editing and publishing'. Mrs Cerf oversaw juvenile publications at Random House, the firm that her husband had founded more than thirty years before. The gist of her talk was that 'juveniles offer an ever-growing market to the capable writer—a market that has difficulty finding the kind of material that makes worthwhile and saleable books for youngsters'.[19] Like the School's advertisements, the magazine reinforced the myth that publishers were in desperate need of good writers. In sum, the main role of the Guiding Faculty was not to shape the curriculum, guide students, or supervise instructors. Its main role was to endorse the FWS products and to grant credibility to the School's message.

Many students noticed the gap between the writers-are-in-demand myth and the ultra-competitive reality of the publishing field, leading to frustration and disenchantment. In a 1963 editorial of the *Famous Writers Magazine*, Gordon Carroll—the director of the School—wrote that letters arrived every day from every corner of the country, asking for help and guidance on getting published. 'We answer the requests by saying that we are a teaching organization, not a marketing service, and therefore avoid entering the counselling arena,' declared Carroll before advising students to read the marketing manual *How to Turn your Writing into Dollars* (5). Five years later, Carroll addressed the issue of discouragement in another editorial. He gave the examples of students in truly difficult circumstances: a blind and partially paralysed man who typed with a device held between his teeth and listened to FWS lessons thanks to a tape provided by a 'talking book' organization; a middle-aged woman confined to a wheelchair, who had to lean sharply to one side to type with two fingers on each hand; and prisoners serving life sentences, who found the energy to write despite the lack of privacy and hope. Those who 'enjoy good health and cheerful surroundings' should stop complaining, said Carroll, and turn back to their typewriter with renewed faith (5).

Yet, few discouraged students followed this advice, and they simply dropped out. In 1970, the School estimated that two-thirds of enrolments did not complete the course. But with 65,000 students and a small number of instructors, the dropout rate was probably higher (around 90 per cent, according to Jessica Mitford). The Famous Writers School employed more salesmen than instructors: a ratio of 3 to 1 in the mid-1960s.[20] Once students had enrolled, they were contractually obliged to pay for the entire three-year course. Despite the rising tuition fees

---

[19] 'Seminars and Sessions', *Famous Writers Magazine*, Spring 1963, p. 44.

[20] 'The number of field representatives ... has mounted, from 219 at the end of fiscal 1963 to 374, while the number of instructors has risen from 77 to 124.' The same article also indicated that enrolment in the FWS had 'virtually doubled in the last 19 months, from 14,196 at the end of fiscal 1963, to 28,281 (on Apr. 30).' 'Growth of Famous Artists Schools Reflects Impact of Culture Boom', *Barron's National Business and Financial Weekly*, 5 July 1965, pp. 45, 27.

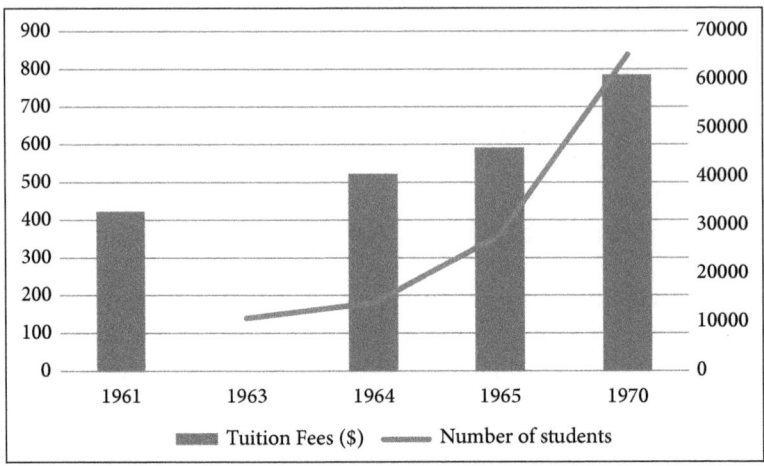

Fig. 5.1 Famous Writers School Tuition Fees and Enrolment, 1961–70.
Source: Author's own.

(from $425 in 1961 to $785 in 1970), the number of students increased rapidly (Figure 5.1). 'We couldn't make any money if all the students finished,' Famous Writer Phyllis McGinley told Mitford (50). There are many reasons for the high dropout rate including the low quality of the lessons, the length of the course and the absence of continuity as students received feedback from different instructors. The gap between the expectations created by the School, and the reality of the literary market disappointed many students, particularly those from marginalized groups—groups that were explicitly targeted by the School.

Despite charging very high tuition fees, the School presented itself as an ethical enterprise, as a quasi-charity that was helping the have-nots get better opportunities. Advertisements insisted on the 'help' and mentorship that the Guiding Faculty was generously giving to would-be writers. 'These leading authors and teachers in every branch of writing have branded together to create a school of professional writing to help you develop your skill, talent and craftsmanship; and to pass on to you their secrets of achieving commercial success and recognition', claimed one of the first advertisements for the School.[21] This service was described as an altruistic way for famous writers to share their experience. Reflecting on their long, hard path to the top, the Guiding Faculty had concluded that the trial-and-error method was not the best. They wanted to do some good by teaching the tricks of the trade to less experienced writers. 'Your life is many stories … let us help you write them,' declared a 1971 ad, once again using the language of assistance.[22]

---

[21] Advertisement for the Famous Writers School, *The New York Times*, 11 Sept. 1960, p. 145.
[22] Advertisement for the Famous Writers School, *The New York Times*, 1 Mar. 1970, p. 320.

The cost of this service was never discussed in advertisements. Instead, the focus was on the 'aptitude test' used to select worthy students. 'To help find people with an aptitude for writing that is worth developing, the twelve famous writers have created a revealing test to show you whether you should think seriously about professional training,' announced a 1960 ad. 'If you do have this aptitude, we will tell you so. If you don't, we will frankly tell you that, too.'[23] Of course, this was rarely the case. According to official figures released by Famous Artists Schools, around one out of ten prospective applicants was turned down.[24] But this number was probably much lower. Jessica Mitford gave the example of a quasi-illiterate woman of German origin who received the standard letter of congratulations, inviting her to enrol and start making money with her writing.[25]

Yet, the Famous Writers School and its parent company did help at least one marginalized group: prisoners. In 1961, *The New York Times* told the story of Eugene Francisco, a convict who developed as an artist thanks to the help of his sheriff and a three-year scholarship from Famous Artists Schools (Parke 29). Likewise, the FWS offered free tuition to selected prisoners. In December 1965, Albert F. Nussbaum wrote a letter to *The New York Times* from his cell in Leavenworth, Kansas. As an aspiring writer, Nussbaum had found many opportunities to practice his craft in prison. He was the assistant editor of *New Era*, a prison magazine 'where a man can try his writing wings'. He also praised the Robert Lindner foundation for awarding the annual Prisoner Awards, and the Famous Writers School for providing 'valuable correspondence scholarships to deserving prisoners'. Not only did the FWS encourage convicts, wrote Nussbaum, it also guided their efforts. Outside help was needed to avoid falling back to a life of crime. 'In prison it's easier to learn to be a better criminal than it is to learn to be a better anything else' (BR16).

Nussbaum was well placed to know that. In the early 1950s, he was arrested for possessing a submachine gun and transporting unregistered weapons across state lines. He was sentenced to the Federal Reformatory at Chillicothe, Ohio. There, he met Bobby Randell Wilcoxson, and the two men stayed in contact after leaving prison. They devised a plan to rob banks, using an arsenal of guns and home-made bombs. Operating between 1960 and 1962, they committed several robberies in New York State. On 15 December 1961, their robbery of a bank in Brooklyn ended tragically, when Wilcoxson killed a security guard. The FBI put the two men on its 'Most Wanted List', describing them as armed and extremely dangerous. The Royal Canadian Mounted Police was asked to be on the lookout, and *The Globe and Mail* circulated a description of the fugitives. Nussbaum 'has blue eyes, medium complexion and a snake entwined around a dagger tattooed

---

[23] Advertisement for the Famous Writers School, *The New York Times*, 11 Sept. 1960, p. 145.
[24] 'Growth of Famous Artists Schools Reflects Impact of Culture Boom', *Barron's National Business and Financial Weekly*, 5 July 1965, pp. 45, 27.
[25] Jessica Mitford, Letter to Barbara Kahn, 3 Dec. 1969 (rpt in Sussman 407); see also Mitford's *Atlantic* article (46).

on his upper left arm,' wrote the newspaper, citing the FBI poster. 'He is an expert gun and locksmith and can fly and repair airplanes.'[26] In November 1962, Nussbaum was captured in Buffalo, New York, after he returned to see his wife and baby daughter.

At the time of his arrest, Nussbaum was only twenty-eight years old, and he devoted the rest of his life to writing crime fiction. He particularly admired *The Name of the Game is Death*, a 1962 novel by Dan J. Marlowe, a popular pulp fiction writer. In prison, Nussbaum corresponded with Marlowe, and the two men became friends and collaborated on several projects (Hoffman, 'Playing with Fire'). When Nussbaum was released on parole in the 1970s, he moved to Los Angeles and published short stories in pulps such as *Ellery Queen's Mystery Magazine* and *Alfred Hitchcock's Mystery Magazine*. He also wrote novels, including *Motorcycle Racer* (1977). When Marlowe's health declined, Nussbaum offered to live with him and became his caretaker. In the 1980s, Nussbaum taught creative writing workshops for mystery writers at the University of Southern California. He also participated in mystery conventions. After giving his paper, he was once asked if he enjoyed writing. 'It's OK,' Nussbaum reportedly said, 'but what I'd really like to be doing is robbing banks' (Stodghill).

The Famous Writers School did little to facilitate the extraordinary reinvention of Albert F. Nussbaum, from 'Most Wanted' criminal to professional crime writer and creative writing teacher. Without Dan Marlowe's advice, it is unlikely that the ex-convict would have succeeded in his new career. Nussbaum largely relied on what I have called the *informal mentorship model*, rather than on writing courses. And yet, the FWS offered hope to Nussbaum at a difficult time in his life, when he was serving a 40-year prison sentence. 'There are many men who both need and deserve outside help,' he wrote in his *New York Times* letter. Prisoners were not the only marginalized group targeted by the Famous Writers School. To sell its writing courses, the FWS created an enticing story of easy success and sold this story using the language of empowerment. Although the School recruited its students from all kinds of backgrounds, it put a lot of emphasis on women, promising them fame, fortune, and flexibility. In the early 1960s, female students represented only a small proportion of those who took correspondence courses. The National Home Study Council reported that the typical student 'is male, 27 years old, a high school graduate, employed; has a family and owns a home' (Du Bois). But an increasing number of women were joining the workforce. In 1950, the overall participation rate of women was 34 per cent. The rate rose to 38 per cent in 1960 and 43 per cent in 1970 (Toossi 18). As more women worked, or expected to work outside their home, the demand for education and training increased. Correspondence schools became interested in this growing market. In 1961, the International Correspondence School published its first catalogue aimed specifically at the female

---

[26] 'RCMP Asked to Aid in Hunt for US Men', *The Globe and Mail*, 5 Mar. 1962, p. 4.

audience. The booklet discussed careers and courses for women in such fields as art, accounting, advertising, general business, chemistry, and retailing. Female students represented only 6 per cent of its market, but the firm hoped that this number would rise as more women worked outside the home (Du Bois).

The Famous Writers School particularly targeted housewives who aspired to join the workforce in a professional role. Many of these women had become disillusioned with their role as wives and mothers. In her 1963 bestseller *The Feminine Mystique*, Betty Friedan argued that social expectations and self-limiting beliefs prevented women from fully realizing their potential. More women were working, but 'they were married women who held part-time jobs, selling or secretarial, to put their husbands through school, their sons through college, or to help pay the mortgage' (17). Fewer and fewer women were entering professional work, wrote Friedan. Unable to find a fulfilling role within or outside their home, many suffered from a problem that had nothing to do with 'the age-old material problems of man: poverty, sickness, hunger, cold' (26).

Starting from 1964, advertisements for the Famous Writers School promised these women not a job, not even a career, but a calling. With writing, they could achieve emotional contentment, social recognition and financial autonomy. Previously, the firm had shown no particular concern for female writers: only two women—Faith Baldwin and Mignon G. Eberhart—were amongst the twelve original members of the Guiding Faculty. This underrepresentation became, ironically, a tool in the School's advertising strategy. Women were underrepresented not because of sexism or nepotism, but because few considered writing in the first place. 'It's a shame more women don't take up writing,' said Baldwin in a *Globe and Mail* ad. 'Unlike many other professions, the welcome mat is really out for women in the writing field.'[27]

Like Albert Dorne's rags-to-riches story, Faith Baldwin's biography was used to convince prospective students that they, too, could become rich and famous. Unlike Dorne, however, Baldwin did not have to overcome poverty. She was born in 1893 in an upper-class, East-coast family. Her father was a distinguished trial lawyer, and she received a good education. When she was twenty-seven years old, she married Hugh Cuthrell, a pilot in the US Navy who later became president of Brooklyn Union Gas Company. The couple had four children and lived for many years on 'Fable Farm', a historic fourteen-room house near Norwalk, Connecticut. Baldwin's first novel *Mavis of Green Hill* appeared in 1921. She wrote quickly, averaging two novels a year. During the Depression, her light fiction appealed to a large audience of women. The formula was often the same: the heroine struggles to find a good man, but eventually finds love and contentment. Several of her novels were made into films with well-known actors—including *Wife versus Secretary* (1936), starring Jean Harlow and Clark Gable. In the interwar period, the division

[27] Advertisement for the Famous Writers School, *The Globe and Mail*, 11 Feb. 1964, p. A3.

between popular and serious writers was not as rigid as it later became.[28] Far from being dismissed as a lowbrow author, Baldwin was approached by *Contempo*, a literary magazine which published a portion of Joyce's *Work in Progress* and a special Faulkner issue in the early 1930s. Asked to review a classic work of Japanese literature, Baldwin told the editor that she was 'galloping frantically through tons of work, in order to get away for a month's vacation'.[29] After the Second World War, Baldwin kept in the public eye: she continued to publish books, and wrote a regular column for *Woman's Day* from 1958 to 1965.

When the advertisements for the Famous Writers School appeared, the seventy-year-old Baldwin was presented as a woman who had leaned in, brilliantly combining family life and professional success. 'Although she has brought up four children,' declared a 1964 ad, 'America's most popular woman novelist has managed to write more than 70 books, including many best-sellers.' Like other Famous Writers, she played the role of the older author eager to advise newcomers. But receiving advice was not enough. Women had to be convinced that writing was an activity worth pursuing in the first place. Baldwin gave three main reasons. First, 'writing is one of the ideal professions for women': no need to go to an office and to leave with half of your mind on the housework. Few professions offered this flexibility, which had allowed Baldwin to run her own house while producing dozens of books. Second, many women had more time than they thought. 'Saying you "could write" if you "had time" is no excuse,' added Baldwin, once again giving her own personal story as an example. Third, only women could write about certain topics from first-hand experience, including, of course, childbirth.[30]

The Famous Writers School also used Mignon G. Eberhart's image to recruit more female students. There were many common points between Baldwin and Eberhart. The two Guiding Faculty members belonged to the same generation (Eberhart was born in 1899, six years after Baldwin) and both came from privileged social backgrounds. They were extremely prolific, writing dozens of novels for a mass readership. While Baldwin wrote what we now call 'romance', Eberhart specialized in detective fiction. Her first novel *The Patient in Room 18*, published by Doubleday in 1929, featured a character that reappeared in later works: nurse and amateur detective Sarah Keate, one of the first female sleuths in mystery fiction. Like Baldwin, Eberhart moved from print to the new media of the time: her novel *While the Patient Slept* was made into a successful film in 1935, the first of several film adaptations of her works (Keene). This widened her audience further and brought her fame, fortune, and freedom. Reflecting her love of travel, her novels are often set in exotic locations, including the Caribbean and the Far East. In short, Eberhart embodied the dream lifestyle of successful writers, a lifestyle at the centre of the Famous Writers School's advertising strategy.

---

[28] See Jaillant, *Modernism, Middlebrow and the Literary Canon* 7–10.
[29] Faith Baldwin to Milton A. Abernethy, 15 Aug. 1932, Box 7, Folder 2, *Contempo* Collection, HRC.
[30] Advertisement for the Famous Writers School, *The Globe and Mail*, 11 Feb. 1964, p. A3.

To sell this glamorous way of life, the Famous Writers School downplayed its intimidating aspects. Advertisements presented Eberhart not as a professional writer, but as a housewife who happened to write. In 1965, a *New York Times* ad featured a photo of Eberhart 'in her comfortable study'. Her dog is at her side, reinforcing the impression of cosiness. While ordinary people had to commute to work or to do household chores, Eberhart spent time in her luxurious study filled with books. She was described as 'a housewife who has managed to write more than 40 books and scores of short stories, and to become one of America's highest paid authors'. Yet, Eberhart was hardly a conventional housewife: she had married three times (twice to the same man), she had no children, and she spent much of her time travelling abroad. This movie-star lifestyle could have scared or alienated many prospective applicants, whose daily routine was totally different. Many women did not want to completely change their lives—remarry, abandon their kids, and travel the world. What they wanted was to keep the same life but have more recognition, more money, and more flexibility. The Famous Writers School told them that they could remain housewives, if they wished, and add some glamour to their routine. They, too, could become as successful as Eberhart, who 'enjoys frequent movie and TV sales'.[31]

Using Faith Baldwin's and Mignon Eberhart's image, the Famous Writers School wanted to empower women who felt marginalized and unappreciated, telling them that their frustration could be turned into a productive force. Successful writers 'had the "divine discontent" it takes to succeed in writing,' declared a 1963 ad. The School then gave a definition of 'divine discontent'—a phrase coined by Charles Kingsley. It starts with the impression of being an observer in life, with a kind of distance that is disquieting at first. This leads to a 'recurring ache to put into words the people you've known or the life you have lived … to express your faith or your philosophy … to share your proudest thoughts and experiences with other human beings …'[32] The ad used the vocabulary of pain and desire to show that the initial suffering was necessary to achieve great work. In other words, women and other discontented groups could use this negative energy productively, sharing their feelings with others through writing.

How did women react to the FWS's advertising strategy? What did they think of the *write-what-you-know* message carried by Eberhart and Baldwin? As a self-confessed Christian traditionalist and 'reactionary', Baldwin was an unlikely feminist (Fredericksen). Far from being a radical denunciation of sexism, the advertisements were written in the mild, confessional style of women's magazines, a sector that Baldwin knew well. Baldwin did not appear angry, just disappointed with the present situation and hopeful that more women would join the writing field in the future. Describing the photo on the ads, Jessica Mitford wrote that

---

[31] Advertisement for the Famous Writers School, *The New York Times*, 25 July 1965, p. SM49.
[32] Advertisement for the Famous Writers School, *The New York Times*, 17 Nov. 1963, p. BR30.

Baldwin 'look[ed] up from her typewriter with an expression of ardent concern for that vast, unfulfilled sisterhood of nonwriters' (45).

Not everyone shared Mitford's disdain for the FWS's message. In a 1972 article, the feminist scholar Elaine Showalter used a quote from the 1964 ad—'Actually, writing is an ideal profession for women …'—to illustrate the lack of professional opportunities faced by female writers. Trapped in their homes, many women were overwhelmed by feelings of anger, frustration, and resentment. 'With so little opportunity for experience, so little space in which to channel psychic energy, women, as the ad from the Famous Writers School so shrewdly recognises, *need* writing as an escape-valve for their desperate need for self-expression' (345). Far from dismissing Baldwin and the Famous Writers School, Showalter took the message of entrapment and need for emotional release seriously. Advertisements for the FWS struck a chord amongst many women, raising awareness that domestic topics were worth writing about.

In 1973, a thirty-eight-year-old doctoral student called Jeannine Dobbs finished her dissertation on the female experience in American poetry. This was an important subject, Dobbs argued, as more and more women were writing about the home and family life. She gave the example of Rosellen Brown's poem 'The Famous Writers School Opens Its Arms in the Next Best Thing to Welcome' (*Some Deaths in the Delta*, qtd in Dobbs 2). There is some irony here, with the poet admitting she is obedient while looking for freedom and emotional escape through writing. But Dobbs had little interest in the irony. She described the poem as 'a good example of using what you know' (2). Other feminist scholars agreed: Brown's poem was later reprinted in *Women Working*, an anthology published by the Feminist Press in New York.

The Famous Writers School exploited the feminist message to sell its overpriced courses. Its 1970 book *Writing, Revising and Editing* included an essay by Janet Van Duyn, 'Why Women Want to Write'. Women, wrote Van Duyn, are trapped in a catch-22 situation:

> If she stays home and likes it, she's imprisoned in some kind of 'mystique'. If she goes out and likes it, she's restless, irresponsible, even disturbed. If by some miracle she manages to do both, she's a phenomenon and therefore suspect.
>
> (36)

Here, the reference to Friedan's *The Feminine Mystique* is explicit. Drawing on Virginia Woolf's *A Room of One's Own*, Van Duyn went on to give an overview of the female condition through the centuries. She concluded on an upbeat note: a woman's world was changing and enlarging at an unprecedented rate, and more women were achieving stature as writers thanks to the help of the Famous Writers School.

But this commercialization of feminism was not entirely negative. The pages of the *Famous Writers Magazine* are full of stories about domestic life, written by

FWS students. One woman, Norma C. Cirves, had sold a short story after her graduation in the 1930s, then worked as a stenographer during the war before remaining as a suburban housewife and mother during the next two decades. The story she published in the magazine is about a young boy who runs away from home ('Runaway'). The FWS did not give Cirves the fame and fortune promised in advertisements, but it offered publication and readers. More importantly, perhaps, it told women that their own experiences were valuable and worthy to be written about. It also encouraged them to find female role models. At the Harry Ransom Center in Texas, I found the student information record of a forty-six-year-old housewife with five children. 'I want to write good short stories, with the same quality, humor and pathos as those of Margaret Cousins,' declared this student.[33] As a successful editor and writer who worked for the FWS, Cousins inspired other women to share their stories.

While advertisements emphasized the pleasure of self-expression, the School's course materials insisted that writing was hard work. Paul Engle, who joined the Guiding Faculty in 1968, discouraged students from relying too much on their raw experience. Writing, like all arts, required discipline and constraint. In an essay published in the *Famous Writers Annual* (1970), Engle declared that the writer 'is not trying to put his own self into words but to create a work of art'. And, he added: 'the less of his own self involved or expressed, the better' ('Learning from Other Writers' 230). This was not the first time that Engle had dismissed indulgent writers eager to share their feelings. Writers need a minimum of calmness, he argued in his 1961 essay 'The Writer and the Place'. Without calmness and control, the work lacked form and the 'moving cry becomes only screaming' (4). Through the voice of Engle and other Guiding Faculty members, the FWS told discontented women that their emotional turmoil could be turned into art, but that this process would require self-discipline and perseverance. The discrepancy between the advertisements and the harsh reality of a writing career did not go unnoticed. Shortly after the creation of the School in 1960, Granville Hicks launched an attack in the *Saturday Review of Literature*. In his youth, Hicks had openly espoused communism: he worked as literary editor of *New Masses*, before resigning from the Communist Party in 1939. He remained concerned with social justice, and his criticism of the Famous Writers School is framed as a defence of the weak against the strong. 'The chances are the student who enrolls in the Famous Writers School may not get his money's worth—and the money involved isn't peanuts,' he said ('Mail-Order Creativity' 35).

Having taught writing in colleges and at writers' conferences, Hicks believed that a writing course served three main functions. First, it could give encouragement to write regularly, and the assurance that someone will read what is written. Second, a course or a writers' conference offered an opportunity to meet peers.

---

[33] Famous Writers School, Student Information Record, 1 Nov. 1963, Box 28, Folder 7, Margaret Cousins Papers, HRC.

Other would-be writers could then be turned into readers, forming a little audience when the text is read in class. Third, the course instructor could provide useful hints and help the writer develop talent. A correspondence course performed the first function, and part of the third function. Its main flaw was the lack of human interaction. There was no 'companionship of other beginning writers' and 'no personal contact between student and instructor' (12).

These limitations, common to all correspondence courses, would have been acceptable if two conditions were met: if high standards were set for the selection of students, and if the instructors were conscientious. After looking at the School's Aptitude Test, Hicks rightly concluded that most prospective applicants would be accepted. And since students sent only twelve assignments, it was impossible, even for the most able instructor, to help them develop their talent. The Famous Writers School could not deliver what it promised, Hicks concluded. There was no magic formula for success. 'Because I have great sympathy for would-be writers, I wish the twelve famous authors weren't involved in tempting them in just this way' (35).

In the 1960s, the *Saturday Review of Literature* had a circulation in excess of 500,000,[34] and Hicks's article was widely read. I found a copy of this article in the papers of Brewster Ghiselin at the University of Utah. To reach as many writers as possible, the Famous Writers School had sent a form letter to Ghiselin, a distinguished poet and creative writing professor. 'To help you find out whether you do have writing aptitude worth developing,' said the letter, 'the Twelve Famous Writers created a revealing sixteen-page Talent Test.'[35] The test was costly to print, but the School would send it free of charge and have a professional writer on their staff grade it without any cost or obligation whatsoever. As an experienced writer in his late fifties, Ghiselin had, of course, no interest in this aptitude test, and Hicks's article reinforced his conviction that the School was a sham. The same form letter—which began with 'Dear Friend'—was sent to Frank Dobie, a seventy-three-year-old writer from Texas. Dobie was so infuriated that he wrote back to the School. 'Dear Sir, I am not your friend,' he said. 'Please cease sending me your crap for gulls.'[36]

Neither Dobie nor Ghiselin fitted with the typical profile of the FWS student: a would-be writer who had no idea of how things really worked in the publishing industry. So why did the FWS send them advertising materials? One way to answer this question is to compare the School's marketing strategy to that of the paperback publishers. In the late 1930s and 1940s, these publishers had proved that there was a wide market of people interested in books—but who lacked access to bookstores (or the confidence to visit a bookstore). The paperback revolution transformed a

---

[34] Siracusa 155.
[35] Famous Writers School, Circular Letter, undated, Box 7, Folder 13, Brewster Ghiselin Papers, U of Utah Special Collections.
[36] Frank Dobie to Famous Writers School, 29 May 1962, Box 98, Folder 1, J. Frank Dobie Papers, HRC.

distribution network that had so far neglected small towns and rural parts of the country. Books were now sold for as low as 25 cents in news stands and other stores, reaching the mass market. Non-readers could be transformed into readers. And these readers could, in turn, be transformed into would-be writers. For the Famous Writers School, *anyone* who had an interest in reading was a potential client. The School cast a very wide net, advertising in large-circulation periodicals and on television, inserting postcards in paperback books and sending form letters to millions of potential customers. Dobie and Ghiselin were caught in this wide net. But for the School, these isolated cases were irrelevant, and did not distract it from its objective: creating a mass market for writing courses.

Responding to Granville Hick's criticisms, Albert Dorne defended his School in three main points. First, not everyone could attend writers' conferences or creative writing classes. For students in small towns and rural areas, and for those with a busy schedule, the Famous Writers School offered a valuable service. Second, Dorne said: 'we don't claim to teach *creative* writing' (27). The FWS focused on teaching practical writing tips to improve the student's communication skills. The aptitude test was for absolute beginners, not for experienced writers like Hicks. Third, the School believed in setting high goals for their students—which is why advertisements relied on the success stories of writers at the top of their field.

There was nothing wrong in telling people they could become better craftsmen, replied Hicks one week later. But the advertising programme of the Famous Writers School suggested a different kind of hope. People were encouraged to hope that they can become rich and famous. 'One of the most persuasive elements in the whole campaign is the support lent to the School by the Famous Writers,' wrote Hicks. 'I do indeed wish that they were not involved in it' ('Letters to the Editor' 29). Although he did not mention Cerf directly, Hicks probably wondered why such a distinguished publisher endorsed the FWS. Both men belonged to the same generation, and in the late 1920s, Hicks had used Modern Library books published by Cerf to teach contemporary literature.[37] For Hicks, Cerf and the Guiding Faculty shamelessly exploited powerless would-be writers.

Drawing on quantitative evidence, other critics showed that writing was not a profitable enterprise. In a 1963 article entitled 'Let the Would-be Writer Beware', David Dempsey cited figures from the Authors League of America, whose members earned on average $3,105 annually. Making money out of fiction writing was particularly difficult, and yet only 10 per cent of FWS students took the specialized courses in business and advertising writing (22). Dempsey added that the average age of students was over forty years old (23). Denying the reality of a saturated literary field, the FWS was selling dreams of success to the middle-aged and elderly. In 1969, Robert Byrne wrote the first book-length attack on the Famous Writers School and other businesses that targeted would-be writers. 'The average full-time

---

[37] Granville Hicks to Modern Library, 25 Jan. 1928, Catalogued Correspondence, RH.

free-lancer earned just over $3,000 per year, not counting expenses,' Byrne noted. And he added: 'That income very nearly qualifies him for emergency welfare assistance' (17–18). So why did so many people believe the dubious claims of these firms? Byrne gave two main reasons (19). First, many would-be writers were addicted to daydreaming, and did not care about reason. And second, income figures and other hard facts about the writing profession were difficult to find. As we have seen, the Famous Writers School claimed that writers earned a minimum of $6,000 per year—nearly double the actual average income.

In a saturated writing market, there was one profitable field: hard-core pornography. 'Half a dozen publishers of pornographic paperbacks have sprung up in recent years,' Byrne said, 'some of them issuing as many as fifteen new titles a month' (27–8). Indeed, the last trials against obscenity had exonerated titles such as *Lady Chatterley's Lover*, *Tropic of Cancer*, and *Fanny Hill*—opening the door for the publication of prurient texts. And yet, the Famous Writers School was too conservative, too 'square' to tell students about this growing market. For Byrne, the stories published in the *Famous Writers Magazine* were irrelevant in a world marked by violence and social upheaval (48). What was the point of publishing a story about a boy's love for his dog, at the time when young Americans were dying in Vietnam? This countercultural message was reinforced by Byrne's choice of publisher for this book. *Writing Rackets* was published by Lyle Stuart, who also issued *Naked Came the Stranger* (1969), *The Sensuous Woman* (1969) and *The Anarchist Cookbook* (1970).

Whereas Byrne's book reached only a small audience, Jessica Mitford's 1970 article made a huge impact and contributed to the downfall of the Famous Writers School. Mitford was not the first to criticize the School's high tuition fees and false advertising. But she was the first to obtain interviews with the Guiding Faculty, and to show that they played almost no role in the running of the School. The Famous Writers were mere figureheads who appeared on advertisements and lent their names to the firm. They were expected to go to Westport from time to time, but these visits were mostly photo opportunities for the *Famous Writers Magazine*. Amongst these Famous Writers was Paul Engle, who pleaded ignorance. 'I'm the least informed of all people,' he told Mitford before explaining the difference between the guiding faculty 'which doesn't do very much' and the teaching faculty 'which actually works with the students' (47).

Following the publication of Mitford's article, Iowa Attorney General Richard Turner filed a suit against the Famous Writers School. The suit asked that the school be enjoined from selling writing lessons in Iowa pending an investigation to determine whether the School is 'a fantastic fraud,' as Mitford had implied. Kristelle Petersen of the *Daily Iowan* then wrote a very critical account of Engle's role in the School. Like Mitford, Petersen pointed out Engle's ignorance of all financial aspects, sales and advertising methods, as well as admission procedures and the enrolment figures of the School. The income that Engle received was for a vaguely defined role as advisor of the teaching faculty. 'If I have value,' he told Petersen, 'it is because I have had the kind of experience the other Guiding Faculty has not had—real experience with teaching writing. I talk about the importance of revision and how reluctant people are to revise and that this is even tougher to do by mail.' Engle had organized two correspondence courses in poetry and fiction at the University of Iowa in the mid-1960s, at the time when he was still director of the Writers' Workshop. These courses were not profitable enough and were later dropped. 'My experience in attempting to teach writing by mail was much like the FWS course,' he said. In short, Engle drew an explicit parallel between the Famous Writers School and the correspondence version of the Iowa Creative Writing programme. The skills that he had honed as creative writer and professor could be easily transferred to the mail-order writing business.

For Nelson Algren, the similarity between university workshops on the one hand, and FWS courses on the other was deeply troubling. 'The Creative Writers' Workshops are the campus extension of the Famous Writers' philosophy,' he wrote in a 1975 article in *The New York Times*. Algren had taught creative writing at Iowa ten years before, and he deeply resented a key assumption of the workshop: that writers need feedback from others to make progress on their work. Serious writers don't need to know how other writers work. They just do it their own way, as creative individuals rather than members of a group. 'Creativity, by its own essence, is a solitary enterprise,' Algren said ('On Kreativ Righting'). This was exactly what Faulkner had argued a quarter of a century before. But Algren added an important point: creative writing workshops were exploiting naïve would-be writers, offering false hope in exchange for regular payments. He noted the similarities between advertisements for the Famous Writers School and for Engle's courses at Iowa (*The Last Carousel* 76). In both cases, aspiring writers were told first to return an aptitude test, and second, to send some money.

The rapid decline of the Famous Writers School in the 1970s was due to three main reasons: the reckless expansion of its parent company in overseas markets stretched its finances; the firm was left vulnerable when the economy slowed down; and it had to face a series of investigations for misrepresentation and misleading advertising. In 1970, the *Sunday Times* reported that the US Federal Trade Commission was looking into the School's advertising practices. Angus Wilson, who considered backing a similar school in Britain, was reportedly disturbed by these allegations.[38] Later that year, Wilson and Malcolm Bradbury launched the pioneering MA in creative writing at the University of East Anglia. Like their American counterparts, British writers dissociated themselves from correspondence courses that promised literary glory. In an article for the satirical magazine *Punch*, Richard Gordon wrote about his experience with the UK-version of the Famous Writers School. 'In Britain, you do not style yourself the Famous anything,'

---

[38] 'The You-Too-Can-Write-A-Best-Seller Row', *The Sunday Times*, 15 Feb. 1970, p. 32.

he said, 'We became the International Writers School' ('How I Became a Famous Writer' 930). Gordon went on to mock the School's aptitude test. 'Suitability was discovered from such questions as, *Name three of your favourite authors*, and *Do you own, or have use of, a typewriter?*' (931). By the mid-1970s, the ailing School had completely abandoned the aptitude test, and asked prospective applicants to send a motivation letter instead. 'It could be the most important letter you'll ever write!' declared an ad in *The New York Times*.[39]

The demise of the Famous Writers School had a lasting influence on the way creative writing courses (within and outside the university system) are advertised. Although it is no longer acceptable to explicitly promise fame and fortune to potential candidates, these aspirations have not disappeared. The discourse on success and freedom remains as attractive as it was in the 1960s, when the FWS was in its prime. The FWS exemplifies the social and cultural shift to a model of *radical individualism*, a model that continues to this day to impact creative writing programmes. Moving away from the model of professionalization that emphasized self-sacrifice and discipline within a group, creative writing programmes started celebrating personal development, individual success, and self-fulfilment. Yet, Nelson Algren and others pointed out the contradictions at the heart of the creative writing institution. For these commentators, creativity was a radically individualist endeavour that could not be practised within a university writers' workshop. The entire creative writing enterprise was a sham, similar to the Famous Writers School. What Algren et al. did not take into account, however, was that creative writing programmes provided at least one benefit to their students: access to networks, as the following chapter illustrates.

---

[39] Advertisement for the Famous Writers School, *The New York Times*, 25 Apr. 1976, p. 439.

PART II
UK

6
Myth Maker

Malcolm Bradbury and the Creation of Creative Writing at UEA

The story is familiar and goes something like this: in 1970, the young Ian McEwan saw an advertisement for a new postgraduate course in creative writing at the University of East Anglia. He gave a call to Professor Malcolm Bradbury, sent a writing sample, and became the first (and only) student of the first MA in creative writing in the UK. McEwan, of course, went on to become one of the most successful British writers of literary fiction. And Bradbury was knighted in 2000, shortly before his death, for his services to literature.

This is a good story, which emphasizes the extraordinary luck of both McEwan and Bradbury. But it is also a retrospective narrative, which obscures the fact that university creative writing in Britain was not entirely new. As Kathryn Holeywell has shown, creative writing was offered for assessment at UEA in the 1960s.[1] And in Autumn 1969, Lancaster started offering a creative writing option for undergraduates. From 1970, students who took this option got a mark, which counted towards their degree. David Craig (the founder of the programme) wrote: 'if we believe that creative writing deserves to be on the syllabus for its validity as an expression of the whole person and an exacting challenge to the honesty of our intelligence, then it also deserves to count, which means to be marked' ('Creative Writing at Lancaster' 84–5). Informal courses had long existed—for example, in the 1950s, David Lodge took a course on 'Essay Writing' at University College London, which included practical criticism and writing exercises (*Quite a Good Time to Be Born*, chap. 9). Outside academia, the Arvon Foundation started offering creative writing courses to a wide range of publics as early as 1968.

It is certainly true that postgraduate courses in creative writing were unheard of in the UK. But programmes with formal supervision, within a taught creative writing MA, did not appear in 1970. As McEwan himself has repeatedly said, he studied

---

[1] 'Evidence that [Angus] Wilson offered informal creative writing instruction at UEA as early as 1963 as well as the revelation that he utilised creative writing for the assessment of at least one academic course in the School of English proves that creative writing at UEA has a much longer history than has previously been suggested' (Holeywell 21–2).

literature with the option to submit fiction instead of a critical dissertation.[2] He also had no more than a few informal meetings with Bradbury—nothing that resembled a structured writing programme. The casual nature of this supervision was far from unusual in a period when universities were less subject to regulation than they are today. But if McEwan signed up for a programme with 'formal supervision in creative writing' (as the graduate handbook for 1970 promises),[3] he simply did not get what he expected. 'My writing life has been one long uphill struggle to persuade the world that I didn't do a creative writing course,' he once declared (qtd in Benedictus).

When we talk about the institutionalization of creative writing in the university system, we need to make two distinctions: was creative writing offered for assessment and accreditation? And was it formally taught (within workshops, for example) and supervised? The first stage of institutionalization occurred in the 1960s at the undergraduate level at UEA, and later at Lancaster. The second stage seems to have happened in the early 1980s, which coincides with the creation of an MA in creative writing at Lancaster. So why do we continue to associate the origins of university creative writing in Britain with a specific year (1970)—despite McEwan's repeated declarations? And why do we continue to place Malcolm Bradbury at the centre of this story—even though there were many other people, at UEA, Lancaster, and elsewhere, who experimented with creative writing courses?

Bradbury contributed to shaping the founding myth of creative writing programmes in Britain—which makes it particularly powerful and enduring. From the 1980s, he told the story repeatedly. 'McEwan was in my creative writing class,' he declared in a typical 1992 interview (Gensane 45). How could McEwan be in a creative writing class that consisted of only one student? Despite the inconsistencies, the story has been influential because, arguably, it fits in a cultural model that we recognize—the model of the older writer who discovers and consecrates young talents.[4]

Accounts of university creative writing in Britain have often been written by friends, colleagues, or disciples of Bradbury, and tend to overestimate his role. Take *Body of Work: 40 Years of Creative Writing at UEA*, a collection of essays edited by Giles Foden and first published in draft on the website malcolmbradbury.com in 2010. Foden, who teaches at UEA, is well aware that the university had already

---

[2] See Benedictus and Hebert for examples.

[3] 'In some years it will be possible to take an M.A. in Creative Writing. This will consist of three courses taken from programme 1 (The Nineteenth and Twentieth Century Novel), including the compulsory "The Theory of Fiction." In addition there will be formal supervision in creative writing. A body of fiction (several short stories or part of a novel) will be substituted for the dissertation.' 'The Graduate Programme', 27 Nov. 1970, UEA/BRAD/11, UEA Collection: Malcolm Bradbury, University of East Anglia.

[4] The story has even crossed borders. Writing about the institutionalization of creative writing at the University of Sydney, the *Australian* mentioned the 'postgraduate writing course' that McEwan took in Britain (Neill).

experimented with creative writing in the 1960s. And yet, the title of the collection implicitly puts the emphasis on 1970 as the starting year for 'creative writing at UEA'. Foden's introductory essay mentions Bradbury in the first paragraph and leaves little doubt as to his central role ('this organic process would probably not have happened if Bradbury had not joined the staff of UEA in 1965' [11]). A review of the book in *The Guardian* is illustrated with a picture of Bradbury in the classroom (Davies).

The overemphasis on a charismatic leader obscures deep institutional forces that were moving British universities towards the American model of higher education. In the wake of the Robbins Report, the new universities of the 1960s were fertile sites of experimentation, and it is not surprising that creative writing appeared at UEA and Lancaster rather than, say, Oxford. Throughout his career as writer-scholar, Bradbury positioned himself on the margins of the establishment. Like Paul Engle at Iowa, he created a new literary powerhouse outside traditional centres. From the start, creative writing in Britain was positioned as an outsider's discipline—built as a reaction against existing models of literary success.

University creative writing in Britain was never a single-man enterprise. It was not until the 1980s that the discipline became so strongly associated with UEA—and this association was largely due to the rise of the whole sub-group sometimes referred to as the 'university set'[5] (Bradbury, but also David Lodge, Angela Carter, Maggie Gee, and former UEA students Rose Tremain, Clive Sinclair, Ian McEwan, and Kazuo Ishiguro). While Bradbury's unique talents should be recognized, it is also essential to pay attention to networks that shaped the discipline of creative writing.

Surprisingly, the origins of creative writing in the UK have attracted very little scholarly scrutiny. Michelene Wandor presents her book *The Author is Not Dead, Merely Somewhere Else* (2008) as 'the first history of CW in formal, higher education in the UK' (4), but it lacks evidence from the archive. And whereas Holeywell's short article focuses on the period from 1963 to 1966, this chapter has a broader timeframe, from the early 1960s to Bradbury's death in 2000. I discovered unknown documents in the Malcolm Bradbury papers at Indiana University, various archives at UEA and the Booker Prize archive at Oxford Brookes University. I also interviewed, in person and on the phone, many people associated with the first creative writing programmes. When an interview was not possible, I sent out questionnaires and got responses from David Lodge and David Craig. These various research methods shed light on the complex history of creative writing in Britain, a history tied to the changing nature of the university system and to the emergence of opportunities for certain groups of enterprising academics and writers.

---

[5] See D. J. Taylor's *A Vain Conceit: British Fiction in the 1980s* (qtd in McKay).

6.1 Malcolm Bradbury and UEA's Mid-Atlantic Men

Instead of presenting Malcolm Bradbury as an exceptional leader who founded the first creative writing programme in Britain and launched Ian McEwan's career, it is important to look at the broader picture. My point is that the characteristics that made Bradbury interested in creative writing as a discipline (including his extensive experience of the American higher education system) were shared by many of his colleagues in Norwich. I want to look at Bradbury's career within the larger context of the development of UEA, an experimental university that attracted non-traditional professors with new ideas and international experience.

Remembering his youth in the 1950s and early 1960s, Bradbury described himself as 'a regular transatlantic traveller … a typical example of a constant figure of the time, Midatlantic Man' (*Stepping Westward* iii). As a nineteen-year-old student at University College Leicester, he had won a scholarship to go to Canada to research commercial radio. Two years later, in 1953, CBC (Canadian Broadcasting Corporation) broadcast his play 'A Plane Out of Iceland'.[6] Bradbury finished his BA that year and went on to do an MA, then a two-year research degree, at Queen Mary College in London. While continuing to work on his fiction, he was writing a thesis on English little magazines of the early twentieth century. 'I took up this particular topic because the whole question of whether literary magazines had any serious part to play in contemporary cultural life was at the time widely under discussion,' Bradbury later said, thus stressing his long-lasting interest in literary institutions and in the material conditions that allow artistic creation ('Critical years' 31). His research on modernist magazines gave him a chance to meet T. S. Eliot, who wrote him letters of introduction to Ezra Pound and important New Critics: Allen Tate, John Crowe Ransom, and Cleanth Brooks. Towards the end of his degree, Bradbury started applying for scholarships to go to the United States to expand the scope of his project towards American little magazines. In his proposal, he mentioned his interest in New Criticism and his intention to 'gain access to books, and to people' useful to his project.[7] One of his former professors at Leicester, Colin J. Hornex, wrote an enthusiastic reference letter: 'There is some reason to hope that Bradbury will be a writer more heard of in the future and I recommend a stay in America while he is still in his formative years.'[8]

Bradbury's first year in the United States, in 1955–56, was indeed a turning point. He was offered a teaching assistantship at Indiana University and wrote a series of articles on Anglo-American relationships for the *Guardian Journal*.

---

[6] 'Author's Success', *Evening Post*, 27 Nov. 1953.
[7] Bradbury, 'Curriculum Vitae', c. 1954, Box 32, Folder Indiana U. Misc., Bradbury M. mss. II, Indiana.
[8] Hornex, 'Mr Malcolm S. Bradbury', 29 Dec. 1954, Box 32, Folder Indiana U. Misc., Bradbury M. mss. II, Indiana.

He described crossing the Atlantic on a luxury boat ('an opulent floating luxury hotel, with its shops, cinemas, sports and unlimited relaxation') and meeting likeminded people, 'English, American and French, participating in such exchange schemes and travelling on grants awarded by the Fulbright Act'. 'For all these people,' wrote the young Bradbury, 'the change is both exciting and momentous; they are learning in this way the new internationalism that is necessary in these times when communications between nations are essential' ('Cultural Ties in the Making'). Many things fascinated Bradbury in America—from dry-cleaners to young women. One of the most important things he learnt was that universities could be havens for writers. Taking the example of the New Critics, who 'were influential teacher-writers,' Bradbury later said: 'the idea that writers could work together, share techniques, learn from each other's styles, treat each other as serious practitioners, was an improvement over the British custom of isolated amateurism. I came back over the Atlantic a sceptical convert, thinking we might do better at home.'[9] American universities offered opportunities for writers to share ideas, but also to make a living. In 1968, shortly after coming to Norwich, Bradbury wrote:

> When I got to America ..., I found at once that it was easier to be the kind of writer I wanted to be ... The States wasn't only the source of some of the liveliest and most relevant arts and ideas, but also of some of the most generous financial support for them: the great grant-giving nation, the country where the writer had a place on campus, a good range of fee-paying media, and good supplementary royalties. In particular, it was easy for the writer-teacher like myself to get to the States, by teaching or on fellowships, and once there to receive every encouragement for being a writer. The explicit regard for creativity there was of the greatest importance to me, since it was virtually not to be had in England at all. But even more the States suggested to me that there was a working relationship to be made between the two things that interested me most—writing and university teaching—and that the university campus could indeed be bohemia, a place of intellectual and artistic ferment in which it was also possible to preserve a high degree of independence, economic and intellectual.
>
> ('One Man's America' 63)

Being a writer was a 'lonely amateur occupation' in Britain, but it was a professional, financially viable activity on American campuses. Bradbury's reference to 'bohemia' is, of course, significant for someone whose research expertise focused on modernism. While the modernists had viewed Paris, London, and New York as attractive centres, younger American writers turned towards the Midwest and

---

[9] 'Class Act: Malcolm Bradbury Looks Back on His 25 Years as Head of a Creative Writing Course', *Telegraph Magazine*, 7 Oct. 1995, pp. 36, 38.

the South. At the University of Iowa, Paul Engle untiringly sought out funding for the creative writing programme. In the 1960s, sponsors included a wide range of companies and organizations, from the Northern Natural Gas Company of Omaha to the US Steel Foundation. This economic model, based on a mix of private and public grants, impressed the young Bradbury—even though, as we will see later, he was never as enterprising as Engle in the search for funding for UEA's creative writing programme.

When the University of East Anglia was created in 1963, it became (along with other 'plate-glass' universities) a haven for academics eager to shake up the traditional British university system. The first Vice Chancellor for the new university, Frank Thistlethwaite, had lived in the United States as a young man (he won a Commonwealth Fund fellowship in 1938 to study at the University of Minnesota) and had married an American woman (Sanderson, 'Thistlethwaite'). Bradbury later presented Thistlethwaite as the 'founding father of American Studies in Britain' who 'had encouraged the university in an academic plan in which interdisciplinary connections were central. In the arts schools, this meant primarily a link between history and literature' ('How I Invented America' 133). Thistlethwaite valued interdisciplinarity, and surrounded himself with colleagues who had first-hand experience of the American university system—including his former Cambridge classmate, Ian Watt. Between 1948 and 1962, Watt had studied at the University of California, Los Angeles and Harvard University, then taught English at UC, Berkeley. He left California to move to Norwich, becoming Dean of English Studies during the first academic year (1963–64). As Holeywell has shown, Watt was instrumental in the hiring of Angus Wilson as the first professional writer to teach in a UK university (15).

Watt also encouraged Nicholas Brooke, a Shakespearian scholar, to come to UEA and contribute to the development of English studies. As his former student Lorna Sage recalls, Brooke was 'anti-order' and 'may have been predisposed to relish insecurity, just because his family were so set in Cambridge'. The son of a distinguished professor of medieval history, Brooke started teaching at Jesus College, Cambridge, before taking up a lectureship at Durham University. Despite close friendships with some of his colleagues, 'Durham was too collegiate and churchy for his tastes' ('Obituary'). Reading Sage's portrait of Brooke, one gets the impression of a man who found his place at UEA precisely because he was an outcast in more conservative universities.

For Brooke, going to UEA in the early 1960s must have been a daring decision. Victor Sage, who was then studying at Durham with his wife Lorna, gives a sense of what UEA was like at that time:

> Nicholas Brooke anyway came here, and they said to us, would you like to come here to do postgraduate work and he said: 'Oh no, don't come this year because

we haven't got any books.' So this place was in that situation, where it was going to have to build a university library so it was not quite ready, it had no infrastructure ...¹⁰

The lack of infrastructure was still an issue in 1965, when Brooke offered an appointment to Malcolm Bradbury, then a lecturer at the University of Birmingham. Making decisions was never an easy thing for Bradbury, and in the archive at Indiana University I discovered two letters, both dated 18 February 1965—one in which he accepts the position despite 'family problems' and another one in which he rejects it:

> After a long struggle about the decision, I've had to decide that I can't really come to East Anglia just at the moment. As you know, it was, for several reasons, hard for me to weigh the matter, but yesterday we heard that my wife has to have two operations, involving a long spell in hospital, and it was for these family reasons that we decided that this was not a good time for us to move. It sounds inept to say so, but if in a year or so the developments in American literature continue, I should be most interested to be considered then.¹¹

In addition to his wife's health problems, Bradbury had to ponder over his friends' insistence that he stay at 'Brum' (the University of Birmingham). David Lodge, who was then holding a fellowship in the United States, wrote to him a long letter listing all the reasons why he should reject UEA's offer:

> (1) Norwich, though not as daft as Colchester, is pretty experimental and far-out, and educationally, you're a conservative. (2) in a new university the only compensation for the lack of resources, library etc is the satisfaction of shaping syllabuses, building up the strength of the department etc—is this really you? (3) I've never been to Norwich but I bet it's dead from the neck up—and down for that matter—and that most of the interesting people in the University will spend all their time in London. (4) Birmingham is one of the few provincial centres where there are opportunities for significant cultural activity, and the university has a lot of solid assets. You and I and Jim have, I think, already seen that through contact with the local theatre and the BBC—there are all kinds of possibilities for getting started a non-metropolitan spring of literary activity. The Department, when all's said and done, is a happy one as they go.¹²

---

¹⁰ Victor Sage, Interview by author, 27 Oct. 2014, Norwich.
¹¹ Bradbury to Brooke, 18 Feb. 1965, Box 2, Folder 1965, Jan.–Feb., Bradbury M. mss. II, Indiana. I am grateful to Dominic Bradbury for permission to reproduce this letter.
¹² Lodge to Bradbury, 12 Feb. 1965, Box 7, Folder Correspondence Lodge 1962–1968, Bradbury M. mss. II, Indiana.

Lodge was right to point out that UEA, a new 'plate-glass' university, was very different from 'red-bricks' such as the University of Birmingham. But he misjudged Bradbury's ability to adapt and thrive in an 'experimental' university. And, as the rest of his letter shows, he also mistakenly thought that the Norwich job would be detrimental to Bradbury's writing:

> I think it comes down to a question, which has been occupying me of late, too, and that is: is your ambition directed <u>ultimately</u> at success in <u>academe</u> or in creative writing? Of course one can combine them—as we do—but sooner or later, I feel, one has to decide which is to get the lion's share of one's time and energy. If it's <u>academe</u> in your case, if you would like to get a Chair as soon as you possibly can, I guess the Norwich job might help; but if, as I believe, it's writing that's your real interest, then I believe your present position at Brum is much better.[13]

As the correspondence between Lodge and Bradbury makes clear, UEA was primarily interested in developing its offering in American studies. But creative writing programmes had, of course, originated in the United States, and the discipline was already taught at UEA. Once established in Norwich, Bradbury benefited from a flexible system that allowed him to experiment with new courses, and to combine his work as a writer and as a critic. 'I thought we would stay for two or three years while the university was starting but we rooted,' Bradbury later said (Collins 8).

One reason why Bradbury fitted so well at UEA was his enthusiasm for the American university system, a system that encouraged interdisciplinarity and flexibility. At Iowa, Paul Engle stressed this ambition to cover all areas of human activity: 'If it is proper to teach children chicken-sexing, which calls for extreme acuteness of eye, and weaving, which can be a matter of the most gracious taste in design, then why is it not appropriate to teach originality in writing?' ('The Writer and the Place' 2). The American modular course system of teaching and examining meant that a creative writing course could be added without designing an entire programme. This was really a central difference with the British system, based on extreme specialization and final-year assessment. As David Lodge puts it, 'most universities examined undergraduates at the end of a three-year course exclusively by a set of three-hour written examinations, a method which obviously could not be applied to creative writing.'[14] From the start, UEA adopted a model close to the American system, with degree options, ongoing assessments, seminar-based teaching and, from 1971, American-style writers-in-residence (with the Henfield Writing Fellows). Bradbury and Wilson also suggested the possibility of

---

[13] Underlines are in the original.
[14] Lodge, Questionnaire returned to author in June 2015.

introducing a creative writing option for postgraduate students, which famously attracted Ian McEwan to Norwich.

6.2 Ian McEwan and the Rise of the 'UEA Clique'

In October 2014, I attended the talk that McEwan gave at the UEA Autumn Literary Festival and the following Questions & Answers with a group of American exchange students as well as local 'MA Prose students, prose faculty and Fellows only'. Predictably, someone asked a question about McEwan's experience as a student at UEA. 'They claim me as the first student of creative writing,' McEwan said, but 'there was no course'—'We never went in his [Bradbury's] room to discuss my work'.[15] Archival documents show that McEwan took four modules of the MA in The Nineteenth and Twentieth-Century Novel: The Theory of Fiction; Symbolism and American Literature; The English and American Novel 1945–present; and A Comparative Study of Some English and European Novelists.[16] The only 'creative' aspect of the course was the possibility to submit creative writing instead of a critical dissertation. Although there was no workshop provision, this existing dialectic between critical and creative work would later be central to the development of the MA in Creative Writing.

A few months after McEwan's talk, I interviewed him over the phone. When I asked him why he spent so much time at UEA (giving talks, meeting students, answering questions from researchers like me), he replied:

> UEA was very good to me. It gave me the most wonderful year of my life. It started my literary career, I had its undivided attention in the form of Malcolm [Bradbury] and Angus [Wilson]. I made many, many good friends there. It became an important locus of my life—and for that reason, I don't want to turn my back on it. I owe it a great deal. *It never quite was what the UEA PR machine—it never quite was what it described.* There was no course back then … but it wouldn't have happened without UEA. So even though the place has changed – it's a lot more impersonal, far more students and so on – I still feel very connected.[17]

McEwan gives the impression that some impersonal force ('they', 'the UEA PR machine') created the myth of creative writing programmes in Britain, casting him in the role of the first student. And he hardly exaggerates when he says that he has repeatedly tried to convince the world that he did not study creative writing.

---

[15] McEwan, Questions and Answers, 22 Oct. 2014.
[16] UEA/BRAD/11.
[17] McEwan, Interview by author, 9 Mar. 2015, via phone (emphasis added).

As early as 1983, McEwan was already telling the same version of the story. The Book Marketing Council had just released the names of the 20 writers to be mentioned in its 'Best of Young British Novelists' promotion campaign—including many writers associated one way or another with UEA (McEwan, Ishiguro, Rose Tremain, Clive Sinclair, and Maggie Gee). In an article entitled 'Mr Bradbury's Finishing School,' *The Guardian* declared:

> The very first student on the Norwich list was Ian McEwan, who has shown some resentment that he is held up as one of their successes when, as he sees it, the fiction written on the course amounted to about one sixth of his MA work, and the course itself amounted to about three drinks with Bradbury and general discussion of what he was doing.

McEwan told the interviewer: 'no one wants to see himself as the product of a course; it strikes at the mythology of individualism.' But he also recognized that his year at UEA had been 'invaluable', particularly in terms of practical advice on starting a literary career: 'It was very useful that Malcolm suggested some literary editors I could send stories to, that was quite marvellous' (Hebert).

It is perhaps the ambiguity of McEwan's account—pride and gratefulness mixed with resentment—that makes it less compelling than the creative-writing-started-in-1970 story. And even if McEwan did not study creative writing per se, he benefited from an exceptionally nurturing environment at UEA. Archival documents confirm that Bradbury, Angus Wilson, and Alan Burns (who held the first Henfield Writing Fellowship) took a keen interest in his work. In May 1971, Wilson wrote to Bradbury:

> Alan Burns is doing splendid things—the magazine, in particular, seems to have acted as a great stimulus … He already speaks enthusiastically of Ian McEwan. I also admire his work greatly. I am lunching with him today to talk to him about it.[18]

Here, Wilson presents himself both as a fan of the young McEwan and a mentor eager to give advice over lunch. Three months later, he wrote to Alan Ross at the *London Magazine* and enclosed 'for the interest of your editorial staff a piece written by one of my students at Norwich which seems to me to have great virtues'. 'To have an opinion from one of your editors,' added Wilson, 'if you think it at all worth encouraging would be of great service' (qtd in Drabble 421). After graduation, Wilson helped McEwan get funding from the Arts Council. The £1,000 grant—the equivalent of an income of around £28,000 in 2020 (Officer and Williamson)—'was very important at an impoverished time' (Benedictus).

---

[18] Wilson to Bradbury, 25 May 1971, Box 7, Folder Correspondence W-Z, Bradbury M. mss. II, Indiana.

When Jonathan Cape published McEwan's inaugural collection of short stories *First Love, Last Rites* (1975), Wilson supplied a blurb quoted in advertisements: 'An important new writer ... sensitive without shapelessness and intelligent without smart aleckry.'[19] Anthony Thwaite—the 1972 Henfield Writing Fellow at UEA—reviewed the book in *The Observer*: 'the eight [stories] ... look as if some of the characters from early Angus Wilson had been painted by Francis Bacon' ('Brilliant Performance'). Nowhere in the review was it mentioned that McEwan, Wilson, and Thwaite himself belonged to the same UEA network. It is a good example of what the sociologist David Morgan has called the 'hidden work' in the production of culture (31): casual readers tend to think of the author as the unique producer and ignore the social relationships between the writer and other actors of the literary field.

Bradbury also provided advice and encouragement to McEwan in the years following his graduation. He sent one of McEwan's stories to the *Transatlantic Review*, which paid £5 for its publication, and he brought his former student to the attention of the *New American Review* (Benedictus). McEwan was not, of course, the only one to benefit from Bradbury's help. In December 1973, for example, Bradbury recommended one MA student's play for the Radio Times Drama Awards Scheme.[20] The student (Peter Harris) kept in touch with his mentor until at least 1975, when he told Bradbury that he had set up a writers' workshop in Bath.[21] But the link between Bradbury and McEwan proved particularly enduring. In a 1979 review in *The TLS*, Bradbury compared Clive Sinclair's recently published book *Hearts of Gold* to McEwan's *First Love, Last Rites*: 'it is not an inappropriate link to make, since both McEwan and Sinclair participated in a creative writing group at the University of East Anglia' ('The Textuality of Sexuality').[22] As late as 1981— more than ten years after McEwan's arrival in Norwich—Bradbury wrote to Peter Mayer, the CEO of Penguin Books: 'I've ... got one or two young writers who took my graduate course here in Creative Writing I'd like to talk to you about. It's been a good course (most notable product is Ian McEwan).'[23]

McEwan's extraordinary luck was to join what became known as the 'university set' at the time when this small group of writers was on the rise (with Angus Wilson a notable exception).[24] In 1970, Bradbury was a well-respected professor and writer, but certainly not the bestselling author and TV personality that he would become later. When *The History Man* was published in 1975,

---

[19] *The Times Literary Supplement*, 28 Mar. 1975, p. 328.
[20] Bradbury to Radio Times, 17 Dec. 1973, LIT/CW/4, AMWLT, UEA.
[21] Harris to Bradbury, 7 Sept. 1975, LIT/CW/4, AMWT, UEA.
[22] Sinclair did not study for the MA in creative writing (he did a BA at UEA, graduating in 1969, and then came back as a PhD student).
[23] Bradbury to Mayer, 6 Feb. 1981, Box 4, Folder Correspondence 1981 Jan.–May, Bradbury M. mss. II, Indiana.
[24] Victor Sage attributes the eclipse of Angus Wilson's reputation to the fact that his novels were read as social realism, a genre in decline from the 1970s. Interview by author, 27 Oct. 2014, Norwich.

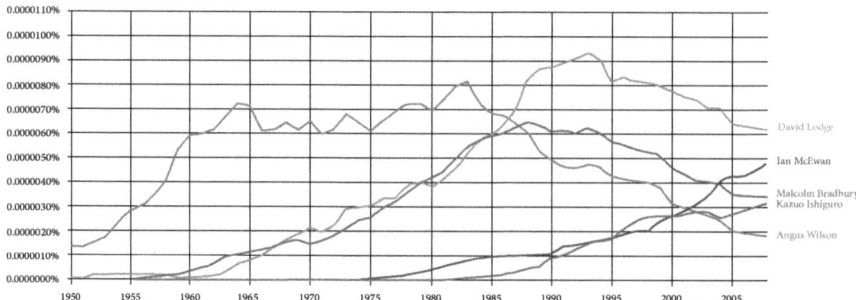

Fig. 6.1 Graph displayed on Google Books Ngram Viewer, for the phrases 'Malcolm Bradbury, Ian McEwan, Kazuo Ishiguro, David Lodge, Angus Wilson', between 1950 and 2015 from the corpus 'English'.
Source: Author's own.

it sold around 10,000 copies in hardback. When it was adapted for the BBC four years later, '10,000 turned in one night into 10 million'—Bradbury told one interviewer with characteristic exaggeration (Gensane 44). A search on Google Books Ngram, which shows the occurrence of selected phrases in a huge corpus of books, confirms Bradbury's rising reputation, which continued until the late 1980s (Figure 6.1).

David Lodge also enjoyed increasing recognizability and commercial success. A long-lasting friend of Bradbury, Lodge was asked to examine McEwan's MA dissertation. 'OK, I'll examine your creative writing chap,' Lodge wrote to Bradbury in September 1971. 'It should be interesting, though rather difficult to know what kind of standard to apply. It would seem rather hard on the chap to viva him just in order to get over to Norwich to see you, but I'll bear the possibility in mind.'[25] Here, Lodge pointed out an issue that remains at the centre of the discipline today: the difficulty of marking creative writing essays according to 'objective' criteria. A little-known writer in the early 1970s, Lodge later published a series of best-selling books, including the trilogy of academic novels *Changing Places: A Tale of Two Campuses* (1975), *Small World: An Academic Romance* (1984) and *Nice Work* (1988). He has stayed in touch with McEwan over the years (their correspondence can now be consulted at the Harry Ransom Center in Texas).

At UEA, McEwan also met several young academics who went on to distinguished careers. Jon Cook was then a fellow student and got his first academic post in 1973[26]—before climbing the professorial ladder. Like Cook, Victor Sage stayed at UEA for his entire professional career. A young English scholar who was also writing fiction, Sage met McEwan in the Autumn of the MA year. They both

---

[25] Lodge to Bradbury, 11 Sept. 1971, Box 7, Folder Correspondence Lodge 1969–1994, Bradbury M. mss. II, Indiana.
[26] Cook, Interview by author, 6 Oct. 2014, Norwich.

published pieces in a local magazine and saw each other several times in the Spring socially. They became closer after the MA was finished and met again in London in Autumn 1971.[27] 'We were very interested in each other's work,' McEwan declares, 'so he became an important part of the writing community for me.'[28] As Sage notes, McEwan was eager to meet people during his time in Norwich, and he succeeded in building strong relationships in the writing and academic worlds. In the long term, these contacts in academia helped consolidate McEwan's place in the literary canon. As John Guillory points out, 'the process of canon formation has an institutional context, the school' (45). Courses on recent British fiction often include primary texts by McEwan, as well as secondary readings such as *Contemporary Critical Perspectives: Ian McEwan* (Continuum, 2009), which features an interview of the writer by Sage and Cook.

In short, what McEwan gained from his year in Norwich was not primarily an education in creative writing or even mentorship by Malcolm Bradbury ('by contemporary standards, a less than model teacher', as Peter Ho Davies puts it). What McEwan gained was access to a *network* of successful—or soon-to-be-successful—writers and tastemakers, within a specific institution. He was not the first student in creative writing in Britain, but he benefited from social relationships that helped him publish and promote his work (what David Morgan has called 'friendship work' in relation to the production of culture [19]). And McEwan was helped by this web of distinguished writers (Bradbury, Wilson, Burns, Thwaite), fellow students (Cook) and young lecturers (Sage) because he belonged to a specific institution: the University of East Anglia. He was not an isolated would-be writer; he was already there, at the centre of an institution that would continue to rise within the larger literary field. Although McEwan never made a secret of the help he received, he has also tried to preserve his autonomy as a writer—resisting any attempt to present him as part of the 'UEA clique' or as Bradbury's protégé.

McEwan is not the only writer who has gained access to publishing networks, and then tried to downplay these relationships in order to present himself as a 'self-made' writer. Even authors who are pure products of creative writing programmes still often see themselves as outsiders—emulating the literary rebels who founded these programmes. Other examples include Kazuo Ishiguro and Saul Bellow, who both benefited from the model of professionalization of the writing career within universities but remained ambivalent or even hostile to these programmes.[29] William Faulkner and Ernest Hemingway, who launched their career thanks to the *informal mentorship model*, then defended an individualist vision of creativity.

---

[27] Sage, Email to author, 17 Mar. 2015.
[28] McEwan, Interview by author, 9 Mar. 2015, via phone.
[29] See Chapter 8 for an overview of Ishiguro's ambivalence towards creative writing programmes, an attitude that changed when he was awarded the Nobel Prize.

What happened to writers who showed gratitude towards their mentors? Women are perhaps more likely to shun the 'self-made' myth and openly talk about the help they have received. Let's take the example of Rose Tremain. After studying at UEA in the 1960s, she published her first novel *Sadler's Birthday* in 1976. Her career in the 1980s closely resembled that of McEwan and Ishiguro: she was amongst the 1983 'Best of Young British Novelists', and she appeared on the Booker Prize shortlist (her novel *Restoration* lost out to Ishiguro's *The Remains of the Day* in 1989). Her career has been successful, but less successful than her UEA peers. In 2018, a *Guardian* journalist asked her if the fact that she has never won the Booker Prize bothered her. 'Well, it does slightly,' she said. 'I think, really? All those books which have had on the whole, such great acclaim, why has that never happened? But it annoys me that it bothers me. And now we've got the Americans in it, it's gone, hasn't it?' (Allardice). Despite being a prolific, critically acclaimed writer with a large audience, Tremain has not obtained an award that both Ishiguro and McEwan got. There are many ways to explain this. First, Tremain is mainly known for historical fiction, a genre that is not traditionally favoured for the Booker. Another explanation is that she has repeatedly acknowledged her debt to her mentors at UEA, Angus Wilson and Malcolm Bradbury—including in an article published when she was part of the Booker Prize selection committee in 1988 ('Angus Wilson, Malcolm Bradbury and the Dead Cat'). In a literary world that over-values individualism and originality, it is possible that Tremain's honest acknowledgement of her mentors made things more difficult for her.

6.3 The Booker Prize and the Rise of UEA's Creative Writing Programme

In 1981, Ian McEwan's *The Comfort of Strangers* was shortlisted for the Booker Prize—chaired that year by Malcolm Bradbury. It was the beginning of a decade of expansion for UEA's creative writing programme, after years of stagnation. Kazuo Ishiguro, who graduated in 1980, noted that the MA 'hadn't run the previous year because not enough people had applied' (Hunnewell). In fact, there were five graduates in 1979, but none in 1978 (or 1972, 1976, or 1982).[30]

UEA presumably spent few resources to promote the programme (Ishiguro remembers coming across 'almost by accident ... a little advertisement' for the course [Hunnewell]). It took a very long time for the MA to get established, as Bradbury recognized in a report that I discovered in the UEA archives: 'We were not sure it would work in Britain; we were fearful of ending up with weaker students than those elsewhere. For quite a time we were assessing its worth from year

---

[30] Thanks to Andrew Cowan for this information.

to year.'[31] In Autumn 1982, when Bradbury wrote the report, he found it surprising to have eight students: 'The surprise comes because every single offer made was taken up, and what is more nearly every single applicant who came had very high academic qualifications.' To explain the growing attractiveness of the programme (including amongst American students), Bradbury mentioned the success of graduates: McEwan, Ishiguro, Clive Sinclair, and Rose Tremain. The aim of the report was to convince the university's management to increase the resources allocated to the programme—for example, by hiring staff to help with the growing number of applications and to supervise dissertations during the summer term. Bradbury gave the example of Washington University in Saint Louis, which had eight faculty members and a Visiting Professor (a role he had recently taken up). Once again, when thinking about UEA's creative writing programme, Bradbury turned towards the United States for inspiration.

There was one central difference, however, between the British and the American model: funding. Harnessing America's enterprising culture, Paul Engle had been immensely successful at raising funds for the Writers' Workshop. In the dedication to *On Creative Writing*, he thanked the 'heartening variety of individuals, foundations, and corporations' that 'have given funds to the Program in Creative Writing at the University of Iowa, so that young writers from all regions of the USA and many areas of the earth could come here and make an international community of the imagination' (vii). In contrast, Bradbury admitted in his report that his fundraising activities had brought few results:

> I have at various times attempted to raise the money for this in other ways: from the Arts Council, from specific publishers, from Booker McConnell, the donors of the Booker Prize, etc ... I have had much moral support but no guaranteed cash. I suspect a systematic attempt to trawl several publishers would be one way of doing it, but this would take time. And in my view it is in the end a Registry job.

Of course, Bradbury was working in understaffed conditions very different from his American colleagues: he was expected to teach (albeit part-time), deal with admissions and with the administration of the creative writing programme, while continuing his multiple activities: writing fiction, giving talks, travelling to faraway locations for the British Council. But the fact remains that, unlike Engle, Bradbury did not see fundraising as one of his priorities. It is significant, because it meant that UEA attracted mostly students who could get a government grant (Ian McEwan, Kazuo Ishiguro) or who came from well-off families. Ironically, while the young Bradbury had benefited from fellowships to study on American campuses, he made little consistent effort to create similar conditions for his own students.

---

[31] Bradbury to 'Roger', 11 Oct. 1982, LIT/CW/9, AMWLT, UEA.

Bradbury's strengths lay in his vision for the creative writing programme, and in his extensive network of contacts. In his 1982 report, he recommended that 'an undergraduate course in Creative Writing should be systematically provided', citing the example of Washington University in Saint Louis. Bradbury rightly anticipated the growing appeal of the discipline amongst all students—at the time when Minors and Majors in creative writing were becoming increasingly popular in American universities.[32]

At the beginning of the 1980s, Bradbury was also a well-known, well-connected writer who often used his position in the literary field to help his former students and colleagues. Analysing the creation of literary value in the marketplace, Pascale Casanova points out the importance of the name of the writer who consecrates a more junior colleague:

> Value in the literary world is directly related to belief. When a writer becomes known, when his name has acquired value in the literary market—which is to say, once it is believed that what he has written has literary value, once he has gained acceptance as a writer—then credit is given to him. Credit … is the power and authority granted to a writer by virtue of the belief that he has earned his 'name'.
>
> (*The World Republic of Letters* 16–17)

Bradbury repeatedly used his name and authority to push writers associated with UEA. In the speech he gave as Chair of the Booker Prize in 1981, he mentioned McEwan and Angela Carter amongst those 'who have shifted the novel sharply away from the median realism and provincialism that was so influential in the 1950s, toward largeness, moral strangeness, fantasy and grotesquerie'.[33] Bradbury's activism to promote his literary circle did not go unnoticed. For example, the satirical magazine *Private Eye* argued that *The Comfort of Strangers* was on the shortlist only because of McEwan's connection with UEA (qtd in Lee).

Shortly after chairing the Booker Prize, Bradbury actively helped another former student, the twenty-seven-year-old Ishiguro, get media attention for his first novel. A poster for a discussion between Ishiguro and Bradbury at the ICA (Institute of Contemporary Arts) in London describes *A Pale View of Hills* as 'an extraordinary first novel, by a young Japanese writer of exceptional talent, which brings the sorrows of war-torn Nagasaki to the depths of the English countryside' (Figure 6.2). There follows a blurb by Angela Carter, who was Ishiguro's instructor

---

[32] According to the Association of Writers and Writing Programs, in 1975, there were twenty-four higher education institutions offering Minors in creative writing and three offering Majors in creative writing for undergraduate students in the USA. These numbers rose to 155 and ten respectively in 1984 (Fenza).

[33] Bradbury, 'The Booker Prize Speech', 20 Oct. 1981, BP/1/13/1/2: Administrative Papers, 1981, Papers of the Booker Literary Prizes, Oxford Brookes University.

Fig. 6.2 Kazuo Ishiguro, Interview by Malcolm Bradbury, ICA, London, 17 Mar. 1982, Poster.
Source: Box 48, Folder Interview with Bradbury, Bradbury M. mss. III, 1950–2000. Courtesy Lilly Library, Indiana University, Bloomington, Indiana.

at UEA and who introduced him to the literary agent Deborah Rogers (he remained her client for thirty-four years, until her death in 2014).[34] As the recording of the ICA event shows, Bradbury promoted the MA in creative writing while celebrating his former student's success. 'Like Ian McEwan and Clive Sinclair,' said

---

[34] See Hunnewell and Trewin.

Bradbury, 'he was one of what proved to be an incredible group of writers who came to that course—brilliant to start with—and had a chance to write through a year.'[35] During the interview, when Ishiguro said he did not read enough to be influenced by other writers, Bradbury adopted a professorial tone to stress that the young man had been encouraged to read widely while at UEA. In short, Bradbury kept reminding audiences that Ishiguro was his former student, a brilliant product of a brilliant course (*The Guardian* later compared him and Angela Carter to 'proud parents' 'zealously' defending the young writer [Targett]).

Ishiguro was also amongst the 'Best of Young British Novelists' chosen in summer 1982 (the promotional campaign started a few months later, in early 1983). There is evidence to show that Bradbury had close ties with the Book Marketing Council, which organized the campaign. In February 1983, Desmond Clarke, the Director of the Council, sent him the press pack that had been distributed to media contacts, and told him: 'My target is to sell at least 250,000 copies of their books during the period of the promotion.'[36] The project certainly attracted a lot of media interest, on both sides of the Atlantic. According to *The New York Times*, 'more than 2,500 booksellers participated in the campaign, and the Book Marketing Council reports that sales of the books of the writers mentioned increased by 328% during the campaign' (Kakutani). The initiative helped raise the profile of UEA's creative writing programme (which was mentioned repeatedly in the press pack), leading to increased enrolments in the following years.

The growing visibility of the programme is also intertwined with the rise of the Booker Prize. Both institutions originated in the 1960s and shared the same ambition to promote literary fiction to a large audience. Bradbury compared the 'slow process' that led to the establishment of the Booker as a major prize to the similar difficulties encountered by the UEA programme in the 1970s:

> We were lucky to have Ian McEwan right at the beginning, but during the Seventies it poddled along and it was only at the end of that decade that things looked up and there was an obvious new mood. The same was true for the Booker. Initially, I think it was the stature of judges like Saul Bellow and Stephen Spender which attracted interest rather than the prize winners. It really took about 10 years for the Booker to take off. By then, you could almost feel the stakes rising and you could also feel a new generation of writers surging into the limelight.
>
> (Snelling)

Ishiguro was part of this 'new generation of writers' who benefited from the rise of these two institutions, UEA's creative writing programme and the Booker Prize. His second novel, *An Artist of the Floating World*, was shortlisted for the prize in

---

[35] See Ishiguro, *Interview by Malcolm Bradbury*.
[36] Clarke to Bradbury, 10 Feb. 1983, Box 48, Folder Best of British Authors and Publicity, Bradbury M. mss. III, 1950–2000, Indiana.

1986. It led to such an increase in media interest that Ishiguro had to cut himself off from all distractions to write his next book ('How I Wrote'). *The Remains of the Day* won the Booker in 1989, an award that was often presented as the victory of an institution, UEA. As one commentator put it, 'the Ishiguro victory is an endorsement for Professor Malcolm Bradbury, who launched the school of creative writing at East Anglia University' (Radford). Bradbury presided over the Book Trust panel, which chose the judges—including Maggie Gee and Helen McNeil, who both had a close association with UEA.[37] Rose Tremain was also amongst the contenders. Suspicions of cronyism were exacerbated by the fact that Bradbury's friend David Lodge served as chairman of the judges. But far from tarnishing the image of Bradbury and his creative writing programme, the controversy helped present UEA as the antechamber for literary success. A report held in the Booker Prize archive shows that the 1989 award given to *The Remains of the Day* added an additional 50,000 copies in hardback and an estimated 150,000 copies in paperback.[38] 'In reviews and anthologies,' wrote the *Sunday Times*, 'Bradbury has promoted several of his most promising pupils and friends, helping to turn them into literary stars' (Palmer). A graph (Figure 6.3) presented Bradbury as a Godfather at the centre of 'the University of East Anglia mafia', a term which suggested illicit deals and oppositions to other gangs (including 'the Granta set' and 'the Telegraph clique').

As I have argued in this chapter, Bradbury did not single-handedly turn his students into literary celebrities. His activities should be viewed in a broader institutional context. What McEwan had called 'the UEA PR machine' proved remarkably efficient at promoting the creative writing programme in the 1980s. In particular, archival documents show that Michael Benson, the university's Information Officer, consistently associated the 1989 Booker Prize award with UEA, where Ishiguro had studied nearly a decade before. He nudged Bradbury to write an article on Ishiguro,[39] and in an interview with the *Eastern Daily Press*, he said that the award 'underlines the excellence of our creative writing programme, which the university has run for the past 25 years'.[40] Interestingly, Benson traced the origins of creative writing at UEA back to the 1960s. At that time, the myth of 1970 as the starting point of the programme had not yet been firmly established.

Ishiguro's consecration was announced in October 1989 and that same month, UEA organized a seminar on 'Literary Prizes and Literary Culture' to mark the twentieth anniversary of the Booker Prize.[41] Since Ishiguro had been a favourite

---

[37] Gee held a Writing Fellowship in 1982 and McNeil was then working as Lecturer in American Studies at UEA.
[38] Andrew Thompson to Christina Shaw, *c.* 1990, BP/1/21/1/2: Administrative Papers, 1989, Papers of the Booker Literary Prizes, Oxford Brookes University.
[39] Benson to Bradbury, [*c.* Oct. 1989], LIT/CW/6, AMWLT, UEA.
[40] 'UEA Delight at Booker Prize Result', *Eastern Daily Press* [Oct. 1989], LIT/CW/6, AMWLT, UEA.
[41] Centre for Creative and Performative Arts, 'Newsletter: A Celebration of Writing, Twenty Years of the MA in Creative Writing at the University of East Anglia', 9–11 Nov. 1990, LIT/CW/13, AMWLT, UEA.

148   LITERARY REBELS

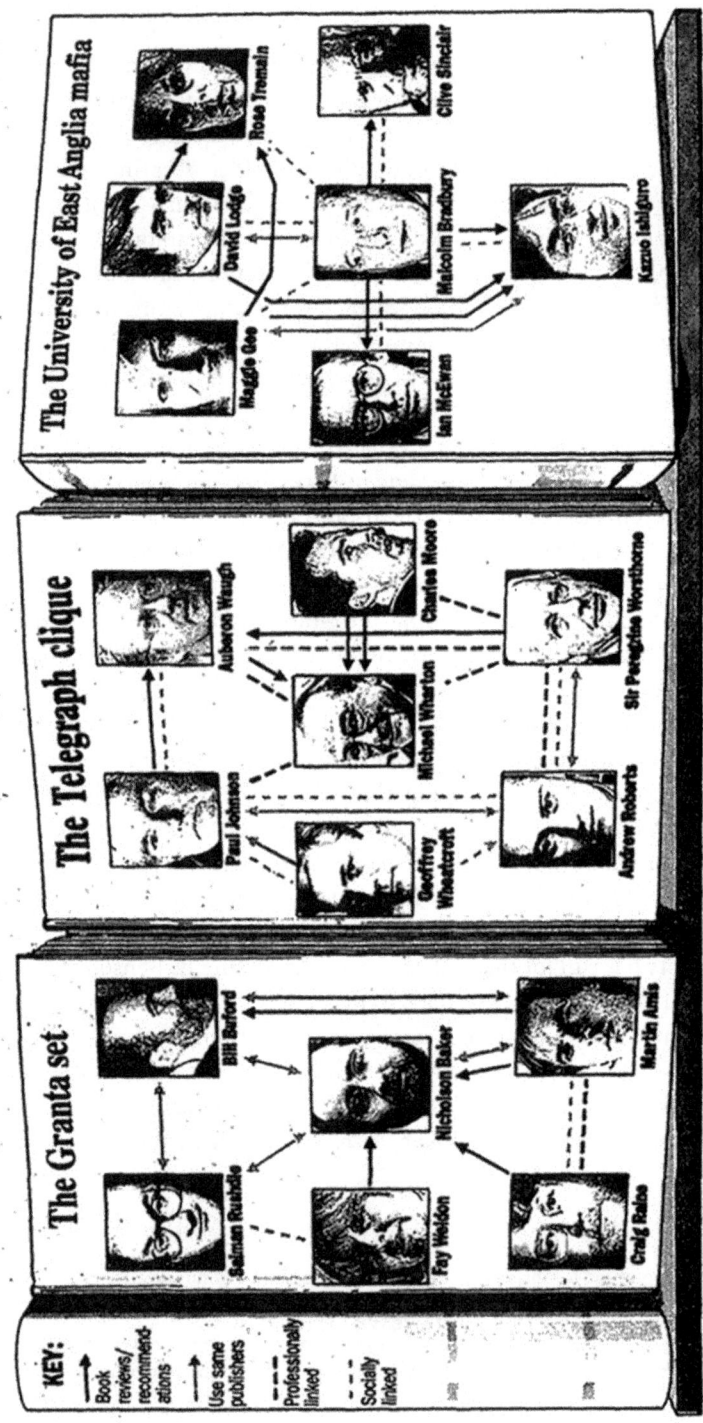

Fig. 6.3 Graph representing 'The University of East Anglia mafia' and other literary groups.
Source: Palmer 1992. Credit: *The Sunday Times*/News Licensing.

for months before the announcement of the prize,[42] the timing of the seminar was hardly coincidental. Even if he had not won the prize (a distinct possibility, with heavyweight contenders such as Margaret Atwood), UEA could still celebrate the shortlisting of two alumni. The seminar was hosted by the newly created Centre for Creative and Performing Arts, which helped with the running of the MA and PhD in creative writing. By the late 1980s, UEA had reached a level of institutional self-consciousness that produced a discourse celebrating the creative writing programme and associating it with other successful literary institutions such as the Booker Prize.

Economists talk of 'path dependency' when, once a choice has been made and a way has been chosen, it is thought more efficient to continue along the already set path rather than reassess the various options. As Benson's discourse shows, one path would have been to celebrate the fact that creative writing was taught at UEA in the 1960s. The other path was to privilege 1970 as the starting date, with Ian McEwan as the first student. In his 2002 *The History of the University of East Anglia Norwich*, Michael Sanderson wrote that the MA in creative writing 'started in 1970 with a single student, Ian McEwan, a Sussex graduate. His extraordinary success in that year and subsequently helped to kick-start the new course, accepted in the University and of ever increasing reputation at large' (90). It is certainly true that McEwan became a successful writer at a young age, helped by Wilson, Bradbury, and others. But there was no guarantee that the 1970 myth would be the best to promote UEA, since it privileged one student over others, such as Rose Tremain who had studied there in the 1960s.[43] So why was it chosen? One possible answer is that the ageing Bradbury increasingly saw the MA programme as one of his most important achievements. Whereas creative writing was taught to UEA's undergraduates when he was still at the University of Birmingham, he had undoubtedly shaped the postgraduate programme. As Tremain told him, 'the course is so much **yours** and whoever takes over from you is going to have a difficult time'.[44] Although Bradbury gave credit to Angus Wilson, he also placed himself at the centre of the 1970 myth ('McEwan was in my creative writing class'). When he died in 2000, the title of his obituary in the *Economist* was 'The Creative-Writing Man', as if his main claim to posterity was the creation of the UEA programme and the 'discovery' of McEwan.[45]

---

[42] 'Books and the Booker', *Washington Post*, 6 Aug. 1989, p. J15.
[43] Tremain was often thought to have studied creative writing in 1970, which shows once again the appeal of the myth. See her letter to Bradbury, 9 Feb. 1993, Box 37, Bradbury M. mss. III, 1950–2000, Indiana: 'If I **had** still been a student at UEA in 1970 (as the press would have me be) I would have applied to do the course and possibly started writing reasonably good novels long before I did' (emphasis in original).
[44] Tremain to Bradbury, 9 Feb. 1993, Box 37, Bradbury M. mss. III, 1950–2000, Indiana (emphasis in original).
[45] 'The Creative-Writing Man', *Economist*, 2 Dec. 2000, p. 41.

The founding myth of 1970 shows that from the start, creative writing was positioned as a discipline on the margins. It was a reaction against traditional routes to literary glory: a family with strong social connections à la Woolf, a nice home in Bloomsbury, a degree from Oxbridge and so on. If Bradbury had set up his creative writing programme in London or the South East, the myth would have lost much of its appeal. For it was tied to the geographical isolation of East Anglia: 'situated on the edge of the fens, Norwich was known mainly for the virulence of the cold winds blowing off the North Sea before Sir Malcolm set up his postgraduate course,' declares the *Economist*.[46] This position on the edge offered the perfect setting from the David versus Goliath story that Bradbury promoted for three decades: the story of a discipline that offered opportunities to the 'have nots' of the literary field.

[46] Ibid.

7
Lorry-Driver Poets and Student Radicals
Inventing the 'Writer-in-Residence' in Britain

What is a writer-in-residence? In the 1950s and 1960s, the British press oscillated between three definitions. First, there was the case of young men (they were almost always men) going to places like Stanford or Iowa to work on their writing and study under famous writers. Then, there were established authors like Robert Frost and William Faulkner being invited on campuses to mingle with students and staff and give informal talks. And finally, the new breed of writer-in-residence was 'a member of the "teaching" staff, conducting regular classes, tutorials or seminars specifically tailored to train and encourage fledgling writers.'[1] In short, the framework was sufficiently vague to apply to all kinds of situations: to emerging and well-known writers, to university departments that could afford to pay a writer without immediate return, and to those that needed additional teaching help.

American programmes in creative writing offered one model for the rise of the 'writer-in-residence' in Britain. A second model was informed by progressive educational ideas. Funded by the Arts Council and other organizations, writers-in-residence advised underprivileged populations: from lorry-driver poets to dry-cleaners-turned-novelists. With the rise of the discourse on creative writing in academia as a source of conformity, all institutions started becoming suspicious—including the Arts Council. The only way to be completely autonomous was to reject funding from institutions and survive in the marketplace, argued the novelist and playwright Jack Trevor Story after a stint as writer-in-residence in Milton Keynes.

For writers of the generation of Malcolm Bradbury (born 1932) and David Lodge (born 1935), the term 'writer-in-residence' was inseparable from the American context. Take the example of Dan Jacobson, a South African writer who had settled in London. In 1956, Jacobson was twenty-seven years old and had already published two novels and a number of short stories. His growing reputation had helped him secure a $2,500 fellowship to go to Stanford University's creative writing centre. There were six people who received the award for the 1956–57 academic

---

[1] 'Writing Schools', *The Times Literary Supplement*, 8 Apr. 1965, p. 275.

Literary Rebels. Lise Jaillant, Oxford University Press.
© Lise Jaillant (2022). DOI: 10.1093/oso/9780192855305.003.0008

year, and the others were from the United States.[2] This was a unique opportunity for Jacobson to build relationships with influential and emerging American writers (he attended Wallace Stegner's class and met the young Richard Elman, who would later write about him in his memoirs [35]). When he came back to Britain, Jacobson wrote *No Further West*, a short book about his year's stay in Palo Alto—a 'stretch of billboards, shopping centres, supermarkets, used-car lots, drive-ins, factories, filling-stations and motels sprawling along the Camino Real south of San Francisco', as the *TLS* reviewer put it (Beaver, 'Unknown California'). For many UK-based commentators, the idea of a creative writing fellowship to spend time in a university had a foreign flavour. And this sense of strangeness was often close to suspicion, even outright hostility. As Bradbury would later say of creative writing, 'it was generally regarded as a dangerous American invention, like the vacuum cleaner and the hoola hoop—and certainly not one that had a place in the literature department of a British university' (*Class Work* viii).

The emergence of the 'writer-in-residence' in the United States and its eventual exportation to Britain have been largely understudied. In the British context, Michelene Wandor cites Alan Brownjohn's unpublished report 'Writers in Education 1951–1979' but she does not add new evidence to explain how and why writers were introduced in schools and universities (*The Author Is Not Dead* 10–11). The American context has also been neglected. The terms 'writer-in-residence' and 'poet-in-residence' do not even appear in Eric Bennett's *Workshops of Empire*. Mark McGurl uses the term interchangeably with 'creative writing teacher' (115), but later mentions in passing that Robert Frost is 'perhaps the first true "writer in residence" in American literary history' (184). This is confirmed in D. G. Myers' *The Elephants Teach* (96). The Oxford English Dictionary also cites a 1927 reference to Frost as 'poet-in-residence' at the University of Michigan.[3] But in *Everyday Reading: Poetry and Popular Culture in Modern America*, Mike Chasar tells a different story. The first writer-in-residence was in fact Percy MacKaye (1875–1956), who served at Miami University in Ohio in the early 1920s. MacKaye was encouraged by Miami President Raymond Hughes, 'who spoke before the National Association of State Universities in 1920 and suggested providing fellowships to creative artists' (258 n10). For Chasar, this precedent led directly to Frost's appointment at the University of Michigan.

The flexible definition of 'writer-in-residence' made it possible to adapt the model to the British context, where university creative writing had so far been held in deep suspicion. Setting up a fellowship for a writer did not require a long-term financial commitment (a few months were enough). Moreover, the writer could make themselves useful by teaching literature and providing advice to students. In 1963, a press release from the University of East Anglia announced the hiring

---

[2] 'Award for Londoner', *The Times*, 12 June 1956, p. 3.
[3] 'Poet, n.', *OED Online*, Oxford UP, Mar. 2016.

of Angus Wilson as the first writer-in-residence in Britain. From the mid-1960s, Regional Arts Associations also provided funding to send writers to schools and universities. In 1967 and 1968, Northern Arts set up a Writer's Fellowship at the Universities of Durham, Newcastle, and Hull (Wandor, *The Author Is Not Dead* 11). At around the same time, the Arts Council launched a 'Writers in Schools' programme. In 1970, the Scottish dramatist Tom Wright was appointed jointly by the University of Strathclyde and the Scottish Arts Council to a creative writing fellowship in the department of English studies.[4] Shortly after, UEA awarded the first Henfield fellowship for an established writer. And in 1972, a grant from the Calouste Gulbenkian Foundation enabled Brian Cox to hire the young poet and publisher Michael Schmidt at the University of Manchester.

Although these programmes took a wide range of forms, they were influenced by two models that overlapped at first, and then grew increasingly distinct. The first one was inspired by elite American programmes in creative writing. The second model was informed by progressive educational ideas, which also triggered the expansion of the comprehensive school system. Creative writing came to be seen as a response to a stifling English curriculum dominated by canonical texts. The writer-in-residence could be a friendly and approachable presence in schools and universities, someone who helped young people from all kinds of social backgrounds to find their voice. In the early to mid-1960s, the 'American' and the 'progressive' models had largely overlapped. Angus Wilson, for example, justified his decision to join the University of East Anglia by appealing to egalitarian notions of education. He also had experience lecturing at American universities, and UEA compared his position to that of Faulkner and Frost. Malcolm Bradbury, a self-described Midatlantic Man,[5] had taught in the extramural department of the University of Hull, where he met Brian Cox. Bradbury's knowledge of vocational courses partly explains his interest in creative writing as a way to renew the traditional academic curriculum.[6] Both Bradbury and Cox were from lower-middle-class backgrounds, and they shared a life-long commitment to education as a route to social mobility and individual empowerment. But they were also profoundly hostile to radical left-wing movements that underpinned much of the educational activism of the late 1960s and 1970s.[7]

In the Black Papers published in *Critical Quarterly* from 1969, Cox criticized the excesses of progressive education and defended a conception of education based on selection and excellence. Archival documents also show that Malcolm Bradbury anonymously contributed to the first Black Paper—a fact that he never

---

[4] 'Fellowship for Dramatist at Strathclyde', *The Times*, 29 June 1970, p. 10.
[5] 'Malcolm Bradbury on *Stepping Westward*' (in *Stepping Westward*).
[6] Giles Foden, Interview by author, 5 May 2015, Norwich.
[7] David Lodge wrote: 'I was right in predicting that Malcolm would find aspects of the radical ethos of UEA uncongenial, but that was precisely what provoked his masterpiece, [his 1975 novel] *The History Man*' (*Lives in Writing*, Malcolm Bradbury).

publicly revealed.[8] This common view on education had an impact on their conception of the writer-in-residence. When Cox introduced a writing fellow at the University of Manchester, he did not expect him to teach creativity to underprivileged populations. What Cox wanted was a writer who could help develop the new Poetry Centre and establish Manchester as a serious competitor to traditional literary centres in London and Oxford. And when the Henfield fellowship was set up at the University of East Anglia, Bradbury aimed to attract a distinguished author who would strengthen the existing creative writing provision. He looked towards the United States in an effort to put Norwich on the literary map. In short, he was doing (on a much smaller scale) what Paul Engle had done at Iowa: find the funding, bring the writers and send out press releases. As senior academics, then, Bradbury and Cox were in a position to shape the role of the writing fellows they hired.

This chapter begins with the representation of the writer-in-residence in Britain in the 1950s and 1960s. The British press often presented it as a threat to creative freedom, a sort of gilded cage for writers eager to obtain financial security—a representation challenged by Dan Jacobson and others. It then focuses on UEA's appointment of Angus Wilson in 1963, a position inspired by the US academic system. The creation of the Henfield fellowship seven years later was one additional step in modelling UEA as an American-style university. The University of Manchester, a more traditional institution, also introduced a writing fellow in the early 1970s. The idea of a writer-in-residence showed it was possible to introduce novelty in higher education, without abandoning values dear to Brian Cox: the principle of selection and the pursuit of excellence. At UEA and Manchester, writing fellows were involved in little magazines and small presses, which offered a platform to publicize literary activities within and outside the university. But some students felt that this model of the writer-in-residence had been imposed on them without proper consultation, and called for the appointments of younger writers with a radical agenda. Following a 'progressive' model, the Arts Council launched a programme of support for writers-in-residence, who often worked with underprivileged populations far from traditional literary centres.

7.1 A Dangerous American Invention?

American voices critical of the creative writing institution—with its classes, professors, and writers-in-residence—found an eager audience in Britain. In a 1953 article in *The Listener* (the weekly magazine established by the BBC), Mary

---

[8] Bradbury to Cox, 28 Jan. 1988, GB 133 COX6/10, COX.

McCarthy denounced the 'business of highbrow writing' inseparable from the rise of New Criticism on US campuses: 'even in the mid-west tall-corn country, the Bible Belt, the prairies, the gaunt mountain towns, there is hardly a college too primitive to have its own formidable New Critic in residence' (901, 902). McCarthy was critical of academia in general (her own campus novel, *The Groves of Academe*, had just been published in Britain). She particularly criticized the institution of creative writing, an institution that had an alarming resemblance to totalitarian regimes: 'The very youthfulness of many of the new-style pedants, the soft pink cheek and crew haircut, coupled with the air of assurance and the business-like style of operation, strikes terror into the literary heart.' And she added: 'American efficiency is chilling, a foretaste of science-fiction millennia, when it moves in, with its equipment, its loudspeakers and tape-recorders, on the intangibles, while it talks briskly of the "strategies" of a poem.'

This dystopian picture should be read alongside descriptions of mass culture by Dwight Macdonald and others. 'Mass culture is imposed from above,' Macdonald wrote in 1953. 'It is fabricated by technicians hired by businessmen; its audiences are passive consumers, their participation limited to the choice between buying and not buying' ('A Theory of Mass Culture' 60). Standardized products served to control these passive, femininized masses by appealing to their lowest instincts. Pulp novels, for instance, satisfied people's attraction to violence, lust, and greed. For Macdonald, the true threat to high culture came not from unsophisticated crime fiction, Hollywood films, and other forms of mass culture, but 'from a peculiar hybrid bred from the latter's unnatural intercourse with the former' ('Masscult and Midcult' 35). This hybrid—which he called 'Midcult' in a 1960 essay—was particularly dangerous, because it closely resembled serious high culture. In other words, this 'middle culture' or 'middlebrow culture' was a form of sophisticated mass culture (*Interviews with Dwight Macdonald* 84). Macdonald gave the example of *Life* magazine, which mixed high and low cultural forms, resulting in 'homogenized culture' ('A Theory of Mass Culture' 62).

For Dwight Macdonald, the post-Second World War world was not a hospitable environment for serious writers and artists. 'I certainly don't think our literature is flourishing, certainly not as compared to the twenties,' he once said (*Interviews with Dwight Macdonald* 84). The *informal mentorship model* of the interwar period was preferable, because it focused on a one-to-one relationship, rather than a larger group gathered in a writing workshop. Macdonald was well aware of the development of creative writing programmes. In 1957, he even taught a creative writing course at Northwestern University, as part of a programme that brought 'distinguished non-academic persons' to campus. Saul Bellow followed him in 1958 (Leader, *The Life of Saul Bellow*). Both men distrusted the model of professionalization in universities, which could lead to the standardization of culture (see Chapter 4). At the time when Ernest Hemingway had become a model in the creative writing classroom,[9] Macdonald warned his own students against Hemingway's 'constant editorializing' ('Masscult and Midcult' 40). He saw *The Old Man and the Sea* as a perfect example of Midcult—standardized, insipid, and masquerading as serious cultural form. In 1959, Paul Engle brought Macdonald (alongside Ralph Ellison, Mark Harris, and Norman Mailer) to the University of Iowa to participate in a symposium on 'The Writer in Mass Culture'. Macdonald declared: 'good writing has always been done for an elite audience and never for everyone' (qtd in Glass, 'Middle Man' 256).

Creative writing programmes were not designed for an elite. On the contrary, they had been developed as democratic institutions, open to anyone who had the ability, discipline and drive to become a professional writer. They can be seen as middlebrow institutions, that mediated between high and low cultural forms. As Catherine Keyser puts it, 'the term middlebrow referred perhaps more clearly to mass-market venues and middle-class audiences than to formal characteristics of literary style' (9). In *Modernism, Middlebrow and the Literary Canon*, I focused on the Modern Library series as an American middlebrow enterprise, that sold difficult modernist text to a large audience, celebrated bourgeois status, and engaged with celebrity culture. Similarly, creative writing programmes promoted a middlebrow cultural pedagogy, with an emphasis on modernism and serious artistic forms turned towards a broad public rather than a closed coterie. For Macdonald, the future of high culture in such an environment was 'dark' ('A Theory of Mass Culture' 70).

Like Macdonald and other New York Intellectuals, Mary McCarthy had grown disillusioned with Marxism and she had an apocalyptic vision of mass culture as a form of top-down control on individuals. What seemed to her particularly scary with university creative writing was the expansion of this control towards the highbrow sphere. The commodification of serious writing in universities and the rise of the 'poet-artist-critic in residence' risked destroying the autonomy of writers, their ability to offer a critical view on their society. As more and more writers had forgotten 'how to starve', they no longer paid attention to the price of financial security (902).

This kind of alarmist discourse had echoes in other British periodicals. When William Faulkner was appointed 'writer-in-residence' at the University of Virginia, *The Times Literary Supplement* questioned the meaning of the term: 'Whatever else this means, and much has been written of this retreat into the ivory towers, the cultural museums, it has meant a limitation of experience, a finicky attention of form, ambiguity, complexity, a continued worship of the canons of New Criticism' (Beaver, 'The American Way'). The sub-text was clear: writers in Britain had fewer financial opportunities, but more freedom to explore life outside the university

---

[9] See Bennett, 'Ernest Hemingway and the Discipline of Creative Writing, Or, Shark Liver Oil'.

system, a system detrimental to creativity.[10] Despite these warnings, British writers continued to flock to America to hold creative writing fellowships. 'There are surely few aspiring young writers who would be willing to reject a *Lehrjahre* at Stanford,' wrote *The Times* in 1965.[11]

Dan Jacobson was amongst those who took up the opportunity to go to Stanford and came back to tell the tale. In *No Further West*, he described the reaction of people in England when they heard he had attended creative writing classes in America:

> Their faces sometimes positively light up with hope. Here, one can almost see them thinking, they have something American which it is altogether safe to patronize, scorn, or simply laugh at. And there is something so wistful about this English hope that I am almost sorry to have to say that I am not at all certain that it is justified.
>
> (82)

After capturing the mix of contempt and envy that the American model inspired in Britain, Jacobson listed the arguments against creative writing programmes, including the impossibility of marking creative essays or of accommodating the subject amongst scholarly disciplines:

> [W]hile undergraduates do make a habit of writing, for them to be able to use these writings as a part of their progress towards their degrees is not merely unscholarly but positively anti-scholarly, defeating the very purpose of the university, which is to train and teach its students, not to indulge them ... [F]or grown-up men to encourage them to write, and to let their writing be part of the work for which they are awarded their degrees—this is sheer indulgence by all who are involved in it, another example of that peculiarly American want of proportion when it comes to dealing with the arts or the education of their young, the American lack of respect for privacy, loneliness, and single-handed effort.
>
> (83-4)

In this line of argument, undergraduates are presented as spoilt children who lack the motivation to study difficult academic subjects and prefer to indulge in pleasurable pastimes like writing. And professors take the role of indulgent parents who encourage them instead of guiding them in the right direction. For Jacobson, this criticism of creative writing programmes ignored the fact that American students worked hard at improving their craft. They 'may be wrong in believing

---

[10] This charge was repeated more recently in D. J. Taylor's *The Prose Factory*. For example, Taylor argues that Angus Wilson's position at the University of East Anglia led to his creative decline (368). See also Taylor's article 'Angus Wilson: From Darling to Dodo'.

[11] 'Writing Schools', *The Times Literary Supplement*, 8 Apr. 1965, p. 275.

that there is nothing they cannot do if only they put their minds to it' (85), but this optimism was accompanied by determination, effort, and perseverance—a characteristic of American society that Jacobson found enthralling.

Whereas Jacobson used rational arguments to debunk clichés of creative writing as a 'soft' discipline, Malcolm Bradbury showed the funny side of these prejudices. Drawing on his own experience of the American university system, his satirical novel *Stepping Westward* (1965) centres on James Walker, a thirty-something provincial novelist affiliated with the Angry Young Men. Bored with his uneventful life, Walker accepts an invitation to be a resident writer at Benedict Arnold University, somewhere east of the Rocky Mountains. He discovers a country with seemingly endless erotic opportunities and soon writes to his wife Elaine, asking for a divorce. The informal style of seminar teaching also suits him, despite the low academic level of his students ('Some of em can hardly write their names in the dust with a stick,' Harris Bourbon, the Head of the English department, confesses [chap. 5]). But Walker's refusal to sign a loyalty oath leads to his downfall and eventual return to England.

At first sight, the plot was hardly original: as *The Times Literary Supplement* put it, 'there have been a number of tweedy natives—such as Mr Lancaster's Littlehamptons, Mr Amis's *One Fat Englishman*—shipwrecked on those far Atlantic shores, and Mr Bradbury is content to follow in the tradition of the cliché' (Beaver, 'A Familiarish Destiny'). Kingsley Amis, who had pioneered the campus novel in Britain with *Lucky Jim* (1954), was undoubtedly a major source of inspiration for Bradbury. But Bradbury's hero is not an academic or a publisher (as in *One Fat Englishman*). He is a writer both unfamiliar with the university system and with the discipline he is asked to teach. *Stepping Westward* can thus be read as the first British campus novel about a writer-in-residence.

From the start, Walker struggles to understand his new job and explain it to others. After announcing to Elaine that he has been offered a position as 'creative writing fellow,' he adds: 'I go and sit around and write creatively and they pay me seven thousand dollars for doing it.' It is true, he tells his wife, that he previously thought that university creative writing was ridiculous. But 'every man has his price. Mine happens to be six thousand nine hundred dollars' (*Stepping Westward*, chap. 1). This high salary is made possible by the funding structure of Benedict Arnold University, which partly relies on individual donors. 'There are a lot of rich people there,' a colleague tells Walker. 'And they have a writer because they are rich' (chap. 2). The financial aspect is only part of what attracts Walker to America. Eager to free himself from domestic commitments, he soon discovers that American girls are fascinated by creative writers. Julie Snowflake, a student he meets on the boat to New York, tells him that her campus is full of writers. 'A lot of girls like to sleep with them because it's honorific,' she adds (chap. 2). Although Julie says she does not share this opinion, she later has an affair with Walker.

In addition to financial and sexual opportunities, creative writers enjoy a lifestyle free from social conventions—which creates tensions with scholars at Benedict Arnold University. 'This was an age in which the literary life was a form of delinquency,' comments Harris Bourbon, 'and all kinds of questions had to be asked about the way writers acted' (*Stepping Westward*, prologue). His colleague from Business Administration suggests that former writing fellows have tarnished the image of the university. 'One man used to lie naked on the front lawn of a house he'd rented in a first-class section of town,' he tells Ralph Coolidge, the President of the university. 'My wife pointed him out to me several times. It was said that realty prices dropped substantially the whole year he was in that section. And I'm told that the man before him was not heterosexual' (prologue). After behaving badly, these writers went on to publish campus novels satirizing President Coolidge and others. But far from taking offence, Coolidge keeps a collection of these novels, which have brought publicity and increased student enrolments. Bernard Froelich, an English critic, is also convinced of the value of writing fellows, albeit for different reasons:

> He thought these writers proved the superiority of creation over criticism, a thing that English Departments quickly forgot about, and every excess they achieved, every shock they gave to Bourbon, provided Froelich with a peculiar pleasure. When they took off their clothes at freshmen mixers and seduced the wives of the faculty members down by the lake on campus, Froelich could do nothing but rejoice; this was the lesson of the wildness of the world in a community that believed in reducing art to simple order.
>
> (*Stepping Westward*, prologue)

The uneasy relationship between 'creation' and 'criticism' was a timely subject in the 1960s, leading to the separation of the Iowa Writers' Workshop from the English department. *Stepping Westward* is thus anchored in real-life debates about the place of writers in universities.

The novel also reflects contemporary concerns about the 'business of highbrow writing' expressed by Mary McCarthy and others. Indeed, Benedict Arnold University struggles to hire a competent writer-in-residence because of the competition from other institutions. As Harris Bourbon points out:

> All the leading neglected writers had been snatched up long before by Wellesley and Bennington and Kenyon and Hillesley. The only poets and novelists who were neglected were so goddam bad they had to be, and those who wouldn't have taken the appointment at any price because they believed that success was the mark of failure, or that to live on campus was a fate worse than death.
>
> (*Stepping Westward*, prologue)

Here, writers who refuse to participate in the academic market are presented as slightly ridiculous and delusional. Universities offered immense opportunities to writers, opportunities that only the most narrow-minded could reject.

Unable to hire an American writer, Benedict Arnold University turns towards Europe—but James Walker proves to be a disappointment. Froelich manages to put the blame on Bourbon for hiring Walker in the first place and becomes the new Head of the English department. In the last scene, Froelich suggests replacing the writing fellow with a literary quarterly—which would further help his own ambitions. *Stepping Westward* ends with Walker's failure to adapt to the American system and with the downsizing of his job.

Yet the message of the book is not about failure, as David Pryce-Jones rightly pointed out in his *Financial Times* review. On the contrary, it showed the impressive expansion of creative writing programmes, which had led to a tight market for talented writers and to the opening up of opportunities for British writers. Having just returned from one year teaching the subject in America, Pryce-Jones wrote that 'English authors litter the campus'. He made no difference between writers and scholars, citing the example of the historians Arnold Toynbee and Denis Brogan who had recently held visiting professorships in America. For Pryce-Jones, it was clear that Bradbury was 'speaking for the many' with his story anchored in real-life experience (16). This review is significant for two main reasons: first, it showed that for writers born in the 1930s (such as Pryce-Jones and Bradbury), spending time in an American university was no longer unusual. With the generalization of this experience, prejudices against creative writing were also disappearing—opening the door for the expansion of the discipline in Britain.

7.2 Angus Wilson, the First Writer-in-Residence in Britain?

In 1965, the year *Stepping Westward* was published, Bradbury joined the University of East Anglia—the first British university to employ a professional writer, Angus Wilson. In the early 1960s, Wilson was one of Britain's best-known literary authors. After the publication of his first novel *Hemlock and After* in 1952, he wrote *Anglo-Saxon Attitudes* (1956) and *The Middle Age of Mrs Eliot* (1958), which won him a large audience. He was also travelling extensively, lecturing (often without notes) at international events such as the PEN Club conference in Tokyo in 1957. The position that Ian Watt offered him was inspired by the American model: Wilson would teach two courses per year ('Writing and Practical Criticism' in the Autumn, and 'Dickens and Dostoevsky' in the Summer), and he would 'advise and confer with students who are interested in "creative writing" and in other ways to further the cultural aspects of the life of the University'.[12] Aware that Wilson needed to allocate time to write, Watt promised that only one day a week would be required.

---

[12] Ian Watt to Angus Wilson, 2 Jan. 1963, Box 2, Series I, Papers of Angus Wilson, UI.

The reference to the American model was explicit in UEA's press release of January 1963:

> In the United States distinguished writers—William Faulkner, Robert Frost are two examples—have long been associated with Universities, usually with the unofficial title of 'Poet in Residence' or 'Writer in Residence'. Their duties usually comprise the teaching of courses in creative writing and various more general contributions to the cultural life of the University community. This kind of appointment has not been the custom in England. One reason for this is probably that there is considerable doubt, in the first place, as to whether it is possible to teach creative writing and, in the second, as to whether, if it were so, it would be among the proper functions of a University.

Although there had been writers in universities before,[13] Wilson's appointment was presented as entirely pioneering. In this 'new kind' of position, he would be available 'to encourage and criticise the work of student writers as well as to assist in the development of the cultural life of the University'.[14] For UEA, hiring a famous writer was a publicity coup that had been decided at the highest level ('I have always hoped to associate you in some way with the University,' wrote the Vice Chancellor to Wilson).[15] It positioned the Norwich institution as an American-style university, breathing new life into a conservative academic landscape. Referring to Watt's long experience in the United States, Wilson later said: 'no English person would have asked a writer to teach at a university' (Fisher 11).

The position of writer-in-residence was so ill-defined that Wilson struggled to explain his role, presenting himself alternately as a 'visiting writer', a 'creative writing lecturer', and a 'university lecturer'.[16] One source of confusion was the nature of his contract with the university: in the United States, writers-in-residence were generally hired for a short period of time, whereas Wilson's post at UEA was for three years in the first instance. In practice, Wilson was hired as a faculty member with an expertise in creative writing. In a letter to *The TLS*, the writer Vincent Brome praised this appointment as an example of 'cross-fertilization between the academic and writer'. And, he added:

> Shouldn't we, for once, sink our snobbery, and imitate American academic life to the extent of creating a number of Resident Writers or Fellowships which would

---

[13] 'Obviously there have been hundreds of writers at Oxbridge many supported by prizes and fellowships and ordinary institutional practice—it is a history that stretches all the way back to [Alfred, Lord] Tennyson, even further to [Andrew] Marvell ...' Giles Foden, Email to author, 17 Aug. 2016.
[14] UEA press release (first draft), 25 Jan. 1963, Box 2, Series I, Papers of Angus Wilson, UI.
[15] Frank Thistlethwaite to Angus Wilson, 22 Jan. 1963, Box 2, Series I, Papers of Angus Wilson, UI.
[16] 'Londoner's Diary', *Evening Standard*, 31 Jan. 1963, n.p.; Wilson to Mr Van Gijn, 28 Mar. 1963, Box 2, Series I, Papers of Angus Wilson, UI; Wilson, Reasons for accepting post as a lecturer in literature at the University of East Anglia, Notebook 121, Box 15, Series III, Papers of Angus Wilson, UI.

> help to prevent the more remote exploration of dead writers from fossilizing too much of literary research, and encourage the creative writer today?
>
> (415)

Like Wilson, Brome thought that the British had no reason to look down on the American academic system, a system that encouraged both literary creation and scholarship.

However, Wilson did not share Brome's contempt for the study of dead writers. In a 1964 interview, he explained that he considered himself an academic, and that he had 'all his ideas about literature, about Dickens, Jane Austen and so on, clear and projected in his head, ready to be projected to an audience'. In the same interview, he rejected the entire discipline of creative writing. 'How *can* you teach "creative writing" as a subject?' he asked (Wade 28). Wilson's ambivalence about this discipline stems from his desire to be seen as a genuine professor, rather than an invited writer with no real academic credentials. Indeed, his long-standing academic ambitions largely explain why he accepted UEA's offer, signing a deal that was probably more beneficial to the university than to himself. In 1963, at the height of his fame, Wilson did not need the security of an academic post that was far from lucrative (he was appointed at the Lecturer level, on a part-time basis). At the financial level, then, he arguably had more to lose than to gain: the time spent on campus could have been invested in writing commissioned articles or working on a novel. By joining UEA, he would make the new university profit from his celebrity without benefiting from a generous compensation or a prestigious title.

So why did Wilson accept UEA's offer? His academic ambitions dated back to his student days, as he explained in an unpublished document that I discovered in his papers at the University of Iowa. He wrote that when he left the University of Oxford in 1935, he wanted to be an actor but he was told that he was 'too scholarly'. He then said he wanted to be a University lecturer—for this he was told that he was 'not scholarly enough'. After a career at the British Museum library, he gave up his civil service post in 1955 to write full time:

> Since then, as a free-lance writer, my life has continuously expanded—stage plays, television plays, above all lecturing and travel. Lecturing and playwriting have fulfilled my frustrated wish to be an actor. Now, with my weekly visits to the University at Norwich, my other frustrated ambition will be fulfilled.

Wilson was attracted to academic life in general, and to UEA in particular. He gave two specific reasons why he was so excited to join this institution. New universities prepared young people 'for life in any profession or business', rather than limiting themselves to the transmission of scholarship. This broad social mission entailed the reinvention of academic disciplines, including literary studies. 'I can give an extra dimension, a fresh vitality to the literary studies of the young men and women whom I shall teach,' wrote Wilson. And he added: 'At least I shall never let them forget that great literature has come out of the joys and agonies of human beings. If, too, there are by lucky chance some students with a real gift for imaginative writing, my experience will be at their service.' But Wilson's motives were not entirely altruistic. The second reason that made UEA attractive was the promise to gain access to students radically different from the young people Wilson had met at Oxford in the 1930s. Their worldviews and social backgrounds would open up new territories and provide materials for his fiction.

This previously unknown document shows that Wilson carefully weighted the pros and the cons of accepting the Norwich post. He was aware that this appointment would have an important impact on his life, but he was prepared to accept the consequences. 'As to changing my way of life, I seem to have done nothing else since I entered middle age,' he wrote.[17] At the age of fifty, he was ready for a new career, a career that would put him in contact with students such as the young Rose Tremain.

The course that Wilson taught in the first semester, 'Writing and Practical Criticism', included a creative assignment: students had to read George Orwell's 'Shooting an Elephant' and write an analogous autobiographical experience.[18] The mark for this essay then counted towards the final grade for the module. This programme had been designed not by Wilson, but by the module leader Ian Watt. Interestingly, even scholars who were teaching on this course had to mark one creative writing essay. Watt's module emphasized the relationship between creative and critical work, and encouraged students to put themselves in the shoes of writers. Creative writing was already taught and assessed in the 1960s, long before UEA launched the first MA in creative writing in 1970.

7.3 The Henfield Fellowship at UEA

When he talked about the Henfield fellowship, Malcolm Bradbury presented it as an activity associated with the new postgraduate programme in creative writing. 'I am, of course, very keen that the Fellowship should have the function of promoting both writing in the university and the writer appointed,' wrote Bradbury to Wilson in April 1971, shortly after the appointment of the first holder of the fellowship Alan Burns.[19] The satirical magazine *Punch* presented Burns as 'the first ever "writer in residence" at an English school'. Although Wilson's hiring had been

---

[17] Wilson, Reasons for accepting post as a lecturer in literature at the University of East Anglia, Notebook 121, Box 15, Series III, Papers of Angus Wilson, UI.
[18] 'Writing and Practical Criticism' syllabus, 1963, Box 1, Series VI, Papers of Angus Wilson, UI.
[19] Bradbury to Wilson, 2 Apr. 1971, Box 1, Series VI, Papers of Angus Wilson, UI. Underline in original.

described in similar terms seven years earlier, UEA was once again placed at the centre of the institutionalization of creative writing.

At a time when the role of the writer-in-residence was still not clearly defined, *Punch* suggested two options:

> If he plunges straight into helping the children to improve their masterpieces, teaching them how to produce vastly original novels and plays, and telling them all about the best of contemporary literature then that's that.
>
> But if he has the sense to restrict himself to telling his pupils which magazines pay the best rates, how to lunch an editor, where to find the best accountants, when to snap up film rights and how to meet the producers and publishers that matter—and anyone who's ever listened to writers knows that all they ever talk about is money, influence and the drivel written by their rivals—then he's the man for us.[20]

It is difficult to imagine a writer like Alan Burns sharing tips on the most lucrative magazines. After publishing his first book in 1961, Burns was awarded Arts Council maintenance grants for two years followed by a bursary in 1969. He had a reputation as a difficult writer, whose literary experimentations had earned him the respect of his peers without widening his audience. 'The chances are you've never heard of him,' wrote *The Guardian* in 1970. In the same article, Angus Wilson described him as 'one of the two or three most interesting new novelists working in England' (Hall). In short, Burns was at the far end of what Pierre Bourdieu has called 'the field of restricted production' (*The Field of Cultural Production* 39). A former lawyer, Burns had 'substantial economic and social capital' that allowed him to choose and remain in an economically risky position in the literary field (67).

With several novels and a solid reputation, Burns seemed an excellent candidate for the Henfield fellowship. As Bradbury wrote to Cox, they were looking for 'someone distinguished but also capable of talking usefully to students, and with a particular project of his own that he wants to get on with'. At UEA, Burns was expected to give lectures and to teach seminar groups. 'We do draw the writer into some of our formal teaching,' declared Bradbury, 'but this is because we run a Creative Writing MA. We encourage him informally to do the same at under-graduate level.'[21] Burns was housed on campus, which gave him opportunities to keep in touch with students. In particular, he helped found and edit a student magazine of creative writing, to which the young Ian McEwan contributed.

The brief life of *Amazing* magazine was described by Robert Stuart Short in another UEA publication, *Kett*. Short saw its failure as a symptom of malaise in

---

[20] 'Lesson One: Count The Change', *Punch*, 13 Dec. 1972, p. 863.
[21] Bradbury to Cox, 10 Nov. 1972, GB 133 CQA1/1/116, CQ.

the university, plagued by sit-ins and disruptions of exams. As he pointed out, the *Amazing* magazine started with a good idea: to build up 'a truly original figuration' of life at UEA by means of anonymously contributed fragments of wisdom and description—'letters to relatives—cuttings from official and unofficial documents—parts of essays and teachers' comments—snatches of overheard conversation recorded on tape in common-rooms, seminars or on building sites—graffiti—narratives of dreams provoked by the locale'. To collect these fragments, the magazine's editors set up large post boxes around the campus, but when the boxes were broken open they were found to contain only traditional poems and short stories. As Short wrote: 'The general will was missing. The Old Adam of Romantic individualism had reasserted itself. The squads of anonymous collectors broke ranks. Soon, everyone was asking to see his signature at the head of his particular bit or piece.'[22]

The first and only issue of *Amazing* magazine can now be found in the UEA archive. The top leaf of this stapled publication is a copy of a letter addressed to the University Authorities. 'It has come to our attention that certain individuals within the University community are engaged in activities which may have a deleterious effect on general morale and good order,' declared the letter before asking the authorities to keep their ears to the ground to gather information on this 'so-called Surprising Magazine'. As the signature 'Affectionately, "Caligari"' made clear, the letter was in fact a parody, mocking the fear of student radicals and their disrupting effect on the university system. The content of the magazine was influenced by the counterculture of the time. It included a pleasure guide to UEA by Robert Short, and a short story, 'Cocker at the Theatre', by McEwan—which described an audition for a sex scene in graphic detail.[23]

Burns' involvement in the magazine does not mean he endorsed its content. In fact, during a telephone interview, McEwan told me that Burns 'wasn't very keen on [his] stories', but nevertheless gave him 'a lot of encouragement'.[24] Burns also suggested he read Beckett's work after noticing that McEwan seemed 'unconsciously influenced' by the author of *Molloy* (McEwan, *Class Work* xviii). Thirty years later, Burns was described in McEwan's novel *Sweet Tooth* as 'by far the best experimentalist in the country' (184). The enduring relationship between Burns and McEwan highlights the success of the first Henfield fellowship—a fellowship that aimed to serve both the writer and the students interested in writing. By contributing to *Amazing* magazine, a publication playfully positioned against the 'university authorities', Burns had shown that the opposition between students and staff could be bridged through dialogue and common projects.

[22] Qtd in 'The State of English, IV: University of East Anglia', *The Times Literary Supplement*, 3 Mar. 1972, p. 251.
[23] *Amazing* magazine, Student newspapers, UEA collection. 'Cocker at the Theatre' was included in McEwan's collection of short stories *First Love, Last Rites* (1975).
[24] Ian McEwan, Interview by author, 9 Mar. 2015, via telephone.

Yet, some UEA students felt that the fellowship did not serve its purpose. In a 1973 editorial article in the student magazine *Scorpion*, Ron Binns argued that 'the impact of the Fellowships on student writing has, I suspect, been slight'. The fellows were only on campus for one term, and their involvement with students was limited. *Amazing* magazine folded after one issue and the 1972 fellow, Anthony Thwaite, held only two literary evenings and initiated a group poem. For Binns, it was time to ask questions about the appointments and conditions of these awards:

> Is it satisfactory that the Fellow should be chosen by two senior members of faculty without any consultation of the opinions of students who are, after all, the supposed benefactors of the appointment? And is it satisfactory that the workload associated with the Fellowship seems to end with the suggestion that aspiring writers drop by for a coffee and a chat? Would it not be reasonable to make it a condition of the award that the selected writer give some lectures on the current state of British writing in whichever mode he specialises (the novel, the poem, or the play?).

Being involved in the selection of the teaching staff had long been a demand of student activists, a demand that seemed unreasonable to many academics (as 'Fight for Education', the first Black Paper, makes clear). Increasing the number of contact hours with students was another common demand. Binns's article went further and asked for the establishment of an age limit 'to ensure that the writer is not so established as to be writing in, say the style of the 1950s'. This was a lightly veiled attack on Wilson, who was associated with the social realism of the immediate post-war period. For Binns, it was time to appoint 'a relatively young radical post-modernist writer (Essex managed to get Tom Raworth) capable of inspiring, rather than someone solidly successful who may be tempted to treat the award as providing a peaceful summer vacation at UEA'.[25]

If Bradbury heard about these complaints, he simply ignored them. In 'Decline and Fall of the University Idea' (his contribution to the first Black Paper, signed 'B.'), he denounced the 'extremist student lobby' determined to defend '*their* interests' rather than those of the university community (62, 61). He particularly resented the rhetoric of opposition between the students and the faculty, 'who are given the status of a managerial class' (61). For Bradbury, this narrative of class war between staff/managers and students/workers risked transforming the university into a 'Che Guevara Institute of Strategic Studies' (62). Asked to appoint a young radical writer-in-residence, Bradbury chose the Guyanese writer Wilson Harris, one of the oldest Henfield fellows ever (he was fifty-three years of age when he took up the fellowship). From 1971 to 1977, the median age of fellows was forty-one. Bradbury wanted to appoint writers with a solid track record of publications, and he did not hesitate to select his own friends. In *Lives in Writing*, David Lodge

---

[25] Ron Binns, Introduction, *Scorpion* 2, Summer 1973, Student newspapers, UEA collection.

described his 1977 Henfield fellowship as a pleasant way to spend the summer, writing and socializing with the Bradburys. One of his duties was to invite writers to come and talk about their work, and he used this opportunity to meet the playwright Simon Gray (chap. Simon Gray's Diaries).

Former Henfield fellows often kept close ties with the UEA community. The 1972 fellow Anthony Thwaite taught English and American studies for one term each year from 1973 to 1979.[26] And following the Booker Prize award to Kazuo Ishiguro and the attacks against the 'UEA mafia', Maggie Gee wrote to *The Sunday Times*: 'I was never a student at UEA, though as a published novelist ten years ago I did hold a three-month Henfield fellowship there.'[27] The successful careers of Henfield alumni reinforced the perception that Norwich was now an important literary centre, a sort of British Iowa that could make and break reputations.

7.4 Funding a Writer at the Poetry Centre, University of Manchester

While the establishment of a writer-in-residence contributed to the institutionalization of creative writing at UEA, it was an integral part of Brian Cox's plan to develop the Poetry Centre at the University of Manchester. Like Bradbury, Cox had first-hand experience of the American educational system. In 1965, after returning from an academic trip in the States, he wrote to Richard Hoggart at the University of Birmingham, asking for a reference. After more than ten years working at Hull, Cox's experience in the US had made him realize it was time to move on. Hoggart wrote that this kind of disillusion with the British system was common: 'David Lodge will be coming back in about a week from his year on a Harkness Fellowship. I expect he will have many of the same feelings as you do (though Birmingham certainly does have something of the air of possibility and experiment which you get in America; and it's not so generally damp in its atmospheres as Hull).'[28]

At the University of Manchester, which he joined as a professor in 1966, Cox found the opportunities he was looking for. The controversy that followed the publication of the first Black Paper in 1969 gave him a national platform, and shortly after, he set up the Poetry Centre thanks to a grant from the Arts Council. At a time when many London publishing houses were neglecting their poetry lists, the Poetry Centre offered a chance to put Manchester on the literary map. It organized large poetry readings, published *Critical Quarterly*, and started building up a manuscript collection (which can now be consulted at the John Rylands Library).

---

[26] Anthony Thwaite, Interview by Sarah O'Reilly, 29 Aug. 2008, Authors' Lives, British Library.
[27] *The Sunday Times*, 24 May 1992, p. 7.
[28] Richard Hoggart to Brian Cox, 20 Sept. 1965, GB 133 COX6/10, COX.

And in 1972, Cox was awarded funding to bring the twenty-five-year-old poet Michael Schmidt and his press, Carcanet, to Manchester.

Schmidt's move from Oxford to Manchester highlights the new opportunities that were opening up for writers outside traditional literary centres. Schmidt came from a wealthy, cosmopolitan family: both his parents were American, but he had grown up in Mexico and later identified as Mexican. After studying at Harvard for one year, he transferred to Oxford where he became president of the Poetry Society. In 1968, he took over a student magazine called Carcanet, which had been set up six years earlier to link Oxford and Cambridge writings (Jaillant, "Invisible Poetry"). The contacts Schmidt made at the Poetry Society allowed him to expand the reach of the magazine well beyond the student community. In 1969, he decided to produce a series of seven pamphlets dedicated to the work of poets based in Oxford, and he went on to publish books under the Carcanet imprint. Schmidt energetically promoted his new enterprise and made new contacts outside Oxford. Following the recommendation of the poet Gareth Reeves, he sent a copy of the Carcanet magazine to Cox and told him about his projects of issuing bound and numbered copies of the works of new poets.[29] Cox then accepted two of Schmidt's poems for publication in *Critical Quarterly*[30] and the two men met in person at the Literature panel of the Arts Council.

For Cox, the prospect of attracting a young entrepreneurial poet to Manchester was appealing, and he started exploring funding options. After asking for more information about the Calouste Gulbenkian Foundation, Cox sent them an application for a three-year grant, with the overall aim of developing the poetry and cultural scene in the North of England. If Carcanet Press joined the Poetry Centre, Cox wrote in his proposal, 'we should become one of the most exciting poetry centres in the English speaking world, and our work would have a high international reputation. The Arts in the North would benefit enormously and we already have backing from the North West Arts Association.'[31] Schmidt also insisted on the opportunities that the North offered. 'I think Manchester is ripe for our sort of revolution—far riper than staid Oxford or unanchored London,' he wrote to Cox. 'The bomb sites I am sure will soon put forth blossom and houses.'[32] This imagery of revolution and war highlights Schmidt's positioning in the avant-garde, at the forefront of new poetic developments.

Unlike the Henfield fellow at UEA, Manchester's writer-in-residence was to be treated as a permanent member of staff. The Calouste Gulbenkian Foundation accepted to fund a three-year writing fellowship for Schmidt (from 1972 to 1975), with the understanding that funding would thereafter come from the Arts Council's Compton Bequest.[33] In his correspondence, Cox also stated that

---

[29] Schmidt to Brian Cox, 1 Oct. 1969, GB 133 COX8, COX.
[30] Cox to Schmidt, 25 Jan. 1971, GB 133 CQA1/1/116, CQ.
[31] Cox to A. Wraight, 7 Mar. 1972, GB 133 COX5/1, COX.
[32] Schmidt to Cox, 12 Feb. 1972, GB 133 CQA1/1/116, CQ.
[33] Cox to Wraight, 21 Apr. 1972, GB 133 COX5/1, COX.

he wanted Schmidt to stay at Manchester on a long-term basis.[34] And while UEA expected the fellow to teach in the creative writing programme, Cox insisted that Schmidt concentrate on his own work, including managing the Carcanet Press. As Schmidt told me:

> I was a half time appointment, and Brian said: you do not want to attend departmental meetings, he kept trying to protect me against all the things that make universities horrible. But after a while, I insisted I wanted to go to the meetings, and I insisted I wanted to be full time …[35]

In particular, Schmidt was eager to do some teaching. As he wrote to Cox in 1972, he had been promised tutorial teaching at Oxford, but it never materialized.[36] At Manchester, he taught various courses, including a course on recent poetry, and he also saw students to discuss their own writing.[37] But the phrase 'creative writing' was not even mentioned in Schmidt's and Cox's correspondence until 1976 and the appointment of an Arts Council-funded writing fellow.

At the time when Paul Mills took up this creative writing fellowship at Manchester, the discipline was not fully institutionalized. The new fellow taught on a contemporary poetry course, giving lectures and leading seminars. He also started an informal discussion group for students interested in writing and a 'surgery' where they could come and talk about their own work.[38] When the Arts Council refused to renew the fellowship for a second year due to financial constraints, Michael Schmidt took over the teaching of the creative writing course. However, it seems that students were not formally assessed for their creative work until the late 1980s, when Schmidt started giving undergraduate workshops with the novelist Richard Francis (they set up the MA in Novel Writing in 1993).[39] The late emergence of creative writing at Manchester shows that red-brick universities were much more reluctant to institutionalize the discipline than newer universities such as UEA or Lancaster.

7.5 The Arts Council and the Democratization of the Writer-in-Residence

From the mid-1970s, the Arts Council funded creative writing fellowships in Universities, Polytechnics, and Colleges of Education. By the end of the decade, these schemes were so widespread that the model of the writer-in-residence was parodied on television. In 'I'd Turn Back If I Were You, Dorothy', the novelist and

---

[34] Cox to the Bursar, 29 Aug. 1972 and Cox to F. J. L. Duncan, 28 Aug. 1975, GB 133 COX5/1, COX.
[35] Schmidt, Interview by author, 24 Nov. 2015, Manchester.
[36] Schmidt to Cox, 16 Feb. 1972, GB 133 CQA1/1/116, CQ.
[37] Cox to C. Dupre (International PEN), 1 Oct. 1975, GB 133 COX5/1, COX.
[38] Paul Mills, Application for renewal of Creative Writing fellowship, 1977, GB 133 COX5/1, COX.
[39] Richard Francis, 'About Me', https://richardfrancis.wordpress.com/about/. Accessed 30 Apr. 2021.

playwright Jack Trevor Story satirized his temporary hometown, Milton Keynes. Installed on an Arts Council fellowship, his task was to stimulate creative activity, represented in the programme by a lorry-driver poet (introduced as the Poet-Lorry-ette of Milton Keynes).[40]

This programme of creative writing fellowships finds its origin in the 'Writers in Schools' scheme that the Arts Council developed in the late 1960s. Leonard Clark, who suggested the idea to the Literature panel in 1967, wanted to encourage artists to share their creative practice with children. The sculptor Henry Moore had once gone, at his suggestion, into a school in Castleford, Yorkshire. Moore gave the children each a lump of clay and said: 'we won't talk about it, we will do it.' This visit, said Clark, had left a lasting mark on the art of that school.[41] In his proposal, Clark suggested a national plan of funding and the creation of 'a register of writers who would be willing to give their services in the areas where they live and work'.[42]

Clark's proposal fitted well with the political climate of the time. Jennie Lee, Minister for the Arts in the Labour government of Harold Wilson, told a 'school of the future' conference organized by the National Union of Teachers that it was becoming essential to bring the activities of the world into the classroom. She added that the Arts Council proposal would make it easier for schools to arrange for authors and poets to come and read their work, or talk about it.[43] Yet, not everyone was enthusiastic. One member of the Literature panel reportedly expressed the view that 'creative writers have nothing to pass on to children and are not qualified to go into schools'.[44] In a letter to Angus Wilson (who was chairing the panel), the novelist William Sansom wrote that the writers selected would have to speak well and be 'reasonably sober'.[45] Despite these misgivings, the scheme was approved at the beginning of 1968.

In its original form, the Writers in Schools scheme funded one-off visits by writers into educational institutions, rather than longer residences. Eric W. White, the Literature Director of the Arts Council, sent a circular to a number of writers (including Kingsley Amis) to explain the scheme. But White's bureaucratic tone, as well as the low fees, infuriated Amis. In his letter to White, which was published in the *Spectator*, he declared:

---

[40] 'I'd Turn Back If I Were You, Dorothy', directed by Patricia Ingram, ATV, 1977.
[41] Michael A. Walker to Eric White, 10 Nov. 1967, Box 7, ACGB/60/65 Writers in Schools Scheme: General 1969-1985, Arts Council of Great Britain, V&A.
[42] Leonard Clark, 'Writers in Schools' Memorandum, 16 Nov. 1967, Box 7, ACGB/60/65 Writers in Schools Scheme: General 1969-1985, V&A.
[43] 'Arts Not the Icing', *Yorkshire Post*, Box 7, ACGB/60/65 Writers in Schools Scheme: General 1969-1985, V&A.
[44] Qtd in Sue Harries, 'Writers in Schools: A Report on the Scheme in England up to 1983', p. 15. Box 5, ACGB/60/65 Writers in Schools Scheme: General 1969-1985, V&A.
[45] William Sansom to Angus Wilson, 22 May 1968, Box 7, ACGB/60/65 Writers in Schools Scheme: General 1969-1985, V&A.

The Arts Council is, or should be, concerned with improving the conditions of art, and hence the conditions of artists, rather than with things like providing a 'service' to schools and colleges. A writer is not an electrician or a plumber, and it is particularly culpable in people like you to regard him as such.

For Amis, the fee of £15 was 'far less than a reputable journal would pay for a review or article of equivalent length, which can be written without having to go anywhere'.[46] However, other less-established writers pointed out that this fee was higher than what they had previously accepted for similar talks. Some of these writers later complained that they never received any engagements from schools. 'Since I can think of no reason why I should be uniquely excluded,' wrote one disgruntled author, 'the huge majority of engagements must go to a tiny minority of well-known writers.'[47] By treating all writers in the same way, the Arts Council risked angering those with an established reputation but also less-known authors.

For the Creative Writing Fellowships scheme launched in 1974, the Arts Council dealt mostly with institutions, and made no suggestion of writers that might be available. If the proposal was successful, the institution would then select a writer for a residence of one year (renewable for another year). A representative of the Literature panel was generally present during the interviews. In 1976, for example, C. J. Driver represented the Council in the selection of Creative Writing Fellows at both Wolverhampton Polytechnic and York University. Both interviews raised interesting questions about the purpose of the fellowships, declared Driver:

How does one balance the needs or desires of the institution and the needs of the writers? Does one choose a Fellow because he/one looks like contributing to the institution, or because the institution may help the writer? To be particular, can one choose a writer who may have considerable promise but who seems very inarticulate in speech and likely not to get to know many students? Does one choose an attractive and lively writer than an introspective and maybe 'skinless' one, even though one has a hunch that the latter has great promise.[48]

Aware that a creative writing fellow was expected to be communicative and sociable, Jack Trevor Story described playing the role of the lively writer, and then disappointing people who caught him off guard (80). Introversion, he wrote, was the natural attribute of productive writers. Only those who preferred to talk about writing flourished as creative writing fellows (81). Catching Story in a moment

---

[46] Kingsley Amis to Eric White, 11 May 1969, Box 1, ACGB/60/65 Writers in Schools Scheme: General 1969–1985, V&A.
[47] Paul Ableman to Josephine Falk, 5 July 1973, Box 2, ACGB/60/65 Writers in Schools Scheme: General 1969–1985, V&A.
[48] C. J. Driver, Report on the selection of creative writing fellows, 30 July 1976, File 1, ACGB/60/5 Creative Writing Fellowships: General Correspondence 1973–1981, V&A.

when he is trying to write, someone tells him: 'I've found you another novelist. She's eighty-five and she's got six books that have never been read by anybody. She used to be a dry cleaner' (80). Behind the comedy lies the hard reality: advising those would-be writers is a waste of time, time that could be spent actually writing.

While Jack Trevor Story presented his Arts Council-funded position as detrimental to his work, Angela Carter had a more positive view of the fellowship. Based at the University of Sheffield from 1976 to 1978, she wrote a glowing report at the end of her first year. 'I've ... been able to make some experiments with the methodology of actually teaching creative writing, with very hopeful results,' she declared, 'and I shall pursue this further next year.'[49] She also benefited from her conversations with the folklore group in the English Department at Sheffield and wrote her short story 'The Company of Wolves' (a retelling of the Little Red Riding Hood tale). Kenneth Graham, the Head of department, was also pleased with Carter's contribution: 'Her own interests in the Gothic led to her full involvement in one of our Special Subjects for third year students, "The Gothic Imagination".'[50] In short, Carter brought her own creative expertise to the department while also benefiting from her colleagues' and students' existing interests. The examples of Carter and Story show that the writers-in-residence supported by the Arts Council were not a coherent group. While Carter worked at a red-brick university, Story was expected to advise working-class people who had little hope of being published.

Whereas Jack Trevor Story satirized his advisees, others mocked writers-in-residence who contributed little to their host institutions. In 1975, *Punch* published a series of cartoons of imaginary writers-in-residence at a public library. 'Cyril St John Dizzard', for example, refused to give a poetry reading 'on the grounds that this would constitute a public performance from which no benefit would flow to the poet involved'. Dizzard then consented under pressure 'to read out to three old-age pensioners a chapter from an out-of-copyright handbook on the care and maintenance of hot-air balloons' (Figure 7.1). This satire of selfish writers-in-residence shows that the position was now widely spread across the country, thanks to funding from the Arts Council and other organizations (including the Greater London Arts Association).

When the Arts Council schemes were suspended in the 1980s in a context of drastic budget restrictions, many criticized the move as an attack on the poor and less educated. One writer-in-residence declared:

> Kids would come wandering into my office, wanting to know could I help write their holiday notes, their job applications, college applications. I met apprentices

---

[49] Angela Carter to Josephine Falk, 30 June 1977, ACGB/60/9 Creative Writing Fellowships Reports 1976–1980, V&A.

[50] Kenneth Graham to Falk, 22 Feb. 1979, ACGB/60/9 Creative Writing Fellowships Reports 1976–1980, V&A.

on day release, less able (usually socially deprived) students, people who had their eyes set firmly on university. In all of these situations I was introduced not as an extra lecturer but as a novelist, not as an expert in English Lit, but as a living, working writer.

(Milne)

The writer-in-residence model developed by the Arts Council also benefited authors excluded from literary circles. 'My own horizons are being expanded in a remarkable way,' wrote Ursula Fanthorpe about her fellowship at St Martin's

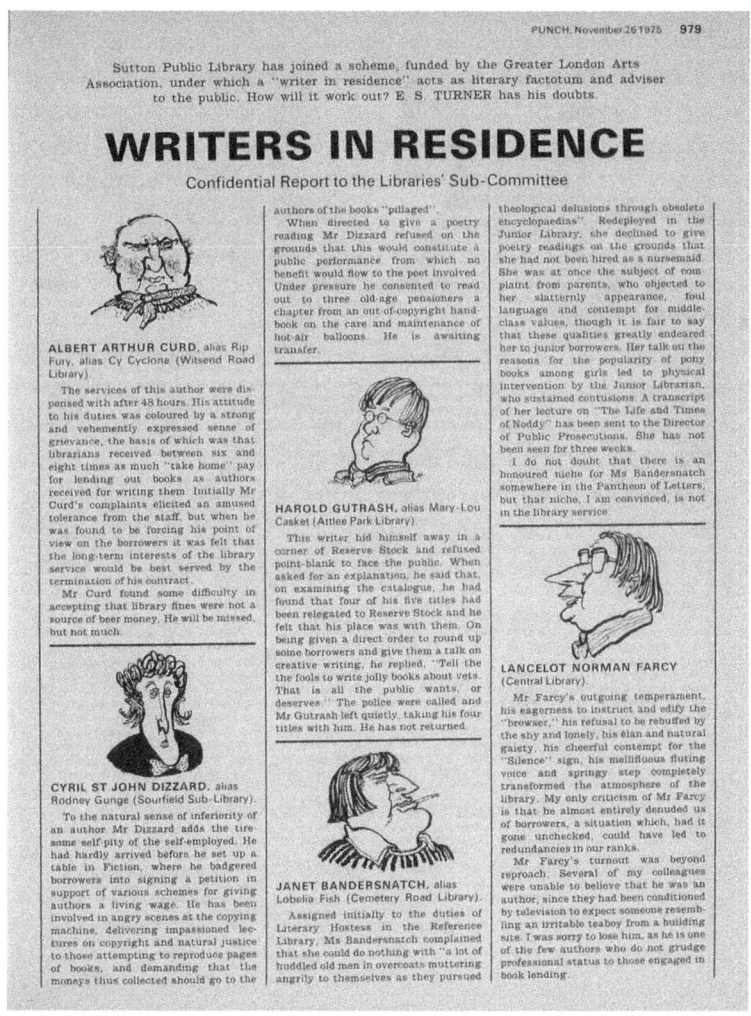

Fig. 7.1 E. S. Turner, 'Writers in Residence', *Punch*, 26 Nov. 1975.
Credit: *Punch* Cartoon Library/TopFoto.

College in Lancaster. 'Normally I work from 9 to 5 in a Bristol hospital as a clerk, then travel 20 miles home to Wotton-under-Edge,' she added. Being treated as a writer was, for Fanthorpe, an extraordinary experience: 'At work I'm the receptionist.'[51] This warm letter boosted the morale of Arts Council staff, who had been discouraged by the decision to reduce support for literary activities.[52] Fanthorpe's fellowship was indeed a success story: already in her fifties when she took up this position, she was recognized late in life (amongst many honours, she was the first woman to be nominated as Oxford professor of poetry in 1994).

But on the other side of the debate, the 'progressive' model of the writer-in-residence seemed a waste of public funds. Particularly damaging were the criticisms from within. Jack Trevor Story's television programme 'I'd Turn Back If I Were You, Dorothy' reached the mass market, raising questions about the need for a writer-in-residence scheme. The *Daily Mail* presented his account of Milton Keynes as a 'horror story'.[53] Despite his poverty (he had recently gone bankrupt), Story claimed that the only way to be completely free was to reject funding from the Arts Council and similar institutions. Genuine writers had to survive in the marketplace, he argued.

To a large extent, the 1980s saw the triumph of an 'American' conception of the writer-in-residence, a view pioneered by UEA twenty years before, a view that put excellence and competition above democratization. Lorry-driver poets and student radicals were on their way out. That does not mean that writers disappeared from schools and libraries: the rapid expansion of the discipline of creative writing in the 1990s opened up new opportunities for authors, including in the primary and secondary education system. Like the vacuum cleaner and the hoola hoop, the writer-in-residence was an American invention that took root in Britain.

---

[51] Ursula Fanthorpe to Josephine Falk, 9 Jan. 1985, ACGB/60/1 Writers-in-Residence Scheme: Correspondence with Host Institutions 10 boxes 1974–1985, V&A.

[52] Falk to Fanthorpe, 23 Jan. 1985, ACGB/60/1 Writers-in-Residence Scheme: Correspondence with Host Institutions 10 boxes 1974–1985, V&A.

[53] 'Jack's Horror Story', *Daily Mail*, 8 Aug. 1977, p. 19.

8
Kazuo Ishiguro
'The First Product of a Creative Writing Course to Win the Nobel'

Creative writing programmes have continued to position themselves on the margins of the literary field—despite obvious signs that they are now part of the 'system'. On 5 October 2017, Kazuo Ishiguro learnt that he had won the Nobel Prize for Literature. The laureate seemed as surprised as everyone else. 'I thought it was a hoax,' he said.[1] Born in Japan in 1954, the British novelist had not been amongst the favourites. When *The Guardian* opened its live feed at 10:47 BST, the reporters gave a short profile of potential winners: the Kenyan writer Ngugi wa Thiong'o; the Korean poet Ko Un; the Chinese novelist and short story writer Yan Lianke; the Japanese novelist Haruki Murakami. Their ages ranged from fifty-nine to eighty-four years (the Nobel rarely goes to anyone younger), and they came from Africa and Asia. The last four prizes had gone to Westerners—including the American musician and songwriter Bob Dylan in 2016—and many thought that the Nobel Committee would now turn to the non-Western world. But the favourite was a woman, the 77-year-old Canadian novelist Margaret Atwood, 'arguably the most famous name on this year's list'. The betting company Ladbrokes gave her 7/2 odds (Cain).

One of the first things that Kazuo Ishiguro did after winning the prize was to apologize. 'I apologise to Margaret Atwood that it's not her getting this prize. I genuinely thought she would win it very soon. I never for a moment thought I would. I always thought it would be Margaret Atwood very soon; and I still think that, I still hope that,' Ishiguro told the Canadian *Globe and Mail* (Lederman). After the apologies came the gratitude. In his lecture delivered in Stockholm, Ishiguro situates the start of his writing career in 1979, when he began 'a one-year postgraduate Creative Writing course at the University of East Anglia'. The choice of words is important here: unlike Ian McEwan, Ishiguro explicitly presents himself as the product of the Program Era. The story of his transformation into a professional writer relies on clichés. First, there is the room in Buxton, a small village in

---

[1] '"I thought it was a hoax": Kazuo Ishiguro on Winning the Nobel Prize in Literature', *The Guardian*, 5 Oct. 2017.

Norfolk where he was living during his time at the University of East Anglia. 'My little room was not unlike the classic writer's garret,' Ishiguro says. Then come the mentors. Like so many writers in the past, Ishiguro learnt from already established professionals. But the novelty of his story comes from the setting, which takes place in a university, within the context of a creative writing course. About his early attempts to write about Japan, Ishiguro declares: 'I remain to this day profoundly grateful to my fellow students, to my tutors, Malcolm Bradbury and Angela Carter, and to the novelist Paul Bailey—that year the university's writer-in-residence—for their determinedly encouraging response' (*My Twentieth Century Evening—and Other Small Breakthroughs*). It is thanks to his first two Japanese-inspired novels—*A Pale View of Hills* and *An Artist of the Floating World*—that Ishiguro established his reputation. Without UEA, Ishiguro would not be the writer we know today.

How could such an original writer emerge from a creative writing programme? After all, creative writing has long been derided as factory-like, producing standardized prose and bland poetry for a limited audience of academic peers and highbrow readers. And why did the newly en-Nobeled Ishiguro give such a promotional boost to the University of East Anglia? He could have thanked individuals (Malcolm Bradbury, Angela Carter) without referring to the institutional context of the university. Instead, he chose to transfer his immense cultural capital to a university that is little known outside Britain. 'Well: it's not every day that you get mentioned in a Nobel Prize acceptance speech!' tweeted Literature@UEA—the Twitter account of the School of Literature, Drama and Creative Writing.[2]

The day the award was announced, the British-born critic James Wood wrote in *The New Yorker*: 'a graduate of the University of East Anglia's creative-writing school, where he was a student of Angela Carter, [Ishiguro] may well be the first product of a creative-writing course to win the Nobel' ('Kazuo Ishiguro'). Ishiguro may or may not have read this article. What is certain is that a few weeks later, in his speech in Stockholm, he proudly endorsed his university training. In doing so, he promoted a model of a literary career that has long been resisted in Europe.

This Anglo-American model of creative writing education is at odds with the European way traditionally followed by the Nobel Prize Committee. It would be difficult to imagine the French writer Patrick Modiano (who won the Nobel in 2014) emerging from a creative writing course—a discipline that did not exist in France until very recently and is still somewhat controversial. Shortly before the award to Modiano was announced, Swedish Academy member Horace Engdahl criticized the grants and financial support that universities and other institutions give to writers. 'Even though I understand the temptation, I think it cuts writers off from society, and creates an unhealthy link with institutions,' he told the French newspaper *La Croix*. 'Previously, writers would work as taxi drivers, clerks, secretaries and waiters to make a living. Samuel Beckett and many others lived like this.

---

[2] Tweet, Literature@UEA, 8 Dec. 2017.

It was hard—but they fed themselves, from a literary perspective.'[3] Yet, three years later, the new Nobel laureate proudly endorsed his link with an academic institution. The Japanese material that Ishiguro used for his first two novels did not come from his professional experience as a social worker. Instead, he relied on memories from his childhood and gave them form through practice and the encouragement given by his tutors and fellow students at UEA. Far from cutting writers from the real life, universities can produce leading writers, critically acclaimed and commercially successful—a fact that the Swedish Academy recognized with the 2017 prize.

Following the work of James English and Pierre Bourdieu, I see the Nobel Prize as a 'competitive struggle' that consecrates writers who embody a particular literary model or ideology.[4] Scholars such as Rebecca Braun have situated the Nobel Prize within a European, anti-American framework. For Braun, the Nobel Prize 'is both a product of and major contributor to a mid-European, non-market-driven model for valuing high-end cultural achievement' (320). This might have been the case in the 1990s and 2000s, with awards made to European provocateurs such as Günter Grass and Elfriede Jelinek. But in 2015, the literary scholar Sara Danius, who has a PhD from Duke University, took over as Permanent Secretary of the Swedish Academy. The Secretary often defines an epoch in the history of Nobel Prizes in Literature. After the Second World War, Anders Österling explicitly made amends for the previous neglect of modernist writers by consecrating T. S. Eliot, André Gide and William Faulkner. The first award that Danius made—to the Ukrainian writer Svetlana Alexievich, in 2015—fits well with the non-market-driven model long favoured by the Swedish Academy. But in 2016, the Nobel went to Bob Dylan, who has sold millions of records worldwide. And the following year, the prize consecrated Ishiguro, a writer whose novels have been adapted by Hollywood with star casts (Anthony Hopkins and Emma Thompson, in *The Remains of the Day*; Keira Knightley and Charlotte Rampling, in *Never Let Me Go*). Awarding the prize to Ishiguro, Danius hoped this choice would 'make the world happy' (Charles)—presumably because Ishiguro combines readability and mass-market appeal with highbrow credentials.

Sara Danius resigned a few months later following a scandal involving the husband of an academy member, and the 2018 award was cancelled. She was replaced by Mats Malm in April 2019. Later that year, the new Secretary announced that Olga Tokarczuk and Peter Handke had won the Nobel Prizes in Literature for 2018 and 2019. After a scandal widely seen as damaging to the credibility of the prize, the Committee sought to achieve a balance between gender and, perhaps, political opinions: Tokarczuk is a figure of the Left in Poland, while Handke is a right-leaning Austrian writer, who delivered a eulogy at the funeral of Slobodan

---

[3] Flood, 'Nobel Judge Fears for the Future of Western Literature'.
[4] See English, *The Economy of Prestige* 50.

Milosevic, the former leader of Yugoslavia. With these awards to writers from Central Europe, the Nobel Committee signalled its return to its traditional model of literary production. With the departure of Danius, the Bob Dylan/ Kazuo Ishiguro parenthesis was closed, and the non-market driven, mid-European model was back.

In this chapter, I argue that Ishiguro's Nobel Prize award and speech was a moment of temporary triumph for the Anglo-American model of creative writing programmes, and a symbolic victory over the European model of literary production long endorsed by the Nobel Prize Committee. The first section positions the 2017 Nobel Prize in Literature within the history of the past four decades, a history marked by diversity and attempts to globalize the award. In the second section, I turn to two institutions that made Ishiguro's success possible: the creative writing programme at UEA, and the publishing house Faber. These institutions encouraged and promoted his positioning as a Japanese-born British writer whose fiction defies established genres. The third section examines Ishiguro as a celebrity and a canonical author whose work is taught at the school and university level. This status has brought constraints that Ishiguro reluctantly accepted—such as the need to preserve an archive at a time when all aspects of the author's life are scrutinized. Ishiguro's ambivalence towards archiving and his choice to sell his own records to the Harry Ransom Center in Texas (rather than UEA) are covered in the fourth section.

8.1 'I'm going to change my name to Gary Smith': Nobel Prize and Diversity

In recent decades, the Swedish Academy has endorsed Nobel laureates from a wide range of national and ethnic backgrounds. Previously marginalized languages and cultures have been recognized: Latin America (Pablo Neruda 1971, Gabriel Garcia Marquez 1982, Octavio Paz 1990), the West Indies (Derek Walcott 1992), Africa (Wole Soyinka 1986, Nadine Gordimer 1991, J. M. Coetzee 2003), Asia (Gao Xingjian 2000), the Arab World (Naguib Mahfouz 1988), Australia (Patrick White 1973). This tendency is also reflected in the citations that justify awards: 'reflecting a continent's life and conflicts' (Marquez), 'brings alive a continent's destiny and dreams' (Neruda), 'introduced a new continent into literature' (White). The Swedish Academy is proud of this diverse record, which partly compensates for decades of neglect of non-European writers following the establishment of the prize in 1901. In his will, Alfred Nobel had requested that in awarding the prizes no consideration shall be given to the nationality of the candidates. 'The Nobel Prize has become the global prize the donor intended,' declared the Academy in 2011 (Svensén 67).

As Pascale Casanova has shown, the prize works because everyone believes in its universality. 'The Nobel Prize is today one of the few truly international literary consecrations, a unique laboratory for the designation and definition of what is universal in literature,' Casanova argues ('Literature as a World' 74). Ishiguro's speech at the Nobel banquet highlights this ability to transcend national and linguistic boundaries:

> The pride we feel when someone from our nation wins a Nobel Prize is different from the one we feel witnessing one of our athletes winning an Olympic medal. We don't feel the pride of our tribe demonstrating superiority over other tribes. Rather, it's the pride that comes from knowing that one of *us* has made a significant contribution to our common human endeavour. The emotion aroused is a larger one, a unifying one.[5]

This speech is framed by references to Ishiguro's family history rooted in Nagasaki and the memory of the atomic bomb. It reinforces the audience's belief that the prize is a force for good that celebrates a common humanity.

The Nobel Prize shows the existence of a 'world literary space' (as Casanova puts it ['Literature as a World' 72]), but this space is not an equal playing field where everyone has a chance to win. In the past twenty years, only five women have received the award. Despite being the bookmakers' favourite in 2017, Margaret Atwood lost. She graciously congratulated the winner on Twitter and advised her followers to read her review of *Never Let Me Go*. It was not the first time that Ishiguro had bypassed Atwood in a literary competition. As we have seen in Chapter 6, his third novel *The Remains of the Day* won the Man Booker Prize competition in 1989, winning over Atwood's *Cat's Eye*. By the late 1990s, Atwood had been selected three times for the Booker, without ever winning. In 2000, her novel *The Blind Assassin* was again on the shortlist alongside Ishiguro's *When We Were Orphans*. Ishiguro told CNN that he disliked the effect the prize had on writers. 'There's a very cruel side to it,' he said. 'I don't think it's any fun, even if you are one of the most respected authors in the world like Margaret Atwood, to keep being nominated and not win. I sincerely hope she gets it this time' (Dunn, 'In the Land of Memory'). Atwood did get the Booker that year. But her failure to win the Nobel Prize in 2017 embarrassed Ishiguro, who is fifteen years her junior. The award clearly showed that a man—whatever his ethnic origin—is still more likely to win the Nobel Prize than a woman.

Reflecting on the reasons why Ishiguro got the Nobel Prize, critics agreed that his originality and defiance of literary trends makes him a worthy winner. Let's take the example of James Wood of *The New Yorker*, who is neither a star-stuck fan of Ishiguro nor an entrenched critic. Wood was disappointed by Ishiguro's 2015 novel *The Buried Giant*—a fantasy set some years after the death of King Arthur. 'Its allegory manages somehow to be at once too literal and too vague' ('The Uses of Oblivion'). Like *The Unconsoled* (a novel that Wood found hard to read), *The*

---

[5] Ishiguro, Speech at the Nobel Banquet, 10 Dec. 2017.

Buried Giant was 'foggy, amorphous, miasmic'. But Wood also praised *The Remains of the Day*, a story told by an old butler who reflects on English country house life in the 1930s and his years serving a Nazi sympathizer. Similarly, *Never Let Me Go*, a dystopian novel about cloned schoolchildren, matched bland style with horrific content. Is this enough to make a worthy Nobel Prize laureate? Yes, Wood argued, for one main reason: originality. 'Ishiguro does his own thing, and his work doesn't resemble anyone else's.' He has written historical novels set in Japan, England, and Shanghai before turning to science fiction and historical fantasy. 'He is undistracted by literary fashion or the demands of the market', which explains his willingness to explore genres despised by many literary authors and their readers (Walsh, 'Harvard's James Wood').

The word 'originality' has been used to describe Ishiguro's fiction since the 1980s. When *The Remains of the Day* was released in the United States, a *New York Times* advertisement included a series of blurbs by prominent literary figures. 'The writer is an original and so is the book which is very funny and one of the saddest I can remember,' Doris Lessing declared. The American novelist Robert Stone added: 'Ishiguro is a highly original and gifted novelist.'[6] This literary originality is intrinsically linked to the author himself, whose ethnic origin and personal story do not resemble existing models.

Ishiguro's two first novels pigeonholed him as a Japanese writer who could explain this culture to Anglo-American readers. Japan was then an economic powerhouse that threatened the dominance of Western firms in a wide range of sectors—from automobiles to TV cartoons. Yet, Japanese culture and way of life remained little known in the West. In his introduction to Yasunari Kawabata's *Snow Country and Thousand Cranes* (Penguin, 1986), Ishiguro told readers to imagine Japanese homes as 'sparse and unfurnished' to make sense of the book:

> Do not confuse Japanese decor with Chinese, and certainly take care not to let your imagination conjure up the inside of your local Chinese restaurant with its swirling dragon patterns and rich colours. Japanese interiors are practically the antithesis of this.

Today's readers will find such advice unnecessary. From retail companies to bestselling books on *The Life-Changing Magic of Tidying*, Japanese ideal home decor has invaded mainstream culture. As a Japanese-born writer educated in Britain, Ishiguro was ideally placed to explain a different way of life and help his Anglophone readers navigate a multicultural society. An early advertisement in *The Guardian* presented him as 'an accomplished interpreter of Anglo-Japanese relations'.[7]

---

[6] Knopf, Advertisement for *The Remains of the Day*, *The New York Times*, 8 Oct. 1989, p. BR14.
[7] Penguin, Advertisement 'Best of Young British Novelists', *The Guardian*, 24 Feb. 1983, p. 24.

Yet, Ishiguro never felt at ease with this role: he repeatedly insisted he knew little about real life in Japan, having left the country when he was a small child. In that respect, Ishiguro is different from Paul Engle, a born-and-bred Iowan who positioned himself as a cosmopolitan regionalist (see Chapter 1). Although Ishiguro continued to speak Japanese at home, his command of the language was imperfect. The country he described in his first novels was an imagined landscape, constructed through his childhood memories and the stories told by his parents. Lacking the rootedness of a strong national identity, Ishiguro resented being viewed as a Japanese expatriate. In a 1989 interview, he described the reception of his second novel in England. 'People have not paid much attention to the ideas and just treated it as an exotic kind of little thing,' he said. 'I've had every kind of Japanese cliché phrase—even Sumo wrestling.'[8]

Ishiguro also rejected the postcolonial label applied to Salman Rushdie or Timothy Mo. 'Like any writer, I resist being put in a group,' he said in 1990.[9] Unlike writers born in India or Hong Kong, he had little to say about the relationship between Britain and its former empire. Moreover, his style was radically different from the magic realism adopted by many postcolonial writers. Ishiguro felt he had more in common with Ian McEwan and the younger generation of British writers who did not view Britain as the centre of the world.

Rejecting both the Japanese label and the postcolonial label left Ishiguro in a precarious position—'between two cultures', as *The Times of India* put it in a 1984 review of *A Pale View of Hills*. The novel was not Japanese, since it has been written in English. Yet, it 'reads like a translation from the Japanese and reveals little or nothing of the author's English background barring his limpid and spare use of the English language'.[10] Likewise, Rushdie has described minority writers as 'translated men' even when they write in English (17). Pascale Casanova has argued that translation is not a transparent process, but a site of struggle between dominant and dominated languages ('Consécration et accumulation de capital littéraire'). For example, the increase of translations from English in France and the decrease of translations from French in Anglophone countries highlight the decline of French as a world language. In a 1990 interview, Ishiguro used the vocabulary of war or struggle to describe the relationship between the two languages he grew up with. 'In my situation the stronger language was English,' he said. 'The only people I had any contact with who spoke Japanese were members of my immediate family, so it was the Japanese that became invaded and contaminated by English.'[11]

Left with an imperfect command of Japanese, Ishiguro chose the dominant world language. This led to difficult questions at the beginning of his career. In

---

[8] Suanne Kelman, 'Ishiguro in Toronto' (Shaffer and Wong 49).
[9] Allan Vorda and Kim Herzinger, 'An Interview with Kazuo Ishiguro' (Shaffer and Wong 70).
[10] 'For Their Eyes Only', *The Times of India*, 17 June 1984, p. 8.
[11] 'Don Swaim Interviews Kazuo Ishiguro' (Shaffer and Wong 93).

Fig. 8.1 Launch of the Faber Fiction Tour, *Listener*, 23 May 1985, p. 18. Ishiguro is first from the right.
Credit: Listener/ Immediate Media Co.

1985, Ishiguro took part in a publishing event, the Faber Fiction Tour, organized by his publisher (Figure 8.1). A limousine was hired to transport authors to various cities to meet readers and promote their work. In Oxford, Ishiguro got a question from a Japanese woman probing the accuracy of his fiction. He pointed out that he grew up in Guildford in the South-East of England, and she seemed disappointed. Another author, Adam Mars-Jones, then suggested Ishiguro had plastic surgery like Michael Jackson 'in the furtherance of his literary persona'.[12] Ishiguro was playfully reminded of the gap between his Japanese physical appearance and his proclaimed lack of knowledge of Japan, the country where his early novels are set. The disappointment of the Japanese woman, who was not cheered up by the Michael Jackson joke, perhaps stemmed from the awareness of belonging to a dominated culture—seen through the lens of English as a dominant language.

With the publication of *The Remains of the Day*, the question of how to place Ishiguro's work continued to trouble critics. How could a Japanese-born author write a quintessential English novel? In January 1990, *Punch* magazine speculated about famous people's resolutions for the new year. 'I'm going to change my name to Gary Smith' was the line for Ishiguro.[13] Once again, he was reminded of the discrepancy between his Japanese origin and his fictional work. Nearly three decades and a Nobel Prize later, Sara Danius placed Ishiguro's work in the European tradition. 'If you mix Jane Austen and Franz Kafka you get Ishiguro in a nutshell,' she

---

[12] 'Out of the Air. Kaleidoscope Radio 4', *Listener*, 23 May 1985, p. 18.
[13] 'Some Previously Unreleased New Year's Resolutions', *Punch*, 5 Jan. 1990, p. 10.

told reporters (Johnson and Pawlak). The Nobel Lecture also mentioned Marcel Proust as a central influence. In short, Ishiguro managed to transform a weakness into a strength. He could have remained a minority writer whose novels resembled translations. The rootlessness of his work might have deprived him of a stable readership, since it did not fit with existing publishing categories. But it also generated a level of interest and publicity unusual for emerging writers. In the long term, Ishiguro's unique positioning helped him secure the Nobel Prize for Literature—a prize built on its founder's cosmopolitanism and disdain for entrenched national identities.

8.2 The Role of UEA and Faber in Shaping an International Writer

Two main institutions shaped Ishiguro's positioning as an international writer (or 'homeless writer', as he once defined himself)[14]: the University of East Anglia and the publisher Faber. With the support of these institutions, Ishiguro wrote and found a market for his early Japanese-inspired work. Let's start with UEA. In Chapter 6, we looked at the important role that Malcolm Bradbury, Angela Carter and the whole UEA network played in supporting creative writing alumni. For the young Ishiguro, Bradbury and Carter were both writing coaches and publicists. They helped him improve his writing, while also sharing their contacts with literary agents and publishers. They worked for a university, and yet, they did not behave as traditional academics. During the Summer term, Angela Carter invited Ishiguro to her own house in South London. 'She talked very much out of her instincts, and she lived much more how a writer should live,' Ishiguro recalled. 'She wasn't based around the university, her approach was not an academic one' (Gordon, *The Invention of Angela Carter* 290). UEA's creative writing programme left a great deal of autonomy to students. 'The whole point of it was that there was no teaching. It was twelve months in which to discover whether or not one really was a writer' (Chappell).

But was it true that there was no teaching? Ishiguro's long discussions with Carter undoubtedly helped him develop as a writer. According to Carter's biographer, they would sit at the kitchen table and talk about technical issues: 'a running debate was about the validity of manipulative suspense devices' (Gordon, *The Invention of Angela Carter* 290). Carter did not always like what Ishiguro was doing, although she—like Bradbury—left him free to experiment. It is this freedom that Ishiguro found particularly useful, since it allowed him to develop an original style. In a 1987 interview with UEA Professor Christopher Bigsby, Ishiguro said:

[14] Ishiguro and Kenzaburo 115.

I think the East Anglia course is very good in the sense that it holds back quite a lot, at least it did when I was there. There was plenty of time for you just to get on with things unhindered and unassisted. There was no pressure to write in a particular style or to address a particular topic. There was an emphasis on a diversity of what constituted good writing, rather than saying here is model A, B, and C, take your pick and reproduce them. It was very much the case that students should try and find something that rang true to them.

This hands-off approach worked well for Ishiguro and has left him with a suspicion of more interventionist creative writing programmes. 'I would have to be sceptical about the idea that you can create a writer simply through courses and exercises,' he told Bigsby.[15] Like the American novelist Tom Wolfe, Ishiguro fears that creative writing courses will turn students into unreadable writers more interested in style and narrative techniques than in telling a good story. In 1991, he expressed relief that university creative writing was still rare in Britain. 'The thing I fear from the creative writing industry and universities in general is that people elevate priorities that I would not consider to be terrifically important,' he said. 'I don't believe that the nature of fiction is one of the burning issues of the late twentieth century.'[16] More recently, Ishiguro has insisted that UEA's creative writing programme was unlike any other: it was the first in Britain, and it did not resemble a factory aimed at producing standardized writers.

Ishiguro's attitude towards university creative writing is best described as ambivalent. On the one side, he has always been grateful to UEA for helping to launch his career. This gratitude has led him to accept regular invitations to give talks and masterclasses to creative writing students in Norwich. Shortly before the publication of *The Buried Giant*, he asked students to give him advice on the choice of the title—reversing the traditional role of the teacher/celebrity writer who is there to talk rather than to listen. He thus followed the example of Bradbury and Carter, who treated their students as young professionals with a voice of their own. On 11 October 2017, a few days after the Nobel Prize announcement, Ishiguro also appeared at the UEA Literary Festival, a sold-out event whose profits went towards student scholarships. For Ishiguro, lending his famous name to raise funds was another way to help his alma mater.

Yet, Ishiguro shares the distrust against creative writing programmes so common amongst professional writers. He is not the first to fear the effect of universities on contemporary writing, accused of being bland and narrow in focus. His attitude is characteristic of the collective bad faith of a writing profession that has benefited from the creative writing industry by accumulating cultural, social, and economic capital. Ishiguro seems to be aware of this paradox. As

---

[15] Christopher Bigsby, 'In Conversation with Kazuo Ishiguro' (Shaffer and Wong 18–19).
[16] Vorda and Herzinger, 'An Interview with Kazuo Ishiguro' (Shaffer and Wong 79–80).

the first product of a creative writing course to win the Nobel Prize, he chose to endorse this apprenticeship in the award lecture. Reflecting on his career, Ishiguro publicly admitted that his UEA education improved both his writing and his ability to reach an audience. In doing so, he legitimized a training that had long been resisted in Europe—including amongst the ranks of the Swedish Academy.

It is thanks to UEA that Ishiguro found both a literary agent (Deborah Rogers) and a publisher (Faber). The introduction to Rogers came through Angela Carter. And it was during his time in Norwich that he heard that Faber was looking for new writers for a collection of stories. 'If I'd been wandering around London I wouldn't have heard about it, little things like that made a difference,' he said (Allen). The aim of the Faber anthology was to publish writers whose prose had not previously appeared in book form, and earlier volumes had included work by Alan Coren, Ted Hughes, Julian Mitchell, Christopher Hampton, and Tom Stoppard. Ishiguro sent to the young editor Robert McCrum three of his recent short stories (A Strange and Sometimes Sadness; Waiting for J; and Getting Poisoned) for publication in the Faber Introduction series. Ishiguro's cover letter explicitly mentioned his mentor at UEA: 'I was told recently by Malcolm Bradbury that you had contacted him in connection with a new Faber collection in your "New Writers" series, and he suggested I wrote to you.'[17]

Shortly after the Nobel Prize announcement, McCrum reflected on his long relationship with Ishiguro, starting with his discovery of the short stories. 'I cannot forget their haunting strangeness, the unique quality of his writing to this day, a weird mix of classic English and minatory Japanese prose,' McCrum recalled. 'Although there was inevitably some influence from Ian McEwan, they were unmistakably the work of a young writer with a new voice.' McCrum described himself as 'a young editor looking for new talent' and Ishiguro as 'hot from the new UEA creative writing course' ('My Friend Kazuo Ishiguro'). The repetitions of 'new' position both the editor and the writer as pioneers in the literary field. Both belonged to the forefront, to the avant-garde of literary fiction. This position has traditionally been associated with low sales but high symbolic capital. Yet, McCrum has reaped huge rewards from his association with Ishiguro, who went on to sell millions of books and to win the most sought-after prizes.[18]

As Pierre Bourdieu puts it, struggles in the literary field aim at monopolizing the power to consecrate groups or individuals—through publication, for example—and therefore to give value and to appropriate the profits of this operation (*The*

---

[17] Ishiguro to McCrum, 31 Dec. 1979, qtd in Faber, *Faber & Faber: The Untold Story* n.p.
[18] 'He has sold 1.67 million books for £11.9m through Nielsen BookScan's Total Consumer Market. His biggest seller is *Never Let Me Go* with the paperback selling 306,246 copies, while his 1989 Man Booker Prize winner *Remains of the Day* has sold 149,421 copies across all editions since 1998' (Onwuemezi and Wood).

Field of Cultural Production 42). But this power is not absolute: the consecrator works within the larger field and must comply with its rules. Would McCrum have discovered Ishiguro if the young writer had sent him an unsolicited manuscript? Probably not, and McCrum does not pretend to be the unique discoverer of Ishiguro. Instead, he places Ishiguro within the UEA network, referring to various influencers: Bradbury, Carter, and McEwan.

After submitting his stories for the Faber anthology, Ishiguro had his first publishing lunch—a ritual marking the acceptance of the new writer into the literary world. 'They asked if I had anything else,' he recalled. He gave them an extract of *A Pale View of Hills*, which was his thesis for the Master's degree at UEA, and they offered him a £1,000 advance. 'It was the same as my student grant at the time, and so I lived off that and wrote the rest of the book' (Wroe). McCrum remembers that the reviews were absolutely remarkable for a first novel. How can we explain such a quick breakthrough? There are many reasons, including the fascination for Japan in a context of Japanese economic expansion, and the awareness that Britain had become multicultural ('everyone was suddenly looking for other Rushdies,' Ishiguro said).[19] The references to the atomic bomb in *A Pale View of Hills* also attracted interest at a time of renewed anxiety of a nuclear conflict. 'I became profoundly thankful for having been born in Nagasaki,' Ishiguro said in 1983. 'My novel taking place in that city was allowing me to achieve an easy kind of global significance.'[20] But there is another important reason for Ishiguro's success: the help that he received from the UEA network and his publisher after the publication of his first novel.

In a 1986 interview, Ishiguro talked about the ease of his acceptance into the British literary establishment. 'Thirty or forty per cent of the reviews my first book received were from people I know' (Tookey). Angela Carter's blurb appeared on the back of *A Pale View of Hills*. Malcolm Bradbury listed it amongst his books of the year.[21] Two former writers-in-residence at UEA (Anthony Thwaite and Paul Bailey) reviewed the book in *The Observer* and *The Times Literary Supplement*. After explaining that Ishiguro had studied under Bradbury, Thwaite went on to describe *A Pale View of Hills* as a 'wholly successful book' that created the illusion of inhabiting the Japanese mind ('Ghosts in the Mirror'). Bailey was equally enthusiastic, referring to the book as 'a first novel of uncommon delicacy' ('Private Desolations'). For a first novelist, Ishiguro was unusually well-connected, and the UEA network allowed him to quickly gain the attention of a large readership.

Faber was also instrumental in Ishiguro's success. The house has long been associated with the finest kind of literary fiction and poetry. This reputation is partly based on its long association with T. S. Eliot—who worked as editor for three

---

[19] Vorda and Herzinger, 'An Interview with Kazuo Ishiguro' (Shaffer and Wong 69).
[20] Ishiguro, 'I Became Profoundly Thankful for Having Been Born in Nagasaki'.
[21] Bradbury, 'Books of the Year'.

decades, continued to write poetry, and won the Nobel Prize in 1948. In the 1980s, the mergers in the publishing industry created multinational groups, with the ability to pay celebrity-sized advances to promising authors. Literary publishing houses did not escape the trend towards consolidation and internationalization. As an independent house, Faber found it difficult to compete financially with these mega groups. To survive, the firm used innovative methods of promotion to reach new markets.

In May 1985, the journalist Bel Mooney praised the 'admirably entrepreneurial' Faber for organizing a Fiction Tour. For Mooney, it was an excellent idea to apply the techniques of show-business promotion to promote younger, lesser-known writers such as Ishiguro. 'There is a fashionable illusion that such activity is … somewhat vulgar, not the kind of thing in which publishing gentlemen (or ladies) should involve themselves,' Mooney wrote. Faber had managed to transform this kind of promotion into 'respectable hype', organized in cooperation with the Regional Arts Associations.[22] Literary houses such as Faber no longer pretended to be radically different from debased commercial enterprises. The Faber Fiction Tour (Figure 8.1) also reinforced the publisher's brand. Readers traditionally pay attention to the author rather than the publisher and promoting each Faber author individually would have been expensive and time-consuming. Instead, Faber tried to convince readers that all its authors were worth reading.

Advertisements and public letters presented the firm as a discoverer of new talents in a field dominated by mega groups obsessed by profit. In 1984, Robert McCrum asked new writers to send two or three of their short stories for publication in the next volume of the Faber Introduction series. Kazuo Ishiguro was mentioned amongst other writers whose early work had been published in this series ('Letters: Short Stories'). In 1987, shortly after publishing giant Random House acquired Chatto & Windus and Jonathan Cape, Faber issued a full-page advertisement in *The Sunday Times*. The creation of mega groups would lead to the neglect of new, unknown writers, declared the ad. 'As one of the diminishing band of independent publishers Faber and Faber takes a more traditional view and continues to take risks on writers of all kinds.' This commitment to new writing was compatible with profit, as the commercial success of Ishiguro and other Faber writers showed. In contrast to global corporations accused of favouring bland blockbusters, Faber anchored its image in 'the time-honoured publishing tradition' of risk taking. In other words, Faber encouraged readers to make an ethical choice and purchase its books as a way to defend an endangered culture.

Faber also benefited from the rising interest in 'world literature'. According to David Damrosch, 'world literature' designates a mode of circulation and of reading, rather than a canon of texts. It is when several literary systems share a single text that it becomes 'world literature' (3). A similar move away from the literary

---

[22] Mooney, 'Respectable Hype'.

characteristics of the text can be found in Martin Puchner's definition: 'world literature is not written but made—made by a marketplace' (49). This category would apply perfectly to Ishiguro's work if he was writing books in Japanese for a global audience interested in translations. The fact that he is writing in English has led Rebecca L. Walkowitz to describe his work as 'born translated'. 'This is a matter of tone,' writes Walkowitz, with Ishiguro's first-person narrators often speaking 'in a vague or convoluted diction that can seem like translatese' (n.p.). Although Faber does not explicitly market Ishiguro's work as 'world literature', his books fit well in a list that includes many international texts in translation, including by Nobel Prize winner Günter Grass.

As with UEA, Ishiguro has repeatedly expressed his gratitude to Faber. In 2010, he accepted an invitation to speak to the students on the Writing a Novel course at the Faber Academy, a creative writing school founded the year before. In a blog post, Richard Skinner—the Director of the Fiction Programme—presented the talk as an intimate conversation between the speaker and his audience. During this two-hour session, Ishiguro 'offered access-all-areas to his thoughts on writing and his work practices' ('Kazuo Ishiguro & The Art of Narration'). The talk provoked a lot of discussion amongst students and led to a mini-conference on Ishiguro's work at the end of the course. In Skinner's story, Faber Academy students are presented as a select group, with rare opportunities to interact with world-class writers and publishing professionals.

Ishiguro's name has been used to lend prestige and sell creative writing courses organized by a university (UEA) and a publishing firm (Faber), but also a newspaper. In 2011, *The Guardian* started offering 'masterclasses' in partnership with the University of East Anglia, 'the UK's leading university for creative writing, where alumni include Man Booker Prize winners Kazuo Ishiguro and Anne Enright'.[23] Despite Ishiguro's ambivalence towards creative writing courses, his success story helped recruit new students, who were charged £500 for a six-week writing course with UEA–Guardian Masterclasses and a whopping £4,000 for a twenty-eight-session course at the Faber Academy.

8.3 From Celebrity to Canonical Writer

Ishiguro is well aware that his celebrity is a commodity, used to sell books, movie deals, and writing courses. In a 1990 interview, shortly after receiving the Man Booker Prize, he said:

> There was a time not so long ago when writers were rather shabby, unglamorous people, who didn't earn very much money. The only people who wanted to interview them were serious literary types. For some reason the perception of

[23] 'About UEA-Guardian Masterclasses Creative Writing Courses', *The Guardian*, 26 May 2011.

the writer has changed, and they've become glamorous people. They've lost the right, along with politicians and actors and other public figures, to be treated with gentleness and respect.[24]

Here, Ishiguro sheds light on the price he had to pay for his literary celebrity: he became a public figure, a writer whose privacy could be invaded at any time by demanding journalists and readers. The loss of privacy came with a second issue: the struggle to find time to write amidst a wide range of other duties, including international promotion tours and interviews. After winning the Nobel Prize, Ishiguro expressed concern at the distractions that the prize might bring. He said: 'I'm hoping it doesn't mark some kind of end. I've had to battle a lot of my writing life between the demands to be a public celebrity author and finding the time and space to do the real work, so I'm hoping the work itself just continues and is no different to where it was yesterday.' The distracting burden of celebrity brought a third drawback: the risk of being cut from younger readers, who might be put off by the Nobel Prize—a prize that often goes to older writers whose best work is behind them. 'I have GCSE people reading my books and I'm very proud to have that younger audience,' Ishiguro declared (Ellis-Petersen and Flood).

The tectonic changes of the publishing industry in the 1980s largely explain the increased pressure of literary celebrity. Intensified conglomeration has been accompanied by new marketing techniques to reach a wider audience—think of the televised Booker Prize dinner, for example. 'Celebrity,' Loren Glass notes, 'makes authorship a corporate affair' (*Authors Inc.* 672). In particular, publishers push for sophisticated brand management, which is then performed by authors. The process resembles a feedback loop rather than a top-down approach. Instead of being victims of unscrupulous corporations, authors are equally invested in the construction and management of their brands. The brand that Ishiguro and his publishing team have constructed over time rests on an anti-conformist story— the story of a deeply private writer who is not comfortable with celebrity. Like his publisher Faber, Ishiguro has positioned himself as a vestige from an earlier period, when authors could enjoy privacy and concentrate on their work without unnecessary distractions.

This persona has obscured the benefits brought by literary celebrity, including monetary rewards and the ability to sponsor other writers and groups—what Bourdieu called the power to consecrate. To the best of my knowledge, Ishiguro has not publicly commented on the cash award that comes with the Nobel Prize: 9 million Swedish Krona. This silence is hardly surprising. Ishiguro projects the image of a literary writer with little interest in sales and money. The influence that he exerts relies on subtle endorsements. Praising the University of East Anglia in his Nobel Lecture did not bring him any monetary gain, but it helped raise the international profile of UEA's creative writing programme—where his daughter

---

[24] Suanne Kelman, 'Ishiguro in Toronto' (Shaffer and Wong 50).

Naomi studied in 2016–17. Like wealthy alumni who give money towards scholarships or a new library, Ishiguro used his power of consecration to help his alma mater compete in the global university marketplace.

Ishiguro's Nobel Prize accelerated his transition from celebrity to canonical writer. In 1995, he received an OBE [Order of the British Empire] for Services to Literature and his work has since been taught at school and university level and analysed in academic publications. Scholars did not wait for the publication of *Never Let Me Go* in 2005 to scrutinize his novels. The University of South Carolina Press published Brian W. Shaffer's *Understanding Kazuo Ishiguro* in 1998. In 2000, two British presses (Manchester University Press and Northcote) issued short monographs by Barry Lewis and Cynthia F. Wong.

But Ishiguro's canonicity is not limited to the Anglophone world. Let's take the example of France, where his work has been enthusiastically received. In 1998, he was made a Chevalier de l'Ordre des Arts et des Lettres, a prestigious award for individuals who have distinguished themselves in the artistic or literary areas. The following year, *The Remains of the Day* was part of the yearly syllabus for the *agrégation* competitive examination in France. Only a small proportion of secondary school teachers are *agrégés*, and the exam is designed to select the best instructors. It is also the first step towards a university career as *maître de conférences* (lecturer) and professor. Thousands of candidates read Ishiguro's novel that year, and his work gained increased visibility in the academic community. In December 1999, he was invited to give a lecture at the Sorbonne by the research centre 'Écritures du Roman Contemporain de Langue Anglaise' with the help of the British Council.

During his talk, Ishiguro expressed anxiety over the homogenization of culture. He gave the example of Norwegian novels that need to be translated into a world language to reach a larger audience. He added:

> what is very dangerous of course, is that something very crucial and vital disappears here, in this homogenisation of literature: some of the very great energies that come out of someone's knowledge of their own locale, the language that is used in their own culture. All these things will perhaps somehow be ironed out. We will end up with … a McDonald's kind of effect, even with serious literary fiction.[25]

This discourse fits well with France's long-standing fight against the influence of the American model of globalization. Four months before Ishiguro's talk, the farmer José Bové and the Confédération paysanne had dissembled a McDonald's restaurant in Millau, an action that received national and international attention. France had long protected its cultural model (think of the Lang law of 1981,

---

[25] François Gallix, 'Kazuo Ishiguro: The Sorbonne Lecture' (Shaffer and Wong 146).

that supports small bookshops by enforcing a unique price for books), and the anti-globalization movement of the late 1990s gave a new impetus to cultural protectionism. Unsurprisingly, then, no one in the audience questioned Ishiguro's defence of minority cultures. And yet, his position was rather paradoxical. After all, he chose to write in English—the dominant world language. During the Sorbonne talk, he openly admitted that his work was designed for a global market. Of the Hollywood movie adapted from his novel *The Remains of the Day*, he said: 'they didn't have to change it very much because it was all ready-made for international consumption.'[26] In short, Ishiguro was not in the position of a Norwegian writer limited by the constraints of a small linguistic community. The kind of opportunities that he had—access to an international audience and a lucrative movie deal with Hollywood—put him amongst the literary elite that benefited from globalization.

Despite Ishiguro's experimentations with science fiction and fantasy, French publishers have continued to market his work as literary fiction for an audience of students, instructors, and educated readers. His work has benefited from the rise of translations from English to French, and his novels are available in reprint paperbacks in the Folio series published by Gallimard. First editions are issued by Éditions des Deux Terres, a subsidiary of Hachette which specializes in translation—including fiction by the bestselling crime writers Patricia Cornwell, Ruth Rendell, and Jeffery Deaver.

Despite its commercial success, Ishiguro's work has been marketed as highbrow fiction. Let's take the example of *The Buried Giant*, issued in a French translation in 2015. The inside flap of the hardcover edition positions Ishiguro in an international, multilingual context: 'Kazuo Ishiguro, born in Nagasaki, arrived in Great Britain aged five.' A short biography of the translator Anne Rabinovitch mentions her doctorate in North American studies. The back cover summarizes the plot, emphasizing the Shakespearean themes that run throughout Ishiguro's work. There are no references to dragons and other fantastical elements. A blurb on the back cover of the paperback edition describes it as an epic novel reflecting on memory and loss. *Le Géant enfoui* is packaged not as fantasy for a mass-market audience, but as a serious work of fiction for sophisticated readers.

8.4 ' I should store everything and sell it to some mug in Texas'

Having risen to canonical status within and outside the Anglophone world, Ishiguro had to decide what to do with his archive. In August 2015, *Reuters* reported that the Harry Ransom Center at the University of Texas (UT) had bought the Ishiguro

---

[26] Ibid. 147.

archive for over $1 million—five times the amount that the British Library paid for the Angela Carter archive a decade before (Herskovitz; Turner, 'A New Kind of Being'). This discrepancy tells us a lot about Ishiguro's perceived market value versus that of his former mentor. It also highlights the considerable financial power of American research libraries over their less fortunate European counterparts.

The market for literary archives boomed in North America in the years after the Second World War, as university libraries competed to acquire the most desirable papers of modern and contemporary writers. In 1957, Harry Huntt Ransom—an English professor at UT—founded the Humanities Research Center (as it was then called) in Austin, Texas. Ransom believed that a great university needed a strong library, and he spent a lot of time and energy building the library collections. Having acquired the Ian McEwan archive in 2014, it made sense for the Humanities Research Center to buy the papers of Ishiguro, another prominent alumnus of the UEA creative writing programme.

More surprising is Ishiguro's decision to part with his papers at this point in his career. In a 2007 interview, Sean Matthews, a British researcher, asked him if he was storing notebooks, scrap papers, and draft versions for posterity. Ishiguro seemed annoyed, telling Matthews it was 'a very vexing question' for him. Up to *The Remains of the Day*, he used to throw away everything. This changed in the 1990s. 'A book collector phoned me and said this was a mistake, that I could get huge amounts of money selling this material. In the future, he said, I should store everything and sell it to some mug in Texas.'[27] When Ishiguro did sell his archive to the Harry Ransom Center, he toned down this story: the book collector who phoned him became a 'friend', and the potential buyer was no longer referred to as 'some mug in Texas' (Herskovitz). More importantly, Ishiguro suppressed his ambivalence towards the archiving process, which was very explicit in the 2007 interview.

Ishiguro told Matthews that he wished he hadn't had this phone call. 'Now I can't throw anything away.' He added that he could not understand why his old papers and drafts would be valuable to anyone. 'It may be interesting for some people to trace the processes of creation and writing, but it doesn't have the same value one gets from reading a novel.' He gave the example of *Crime and Punishment*: knowing something about the genesis of the novel would not enhance his reading experience. 'What is important is to look at writing as a dialogue between author and serious readers, and to understand the satisfaction and fascination that comes from appreciating a work of art.'

The dream of an unmediated dialogue between writer and reader is not new. Virginia Woolf, for example, was equally hostile to professors whose job is to analyse and explain literary works. She aspired to talk to readers directly, without any intermediaries. The site of this dialogue was the literary text, and only the literary

---

[27] Sean Matthews, '"I'm Sorry I Can't Say More": An Interview with Kazuo Ishiguro' (Matthews and Groes 121).

text—which is why Woolf was so reluctant to write introductions and prefaces that would frame the reading experience.[28] Likewise, Ishiguro has long been suspicious of paratextual elements. In his 1986 introduction to *Snow Country and Thousand Cranes*, he addressed readers directly: 'Begin reading, and you are unlikely to feel the need for encyclopaedias or for large numbers of explanatory footnotes; the novels themselves will supply all the information you immediately require, and are in many ways ideal introductions to these peculiarly Japanese territories' (1). In short, Ishiguro encouraged readers to believe in their own ability to understand the text, without the help of anyone. Like the founding fathers of creative writing programmes, he has showed typical ambivalence towards academia and has held literary scholars at a distance.

Ishiguro's ambivalence towards archives and researchers did not entirely disappear after he signed a deal with the Harry Ransom Center. Many writers are content to ship boxes of old papers (and increasingly, hard drives and email accounts) to archival repositories. The Ian McEwan archive, for example, contains highly personal letters and emails—which would probably be closed to the public if his archive had stayed in Britain, a country with stricter data protection laws. Ishiguro guards his privacy zealously, and the archive he sent to Texas is carefully curated. 'He spent weeks sifting through the papers, making notes about the manuscripts and other documents he found in it,' Stephen Ennis, the Director of the Harry Ransom Center, said ('Taking Note of the Kazuo Ishiguro Archive'). These notes—which range from long explanations to short post-it notes—are scattered throughout the archive. In an interview to the *Bookseller*, Ishiguro confirmed that he spent a lot of time reviewing his old papers prior to transfer: 'I thought it would be a neutral exercise,' he said of assembling his archives. 'But it has been an enormous amount of work; I've essentially been going through my whole life' (Tivnan).

Textual scholars might be interested in Ishiguro's notes—although I suspect that many are weary of writers' retrospective interpretations of the writing process. My own experience was disappointing. When I visited the Harry Ransom Center in Summer 2017, I wanted to get a glimpse of Ishiguro's relationships with Malcolm Bradbury and Angela Carter when he was studying at UEA and in the years that followed his graduation. Although I am a great admirer of Ishiguro's novels, I did not make the trip to Texas to know more about the process of textual creation. Instead, I wanted to read his letters and emails—as I had done in the Ian McEwan collection. But instead of personal correspondence, I had to rely on old magazine articles. While I understand Ishiguro's hesitance about sharing unsorted, unpolished and, perhaps, intimate writing while he is still alive, I felt that the archive would have been richer if he had treated researchers as responsible adults, rather than pupils who need to be guided through materials. Ironically, in

---

[28] See Jaillant, *Cheap Modernism* 37.

assembling his archive so carefully, he undertook the role of the professor providing explanations—a role that he has long held in suspicion. His ambivalence towards academia, and his concern for privacy, have had a direct impact on the literary scholarship we can produce using archival methodology.

The announcement of the Nobel Prize of Literature for 2017 was a pleasant surprise for Stephen Ennis and his colleagues at the Harry Ransom Center. In the market for literary archives, prices can go up and down, and buying an archive for $1 million is a gamble. The Nobel Prize confirmed that the transaction had been a good investment and increased the professional standing of Ennis. 'It is one thing for the Ransom Center to collect the papers of Nobel laureates and another thing entirely to collect the papers of future Nobel laureates,' Ennis told UT News, the university's internal publication.[29]

Why does it matter that the Ishiguro archive is in Texas and not, say, at the University of East Anglia? With the acquisition of the papers of McEwan and Ishiguro in 2014 and 2015, the Harry Ransom Center became the place to go for anyone interested in the most distinguished alumni of the UEA creative writing programme. This was, of course, a defeat for UEA and for Professor Jon Cook, who had sought to acquire the McEwan archive for two decades. In a 1998 letter to McEwan, Cook wrote:

> We are also thinking seriously about establishing an archive of contemporary writing here. Doris Lessing wants to leave her papers to the University. I know we've talked about this before but I wanted to ask if, in principle, you would be willing to do the same. The shadows aren't that long yet, I know, and you may have made other arrangements, but I wanted to check if it's something that we can talk about further.[30]

Cook was right about the Doris Lessing archive. Lessing had a long association with UEA: she held the title of Distinguished Fellow in Literature and received an Honorary Degree in 1985. After winning the Nobel Prize for Literature in 2007, she made a substantial initial gift of personal papers to UEA. In 2013, following the writer's death, the University received the remainder of her personal archive—including personal papers, correspondence, notebooks, and diaries. The rest of her archive is at the Harry Ransom Center, which purchased the materials in 1999 and 2015. The example of Lessing shows how the two institutions are competing in the market for literary archives: on the one side, UEA cajoles British writers with

---

[29] 'Students, Researchers and Public Have Access to Archive of Nobel Laureate Kazuo Ishiguro', *UT-News*, 5 Oct. 2017, https://news.utexas.edu/2017/10/05/nobel-laureate-kazuo-ishiguros-archive-is-at-ransom-center. Accessed 30 Apr. 2021.

[30] Jon Cook to Ian McEwan, 27 Nov. 1998, Box 31, Ian McEwan Papers, Harry Ransom Center, U of Texas at Austin.

honorary degrees and other symbolic awards, hoping for a gift of valuable archives in return; on the other side, the Harry Ransom Center seduces authors with dollars and the promise that their archive will be held in world-class facilities and made available to international researchers.

Cajolery was not enough to win the papers of McEwan and Ishiguro, and the Harry Ransom Center now controls the narration around the archive: how documents came to rest in those archives, what documents are particularly interesting and worth consulting. Following the cataloguing of the Ishiguro collection, Stephen Ennis wrote:

> As valuable as the UEA experience was, the archive offers a competing, and more solitary, narrative of how Ishiguro learned to write. It was while away in rural Cornwall, far from the seminar room in East Anglia that his personal breakthrough came with a short story called 'Waiting for J.'
> ('Taking Note of the Kazuo Ishiguro Archive')

Imagine that the Ishiguro archive had ended up in Norwich. Would UEA downplay the role of its own creative writing programme in Ishiguro's career? Of course not. With the departure of valuable collections to Texas, UEA has lost archives central to its own institutional history. It has also lost a privileged position to tell the story of these archives and their creators.[31]

Now imagine that UEA had approached Ishiguro shortly after his 1982 Winifred Holtby Memorial Prize or the 1986 Whitbread Prize. Ishiguro was still in his late twenties/early thirties, but he might well have agreed to transfer his archive to his alma mater. This is, after all, what the young publisher Michael Schmidt did with the University of Manchester in the 1970s. If such an agreement had been reached, valuable documents would have been preserved instead of being thrown away. It is not a coincidence that UEA is now actively preserving the records (including born-digital records) of young writers who have studied or taught in the creative writing programme.

Fortunately for the University of East Anglia, Ishiguro's Nobel Prize speech can be used as a powerful recruitment tool. Look at the website of its creative writing programme, and you will see a section entitled 'alumni'. Click on the cover of *The Remains of the Day*, and you will find a longer list of former students. For the time

---

[31] The Harry Ransom Center is, of course, not the only archival institution that seeks to control the narrative on its collections (both paper and born-digital). Columbia University in New York City presents its archives 'as one of the country's premier collections of publishers' archives': 'because New York City is the center of the nation's publishing industry, we have focused on the local scene but have expanded beyond where relevant or opportune' ('What We Collect', https://library.columbia.edu/libraries/rbml/acquisition.html. Accessed 30 Apr. 2021). This downplays the historical role that Boston played in the development of the publishing industry in the US (Houghton Mifflin was founded in Boston in 1832, and is still based there).

being, Ishiguro has replaced McEwan as UEA's most distinguished alumnus. The Nobel Prize speech is also a godsend for all the creative writing programmes that have recently emerged in Continental Europe and elsewhere. The European suspicion of American-style creative writing factories is now competing against another story: the story of universities' ability to nurture diverse voices in creative writing programmes positioned on the margins of the academic establishment.

9
Beyond Academia
From Arvon to the Faber Academy

Let me tell this story, inspired by John Moat's *The Founding of Arvon*. The date is November 1966, the place is Devon. When John Moat got up, it was cold and miserable. A wet grey spiritless day, as far as he could see from the window of his cottage. He put on a jumper, made himself a cup of strong tea and thought of the work ahead—there were some poems to polish, some letters to answer. At least, the telephone worked now, the British Telecom chap had checked the line and the strange noise had disappeared. He didn't use the phone a lot anyway. Letters gave you a chance to think more carefully, to reflect, edit, and delete. That's how he and John Fairfax had come up with the idea of the writing school—they had talked for hours, and then refined the idea in their letters. They were both teachers, and they hated their jobs—or rather, they hated the education system. It removed literature from life, it denied the existence of living writers. There was a better way. A kind of apprenticeship, or mentorship if you like, with a practising writer teaching the craft of writing. Put young people together in an isolated place, no radio, no silly magazines. Alone with a living writer. That's what the writing school would look like. A chance for teachers to rediscover the pleasure of teaching, a chance for young people to learn fast and discover their own voice.

It was lunchtime now, and Moat was still in his kitchen. A hopeless, unproductive day, that's what it was. He felt restless, unable to concentrate. Someone had mentioned that Ted Hughes was in a hut somewhere fifteen miles down the coast near Widemouth, away from things, working on his own. They had not met yet. Moat knew that he should run into Hughes, that he should at least try to explain the writing school idea to this well-connected, powerful man. He took his boots and his car keys, and banged the entrance door behind him. At Widemouth, he walked on the cliffs for a time and looked at the zestless sea. Then he drove into the village, asked a petrol man where the pub was and drove to it up the hill. As he got out of his car, he saw a tall, handsome man walking into the car park towards the pub. He stood his ground and simply called out, 'Are you Ted Hughes?' The man swung round as if someone had taken a swipe at him. For a moment, Moat's knees shook, and he thought he was going to be dumb. But the moment passed, and he drank some beer with Ted Hughes and they talked easily for an hour. He then

Literary Rebels. Lise Jaillant, Oxford University Press.
© Lise Jaillant (2022). DOI: 10.1093/oso/9780192855305.003.0010

wrote to Fairfax: 'I found him impressive, with a towering turbulent presence, like an Ahab. He has the physical disposition to accommodate his driving demon—I felt it strongly, a Promethean character—steely, preoccupied eyes and jaw jutted to the devil. And out of him a slow gentleness, an unspeculating humour, a tried wisdom, and a soft, very beautiful voice.' Later, on the Arts Council Literature Panel, Ted Hughes must have supported their application for funding—and that's how the writing school, Arvon Foundation, came to be.

Founded in 1968, Arvon originally aimed at offering time and space away from school for young people to write poetry. John Moat wrote that they were inspired to create Arvon 'as a place where individuals, and in particular young committed writers, could be given a sanctuary away from … the creative deprivation imposed by the system of standard education—and there offered … the guidance of writers.'[1] The Arvon project was informed by the same progressive educational ideas that gave rise to writers-in-residence funded by the Arts Council (see Chapter 7). Flash forward four decades and look at the opening of the Faber Academy in London. At £4,000 for a 28-week course (Nicol), the Faber Academy has been accused of 'monetising the slush pile'.[2] Yet, negative criticisms have remained marginal. Open the London *Evening Standard*, and you will regularly find articles celebrating the publishing deals offered to alumni of the Faber Academy and the like. Scholars have paid no attention to this marketization of creative courses fuelled by celebrity culture. As in the case of the Famous Writers School, would-be writers are sold the dream of a glamorous writing lifestyle characterized by fame and freedom, at the centre of the model of *radical individualism*. Drawing on materials in the Arvon archive at the University of Exeter, and on oral history interviews with people associated with non-academic creative writing courses, this chapter goes from the late 1960s with the creation of Arvon, to the present day and the proliferation of creative writing courses sponsored by publishers and literary agents. It is organized thematically, opposing a 'non-profit' axis that brings together Arts-Council-funded charities, to a 'for-profit' axis with organizations such as Faber Academy and Curtis Brown Creative. While creative writing was historically pioneered by non-profits, the field has become an attractive business for commercial enterprises.

9.1 Non-Profits

9.1.1 Arvon

The Arvon Foundation came at a time when *formal* creative writing courses did not exist in Britain. As we have seen, the University of East Anglia employed a writer-in-residence (Angus Wilson) and Lancaster University was also interested in the

---

[1] 'History of Arvon', https://www.arvon.org/about/history/. Accessed 30 Apr. 2021.
[2] Carole Blake, co-founder of Blake Friedmann Agency, qtd in Thomson.

idea of creative writing. But these remained local experiments, little known outside the universities. As far as John Moat and John Fairfax knew, young writers 'were out in the cold'—unsupported by any structure.³ In contrast, young musicians and painters had long been able to formally train under the guidance of experienced artists.

In his late teens, Moat had studied in an art school before telling his mother he no longer wanted to attend. He travelled to France, visiting the painter Edmond Kapp once a week to show him his work and get some feedback. In addition to painting, he wrote a book of childhood memories and sent it to a friend of Kapp, the literary agent David Higham, who offered encouragement. 'At nineteen, I had a distinguished agent,' Moat later wrote. Writing suited him better than painting, and after studying at the University of Oxford, he started 'a king of apprenticeship' with the South African poet John Howland Beaumont. 'The only person who can teach the technique of writing reliably is an experienced writer,' Moat said (18–19).

If there is a constant theme in Moat's life, it is his rejection of the conventional education system. In his 2005 autobiographical account of Arvon, he dismissed his undergraduate years at Oxford as a waste of time, at least from a creative point of view: 'there was nothing I learned that had bearing on my own writing, or in any direct way on the practice or craft of writing' (Moat 18). As a young man, when he was making a living as a teacher and school librarian, Moat was furious at the corruption and perniciousness of educational institutions. In 1971, he wrote to Fairfax:

> I suppose I should tell the bastards straight out I'm simply exchanging certain skills for money—though my attitude is really less bleak—and that I don't want their crap sentiments as to education or relationships in my gut. (For there's something about 'education,' its attitudes, its lack of real catholicity of response to life, its philistinism which doesn't require much scratching to provoke, its conservatism, self-righteousness/self-abasement paradox and so forth that stinks. You can usually smell its agents a good way off!)⁴

This letter concludes with a reference to Ezra Pound's attack on the establishment, and to his courage and commitment to his ideas. In 1971, celebrating Pound was in the air—*The Pound Era*, by the American scholar Hugh Kenner, was published that year. And as we have seen, the first generation of creative writers in the US admired the modernists' radical rejection of conventional education. Tracing a similar path in Britain, Moat saw Pound as an inspiration for his own attempt to regenerate teaching and learning.

---

³ Fairfax MS 272—Course Information, U of Exeter Special Collections.
⁴ Moat to Fairfax, 30 Nov. 1971, Fairfax MS 272—Personal Letters, U of Exeter Special Collections.

Moat liked to present himself as an outcast who had pursued undistinguished studies at Oxford, and later lived in the countryside far from literary cliques. But early on, Arvon benefited from powerful sponsors. Not only did Ted Hughes use his influence to convince the Arts Council to support the new organization, he also taught the five-day residential courses himself—a 1975 advertisement lists him amongst the 'practising artists' who would tutor up to fifteen students.[5] Hughes even let Arvon use his own house, Lumb Bank in West Yorkshire, which is still used as a Centre today.

In the mid-1970s, Arvon was chaired by one of the most influential figures of the City of London—Havelock Hudson, the director of Lloyd's Bank. In a *Sunday Times* article, Hughes praised Hudson's intelligence and ability to live simply—the financier regularly visited Arvon's Devon Centre and took part in communal cooking. 'He's a strong, clear, straight person,' Hughes added, 'and our little society might well have disintegrated once or twice without his strong hand at committee meetings' (Dunn, 'A Premium Poet'). In addition to sharing his expertise, Hudson made financial contributions to Arvon—including a large personal donation in 1974.

In the next decades, Arvon proved remarkably resilient in the face of huge challenges, including funding cuts during periods of austerity. It is still supported today by the Arts Council, as a National Portfolio Organisation with a grant of c. £388,000 per annum in 2018–22. The format of the course has remained the same over the years: fifteen students and two tutors spend five days writing and sharing communal activities. The growing popularity of creative writing courses, and the relative cheapness of Arvon training, have contributed to the longevity of the organization.

In 1999, *The Times* published the testimony of Lottie Moggach who had spent a week at the Totleigh Barton centre. There were only two men in the course, an uneven mix which is 'pretty typical' of Arvon courses. Moggach described the experience as a way for busy women to carve out some time away from the demands of their daily lives. 'For five days, you don't have to think about the day job, or calling the plumber, or explain to impatient families that your "scribbling" is important to you.' This allowed students to take their writing seriously and to position themselves as would-be professionals. 'Everyone wanted to be published,' Moggach said. In addition, the course played a therapeutic role, offering an audience to those eager to share their feelings:

> Many of the students were using fiction as a kind of therapy and, the confessional urge combined with the fact that we would probably never see each other again, meant we all became intimate quickly. (Well, the women anyway. The men seemed a little alarmed at our immediacy.)
>
> ('Words Don't Come Easy')

---

[5] Advertisement for the Arvon Foundation, *The Times Literary Supplement*, 4 Apr. 1975, p. 381.

Here, the therapeutic function of creative writing is presented in gender terms—women tend to be more comfortable with sharing their feelings and developing close ties with others. The reaction of the two men in the course ('a little alarmed') reminds us that the discipline had not always been like that. Remember the masculinist discourse of a Paul Engle or Wallace Stegner, eager to create a virile discipline fit for Second World War veterans. While the post-war version of the discipline offered little space for women, the current interpretation risks leaving men marginalized—at least those men who are baffled by the confessional tone that characterizes much of contemporary writing.

It is difficult to present Arvon, as it exists today, as a fringe organization hostile to the established education system. Creative writing is now widely taught in schools and universities, and few would dispute the educational value of having a living writer teach poetry or fiction to young people. Yet, Ruth Borthwick – Arvon's Head from 2009 to 2019 – was eager to stress that the Foundation remained as radical as it was in the 1960s. 'What we're doing is trying to be as true to the roots as possible,' she told me during an interview at the Free Word Centre in Farringdon, London.[6] This was obvious in her repeated attacks against academia on two main grounds: its selectivity and its cost. Contrasting with the 'elitism' of universities, Arvon courses welcome people who 'self-select to come'. That represents two-thirds of Arvon's work, Borthwick pointed out. A third of their work is with young people who don't self-select to come but who would benefit from the education opportunity. In addition to being inclusive, a five-day course with Arvon is also much cheaper than a year-long university creative writing programme. 'For undergraduates to take on huge amounts of debt to do creative writing is quite surprising to me,' she said. With this high price tag come high expectations, as university students expect to gain contacts in the literary world and to be published.

When I pointed out that many Arvon students also hope to sign a book contract, Borthwick told me that they don't set those expectations. 'It's quite clear that it's about developing your imagination, your creativity—go as far as you wish to go,' she said. Yet, Arvon also invites literary agents as part of some advanced courses. Some students might see that as an opportunity to get their foot on the publishing ladder. Instead of focusing only on their writing, they are encouraged to make a good impression during the reading that concludes the course. Other creative writing programmes, within or outside academia, also routinely organize readings attended by agents. Despite Borthwick's insistence that Arvon is only concerned with the development of creativity, the Foundation encourages students' expectations to get published, at least in some of its courses.

Borthwick was careful to position her organization in non-business terms. When I asked if she saw herself as a cultural entrepreneur, she said: 'I'm not of a generation that would recognize the "entrepreneur." I'm more an activist.' As we

[6] Ruth Borthwick, Interview by author, 30 Apr. 2018, London.

will see later, this contrasts with the pro-market discourse of the Faber Academy and Curtis Brown Creative. If we create a graph to represent these various positionings, Arvon would be on the extreme left of the horizontal axis that shows attitudes towards the literary marketplace. The vertical axis highlights the organization's attitude towards the therapeutic role of creative writing. Arvon is relatively high on this axis, since its main selling point is the supportive community formed during the five-day course ('a transformative experience', Borthwick told me).

9.1.2 The Literary Consultancy

Even higher on the therapeutic axis is TLC (The Literary Consultancy), a manuscript assessment service created in 1996 by Rebecca Swift, a former editor at Virago. That same year, Swift wrote an article on writing groups for *The Independent*. 'Many participants never publish their work, but simply find being in a writing group a stimulating way of spending time,' she declared. These participants were looking for other people who would listen to their problems. This therapeutic function was seldom acknowledged, but that was changing. 'Among *Time Out*'s listings of the many London groups available one recently appeared offering "writing as self-healing,"' Swift added ('Group Sects').

Swift was fascinated by the relationship between would-be writers and readers working in publishing and related industries. This was the topic of the dissertation she submitted for her MA in Psychoanalytic Studies in 1999. 'Polarisation between most people who write and those that publish creates mutual irritation and frustration,' Swift argued. This antagonism sometimes had serious consequences, she said, giving the example of an editorial assistant who was stalked for six months after sending a rejection card to an author. Given the likelihood of being rejected, why do so many people send their manuscripts to publishers anyway? Swift gave a list of 'intrapsychic aims' of would-be writers, starting with their 'attempt to repair psychic legacies from childhood'. The next step was to find a reader who will witness their difficulties and judge them worthy of an audience. Swift positioned TLC as a response to this desire—would-be writers might never get published, but paying for a manuscript assessment would at least allow them to be read.

Swift's attempt to respond to a therapeutic need often met with suspicion. A 1997 article in *The Times Literary Supplement* presented TLC as 'an operation to assist writers even before they approach an agent, let alone an editor—or alternatively an operation to give employment to former editors who have sunk even below agency'.[7] In other words, the organization benefited Swift and other unemployed editors, rather than writers. When TLC received a grant of £105,000 from the Arts Council England in 2001, *The Times Literary Supplement* remained as suspicious as

---

[7] *The Times Literary Supplement*, 7 Mar. 1997, p. 16.

ever. Instead of celebrating the opportunity for 120 free reads offered by the grant, the journalist criticized the company's exploitation of would-be writers:

> Normally, the tyro writer, already broke from forking out for typing, photocopying and postage (not forgetting return postage), is expected to pay The Literary Consultancy a starting fee of £90 for the consolations on offer from 'a team of hand-picked readers,' who offer 'market-informed appraisals'.[8]

TLC's positioning (high on the therapeutic axis) has left it vulnerable to the accusation of exploitation of would-be writers. Unlike therapists whose activities are closely watched and regulated, TLC operates in a market that lacks regulation. 'It's a wild west market with no sheriff,' declares Sarah Dunant, a novelist who teaches at the Faber Academy (Thomson).

Let's take the example of a Publishing Masterclass that took place at the London Book Fair in March 2005. The *Daily Mail* advertised it as 'the perfect present for aspiring novelists, biographers and poets', designed to 'unlock' their potential as writers. Indeed, the subtitle of the Masterclass promised an extraordinary transformation, 'From rejection list to Booker shortlist'.[9] Only the most gullible aspiring writers would have believed this tale of radical transformation into prize-winners. But even those with more modest ambitions were set for a disappointment.

During the masterclass, the speakers did their best to sound discouraging. Swift, who was attending the Masterclass to promote TLC, said her organization only got two writers into print per year. For the journalist John Walsh, the surprising thing was not that so many would-be writers tried to get published, but that they persevered and refused to accept that they had no talent. Walsh, who was chairing the masterclass, declared: 'Publication is the final legitimising of the rampant ego; it tells you that somebody actually *does* want to listen to you banging on about yourself for 200 pages' ('Still Looking for the Happy Ending'). This demand for getting published—and read—does not match the offer for publication, creating business opportunities for organizations that fill the gap between writers and publishers.

9.1.3 The Case of Poetry

Aspiring poets can also enrol in the courses offered by the Poetry School, a registered charity that is part of Arts Council England's National Portfolio Organisation 2018–22. Founded in 1997 by Mimi Khalvati, Jane Duran, and Pascale Petit, the London-based Poetry School initially offered versification courses, on the formal aspects of poetry. Khalvati encouraged students to learn by doing. 'I dare people

---

[8] *The Times Literary Supplement*, 15 June 2001, p. 18.
[9] 'Writing Masterclasses 2005', *The Daily Mail*, 3 Dec. 2004, pp. 74–5.

to write terrible cliché or gibberish,' she said, 'because if you try to do everything at once—try to learn metre but at the same time to produce great lines of poetry—you won't be able to' (Barnard). The main objective was to learn new writing skills and to make connections, rather than to get published. On its website, the Poetry School declares that it operates 'independently of other poetry institutions and publishers (but we love to collaborate with them.)'[10] For example, Michael Schmidt of Carcanet Press was invited to give a lecture on Imagism and Vorticism in January 2001.[11]

The Poetry School occupies a position close to the 'non-business' end of the horizontal axis on Figure 9.1. It offers an accredited MA in Writing Poetry, in partnership with Newcastle University. Students attend masterclasses and workshops in London or Newcastle-upon-Tyne during term time and come together to participate in a one-week Summer School. Delivered as a part-time course over two years, the MA costs a total of £7,410 in tuition fees.[12] This seems particularly high for a course that is unlikely to lead to a lucrative career. Studying for an MA in Poetry is a risky choice, which depends on the possession of, in Pierre Bourdieu's words, 'substantial economic and social capital' (*The Field of Cultural Production* 67). The aspiring poets' disavowal of short-term economic gains is not without beneficiaries. Hiding behind their non-profit mission, the Poetry School and its academic partner profit at the economic level from the students' appetite for poetry writing, an activity associated with taste and distinction.

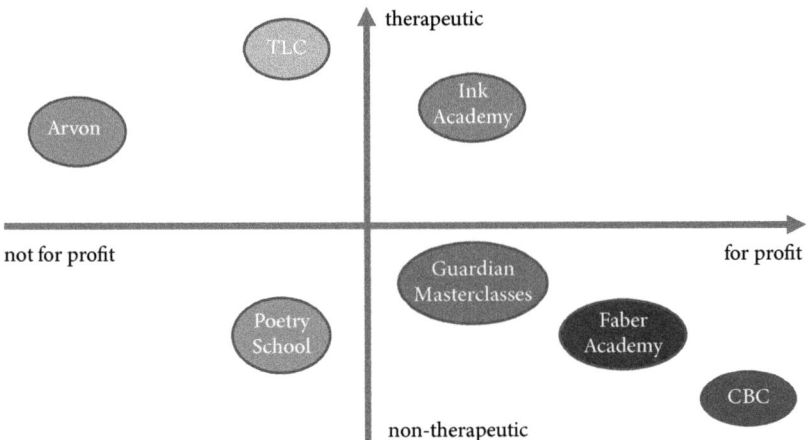

Fig. 9.1 UK-based, non-academic providers of creative writing courses.
Source: Author's own.

---

[10] 'About—Poetry School', https://poetryschool.com/about/. Accessed 30 Apr. 2021.
[11] *The Times Literary Supplement*, 12 Jan. 2001, p. 16.
[12] Writing Poetry MA—Newcastle University, https://www.ncl.ac.uk/postgraduate/courses/degrees/writing-poetry-ma/#fees&funding. Accessed 30 Apr. 2021.

9.2 For Profits

9.2.1 Guardian Masterclasses

A cheaper (but less intensive) option is to enrol in a Guardian Masterclass such as 'Unleash your creativity through writing poetry' taught by Laura Dockrill.[13] Described as a Facebook poet, Dockrill is known for her performances and close links with the singer Adele and other celebrities. The one-day course does not promise any academic benefit. Instead, the masterclass is presented as a fun experience that will leave participants inspired and empowered.

This modest ambition is a far cry from the UEA–Guardian Masterclasses offered from 2011 to 2015. The press release celebrated the alliance between 'Britain's leader in Creative Writing' and 'Britain's leading newspaper' to create a new form of Masterclass education: 'We hope that we'll unearth the next Ian McEwan or Joe Dunthorne and extend this model so different parts of the globe can experience the quality of UEA's education and innovation with the *Guardian*'s great reach and excellent brand recognition' (Acevedo-Scott).

The reference to Ian McEwan reminded prospective students of UEA's excellent record of discovering new writers. McEwan is not only a famous alumnus of the university, he is also a close friend of Professor Jon Cook, who initiated the collaboration with the Guardian Masterclasses. As we have seen in Chapter 6, McEwan has regularly provided endorsements for his alma mater. 'UEA and the *Guardian* already make a significant contribution to the literary culture of this country,' he declared in 2011. 'By working together they will provide a powerful focus and opportunity for people to discover what they can achieve at different stages of their writing lives.'[14] The disappearance of the UEA–Guardian Masterclasses shows the difficulty of this kind of collaboration—in part because of their different positionings on the horizontal axis that opposes non-profits to businesses.

9.2.2 Faber Academy

Created shortly before the UEA–Guardian Masterclasses, the Faber Academy (FA) is part of a long-established publishing house. Both companies used the same strategies to attract would-be writers—promoting successful alumni, while also keeping a certain distance. Claim too much credit, and you run the risk of giving the impression that publication is guaranteed. Claim too little, and would-be

---

[13] 'Unleash Your Creativity through Writing Poetry | Laura Dockrill', *The Guardian*, 6 Feb. 2017.
[14] 'Author Ian McEwan Supports a Series of New Creative Writing Courses Launched by Guardian Masterclasses and the University of East Anglia', *The Guardian*, 26 May 2011.

writers will fear that they will remain unpublished and unread after paying a small fortune in tuition fees.

To sell its £4,000 course Writing a Novel, the Faber Academy uses a blurb from a former client, S. J. Watson, the bestselling author of *Before I Go to Sleep*. 'It was hard work,' Watson says. 'But I not only completed my novel, I also learned how to navigate the choppy waters of the publishing world.' As the FA website makes clear, the course is designed to maximize contacts with professionals in the publishing industry. Students hear talks from Faber's publishing directors and sales managers, and they read to a room of 'London's top agents' once the course is finished. This gives them 'unrivalled access to those who know'. This is the equivalent of paying a premium on LinkedIn to reach out to a hiring manager and make a good impression before even applying for a job. In short, the Faber Academy presents itself as a business-orientated service that allows clients to 'start [their] career' as professional writers.[15]

However, Ian Ellard—the director of the Faber Academy from 2017 to 2019—also stressed that his company did not guarantee any successful outcome. Even when alumni sign a publishing deal, it is rarely with Faber. For example, *Before I Go to Sleep* was published by Doubleday in Britain and HarperCollins in the United States. Although Watson reportedly met his agent—Clare Conville—at the end of the FA course, his thriller would not have fit well on the Faber list, which is mostly known for literary fiction and poetry. When I interviewed him, Ellard insisted on the ability of his firm to self-regulate in a market which is largely unregulated. 'Editorial integrity' is of paramount importance to Faber, he told me. He explicitly linked the notion of integrity to the reputation of the firm:

> It's one of the only things we've got and we have to really, really be careful to cling on to it ... We don't have OFSTED, we don't have any regulator that can come in, tell us that we're doing well and give us a stamp of approval. We've got our reputation and our integrity.[16]

In other words, the Faber Academy wants to preserve its image as a quality, independent publisher—while also offering opportunities to ambitious, commercially orientated writers. The firm is very aware that its highbrow image is not a unique selling point in a market dominated by academia. Its appeal rests in the combination of cultural *and* economic capital. Study for an MA in creative writing at a respectable university and you will gain cultural capital. But only the Faber Academy will offer you access to industry professionals on a regular basis. If you want to become a famous bestselling writer, FA is a 'practical alternative' to a creative writing MA, the website declares.

---

[15] 'Writing A Novel (Evening)', *Faber Academy*, https://www.faberacademy.co.uk/writing-a-novel-writing-course-january-2019-wan18.html. Accessed 14 Aug. 2019.

[16] Ian Ellard, Interview by author, 3 July 2018, via telephone.

While universities refuse to acknowledge that many writers are motivated by money and celebrity, the Faber Academy adopts a pro-business approach. When I asked Ellard why Faber decided to launch its Academy in 2009, he told me that it was 'a deliberate commercial decision': 'We realised that we had a great building, we had a great trusted brand, we had ready access to great writers, and so it made sense to give it a go.' It seems surprising to openly admit that the Academy is the lucrative branch of an old publishing house confronted with a fast-changing landscape. But this pragmatic approach seems designed to attract would-be writers who also want to make money: pay thousands of pounds upfront, in the hope of making much more if your book is published and made into a film.

The 80th Anniversary of Faber in 2009—in the midst of the financial crisis—coincided with a profound rethinking of the company's strategy. In a *Daily Telegraph* article, Stephen Page, Faber's CEO, explained that British publishing was caught in the endgame of the death of the net book agreement in 1995. This led to heavily discounted prices in supermarkets and large retailers. 'It decimated the independent booksellers and drew everyone into a much more mass-market conversation based around bestsellers, which has not been good news for a publisher like Faber,' he said (Clements). Margins were squeezed, and publishing houses had to find new ways to make a profit. Traditionally, publishers dealt with intermediaries, from literary agents to booksellers. They seldom interacted directly with readers. Stephen Page proposed to rethink this model: 'We have started engaging with the reader who wants to be a writer.' In an uncertain landscape, the plan was for non-copyright business to make up 15–20 per cent of Faber's revenue (Thomson).

The market for creative writing courses was unchartered territory for Faber, so Page and his colleagues decided to start with what they had: a strong brand, associated with T. S. Eliot and other modernist writers. The first courses were hosted at the Shakespeare and Company bookshop in Paris (the historical birthplace of James Joyce's *Ulysses*) and in Faber's offices in London, where Eliot used to meet with editors and writers. A weekend course in pastoral East Sussex started with a tour of Charleston, the former residence of painter Vanessa Bell—Virginia Woolf's sister—and country retreat of the Bloomsbury group (McLaren). Faber used its long association with modernism to build its reputation as a credible provider of creative writing courses, but also to distinguish itself from competitors. Arvon courses were cheaper, and offered a similar format (fifteen students, two tutors), but they lacked Faber's modernist aura.

This association with modernism has become less important over time, Ellard told me. 'It's much more interesting for people that we publish Kazuo Ishiguro.' As we have seen in Chapter 8, the author of *Never Let Me Go* gave a Masterclass at the Faber Academy in 2010, and other well-known writers are regular guests. Yet, students are also reminded of Faber's prestigious past—for example, the meeting rooms at the company's headquarters in Bloomsbury are named after works by Eliot, Ted Hughes, and Sylvia Beach. 'For some people, it's a matter of trust, they know that we've been around for a long time and that smart people trust us with their books,' Ellard said.[17] As the brand has expanded outside Britain, it has lost some of its modernist associations to become more focused on living writers and the contemporary publishing landscape. Local versions of the Academy have opened in Canada and Australia. In July 2011, for example, a one-day course on Getting Published offered tips to Australian would-be writers on writing a good proposal and editing their opening chapters. Faber commodifies its prestigious past to sell writing courses with an enticing story—the story that everyone has a 'potential masterpiece' waiting to be written.[18]

The development of the Faber Academy brand has led to a growing emphasis on the selection of students to compete against universities in the profitable market for long-term courses. 'Places on this course are limited and keenly contested,' declares the webpage for the Writing a Novel course.[19] Whether this claim is true or not, it shows that Faber Academy wants to present itself as an elite organization: money alone will not guarantee you a place, you need to apply and be selected. Like the most prestigious university-based creative writing courses, Faber Academy gives the impression that they attract the best—independently of financial abilities. According to the firm, eighty publishing deals for first books have been signed since the Academy started in 2009. Richard Skinner, the FA's fiction director and tutor on the Writing a Novel course, told the London *Evening Standard* that 'not even the University of East Anglia's MA, the UK's best-established creative writing course since the 1970s ..., or the Iowa Writers' Workshop, the world-celebrated literary launch pad featured in the fourth series of *Girls*, can claim an equivalent hit rate over the same period' (qtd in Nicol). The message is clear: if you want to get published, do not waste your time and money on university courses, choose a practical alternative that will launch your career.

In fact, many students go from the university to Faber Academy, and vice versa. Rachel Heng, a graduate from Columbia University, started working on her dystopian novel *The Suicide Club* during a six-month FA course. The book is set in a near future where immortality has become an obsession for the genetically superior upper class. It tells the story of an outlawed group fighting for people's right to live and die as they choose. At the end of her course, Heng read an excerpt to a room full of agents, several of whom expressed interest. She eventually chose to work with Juliet Mushens, the co-founder of Caskie Mushens Literary Agency, who sold the novel to UK publisher Sceptre for a five-figure sum after a five-way auction. US rights were acquired by Holt in a six-figure auction. Despite being described as a 'big future star of the Sceptre list' (Cowdrey), Heng decided to go

---

[17] Ibid.
[18] 'About Us', Faber Academy, https://www.faberacademy.co.uk/about-us. Accessed 30 Apr. 2021.
[19] 'Writing A Novel (Daytime)', *Faber Academy*, https://www.faberacademy.co.uk/writing-a-novel-daytime-novel-writing-course-wnd14.html. Accessed 14 Aug. 2019.

back to the university. In 2017, she started an MFA in Fiction and Screenwriting at the Michener Center for Writers, University of Texas in Austin, and explained her reasons on her website:

> I felt increasingly frustrated—I didn't have enough time to write with my full-time job, wasn't getting enough feedback, didn't have any consistent mentorship. The decision to apply to MFA programs was driven by this frustration, this feeling that what I was doing wasn't enough. I wanted more time, more community, more mentorship. 2–3 years of funded time to focus on my writing sounded like absolute heaven to me.
>
> (Heng, 'On Applying')

Freedom from financial constraints and salaried work—this is what wealthy US creative writing programmes offer their students. Faber Academy will not easily be able to imitate this unique selling point, even though it provides a few scholarships that cover tuition fees.

9.2.3 Curtis Brown Creative

The development of Faber Academy showed that MAs in creative writing did not fill the entire market, and that there was a place for other providers. In 2011, the literary agency Curtis Brown launched a creative writing school, Curtis Brown Creative (CBC). In addition to six-month courses in London or online, CBC offers shorter online courses that are non-selective and cheaper. The driving force behind the school was Anna Davis, who previously worked as Lecturer in creative writing after studying for an MA. This experience left her disillusioned with university-based creative writing courses, for three main reasons.

The first problem is that universities try to fit creative writing within a rigid bureaucratic system. 'It was the accreditation, the marking, that whole system of trying to evaluate people's novels and putting academic-style grades, distinctions, all of that, I found really peculiar,' Davis told me.[20] She felt that a literary agency was a better place to help students improve their writing and educate them in the ways of the publishing industry. 'We're unencumbered by university bureaucracy or the mismatch between academia's ideas of literary worth and the kind of novels people want to buy and read.'

Second, Davis criticized some universities' willingness to accept nearly every student, which results in low standards of writing. 'My impression is that many MA courses that run in the UK at least are not difficult to get onto,' she said. Universities pretend that they select students, but in fact, they are heavily dependent on tuition

---

[20] Anna Davis, Interview by author, 21 May 2018, London.

fees. Since creative writing courses do not cost much to run, they have become a 'cash cow' in some instances. When I reminded Davis that Curtis Brown Creative has also attracted criticism for its high fees (£2,990 for the six-month course), she replied: 'I believe we give good value for money if you directly compare the content of one of our courses to the content of university MA courses, which are of course considerably more expensive.'

The third issue is the quality of instruction. 'You get people who are not even commercially published novelists taking PhDs and becoming lecturers in creative writing,' Davis told me. With limited knowledge of the publishing industry, these instructors cannot help students get an agent and start a writing career. They can, however, advise on how to succeed in academia. MA students are thus encouraged to do a PhD and become creative writing instructors themselves. For Davis, this growing gap between the academic system and the mainstream publishing industry has created market opportunities for other providers.

Like Faber Academy, Curtis Brown Creative targets would-be writers whose main ambition is to get published. When Davis was working in academia, her meetings with students often centred around the same question: whether or not their novel was publishable. In response to this demand, CBC promises would-be writers that they will meet literary agents and other publishing professionals. The course takes place at Curtis Brown's offices near Piccadilly station in London. The security at the entrance gives the impression that only the literary elite ever gets in. Embracing the image of the gatekeeper, Davis said: 'We bring people here, they're coming into the agency, and you can see them energised—just by coming into the agency, just by feeling that they've come through the doors that were locked to them, usually, and that we can open something up and give them a different experience.' For would-be writers, a course at Curtis Brown Creative offers the opportunity to meet published writers and agents, based in London and elsewhere.

While Faber is reluctant to publish writers who have attended its FA courses, Curtis Brown has no problem recruiting clients amongst its own students. The agency represents Nicholas Searle—who did the CBC online course and went on to sign a publishing deal with Viking for *The Good Liar*. Another client, Jane Harper also came out of the online course. By the end of 2021, Curtis Brown Creative stated that they had over 150 published authors among their alumni, and that over half of them are represented by Curtis Brown.[21] 'The agents are looking for talent,' Davis told me. 'We are very keen to find new talents and bring them in.' This discourse reminds us of the Famous Writers School. In both cases, writers are told that writing is a rational career path, that there is a demand for new writing. The speculative reality of the publishing market is carefully hidden, and aspiring writers are encouraged to dream about their future success. For example, literary agents who

---

[21] Anna Davis, Email to author, 30 Dec. 2021.

contribute to the CBC courses tell students about foreign rights as well as film and TV rights.

Curtis Brown uses its submissions portal (the online equivalent of the slush pile) to gather data and attract new clients for its creative writing courses. Would-be writers who just want to submit a proposal to an agent are encouraged to sign up to the Curtis Brown Creative newsletter. They are also asked for information about the creative writing courses they attended in the past—a precious source of information for CBC. The blurring of the boundary between the literary agency and its creative writing branch is problematic. It creates the impression that doing a CBC course will increase the probability of landing an agent. Even those who cannot afford to study with CBC, or who are simply not interested, have no choice but to give their data when they submit their proposal. Since aspiring writers are much more likely to directly approach a literary agent rather than a publisher, CBC's access to data is a major competitive advantage over Faber Academy.

9.2.4 Ink Academy

While Curtis Brown and Faber Academy focus mostly on collective workshops, other providers specialize in one-to-one services. Here again, we see an evolution from non-profit to for-profit organizations. The Literary Consultancy was the first consultancy of its kind ever set up in Britain, and it was followed by a rise of authors' services, including Ink Academy, which offers manuscript assessments and workshops. Aki Schilz—who became the new director of TLC after Rebecca Swift's untimely death in 2016—told me that her organization had a higher purpose than simply making money: 'We're the only literary consultancy that's core funded in the Arts Council England's portfolio,' she said. 'We have never seen ourselves as just a service provider, we are based in the Free Word building'—home to Arvon and other charities. With the Arts Council pushing for more diversity, it is hardly surprising that 'inclusivity and representation' are amongst Schilz's priorities.[22] While funding from the Arts Council was initially used to provide free reads to low-income writers, this group was not very diverse. Schilz is leading various initiatives to increase the visibility of minorities in the creative sector—including rethinking the recruitment process and making events more welcoming.

The Ink Academy, which receives no public funding, is free to focus on its core business: offering editorial services to writers. Whereas TLC provides one-off manuscript assessments via email, Marina Kemp—a former editor who co-founded the company with her sister—insists that 'creative writing can only be

---

[22] Aki Schilz, Interview by author, 20 Apr. 2018, London. Free Word lost its funding in 2021 and the building was shut as a result. As of January 2022, TLC has a virtual office and the team is remote-working.

successfully taught one to one'. While studying for an MA in creative writing, she realized that writers' workshops were much less useful than the tutorials:

> There was a lot of frustration at the amount of time you have to dedicate to read other people's work. It's quite high, because I think that's the way to make it work. Tutors have a [limited] amount of time they can dedicate to one-to-one [tutorials].[23]

Here, Kemp points out a central characteristic of many university courses: the high tuition fees of creative writing programmes are not necessarily linked to a high level of service. Students are encouraged to teach themselves, reading and commenting on each other's work, with little input from teachers. In short, universities are like cable television providers: users buy a bundle of services, wishing they could pay only for the one or two channels that are of interest.

Instead of offering a package, Ink Academy focuses on specific aspects that the users want to develop. Although the company organizes workshops and masterclasses, its main selling point is the opportunity to work one-to-one with tutors (£1,800 for nine sessions over six months). This tends to attract people who, having experienced writers' workshops, now want more individual attention from an experienced writer. 'Lots of our clients have done Faber Academy and MAs, and they've really enjoyed them at the stage they were at,' Kemp says. 'But at some point, they've got the thing they've got to write, and they just need to concentrate on that.' The flexibility of one-to-one tuitions is particularly well-suited to those with young children, so it is not surprising that most of Kemp's clients are women in their thirties and forties. These people are often 'very vulnerable', Kemp adds, 'their writing is a kind of dream that they held very privately for a long time.' Like The Literary Consultancy, Ink Academy offers a quasi-therapeutic service, allowing people to share their stories and to connect with someone who is paid to listen to them.

I asked Kemp about the expectations of these clients: surely, the fact that she had worked for Penguin Random House might lead some clients to expect help with publication? Kemp was clear that they never make promises and very rarely put a client directly in touch with an agent. Instead, they give 'realistic feedback on the publishing process' to make it 'less oblique, and a bit less mysterious, and perhaps less intimidating' for outsiders. For example, Kemp might suggest names of agents who specialize in a certain genre. But this kind of advice can easily be found online, and cold-emailing an agent or submitting a manuscript via their website is unlikely to result in a publishing deal. Kemp agreed that 'it is often hugely about who you know'.

Ink Academy protects itself by giving no guarantee of publication, while also celebrating former clients who have obtained a publishing deal. Following the book

---

[23] Marina Kemp, Interview by author, 26 Feb. 2018, London.

launch for *Milkshake and Morphine*, a memoir by Genevieve Fox, Kemp and her colleagues tweeted: 'Genevieve came to Ink Academy when we were just starting out—we had the absolute pleasure of working on 1st draft of her brilliantly funny, moving memoir.'[24] Fox's book was published by Square Peg (an imprint of Penguin Random House) and was reviewed in major newspapers. This is, of course, excellent publicity for Ink Academy. Go beyond the promotional tweets, and another reality appears: Fox worked for many years as a journalist and she also runs her own creative writing programme/ mentoring service. She is not an outsider who needed advice on getting published. Like Ink Academy, other creative writing providers advertise a small number of success stories, while also managing the expectations of all those who have little chance of ever getting published.

What does the future look like for creative writing courses outside academia? Unsurprisingly, the main trend is digital. This is not an issue for The Literary Consultancy, which does not provide any face-to-face interactions with clients (feedback on manuscripts is sent via email). But for Arvon, the growth of online courses is at first sight incompatible with its immersive experience. As we have seen, the Foundation prides itself on cutting off students from all distractions—radio, television, telephone, and the Internet. Ruth Borthwick had no plan to change this model but was experimenting with online mentoring. 'I don't think that will ever replace the face-to-face living as a community,' she said. 'But it could be something that could keep people going after they had that immersive experience.'[25] Since 2020, Arvon has developed a fourth house online which is now on a shortlist of innovative projects selected by Arts Council England to celebrate the resilience of the arts during the pandemic.

For Faber Academy and Curtis Brown Creative, the digital revolution is not news. FA's writing courses are designed for those who want to 'write in the heart of Bloomsbury (or up a mountain in Peru)'.[26] The firm currently offers six online courses—ranging from three days to twenty-eight weeks. The longer course targets novelists who want to receive feedback on their first 15,000 words, while the shorter courses are for beginners and procrastinators. During the weekend courses, participants use an egg timer and follow the Pomodoro Technique to write in short, intensive blocks. Faber Academy understands that not all aspiring writers have the same needs: some of them live far from London, others have no interest in traditional writing workshops. Its digital offering is conceived as a response to this segmentation of the market and complements the face-to-face courses in Bloomsbury.

---

[24] @ink_academy Tweet, 26 Jan. 2018.
[25] Ruth Borthwick, Interview by author, 30 Apr. 2018, London.
[26] 'Creative Writing Courses in London and Online', *Faber Academy*, https://www.faberacademy.co.uk/creative-writing-courses/location/london/course-length-/2%E2%80%933-months/sort-by/position/sort-direction/desc.html?arrow=1. Accessed 30 Apr. 2021.

Curtis Brown Creative also offers a wide range of online modules, which can be purchased individually or as a package (from 'Starting to Write Your Novel' to 'Edit & Pitch'). Its most expensive offering—the £2,600 six-month online novel-writing course—is described as highly selective and a potential route to a 'major publishing deal'. The examples of successful former students include Janet Ellis, an ex-presenter of the British television programme Blue Peter. Ellis is also mother of singer Sophie Ellis-Bextor, but CBC is adamant that her famous name and connections in the media world did not help her get published. Gordon Wise, her Curtis Brown literary agent, apparently submitted the book under a pseudonym, 'to be sure that editors' motivation for reading and offering was based on the strength of the book itself' (Kam). This hard-to-believe story is designed to convince aspiring writers that only the quality of the writing matters, and that a CBC online course can make a major difference between deal and no deal.

For would-be writers who are not ready to pay thousands of pounds for an online course, the US-based education company MasterClass offers a cheaper alternative. Its business model relies on recruiting high-profile celebrities and creating Hollywood-style videos to introduce users to their 'instructors'. For £170 per year, customers have access to all classes taught by Serena Williams (tennis), Gordon Ramsay (cooking), Margaret Atwood (literary writing), Malcolm Gladwell (non-fiction), James Patterson (commercial writing), Dan Brown (how to write a thriller), and many others. Instructors reportedly make about $100,000 up front when they begin working with MasterClass and receive 30 per cent of the revenue their classes generate (Jarvey).

MasterClass encourages aspiring writers to think that they, too, can become successful by following simple rules and staying positive. James Patterson, described on the Masterclass website as the author of '19 consecutive No. 1 *New York Times* bestsellers',[27] declares in his promotional video that his first novel was rejected by thirty-one publishers. With persistence and effort, everyone can make it to the top. Atwood has a similar message: 'You become a writer by writing, there is no other way. So do it, do it more, do it better.' Likewise, Dan Brown debunks the idea that bestselling status depends on talent, inspiration or even craft. 'Writing a novel is about a process,' he says. 'This class provides practical tools, a road map to turn your ideas into a story.' Fame, freedom, and flexibility—the lifestyle once promoted by the Famous Writers School—is also at the heart of MasterClass. For-profit creative writing courses have evolved from paper-based distance learning to the online world, but the questions they raise remain the same: is it ethical to use a famous writer's image to sell a dream lifestyle, knowing that the 'instructor' probably had little to do with the actual content of the course? Shouldn't aspiring writers be encouraged to be more realistic about their chances of success?

---

[27] https://www.masterclass.com/classes/james-patterson-teaches-writing. Accessed 23 Jan. 2022.

Ian Ellard is right to say that for-profit creative writing programmes have a lot to lose if they fail to provide a high-quality service. No one wants to follow the same path as the Famous Writers School. But relying on companies to self-regulate is not enough. Would-be writers who experience a disappointing course have few options to get some of their money back. Apart from raising a complaint with the company itself, they cannot turn to an independent regulator. This is problematic, especially if the sector continues to grow and attract even more would-be writers determined to become rich and famous, and ready to pay thousands of pounds to achieve this dream. In short, the autonomous creativity associated with the non-academic world comes at a price. For risk-averse writers, the image of blandness and conformity of academia might well turn into an advantage, since it also comes (at least in theory) with quality control and regulation.

Epilogue
The Future of Creative Writing Programmes in Continental Europe

Until the 1990s, universities in Continental Europe resisted the idea that creative writing could be taught. This is no longer the case. In Leizpig, for example, the Institute of German Literature [Deutsches Literaturinstitut] has gained worldwide recognition, thanks to the success of former students but also to its star-filled programme of guest speakers. Synergies with the Leipzig Book Fair, which brings together publishing professionals and members of the public, consolidate the Institute's leading position in the German literary field. But the Institute is not the only place where Germanophone students can practice creative writing. In Vienna, the 'School of Poetry' [Schule für Dichtung] was founded in 1991, as an independent artistic project, and started offering classes the following year. Since 2009, the University for Applied Arts in Vienna has offered a three-year course in creative writing, the first university in Austria to offer an academic course in the subject. In Switzerland, the Literature Institute [Schweizerisches Literaturinstitut] was founded in 2006 as a department of the Bern University of the Arts. It offers Bachelor's and Master's degrees in literary writing for students who write in German and French. Other institutes, such as the Josef Skvorecky Literary Academy in Prague, were founded as private universities.

Literary outsiders were the driving force behind Anglo-American programmes in creative writing, and this positioning on the margins of academia had a huge influence on the institutionalization of the discipline in Continental Europe. This epilogue starts with the example of the Deutsches Literaturinstitut Leipzig (DLL), an institution which finds its roots in the former Communist regime and then reinvented itself in the mid-1990s. Led by Josef Haslinger, an alumnus of the Iowa International Writing Program, the DLL has few links with the literature departments at Universität Leipzig. This institutional structure is, of course, reminiscent of the Iowa model of separation between writers and scholars. In the second section, I examine the case of Paris 8, the first university in France to offer a Master's degree in literary creation. It is not a coincidence that the discipline appeared in a university associated with the margins: both in terms of geographical location (in the Parisian *banlieue*) and in terms of institutional culture (with roots in the political radicalism of May 1968). Like the University of East Anglia in

Britain, Paris 8 sees itself as an avant-garde institution that challenges the literary establishment.

The Leipzig Institute of German Literature finds its origins in the 1950s, at the time when the Communist regime was looking towards the Russian model to build new institutions. In Moscow, the Literature Institute Maxim Gorky, created in 1933, educated writers who would then go on to promote the Party's ideology in their work. In 1955, it became a model for a similar but much smaller institute in Leipzig. The founding director was Alfred Kurella, a man who had worked for years on behalf of Stalin. The new *Institut für Literatur* was named after the Communist writer Johannes R. Becher, who was then Culture Minister of the German Democratic Republic (GDR). Party propaganda was embedded in the new institute's curriculum. Seminars in poetry, prose, and drama educated students to see and describe the world in the right way. Aspiring writers also took courses in literature, cultural studies, art history, music history and Marxism-Leninism, a compulsory subject at all GDR universities. To prevent students from getting too caught up in the world of fiction and philosophy, they were regularly sent to work in the coalmines. From 1955 to 1970, the poet Georg Maurer led the poetry seminars, influencing an entire generation of young East German poets known as the Saxon poetry school [Sächsische Dichterschule].[1]

After the collapse of the Communist regime, the Free State of Saxony decided to dissolve the Institute of Literature on the grounds of its ideological orientation. Students who were still enrolled on 31 December 1990 could finish their degrees, but no new cohort would join them. This decision was highly controversial. During the thirty-five years of its existence, the Johannes R. Becher Institute had educated thousands of writers, including many who rejected the Communist ideology and emigrated to West Germany. This group of alumni included Erich Loest, Jurek Becker, and Hans-Joachim Schädlich, who had experience of American creative writing programmes. They did not understand why the institute had to close its doors just at the time when the idea of training writers was beginning to spread in other European countries. As non-Communist writers, their voice carried an important weight, and the State of Saxony decided to re-launch the Institute of Literature with a new name, a new curriculum, and a new location.

Finding a director for the institute proved a challenge. After a first search which led nowhere, the hiring committee decided to directly approach candidates, including Josef Haslinger, who was then part of the Iowa International Writing Program. 'I didn't want to become a professor at a university in those days, I was writing my novel' [*Opernball*, published in 1995]. Despite this lack of interest, the committee continued to send him letters:

---

[1] See Haslinger, 'Warum Creative Writing?'.

When I came back from Iowa, it was around Christmas in '94, I had all those letters, and I was making my way through those letters and there was this letter from the University of Leipzig ... And this letter said: 'Your hearing is tomorrow' (from the day I opened it) ... So I took the night train and instead of sleeping in the train, I was writing a lecture ... It was about the value of literature nowadays [*Hausdurchsuchungen im Elfenbeinturm*—published in 1996].[2]

Here, Haslinger presents him as a literary rebel, who initially rejects a prestigious academic position. It is only when he realizes that the search committee is determined to hire him that he consents to meet them.

This positioning on the margins of academia is also explicit in an essay that Haslinger wrote in the mid-2000s, ten years after this first experience at Iowa. It was his 'most intense time'—intense at the literary level but also intense in terms of the amount of alcohol he drank. He shared his apartment with the Argentinian author Carlos Feiling and on the first evening, they went to Foxhead, a bar favoured by the city's intellectuals. Feiling was telling him about his encounters with Jorge Luis Borges when the loudspeaker started playing Leonard Cohen's song *Closing Time*. They had to leave the restaurant immediately. 'But it was only two o'clock in the morning,' Haslinger said. 'So we decided to open a bar ourselves. It opened its doors every day at eleven o'clock in the evening, and writers from all over the world then poured into our apartment, some with manuscripts, some with whiskey bottles under their arms. There was no curfew.'[3]

This description of literary life in Iowa follows a familiar pattern: writers are presented as literary rebels, eager to drink all night when ordinary academics are in bed. At the time this essay was published, Haslinger was fifty years old, and he had directed the Deutsches Literaturinstitut for ten years. It would be unusual for scholars with a similar position to write about their own boozy experience at conferences and other professional gatherings. It is true that David Lodge wrote about scholars' unruly behaviours in his campus trilogy, but he used the form of a novel, not an autobiography. In short, Haslinger is reminding his readers that, despite his success in academia, he remains on the margins of the university system. This is the equivalent of an ageing rock star telling anecdotes about his wild youth—a renewed commitment to rebellion based on the fear of having 'sold out' to the system.

Josef Haslinger joined the Deutsches Literaturinstitut Leipzig in 1995 as its new director, after the dismissal of most of the staff. 'The Librarian was the only person from the old Institute who could continue working here.' The institute moved to Villa Wächterstraße 34, a building previously used by the state police. 'The rooms

---

[2] Haslinger, Interview by author, 6 Apr. 2017, Leipzig.
[3] Haslinger, 'Warum Creative Writing?', p. 190 (my translation).

were wired, all the conversations were taped,' Haslinger said.[4] Anchored in the history of the German Democratic Republic, the DLL is not a pale imitation of the American model of university creative writing. Although manual labour is no longer part of the curriculum, the new institute has not entirely erased the legacy of its predecessor. Like in the old institute, students have the opportunity to try out different forms of text—poetry, prose, and drama. They can also experiment with writing for the radio, film, and other media. Whereas many American programmes ask students to specialize in a specific genre, the DLL has a broader focus.

Yet, the Deutsches Literaturinstitut Leipzig is also heavily influenced by the Iowa model of separation between writers and scholars. The old institute was keen to give a strong theoretical education to its students, including a broad knowledge in German, Soviet, and world literature. In contrast, the DLL is isolated from literature departments. When I visited Leipzig in April 2017, a literary scholar based in the Institut für Anglistik told me that DLL students and staff rarely come to their events, even when they invite top writers. And when I interviewed Haslinger, he confirmed that there was 'no relationship' with literature departments:

> We have a lot of readings in our house, it's very rare that a professor from the German department crosses the street. And that's not far away: 100 meters ... We are completely separated. It is fine for us. A literature department has a special task of teaching literature—the history of literature and the forms of literature—not for writers, for readers. And we teach it for writers, this is a different approach. So we are happy that we can make our own programme without taking care of what they think we should do.

As in the case of the Iowa Writers' Workshop, the DLL has enough political clout within the university to deal directly with the central management. This privileged relationship with the university senior managers is based on the success of the institute in attracting talent and media attention. 'They are proud of us,' Haslinger declared.[5]

But the success of creative writing courses in Germany is not without risk. Describing the situation in the United States, Haslinger is critical of programmes that are cut off from real life. Indeed, American literary fiction and poetry survive almost exclusively in an academic environment. 'There are very few journals that are not related to universities and still print literary texts, and there are very few writers who are not permanently or temporarily affiliated to creative writing programmes.'[6] When creative writers want to publish, they often submit their work to friends and colleagues with links to university presses. This system of production and distribution of literary work operates almost exclusively within the academic

---

[4] Haslinger, Interview by author, 6 Apr. 2017, Leipzig.
[5] Ibid.
[6] Haslinger, 'Warum Creative Writing?', p. 186 (my translation).

system. In other words, 'real literary life is increasingly limited to the university environment'.[7] Haslinger's criticism of American creative writing programmes relies on a discourse that we have explored throughout this book—a discourse that associates creative writing in universities with conformity and the lack of creativity. Yet, he also makes clear that the DLL was heavily influenced by professors with experience of Anglo-American creative writing, including himself. Instead of encouraging students to gain real-life experience (perhaps manual labour, as in the old institute), Haslinger values purely academic pursuits, while also criticizing the university system.

Why do Haslinger and others insist on presenting themselves as literary rebels? Why do they continue to criticize an academic system to which they belong? Their position on the margins can be seen as a reaction to the dominant discourse. They keep their distance from an institution that threatens their creativity. They refuse to sober up and behave like scholars. They live with one foot in academia, and the other foot outside. This uncomfortable position can lead to an inversion of the mainstream discourse. The real world is no longer associated with freedom but with conformity, with life spent working in a cubicle surrounded by Organization Men. The academic system becomes the land of the free, an escape from alienated working conditions. In *The Program Era*, Mark McGurl writes that creative writing instructors 'can be seen as offering a form of therapy to some of these students, the "creative types," in advance of their lifelong capture by the usual cubicle' (408). Open spaces have now replaced cubicles as the favoured way to organize white collar work, promising freedom from the old world of conformity and hierarchical structures. Likewise, literary rebels affiliated with universities promise freedom from the cubicle and the painful realities of life outside academia.

In France, the University of Paris 8 Vincennes Saint-Denis, an institution with a long history of political radicalism, was one of the first places to launch a Master's degree in 'création littéraire' in 2013. At around the same time, universities in Toulouse, Le Havre, and Cergy-Pontoise also started offering degrees in creative writing. It is not a coincidence that the discipline emerged in peripheral universities, isolated from the *grandes écoles* and more prestigious organizations. Indeed, the Sorbonne and similar institutions have a much more traditional understanding of literary studies. 'In the old bastions, it's very patrimonial,' Lionel Ruffel, one of the co-founders of the new MA at Paris 8, told me. 'It's the idea that the writer is a kind of inspired genius ... that national distinctions are important, that centuries are important.'[8]

Paris 8 was well placed to challenge this ideology. Founded in 1971, the university finds its origins in the Vincennes University Experimental Centre, created in the wake of the 1968 movement. Associated with leading intellectuals such

---

[7] Ibid.
[8] Lionel Ruffel, Interview by author, 5 Apr. 2018, Paris.

as Hélène Cixous, Gilles Deleuze, and Jean-François Lyotard, the university was designed to be a hotbed of innovation open to the contemporary world. Unlike other higher education institutions, Paris 8 benefited from a large autonomy in the 1970s, and experimented with new topics such as cinema, psychoanalysis, visual arts, theatre, town planning, and artificial intelligence. 'No doubt the remarkable freedom of experimentation and creation, as well as a certain impulse towards solidarity, could not have been maintained without this autonomy,' argues Philip Lewis in the preface of *Folies et raisons d'une université* (14). The title of this book is a reference to the 'craziness' of an institution associated with productive experiments, but also with the worst excesses of the counterculture. The university was accused of being drug-infested, dirty, and dangerous, and in 1980, the conservative government ordered the destruction of its buildings, and its relocation from Vincennes to Saint-Denis—a poor *banlieue* north of Paris.

Like the University of East Anglia in Britain, Paris 8 found inspiration in two models of higher education: the model of openness and democratization associated with the Left in the 1960s; and the model of American universities. Three main innovations were imported from the United States. First, the concept of 'Units of Values' (UV), introduced from the beginning in Vincennes, was based on the 'credits' that American students earn for each course and can transfer to other universities. This model was subsequently adopted in a large number of French universities. Second, flexible boundaries between departments fostered interdisciplinarity and collaborations between history, philosophy, sociology, and literature. Third, the disappearance of the strict hierarchy with professors at the top and students at the bottom led to new forms of teaching—with an emphasis on seminars rather than lectures.

This history of experiments based on the American model influenced the structure of the Master's degree in literary creation. Since the university had long rejected traditional lectures, it made sense to implement practical training in workshops, in order to experiment with new forms of writing. Every fortnight, students receive feedback on their texts. They are encouraged to build a long-term project that will be monitored over the two years of the MA. To complement these workshops, a theoretical training provides the tools necessary to analyse contemporary writings, with an interdisciplinary perspective. The idea is that writing should not be isolated from other arts, particularly visual arts. Finally, professional training includes meetings with book professionals, writers, publishers, translators and critics. Students also receive training on the publication networks that enable the distribution and dissemination of contemporary literature. 'We are all published in good publishing houses, we know these publishers,' Lionel Ruffel told me, suggesting that he and his colleagues provide introductions that connect students with *discoverers of new talent*.[9]

[9] Ibid.

Despite these similarities with the American model of creative writing programmes, the MA in literary creation also presents characteristics specific to the French higher education system in general, and to Paris 8 in particular. First, the low tuition fees contrast sharply with the American system. In 2018–19, Master's students paid tuition fees of 243 euros (271 US dollars). Compare this to the $66,308 that MFA students at Columbia University in New York paid that same year. Second, it would be unthinkable for a French university to hire writers without a PhD for permanent teaching jobs. Although these writers can lead masterclasses and serve in temporary positions, permanent university lecturers and professors are civil servants, hired after jumping through several loops: a competitive exam called *agrégation*, a doctorate, and a *qualification* (to prove that the doctor is indeed qualified to teach at university level). Instructors at Paris 8 are scholars but also practising writers. Lionel Ruffel specializes in non-fiction, while Olivia Rosenthal is a novelist published by the Editions Verticales (part of the Gallimard group). The third difference with most American creative writing programmes is the close connection with art schools and experimental artistic practice. 'We chose not to call ourselves creative writing, it was really very voluntary,' Ruffel said. He positions his programme of *création littéraire* in opposition to traditional literary studies perceived as out-of-touch. Likewise, the Master's in Le Havre is a partnership between the university and the Art school: the former provides theoretical courses (comparative literature, literary translation, aesthetics …), the latter hosts writing workshops.

This focus on artistic experimentations is explicitly highbrow. Through collaborations and workshops, Paris 8 students are encouraged to situate their practice within the Poetry House [Maison de la Poésie] and the Centre Pompidou, located in wealthy arrondissements in Central Paris—far from the deprivation and geographical isolation of Saint-Denis. This transition to a privileged environment is facilitated by the selection of students, a selection that favours literary fiction, upmarket non-fiction, and mixed media. Despite Paris 8's emphasis on democratization, applicants who write in popular and commercial genres seem less likely to be selected. 'For now, it's a bit of a failure, we did not find a good fantasy writer that we wanted to follow,' Ruffel confessed. Positioned on the fringes of academia as a radical criticism of traditional literary studies, the MA in *création littéraire* devalues commercial fiction and the *field of large-scale production*, and encourages students to develop the social and intellectual capital necessary to join the *field of restricted production*.

Let's take the example of two successful alumni of the Master's at Paris 8: Elitza Gueorguieva, who published her first novel *The Cosmonauts Are Just Passing By* with the Editions Verticales in 2016; and David Lopez, whose novel *Fief* (Editions Seuil, 2017) received the literary prize Livre Inter. These two authors are presented as social outsiders: Gueorguieva grew up in Bulgaria and arrived in France when she was eighteen years old in search of better opportunities; Lopez spent his teenage years smoking and killing time with his friends in Nemours, a town in the Parisian region. The Master's in literary creation helped them develop stylistic originality, a key element of upmarket fiction in France. For Gueorguieva, this originality stems from the fact that French is not her native language: guided by her mentors at Paris 8, she was able to turn a potential weakness into a strength. Lopez's use of slang, inspired by rap music, also helped position *Fief* as a stylistically innovative novel based on his experience of deprivation and exclusion.

Developing an original style is not enough to attract the attention of a major Parisian publisher. Aspiring writers also need social capital, for example an introduction by a well-established writer already published by the firm. During her Master's, Gueorguieva was mentored by Olivia Rosenthal and Maylis de Kerangal, both published by the Editions Verticales; Lopez received help from Vincent Message, a lecturer published by Editions Seuil. After gaining access to publication, both Gueorguieva and Lopez then benefited from the publicity machine of the Editions Verticales and the Editions Seuil, and from the growing interest in creative writing programmes in France.

Despite the rise of university programmes at Paris 8 and elsewhere, the discipline of creative writing remains a controversial topic. 'The idea of teaching the art of writing is struggling to make its way in France,' argued the magazine *Bibliobs* in 2012 (Thomann). The following year, France Culture broadcast a radio programme titled 'Shameful Writing Workshops'. One writer, Alain André explained that when he published his first novel with Denoël, the editorial director told him: 'Not a word about your writing workshops on the back cover! It smells too much of sweat.'[10] And in 2014, the newspaper *L'Humanité* asked: 'What can you do with a degree in writing?' (Nicolas).

Three main reasons explain this scepticism: the distrust of the American model; the suspicion of standardization; and the symbolic devaluation of commercial fiction that US creative writing programmes supposedly favour. First, the fear of Americanization has long been a feature of French intellectual life. 'Will the programme in Le Havre be the exact copy of the Anglo-Saxon programmes?' asked the online magazine *Slate.fr* in 2012 (Moullot). Instead of presenting their programmes as American imports, creative writing practitioners have tried to position the discipline within the French tradition. Philippe Ripoll, the coordinator of the Master's in Le Havre, thus declared: 'the writing workshops have a very rich history: we think of the Oulipo' (Dumoulin). Co-founded by Raymond Queneau in 1960, the Oulipo was not a formal workshop within academia, but an informal group that met regularly. The discourse on a French tradition of group-based creative writing makes the discipline more palatable to an audience suspicious of the American model.

---

[10] 'Honteux ateliers d'écriture', *France Culture*, 26 Apr. 2013, https://www.franceculture.fr/emissions/revue-de-presse-culturelle-dantoine-guillot/honteux-ateliers-decriture. Accessed 30 Apr. 2021.

Fig. 10.1 Cartoon, *The Happiness of Being an Author*.
Credit: Antoine Chereau.

Second, creative writing workshops are suspected of producing standardized fiction for the masses. 'The United States applies a pattern of industrial production to all products, whether cultural or industrial, so why would books be different from electronic chips?' declared Eli Gottlieb in 2011 ('À l'école du formatage'). In his comic book *The Happiness of Being an Author* (2018), Antoine Chereau satirized workshops that promise literary success to all participants (Figure 10.1). A cartoon shows a creative writing instructor who tells his students: 'thanks to me you will learn to write a captivating novel that will seduce millions of readers.' A poster on the wall includes endorsements from bestselling Francophone writers—including Marc Lévy, Amélie Nothomb, and Guillaume Musso. This association between creative writing programmes and commercial fiction is the third reason for French hostility to the discipline. *Slate.fr* thus gave the examples of Anglo-American programmes with high tuition fees that 'teach their students to write in a formatted way, promising them to publish best-sellers' (Moullot).

But these criticisms are not sufficient to explain why the discipline of creative writing took so long to get established in France. From hamburgers to shopping malls, the French have adopted numerous American inventions, reinventing them to suit the local taste. Take the example of Big Fernand, a chain of fast-food restaurants that offers made-in-France 'hamburgés'. Clients are welcomed by a 'Fernand de salle', in charge of the presentation of the menu and customer service. With their small moustache, apron, and flat cap that evokes the beret, these hosts have an ultra-French appearance—as Jean-Laurent Cassely has shown in his book *NO FAKE: Counter-story of our Quest for Authenticity*. Everything is done to convince customers that they are in an authentic French restaurant, eating local food served by *hyper-français* staff. So why did France wait three-quarters of a century to adopt university creative writing—one of the last countries in Continental Europe to do so?

Ideological reasons, combined with the rigidities of the French university system, explain the long resistance to the discipline. The sociologist Gisèle Sapiro has written about the 'ideology of the natural-born creator' (*idéologie du créateur incréé*): the ability to write creatively is a gift, not a skill that can be learnt in the education system (15). The ideology of the gift finds its roots in the Romantic era and the development of a vocational model for writers. According to this model described by Nathalie Heinich, writers resembled clergymen and physicians: they were engaged in activities designed to respond to a vocation and an inner desire, with a total investment of the person and the conviction of a gift. Financial remuneration was not a concern. The practice of writing was solitary and could not be shared or taught. For Violaine Houdart-Merot, this vocational regime—marked by an activity on the margins of any community—found an echo in the French university system. 'Since the end of the nineteenth century, literary studies at the university have favoured (with the exclusion of rhetoric) critical reading to the detriment of any practice or form of writing isomorphic to literature' (21). Living writers had no place in this university tradition.

In prestigious universities, creative writing is often accused of being a practical discipline, one that has no place in a curriculum dominated by theoretical knowledge. In a 2013 interview in *Le Monde*, Hélène Merlin-Kajman—a professor of French Literature at the Sorbonne—criticized the new Master's at Paris 8, including the fact that students have to defend with persuasion and conviction their writing projects. 'I fear this annexation of literature to communication,' Merlin-Kajman said (Séry). Designed as a response to falling enrolments in literary studies, Masters in *création littéraire* risked devaluing the discipline. For Merlin-Kajman, then, writing remained a solitary enterprise linked to reading.

The rise of creative writing programmes in France found fertile ground in the crisis of literary studies, but also in the lack of institutional mediation. Since literary agents are rare, 'publishers monopolise access to the writer's profession,' Sapiro declared (Weill). Gatekeepers tend to select the same kind of well-connected writers, leading to standardization. 'The publishing circuit often works like a fairly arbitrary social network system,' Merlin-Kajman noted (Séry). Creative writing courses therefore serve as a mediating institution, a way for would-be writers to differentiate themselves from the thousands of contenders that send their manuscripts to publishers every year.

These characteristics are specific to the French context, but France is not isolated from a broader tendency: the search for personal fulfilment and the rejection of what the anthropologist David Graeber has famously called 'bullshit jobs.' Elise Nebout, the co-founder of the writing school *Les Mots*, in the 5e arrondissement of Paris, compared creative writing to yoga or meditation: it 'can be a way of refocusing,' she said (Bouchy). The next step is to try to turn a hobby into a profession. For Laure Limongi, who teaches on the Master's in création littéraire in Le Havre, many highly educated people are in search of meaning in their professional life (Lecherbonnier). Some of these young professionals leave their jobs to become bakers, restaurateurs, pastry chefs, cheese makers, or brewers—a phenomenon described by Jean-Laurent Cassely in *The Revolt of the First of the Class*. Instead of choosing manual jobs, others decide to turn towards artistic activities, including writing.

To cater to this growing demand, non-academic writing courses were created on the model of the Faber Academy. Launched in 2012, the 'Ateliers de la NRF' are affiliated with the prestigious publishing house Gallimard. The 'Ateliers du Figaro,' organized by the newspaper of the same name, were created in 2017. These courses aim to combine the rigour of a structure modelled on academic writers' workshops, with the freedom traditionally associated with life outside academia. Classes take place in historic buildings in Paris, giving the impression to would-be writers that they will cross the threshold of previously inaccessible literary temples and increase their chances of getting published. The organizers of the Gallimard and Figaro workshops emphasize the luxury and prestige associated with writing in France. Their publicity materials showcase plush rooms in *hôtels particuliers* with views on spacious gardens—a far cry from the image of the university sector in France, with their derelict buildings, over-crowded classrooms, rebellious students and faculty members who insist they are not part of the literary establishment.

With the expansion of creative writing courses (within and outside academia) outside the English-speaking world, there is ample scope for more scholarship on these programmes. Richard Jean So, Fan Dai, and others have pioneered a spatial expansion of the field towards non-Anglophone countries, but we still know too little about the national characteristics of Continental European and Asian programmes. In particular, we need more sustained analysis of these programmes in relation to the economics of world literature in translation and literary prizes, and the varying attitudes towards writing, publishing, and higher education in different countries. Born in the USA, creative writing programmes are now a world phenomenon, with local particularities that deserve more scrutiny.

Conclusion

Rebel Forever? How to Be a Writer in the Program Era

In October 2005, shortly after winning the Orange Prize for her novel *We Need to Talk about Kevin*, Lionel Shriver gave an interview to the US magazine *BOMB*. The interviewer Jenefer Shute asked Shriver about her choice to supplement her income with journalism after studying creative writing at Columbia University: 'I've always wondered how you avoided the peculiarly American trap of teaching creative writing for a living (given that you did fall into the peculiarly American trap of getting an MFA)?' ('Lionel Shriver')

Shriver started by dismissing her degree in creative writing: 'that MFA is the source of enduring shame, even if I didn't mind the process of "earning" it (re: those quotation marks, an MFA, academically, is a joke).' She went on to admit that she got her first literary agent thanks to one of her Columbia workshop instructors, Scott Spencer, so the degree was somewhat useful. 'But I'd have more respect for myself for having gotten a degree in history, for example. At that time, though, I wouldn't have had the discipline for a degree in history or anything else. I primarily wanted attention.'

After dismissing her own experience of studying creative writing, Shriver then confessed that the prospect of teaching the discipline had always made her 'feel suicidal'. And, she added: 'most creative writing workshops are glorified therapy sessions, and very few of your students will go on to publish anything more than their phone number. Moreover … teaching creative writing kills my enthusiasm for writing it. The whole enterprise just starts feeling indulgent, spoilt, embarrassing and pointless.' In short, teaching creative writing is not simply a waste of time. It can also lead to actual creative death.

This dialogue exemplifies the ambivalence towards creative writing programmes and academia that afflicts even those who have hugely benefited from these programmes. Shute (a writer and professor in the English Department of Hunter College, New York, where she taught in the MFA programme in creative writing) could have defended the discipline. Instead, she encouraged Shriver's criticism by presenting the MFA as an 'American trap'. She then agreed with Shriver that many creative writing students crave attention: 'I think that might be the real, hidden reason that so many people end up in MFA programs.' She did not respond when Shriver told her: 'Jenny, I don't know how you can stand it.'

Literary Rebels. Lise Jaillant, Oxford University Press.
© Lise Jaillant (2022). DOI: 10.1093/oso/9780192855305.003.0012

Now, let's imagine that I had been in the shoes of the interviewer. If my interviewee had dismissed literary studies as 'indulgent, spoilt, embarrassing and pointless', I would have objected, saying as politely as I could, that studying literature and the Humanities has many benefits. It seems strange to dismiss your own discipline as a trap, and students as attention-seeking youngsters. But as we have seen throughout this book, literary scholars and creative writers do not abide by the same rules. Scholars do not aspire to be rebels. We are generally content to be organization men and women, who abide by common professional rules. We do not publicly criticize our employer, our discipline or our students. We do not aspire to be free-range intellectuals, independent from the chains of academia. We do not shun the PhD for one-to-one training with independent scholars. In short, the myth of freedom-outside-academia holds little appeal for us.

Lionel Shriver is not the only successful writer who has dismissed her own experience of the academic discipline. And Jenefer Shute is not the only teacher of creative writing who has openly criticized the discipline. In 2014, shortly after being appointed Professor in creative writing at Kingston University, the British writer Hanif Kureishi described the subject as 'a waste of time'. Speaking at the Independent Bath Literature festival, he said that 'probably 99.9 per cent' of students are entirely lacking in talent. Asked if he would consider doing an MA in creative writing himself, he told the audience: 'No. I wouldn't do it like that. That would be madness. I would find one teacher who I thought would be really good for me' (Jones and Clark). Kureishi's remarks highlight the enduring dream of Model #1—the *informal mentorship model*, which seems especially alluring compared to the talentless world of academia (Model #2, with creative writing programmes focused on the professionalization of the writing career). In Chapter 2, we examined the period of transition between Models #1 and #2 through the example of James Culpepper, a young would-be writer in the 1940s.

Shute and Kureishi are not isolated cases of disgruntled teachers of creative writing. In 2009, shortly after winning the National Book Critics Circle Award in Poetry, the fifty-nine-year-old August Kleinzahler gave an interview to *The Guardian*. Like many American poets of the Baby Boomer generation, Kleinzahler has taught creative writing at university and held visiting professorship positions. Yet, he described himself as 'a pariah' in the academic world, and he openly dismissed creative writing programmes as shams designed to lure young and naïve would-be writers:

> I really feel that it's an unsavoury business, sitting in a room and critiquing the poetry of youngsters who aren't yet formed as adults, far less as writers, and who are highly professionalised and ambitious and want to be assured that they're doing something of importance. It's terrible to lie to young people. And that's what it's about.
>
> (Campbell, 'Interview: August Kleinzahler')

If teaching creative writing is so unpleasant and socially harmful, why do it? Kleinzahler replied that he accepts the invitation of 'the creative-writing corporations quite rarely'. The term 'corporations' once again shows the mental framework at stake here. In the *radical individualism model* (Model #3), creative writing programmes are conformist organizations that sell a mediocre product by lying to their own customers.

Freedom can only be found outside academia, but it comes at a high financial cost. Describing her attempt to make a living as a freelance journalist after graduating from her MFA, Shriver says: 'I have for many years lived a terribly insecure financial existence, and have never, ever passed up work, no matter how lowly or poorly paid' (Shute, 'Lionel Shriver'). This trade-off between financial security and creative freedom is explicit in the interview of Kleinzahler. *The Guardian* described his 'dilemma': 'the haphazard life of the bohemian poet set against the potential security of the writer in the university' (Campbell, 'Interview: August Kleinzahler').

Apparently, Jenefer Shute, Hanif Kureishi, and August Kleinzahler did not suffer consequences for their criticism of creative writing programmes. For a literary scholar, openly criticizing your subject, your students and your university would be a suicidal career move. Paradoxically, it can be a career-enhancing move for a creative writer. In other words, dismissing the discipline of creative writing can provide significant benefits in the literary field. Like celebrities who develop a working-class accent to increase their street credibility, teachers of creative writing who openly shun academia signal their ambition to reach the ultimate goal: the freedom and money that comes with a successful writing career outside the university system.

In the *radical individualism model*, being a creative writing teacher in academia brings a reasonable income, but no freedom—hence the risk of losing your creativity. But being a writer outside academia is financially extremely risky. In the UK, the nominal average (mean) earnings for professional writers was just £16,096 in 2018. This figure is low, and masks huge inequalities, with a median income of just £10,497 in 2018. The top 10 per cent of writers still earn about 70 per cent of total earnings in the profession. Having gone to university does not predict higher earnings. The earning power of writers seems to peak for those who are educated to just under degree level. In a literary world where the top prize is to make a good living while writing full-time, having a degree confers no advantage.[1]

For professional writers influenced by the *radical individualism model*, having freedom and money is the ultimate 'positional good'—a way to distinguish yourself from creative writing teachers on the one hand (who have some money but no freedom) and the mass of financially indigent writers (who have plenty of freedom

---

[1] *UK Authors' Earnings and Contracts 2018: A Survey of 50,000 Writers*, 2 May 2019, https://www.create.ac.uk/blog/2019/05/02/uk-authors-earnings-and-contracts-2018-a-survey-of-50000-writers/. Accessed 30 Apr. 2021.

but no money). In his 1976 book *The Social Limits of Growth*, Fred Hirsch observed that in rich economies, most people no longer compete for essential goods. Instead they engage in 'positional competition':

> By positional competition is meant competition that is fundamentally for a higher place within some explicit or implicit hierarchy and that thereby yields gains for some only dint of losses for others. Positional competition, in the language of game theory, is a zero-sum game: what winners win, losers lose.
>
> (52)

In the hierarchy of the literary field, Lionel Shriver occupies a higher position than Jenefer Shute. She has freedom, money, and even celebrity. If Shute was abiding by the rules of literary scholars, she would take pride in her education (she has a PhD in English), her academic position, and the fact that she works in a good university in New York City. Instead, Shute's criticism of her discipline shows that she is following the 'literary rebel' example set up by the founders of creative writing programmes.

Deeply ambivalent towards the university system, Paul Engle, Wallace Stegner, and Malcolm Bradbury continue to influence the way many creative writers see their disciplines. One writer based at a prestigious university in London told me that creative writing is an 'odd fit with English departments'. As a member of a literary studies department, he particularly resented the marking criteria of creative writing essays, based on 'research' and the need of scholarly sources for the best essays. In other words, the marking criteria that apply to literary studies do not fit well with creative writing assignments.

Of course, not all university-based creative writers are dismissive of their discipline and the way it is taught and assessed. Responding to Hanif Kureishi's criticism of talentless students, Will Buckingham (then a Reader in writing and creativity at De Montfort University) wrote an angry article for the *Times Higher Education*. Using emotional language, Buckingham declared: 'What infuriates me about Kureishi's view is not just its overbearing arrogance but also its abject failure of imagination.' Encouraging imagination and creativity is at the heart of creative writing programmes, Buckingham said. He strongly opposed Kureishi's definition of talent as a limited resource that only 0.1 per cent of creative writing students have. 'What worries me is not so much the meaninglessness of this figure as how appallingly dismissive it is of students' potential,' Buckingham added. He preferred to speak of 'talents', that can be nourished in creative writing programmes and then developed as useful skills:

> Far from 99.9 per cent finding their study of creative writing worthless, many graduates of the course on which I teach have gone on to successfully write, publish and perform. Others have set up small magazines and theatre companies.

Some have found themselves working in the publishing world or teaching creative writing. Others still have found that studying creative writing has given them skills useful in other areas: law, medicine or journalism.

('Hanif Kureishi Is Wrong about Students')

The arguments that Buckingham uses to defend creative writing programmes are similar to those that Humanities scholars often use to defend their disciplines. Studying literature, history, and the like develops skills that can then be employed in a wide range of professions.

But if studying is about learning new skills, why should a student choose the Humanities instead of the Sciences? As Justin Stover puts it in his provocative article 'There Is No Case for the Humanities':

Learning to parse Sanskrit undoubtedly entails some general cognitive benefit. But those benefits are always byproducts. No one wants to learn Sanskrit because it will give them a leg up in a fast-moving economy. It will never be a compelling case for the Humanities that they are like a gym for the mind. Forget about attracting administrators—that argument will not even get you any students.

('There Is No Case for the Humanities')

It is not Stover who thinks that the Humanities are useless (he has a PhD in classics from Harvard and teaches at the University of Edinburgh). Rather, he argues that the true value of the Humanities is to select a distinct class of students and scholars: 'the Humanities have always been about courtoisie, a constellation of interests, tastes, and prejudices that marks one as a member of a particular class.' Stover has little respect for Humanities scholarship that incorporates 'the issues du jour in race, class, and gender'. For him, truly valuable scholarship is necessarily specialized and obscure, carried out without any anticipated impact on the outside world.

This defence of the Humanities highlights why it is so difficult for literary scholars and creative writers to work together. One way to collaborate peacefully is to agree that both literature and creative writing are useful disciplines that bring valuable skills that can then be deployed in the real world. But many creative writers do not buy this argument. They may not be as vocal as Jenefer Shute, Hanif Kureishi, and August Kleinzahler, but they secretly think that creative writing programmes have little or no value. On the other side of the creative/critical divide, some Humanities scholars are equally dismissive of the 'skills' argument. They view scholarship as an elite activity designed to produce a distinct class of students and scholars, whose superiority is tied to their prestigious education and ability to master niche topics. In this view, creative writing programmes have no place. As Justin Stover puts it, 'actual artisans, writers, and artists' 'historically have had little university training': there is no need to take an 'Introduction to Food Studies' course in order to become a chef, or a creative writing course to become a gifted writer. Until recently, this argument was dominant in France (as we have seen in the Epilogue). In the Anglophone world, it is more marginal. Life is hard for Humanities scholars who work on obscure topics with no obvious relevance to the outside world. In the UK, the Research Excellence Framework and the criteria for grant applications make 'impact' a necessity. The 'skills' and 'impact' arguments are not perfect, but they at least encourage collaboration with other disciplines rather than separateness.

How can we heal the rift between creative writers and scholars? Throughout this book, I have tried to answer this question by unveiling the historical roots of this divide. Understanding this history may be the first step to bridge the creative/critical divide. I will come to that later but first, let me summarize the three models that have influenced would-be writers in the twentieth century (Figure 11.1). Like new technologies that coincide with previous inventions, new models coincide with older forms. We still listen to the radio, a technology born in the nineteenth century and popularized in the 1920s. Similarly, we are still influenced by the *informal mentorship model*, a model born in France in the nineteenth century and popularized in the Anglophone world in the late 1910s and 1920s.

Just after the First World War, the *informal mentorship model* dominated the literary field. For ambitious writers, finding a mentor was necessary to gain access to rare resources: invitations to literary gatherings (salons, parties, and the like), publication opportunities, and a chance to be reviewed in sought-after periodicals. On 3 December 1921, Sherwood Anderson wrote to Gertrude Stein in Paris: 'Mr Hemingway is an American writer instinctively in touch with everything worth while going on here and I know you will find Mr and Mrs Hemingway delightful

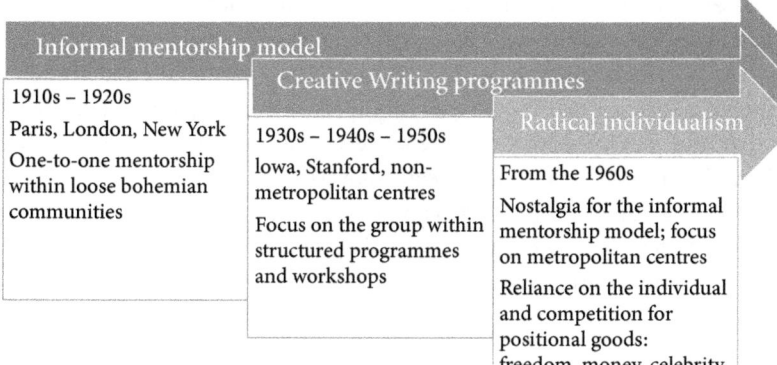

Fig. 11.1 How to become a published writer: Three models.
Source: Author's own.

people to know.'² Here, Anderson made clear that Stein had something to gain by meeting Ernest Hemingway, a promising writer in touch with current trends.

Anderson also wrote a letter of introduction to Ezra Pound. The young Hemingway probably met Pound in March 1922. In 1925, his 'Homage to Ezra' was published in *This Quarter*:

> So then, so far, we have Pound the major poet devoting, say, one fifth of his time to poetry. With the rest of his time he tries to advance the fortunes, both material and artistic, of his friends. He defends them when they are attacked, he gets them into magazines and out of jail. He loans them money. He sells their pictures. He arranges concerts for them. He writes articles about them. He introduces them to wealthy women. He gets publishers to take their books. He sits up all night with them when they claim to be dying and he witnesses their wills. He advances them hospital expenses and dissuades them from suicide. And in the end a few of them refrain from knifing him at the first opportunity.
>
> (qtd in Bruccoli)

Hemingway did not refrain from 'knifing' his literary benefactors (his novella *The Torrents of Spring*, published the following year, was a sharp attack on Anderson). But he remained deeply appreciative of Pound, a poet who worked tirelessly to help his protégés. This figure of the literary mentor—a distinguished writer who connects others with opportunities—is at the centre of Model #1.

The *informal mentorship model* was centred on the one-to-one relationship between mentor and mentee within literary groups. These bohemian communities held particular appeal in the 1920s. In July 1926, the American publisher Alfred Knopf advertised a new edition of Wyndham Lewis's *Tarr*, first published by the Egoist Press in London in 1918. Lewis's modernist novel was described as a quasi-sociological account of the Parisian bohemian community. 'What are they really like? The Latin-Quarter artists,' asked *The New York Times* ad, appealing to readers' curiosity for bohemians 'who spend their days painting in dark studios, and their nights talking outside the cafés of Montparnasse?' The ad promised that *Tarr* was a 'truthful picture of that intense society', thus placing the arch-modernist Wyndham Lewis in the tradition of realist novels.³

The enduring appeal of Model #1 can be seen in *The Workshop: Seven Decades of the Iowa Writers' Workshop*, a volume edited by Tom Grimes (1999). In the introduction, Frank Conroy wrote that, as a young man in the mid-1950s, he went to Paris:

---

² Anderson to Stein, 3 Dec. 1921, Box 13, Sherwood Anderson Papers, Newberry Library, Chicago, IL.
³ Knopf, Advertisement for Borzoi Books, *The New York Times*, 18 July 1926, p. BR20.

I had very little money, lived in an Algerian slum, ate so badly I lost half the hair on the back of my head from a vitamin deficiency, got robbed, got beaten up, and endured various other hardships. Nevertheless I stayed, because I had read about prewar Paris—about Hemingway, Fitzgerald, Joyce, and all the others who used to hang out in 'Boul-Miche' at The Dome or The Select.

(xi)

Conroy wanted to connect with expatriate writers he assumed must be in Paris. 'But of course I was too late,' he wrote. 'There was no doubt an artistic community, but it was no longer open and welcoming, if indeed it had ever been as open as I imagined' (xi). He met no American writers and made only a single friend, a young British painter who survived precariously. After one year, he came back to the US.

When Conroy wrote this account of his initial failure to launch his literary career, he was the director of the Iowa Writers' Workshop, a position that gave him influence and authority over younger writers. Like Paul Engle before him, Conroy presented the *informal mentorship model* as long dead, replaced by creative writing programmes. The mentorship relationship now took place within the university system rather than in bohemian communities. At the University of Iowa, he said, 'older talented writers run the place and do the teaching, or, more accurately, the guiding' (xi). Tom Grimes was one of Conroy's protégés, who went on to direct his own creative writing programme in Texas. Grimes also wrote about his relationship with Conroy in his book *Mentor: A Memoir* (2010).

The rise of creative writing programmes after the Second World War was intrinsically linked to an overall social ethic that valued the group over the individual. As William Whyte put it in *The Organization Man* (1956), 'belongingness' and the 'belief in the group as the source of creativity' were central to this ethic (32, 7). With their focus on group feedback within workshops, creative writing programmes were perfectly suited to the post-war era. In *The Second Mountain* (2019), David Brooks has written admiringly of the post-Second World War period, a period dominated by a 'moral ecology' that 'emphasised humility, reticence, and self-effacement'. Indeed, creative writing programmes were not designed to celebrate egocentric individuals. In his preface to *A Community of Writers* (1999), Robert Dana wrote about his memories of the Iowa Writers' Workshop in the 1950s and 1960s: 'There was a certain modesty that presided over our occasional dreaming, a modesty born of the conviction that writing is hard work, that it requires sacrifice and self-effacement' (ix). Today's creative writing programmes are certainly not associated with humility, but the dominant ethic was different then.

With veterans enrolling at universities in record numbers, many men (usually older than standard college age) participated in writing workshops after the war. These men had started their adult life in a military setting, and the discipline they found at the University of Iowa and elsewhere bore similarities with the army. Philip Roth, who taught at Iowa in the early 1960s, saw the Workshop as serving three purposes: giving young writers an audience, a sense of community, and an acceptable social category— that of 'student' (Grimes, *The Workshop* 4). Each of these purposes focused on the group rather than the individual. The workshop was constructed on a masculinist ethos of service and self-effacement. The objective was not to soothe writers' egos, but to tell them the truth during tough feedback sessions.

The Iowa model was exported throughout the United States. As we have seen in Chapter 3, Wallace Stegner preached hard work and self-discipline to the students of the Stanford Writing Program. He was the perfect embodiment of the values of the 1950s: humility, reticence, and self-effacement. The rise of the *radical individualism model*—exemplified by his former student, Ken Kesey—horrified him. In a lecture delivered in 1980 at the University of Utah, Stegner gave a bleak picture of a country destroyed by selfishness and greed:

> We have lived through times when it has seemed that everything ran downhill, when great corporations were constantly being caught in bribery, price fixing, or the dumping of chemical wastes in the public's backyard—when corporate liberty, in other words, was indulged at the public expense. We have seen the proliferation of government bureaus, some of them designed to curb corporate abuses and some apparently designed only to inhibit the freedom of citizens. We have watched some of our greatest cities erupt in mindless violence. We have built ourselves a vast industrial trap in which, far from being the self-reliant individuals we once were, and still are in fantasy, we are absolutely helpless when the power fails.
>
> (*The Twilight of Self-Reliance*)

Here, Stegner described the dark side of a radical individualism that had destroyed great institutions, atomized society, exploited the environment, and left everyone vulnerable. He listed corporations and government agencies amongst institutions that suffered greatly from the social anarchy of the 1960s and 1970s. He could have added creative writing programmes to this list. In 1982, two years after giving this lecture, Stegner asked for his name to be taken off all Stanford Writing Program leaflets and announcements.[4] The programme that he had founded more than three decades before was now an embarrassment for him. He also arranged for his personal archive to be transferred to the University of Utah, in a State shaped by the Mormon values of 'endurance, discipline, faith' that he praised in *The Gathering of Zion: The Story of the Mormon Trail* (12).

Stegner's lecture highlights the conflict between the values of self-restraint associated with Model #2, and the hyper-individualism of Model #3. He presented this conflict not as a radically new thing, but as a remake of the tensions between two

---

[4] Stegner to John L'Heureux, 24 July 1982, Box 162, WS, Utah.

nineteenth-century American figures: the 'pioneer farmer' and the 'frontiersman'. The first one valued self-reliance but also family, property and rootedness. With his rugged individualism and deep roots in Oxford, Mississippi, William Faulkner would be a good example of this figure—as we have seen in Chapter 2. In contrast, the frontiersman embraced 'recklessness, contempt for law, a hawk-like need of freedom'. For Stegner, his countercultural contemporaries resembled frontiersmen, men like his own father whose intense desire for freedom led to destructive behaviour. 'Any variety of the frontiersman is more attractive to modern Americans than is the responsible, pedestrian, hard-working pioneer farmer breaking his back in a furrow to achieve ownership of his claim and give his children a start in the world,' Stegner said. And he added: 'The freedom of the frontiersman is a form of mortal risk and contains the seed of its own destruction' (*The Twilight of Self-Reliance*).

Despite his revulsion for countercultural excesses, Wallace Stegner was a literary rebel of a sort. He shared many traits with Paul Engle at Iowa, but also with Malcolm Bradbury, who was equally horrified by the social transformations of the 1960s and 1970s. These men owed their successful career to the university system, and they defended this institution faithfully when it was attacked by student activists and other radicals. They knew how to forge allegiances with scholars when needed. They convinced their Senior Management to support their creative writing programmes through funding and visibility across campus. But ultimately, they failed to bridge the gap between scholars and creative writers. This failure is partly due to the rising influence of literary theory in English departments, a trend that dismayed them. But the rift was more profound than that. Even at the height of their power, Stegner, Engle, and Bradbury failed to move the discipline of creative writing to the centre of the academic institution. They remained on the margins of academia, largely by choice, preferring their creative freedom to genuine engagement with other disciplines.

This 'literary rebel' attitude lay the ground for the *radical individualism model* that came to dominate creative writing programmes. In many cases, it also influenced the literature that has been produced in these programmes. Take the example of Ian McEwan's *First Love, Last Rites*. This inaugural collection of short stories dealt with, in McEwan's words, 'sibling incest, cross-dressing, a rat that torments young lovers, actors making love mid-rehearsal, children roasting a cat, child abuse and murder, a man who keeps a penis in a jar and uses esoteric geometry to obliterate his wife'. McEwan showed his stories to his tutors Malcolm Bradbury and Angus Wilson. Far from being shocked, they encouraged this promising student. 'No one thought my stories were outrageous or immoral,' McEwan recalled. 'Bradbury would say something like: "Not bad. When can I see the next one?" '. For McEwan, writing forty years after the publication of the book, *First Love, Last Rites* was the product of the 1960s and 1970s. 'I feel neither nostalgic nor dismissive about those times now,' he declared. 'There were gains and there were, plainly, excesses' ('When I Was a Monster'). The model of *radical individualism* could produce valuable writing that did not pretend to be moral.

The discipline of creative writing could have evolved in a different way. In 1955, the poet Yvor Winters encouraged his creative writing students to take up graduate courses, while Wallace Stegner insisted that they concentrate on their writing. And three decades later, Malcolm Bradbury's *My Strange Quest for Mensonge*—a parody of French theory—did nothing to reconcile writers and literary critics. The opportunity to develop more critical/creative collaborations was missed. The rise of the *radical individualism model* widened the gap between scholars and writers. Creative writing programmes undertook a deep change: they abandoned the quasi-military discipline of the early days and left more space to self-expression. Their anti-intellectualism became more blatant. 'We don't need no education. We don't need no thought control,' sang Pink Floyd in 1979,[5] echoing this anti-academic mood. Creative writing programmes became hotbeds for the cult of the self in a hypercompetitive consumer society obsessed with celebrity and material success.

Bret Easton Ellis is perhaps the most famous example of this evolution. When he was a student at Bennington College in the early 1980s, Ellis joined a workshop taught by Joe McGinniss, and wrote his first novel as a result. McGinniss sent the novel to Morgan Entrekin, a young editor at Simon & Schuster (Baelo-Allué 39). Ellis received an advance of $5,000 for *Less Than Zero*, and he appeared on talk shows in the United States and in England to promote the novel. About 50,000 copies were sold the year it came out (1985), and it was turned into a film produced by 20th Century Fox in 1987. Following the publication of *The Rules of Attraction* (1987) and *American Psycho* (1991), Ellis influenced cohorts of creative writing students. He 'had an enormous influence on the last three years' intake of our students,' declared Malcolm Bradbury in 1999.[6]

A former student of Bradbury at the University of East Anglia, Kazuo Ishiguro launched his writing career at around the same time as Ellis: his first novel *A Pale View of Hills* was published in 1982, three years before *Less than Zero*. Like Ellis, Ishiguro owed his celebrity to creative writing programmes, but also to the changes in the publishing industry—with increasing opportunities for authors of literary fiction. As seen in Chapter 8, the independent publisher Faber built on Ishiguro's success from the 1980s to present itself as a trailblazer in a publishing industry dominated by large corporations following a wave of mergers on both sides of the Atlantic.

In his 1981 book *The Blockbuster Complex*, Thomas Whiteside warned that the publishing sector was increasingly orientated towards mass products, and potential synergies with other industries of mass entertainment. For Whiteside, this

---

[5] Pink Floyd, *Another Brick in the Wall*, Harvest, 1979.
[6] 'Bret Easton Ellis: Leader of the Bret Pack', *The Guardian*, 8 Jan. 1999.

raised the threat of homogenized and degraded literary production, with large publishing corporations eager to find bestselling novels that could then be turned into movies or TV series. In *Orality and Literacy: The Technologizing of the Word* (1982), Walter Ong argued that the total dominance of print culture was coming to an end, replaced by a new kind of oral culture mediated by new technologies. Concerns over close partnerships between publishing, television, and film were reinforced by the rise of bookstore chains such as Borders and Barnes & Noble. For these critics, the massification of the book business endangered independent publishers, booksellers, and writers whose work could not easily be sold to the mass market.

In a 1985 article on 'The Cultural Meaning of Concentration in Publishing', the sociologist Elizabeth Long debunked this line of argument. Mergers had always been frequent in the publishing industry, an industry that has historically been undercapitalized. Concentration was already a feature of the publishing industry in the interwar period. In *Economic Survey of the Book Industry 1930–1931*, O. H. Cheney showed that between 1925 and 1930, four companies accounted for approximately one-fifth of the titles published, and approximately twenty companies accounted for half of them. Synergies between the publishing industry and Hollywood led to the rise of star writers such as Kathleen Winsor, whose 1944 bestselling novel *Forever Amber* published by Macmillan was turned into a Technicolor film three years later.[7] Elizabeth Long situated the publishing industry of the 1980s within this longer historical framework, which increasingly blurred the boundary between high culture and mass market. As she put it, 'the new media have certainly expanded the cultural universe, reached mass markets untouched by books, and pulled some writers and publishers towards new modes of communication and new audiences' (23).

What was the impact of this changing publishing industry on creative writing programmes? In a 1988 article on the University of East Anglia's MA in creative writing, Rose Tremain wrote that literary fiction now commanded 'serious attention and serious money'. Talented young writers hoped to find a publisher 'without the luxury of the one year entirely devoted to writing and critical appraisal'. But UEA's programme remained more than ever central to encourage students with a gift for 'creative imagination'. For Tremain, it was not the publishing industry that had impacted on UEA, but rather the opposite: the programme 'change[d] the way serious fiction is regarded' ('Angus Wilson, Malcolm Bradbury and the Dead Cat').

As an alumna of the University of East Anglia, Tremain was well placed to observe a UK literary landscape that increasingly centred on UEA. She was amongst the judges for the 1988 Booker Prize, which was awarded to Peter Carey's novel *Oscar and Lucinda*. Carey's editor at Faber was Robert McCrum (who became

---

[7] See Jaillant, 'Subversive Middlebrow'.

Kazuo Ishiguro's editor following a recommendation from Malcolm Bradbury). Amongst the Booker shortlist was *Nice Work* by David Lodge, a long-time friend of Bradbury. The following year, the Booker Prize went to Ishiguro's *The Remains of the Day*, bringing renewed publicity to UEA. The film adaptation was released in 1993, highlighting a 'communications circuit'[8] that ran from creative writing programmes, to publishers of literary fiction, to movie companies reaching the mass market.

Paradoxically, the *radical individualism model* that shaped university creative writing from the 1960s and 1970s led to an increased reliance on literary networks and communities. This was not a new phenomenon (remember the bohemian communities of Model #1), but in the ultra-competitive literary world of the late twentieth century, the search for communities often resembled tribalism. As David Brooks notes, 'the tribal mentality is a warrior mentality based on scarcity: Life is a battle for scarce resources and it's always us versus them, zero-sum' (*The Second Mountain*). Tribalism led to accusation of nepotism. As we have seen, UEA was described as a 'mafia', instrumental in the success of Ian McEwan, Kazuo Ishiguro, and others (including Rose Tremain, who has had a successful career albeit not to the level of her male UEA counterparts). Creative writing courses expanded rapidly in the 1980s, with an increasing number of students hoping to receive advice on how to publish their work. Joining a creative writing programme became a way to access rare resources (including literary agents and editors via recommendations from course instructors, for example).

In a context of growth in the publishing sector, creative writing programmes took the role of gatekeepers that would 'select and nurture' the most promising young writers, as Rose Tremain puts it ('Angus Wilson, Malcolm Bradbury and the Dead Cat'). From 1975 to 2000, UK title output had almost tripled,[9] and the number of new and revised titles rose to 183,000 in 2013.[10] Global exports have been crucial to the UK publishing industry and reached £3.5 billion in 2018—59 per cent of total sales income (Rowe). There have been concerns of print books sales decreasing in recent years, but digital formats and audiobooks are on the rise. Total consumer audiobook sales income was up 43 per cent in 2018, reaching £69 million (Rowe). For editors and agents, the problem is not to find writers, but to find those who will make an impact. In theory, creative writing programmes can provide a competitive advantage in a crowded literary field—which largely explains their popularity with would-be writers.

In practice, however, creative writing courses very rarely lead to the ultimate 'positional good': freedom, money, and celebrity outside the academic system. The first problem is the declining market for literary fiction since the beginning of the

---

[8] See Darnton.
[9] *Book Facts 2001* 17.
[10] Flood, 'UK Publishes More Books per Capita than Any Other Country, Report Shows'.

twenty-first century. Drawing from Nielsen BookScan data, a 2017 report from Arts Council England showed falling book sales overall and falling dividends for the sales made since 2001 (Arts Council England 11). In this tough market, the 1,000th bestselling fiction title sold between 3,000 and 4,000 copies a year. The 5,000th bestselling title sold just 320 copies and the 10,000th, between 94 and 99 copies a year—hardly figures to produce an income for its author to live on. The report made clear that 'outside of the top 1,000 authors (at most), printed book sales alone simply cannot provide a decent level of income' (17). It is not a coincidence that several creative writing programmes (including that of UEA) have started offering courses in crime writing. Genre and commercial fiction predominate in ebook format and have weathered the digital revolution slightly better than literary fiction.

Since making a living by writing literary fiction is rarely an option, some authors turn to journalism and freelance writing. And they are hit by the second problem: the falling market for newspapers and magazines, with the rise of freely available content on the Internet. National newspaper circulation in the UK has decreased from 22 million in 2010, to 10.4 million in 2018, a decline of 52.5 per cent.[11] In this declining sector, only those with strong connections at the most prestigious publications earn a sustainable income from this work.

Unable to reach freedom, money, and celebrity with their writing, many turn to teaching. The rising number of MA programmes in creative writing, but also BAs and PhDs, has offered employment opportunities (often on a part-time basis with short-term contracts). Discontents point out, once again, that academia is a threat rather than an opportunity for writers. Discussing the future of literary fiction, the novelist Will Self declared: 'I think that creative writing programmes are a force for conformity and lack of experimentation.' And he predicted that 'as it becomes clear that the massive amounts of writers who are enrolling in these courses are going nowhere [serious fiction] will be a "conservatoire" form, practised by young ladies and gentlemen, and followed by a select group ... like classical music or easel painting'.[12] Will Self comes from a distinguished and well-connected family of civil servants and professors. He has managed to make a living as a literary novelist, supplementing his income as a professor of Contemporary Thought at Brunel University. His dismissal of creative writing programmes shows, in Pierre Bourdieu's terms, the collective 'bad faith'[13] of literary writers who continue to cling to the dream of an autonomous life outside academia—while benefiting from the university system.

---

[11] 'How People in the UK Are Accessing News: 6 Key Findings', *What's New in Publishing | Digital Publishing News*, 2 Aug. 2019, https://whatsnewinpublishing.com/how-people-in-the-uk-are-accessing-news-6-key-findings/. Accessed 30 Apr. 2021.
[12] Flood, 'Literary Fiction in Crisis as Sales Drop Dramatically, Arts Council England Reports'.
[13] *The Rules of Art* n.p.

The feminization of creative writing programmes coincided with the falling market for fiction, particularly in literary fiction. In the United States, adult fiction revenue fell 16 per cent between 2013 and 2018, from $5.21 billion to $4.40 billion. Unsurprisingly, genre fiction did better than literary fiction. In 2015, only one out of four novels that sold more than one million print copies was a literary book: *Go Set a Watchman* by Harper Lee (1.6 million). The other three were *Grey* by E. L. James (romance/erotica, 1.4 million), *The Girl on the Train* by Paula Hawkins (mystery/thriller, 1.3 million), and *All the Light We Cannot* by Anthony Doer (history/war, 1 million) (Milliot and Deahl). In the meantime, enrolment in creative writing programmes has exploded. Between 1988 and 2014, the number of people earning MFAs in creative writing increased more than sixfold in the USA. These new degree-earners were 59–66 per cent female.[14] At the Iowa Writers' Workshop, female students have been more numerous than males since 1983 (Glass and Kelly). For these increasingly female graduates, getting a book deal in a tight publishing sector is difficult. Only a tiny minority will reach bestselling status in a market where fiction is declining, and nonfiction growing (particularly political and self-help books).

What can we do to help struggling writers? Is there a way to heal the breach between writers and scholars? The first step is to challenge the *radical individualism model* that has influenced creative writing programmes since the 1960s. With their deep suspicion of scholars, the founders of the discipline made a particularly fertile soil for this model which values freedom, money, and celebrity outside academia. It is an untenable model: if the university world is such a hostile world that leads to certain creative death, why would anyone accept to teach there? Why not find any kind of job and write in the morning, evening, and weekends, as so many writers did in the past and continue to do? Model #3 is not only illogical, it is also essentially destructive. In a cut-throat literary world, other writers are rivals competing for a book deal in an ever-tightening market. 'Happy Hunger Games! And may the odds be ever in your favour'—could be the motto of creative writing programmes ruled by the *radical individualism model*. Lip service is paid to the need to develop creatively and become a better writer. But the true objective is to get access to networks, connections, and rare resources—being signed by a literary agent, getting a book deal with a prestigious publisher, grabbing the attention of the media. The whole enterprise is fuelled by an inflated cult of the self ('I primarily wanted attention,' as Lionel Shriver said).[15]

Not all creative writers in academia abide by this hyper-individualist model. Some still value self-effacement, service, and humility at the centre of original creative writing programmes. They genuinely think that the point of studying creative

---

[14] Juliana Spahr and Stephanie Young collected the data from IPEDS, a federal database. See 'The Program Era and the Mainly White Room', *Los Angeles Review of Books*, 20 Sept. 2015, https://lareviewofbooks.org/article/the-program-era-and-the-mainly-white-room/. Accessed 30 Apr. 2021.

[15] Shute, 'Lionel Shriver'.

writing is to become a better craftsman or craftswoman within a group structure, that is, the workshop and the larger university system. These writers are convinced that writing is a positive, sometimes life-changing, activity that should be shared with anyone. In 1974, Richard Shelton, a professor at the University of Arizona, established a writers' workshop at the Arizona State Prison. He wrote about this experience in his memoir, *Crossing the Yard: Thirty Years as a Prison Volunteer*. Shelton's colleagues continue to conduct creative writing workshops for inmates. This work has led to publication opportunities for former prisoners, who have made names for themselves through their writing instead of their crimes.

I am not arguing that we should go back to the 1950s. Women and writers of colour were too often marginalized in the original creative writing programmes. Data gathered by 'The Program Era' project show that there were even years with no women enrolled in the Iowa Writers' Workshop (Glass and Kelly). Funding for fellows at the Stanford Writing Program mostly went to men (see Chapter 3). In addition, the Rockefeller Foundation and the Ford Foundation allocated smaller grants to women and writers of colour (see Chapter 4). The institutional legacy of these grant-making programmes and decisions resulted in reduced opportunities for female writers over the long term. Women continued to struggle to publish their work and to reach a wide audience. An analysis of The New York Times Best Seller list points out that three-quarters of bestselling literary fiction books were written by men in the 1950s—a portion that remained relatively stable until the 1980s (Cima).

Historians have challenged the theory that women were victims of the 1950s.[16] But, as Martin Halliwell points out, 'widespread college engagements and falling marriage ages were sure signs that motherhood and housework had become sanctified' (41). For middle-class women who went on to work after college, discrimination in the workplace was rife. In 1950, the Random House editor Saxe Commins wrote to a bookseller who had asked for advice on her daughter's plan to work in the publishing industry. 'First of all, we must consider the fact that she is a girl and, therefore, is qualified to do a woman's work,' Commins declared. 'For the most part women rise to the highest editorial positions in the juvenile department. In all other divisions they are usually employed as secretaries to men or as editorial assistants.'[17] He suggested training in stenography as the best way to find a secretarial job in the editorial division of a publishing house. In this male-dominated world, being pretty was seen as an additional advantage (see Chapter 3 for a discussion of the reference letter that Stegner wrote in 1955 for a former student applying for a job in publishing). With so few women holding senior editorial positions, it is not surprising that female writers did not have the same opportunities that men had.

[16] See Meyerowitz and Kaledin.
[17] Commins to Mrs Marie Fleming, 3 Feb. 1950, Box 276, RH.

That said, today's creative writing programmes have largely forgotten the 1950s values of self-effacement, humility, and service defended by Wallace Stegner and others. With their emphasis on self-aggrandizement, they have promoted an endless quest for status symbols of the material sort (a lucrative book deal) but also of the immaterial sort (obtaining a coveted literary prize and getting reviewed in *The New York Times*, *The New Yorker* or *The Times Literary Supplement*, which may or may not lead to significantly increased sales). This literary world is brutally unequal, with an elite of brand names at the top, and the vast majority of struggling writers at the bottom. Many studies have shown that income inequalities fuel unhappiness,[18] and the numerous articles on the plight of midlist writers (as well as the disgruntled statements of Jenefer Shute, Hanif Kureishi, August Kleinzahler and Will Self) seem to confirm that the current model is not working.

David Foster Wallace showed a way forward in his famous 2005 commencement speech to the graduating class at Kenyon College. Wallace completed an MFA in creative writing at the University of Arizona in 1987. At the time of the speech, he was a professor of creative writing and English at Pomona College in California. His novel *Infinite Jest* (1996) appeared on *TIME* magazine's list of the 100 best English-language novels published between 1923 and 2005. In his talk, Wallace spent no time criticizing academia or praising the 'freedom, money and celebrity' lifestyle that so many writers envy. He did not tell Kenyon College graduates to follow their dreams and trust their instincts. Instead, he told them to turn away from the self-obsession that is our dominant organizing mode at the individual and social level:

> the so-called real world of men and money and power hums merrily along in a pool of fear and anger and frustration and craving and worship of self. Our own present culture has harnessed these forces in ways that have yielded extraordinary wealth and comfort and personal freedom. The freedom all to be lords of our tiny skull-sized kingdoms, alone at the centre of all creation. This kind of freedom has much to recommend it. But of course, there are all different kinds of freedom, and the kind that is most precious you will not hear much talk about much in the great outside world of wanting and achieving ... The really important kind of freedom involves attention and awareness and discipline, and being able truly to care about other people and to sacrifice for them over and over in myriad petty, unsexy ways every day.
>
> (*This is Water*)

Being able to care, showing discipline and sacrifice: those values are no longer fashionable, but they were once at the centre of creative writing programmes. In her book *The Life of I*, Anne Manne argued that one way to challenge the 'culture of

---

[18] See Oishi and Graham for examples.

narcissism' is to build an 'invisible world of care' based on 'a willingness to give time and attention to others'. 'It requires a connected, communal self, cooperating with others for purposes larger than the self.' For creative writers, building close links with scholars will offer a way to be at home in the academic community. Cooperating with others is not easy, and the founders of creative writing programmes left a difficult legacy of distrust towards the university system. What's more, scholars are not always willing to bridge the gap and start productive discussions with their creative writing colleagues. But ultimately, those are small obstacles. The Roman emperor Marcus Aurelius wrote in his *Meditations* (Book V): 'The impediment to action advances action. What stands in the way becomes the way.' It is time for scholars and creative writers to turn away from literary rebels and to write a new story of collaboration, sacrifice, and care.

Afterword by Mark McGurl
Paradoxes of Institutional Belonging

If there were any doubt that there were more exciting discoveries to be made in the archives of institutionalized creative writing instruction, Lise Jaillant's absorbing *Literary Rebels* proves the opposite. Beginning with what we might think of as the usual suspects in the telling of the discipline's history—Paul Engle at the Iowa Writers' Workshop, Wallace Stegner at Stanford, figures who have received sustained attention in recent accounts, including mine, of the phenomenal rise of the discipline from the mid-twentieth century to the present—Jaillant presents her readers with a wealth of new and surprising examples of the kinds of people and places arisen in that period to serve the popular desire to become a writer. So much so as to provoke renewed reflection even on those figures we may have thought we knew, reframing them as part of an enterprise that now extends far beyond the borders of the United States, and has always spilled beyond the walls of the university.

In these pages Engle and Stegner are finally brought into contact with their English counterpart in the founding of important centres of creative writing instruction, Malcolm Bradbury, whose efforts at the University of East Anglia have been so influential in the recent literary history of England. Nothing could have foretold the coming of Iowa City—*Iowa City*?—as an important counterforce to the overwhelming concentration of literary power in New York City. Similarly, the rise of Norwich as the city that would nurture the ambitions of writers like Ian McEwan and Kazuo Ishiguro at a distance from the otherwise overwhelming gravitational pull of London and Oxbridge is a story understandable only in terms of a fascinating collision of broader historical forces with local and individual contingencies. In filling out this picture so astutely, Jaillant widens the scope of our understanding of the phenomenon of creative writing, preparing the ground for further research in the broader Anglophone world and beyond.

But this is just the beginning. It is in her uniquely serious efforts to tell the story of creative writing 'from below' that Jaillant's work establishes its stark difference from, and advantages over, recent studies and offers an example for others to follow. And so we get, near the beginning, a wonderful glimpse of a young man named James Culpepper who sought literary advice in correspondence with William Faulkner, demonstrating the persistence in the 'program era' of more traditional relations of informal mentorship in the training of writers. That the relation in this case came to nothing is itself highly instructive. Culpepper would as far as we know never manage to publish anything, the sum total of his collected works now consisting of the archived correspondence he managed to strike up with a famous elder writer, which correspondence ended not in literary success but complete failure and resentful rancour.

He is a useful reminder that in literary history there are outsiders and outsiders—margins beyond the margins. Shouldn't the presumably millions of unpublished manuscripts produced to the side of that history be considered an integral part of that history? It is a daunting but inescapable thought. So, too, with enterprises like the Famous Writers School, a for-profit correspondence course cynically and superficially associated with some big names but otherwise a means of profiting off popular dreams of literary glory. Refusing to turn away from such phenomena as this, Jaillant's research allows us to ask how and if legitimate creative writing programmes are continuous with it, even as her account of creative writing instruction as non-profit activism at Arvon in the UK presents the other, more idealistic side of the coin.

For me, the most important thing we learn from the reach and variety of Lise Jaillant's case studies is how complex, even paradoxical, the very idea of the institutional outsider can become. Engle, Stegner, and Bradbury were three men—white men—who started their careers as relative outsiders to elite literary circles and established institutions at considerable distance from centres of power. In so doing, they became the ultimate insiders to those prominent programmes. But only, in some cases, to find themselves exiled again. Think here of Paul Engle, leaving behind the programme with which he was so closely associated to start something new and entirely different in conception, the International Writing Program. Or of Stegner retreating from Stanford, where things did not go his way, to his home in the golden hills above campus to nurse his wounds and ask himself how he of all people had managed to become what radicals disdainfully called 'the Man'?

In truth, this paradox is threaded tightly into the very fabric of the enterprise of creative writing, which, as a social but also an artistic reality, stands on the very border between inside and outside, a kind of turnstile. In the ongoing evolution of literature, it helps bring form to novelty, which in turn renovates the forms into which it flows. In the ongoing institutional development of literary life, the subject of Lise Jaillant's important book, it makes space for the outsider on the inside without simply converting her into an insider. It converts her into something more complex than that—a writer.

Mark McGurl

Works Cited

Acevedo-Scott, Landa. *Tibor Jones Brokers UEA–Guardian Masterclasses Deal*, 26 May 2011, http://www.tiborjones.com/news/tibor-jones-brokers-uea-guardian-masterclasses-deal/. Accessed 30 Apr. 2021.

Adams, J. Donald. 'A New Voice in American Poetry: Paul Engle's American Song may Prove a Literary Landmark'. *The New York Times*, 29 July 1934, p. BR1.

AFP. 'French Literary Rebel Houellebecq Releases Serotonin, a Novel that Echoes "Yellow Vest" Protests'. *France 24*, 4 Jan. 2019, https://www.france24.com/en/20190104-french-literary-rebel-michel-houellebecq-releases-novel-serotonin-yellow-vest-protests. Accessed 30 Apr. 2021.

Algren, Nelson. *The Last Carousel*. Seven Stories Press, 1973.

Algren, Nelson. 'On Kreativ Righting'. *The New York Times*, 29 Mar. 1975, p. 18.

Allardice, Lisa. 'Rose Tremain: "I Don't Want to Write for Vengeance. It's Cheap and Angry"'. *The Guardian*, 7 Apr. 2018.

Allen, Robert. 'Kazuo Ishiguro: Japanese Novelist in English'. *The Irish Times*, 20 Jan. 1987.

Altacruise, Chris. 'Stepford Writers: Undercover inside the M.F.A. Creativity Boot Camp'. *Lingua Franca*, vol. 1, no. 2, 1990, pp. 18–21, 30.

Andrews, Clarence A. 'John Towner Frederick: Man of the Midland'. *The Iowan*, Fall 1971, pp. 14–18.

Arts Council England, *Literature in the 21st Century Report*, 15 Dec. 2017.

Athey, Joel. 'Berryman, John'. *American National Biography Online*, Apr. 2014.

Atlas, James. *Delmore Schwartz: The Life of an American Poet*. Farrar, Straus and Giroux, 1977.

Atlas, James. Bellow: A Biography. Random House, 2000.

'B'. 'Decline and Fall of the University Idea'. *Critical Survey*, vol. 4, no. 1, 1969, pp. 60–2.

Baelo-Allué, Sonia. *Bret Easton Ellis's Controversial Fiction: Writing between High and Low Culture*. Continuum, 2011.

Bailey, Paul. 'Private Desolations'. *The Times Literary Supplement*, 19 Feb. 1982, p. 179.

Barnard, Matt. '"Splurge of Emotion" or a Combination of Inspiration and Craft? Poetry's Great Debate and the Lessons of Rhyme and Reason'. *The Times*, 9 Sept. 1999, p. 41.

Batuman, Elif. 'Get a Real Degree'. *London Review of Books*, vol. 32, no. 18, Sept. 2010, pp. 3–8.

Beaver, Harold Lowther. 'The American Way'. *The Times Literary Supplement*, 16 Aug. 1957, p. 500.

Beaver, Harold Lowther. 'Unknown California. Review of No Further West, by Dan Jacobson'. *The Times Literary Supplement*, 26 June 1959, p. 382.

Beaver, Harold Lowther. 'A Familiarish Destiny. Review of Stepping Westward, by Malcolm Bradbury'. *The Times Literary Supplement*, 5 Aug. 1965, p. 673.

Benedictus, Leo. 'The Write Stuff'. *Prospect Magazine*, 15 Dec. 2010, http://www.prospectmagazine.co.uk/arts-and-books/creative-writing-courses-ian-mcewan. Accessed 30 Apr. 2021.

Bennett, Eric. 'Ernest Hemingway and the Discipline of Creative Writing, Or, Shark Liver Oil'. *MFS-Modern Fiction Studies*, vol. 56, no. 3, 2010, pp. 544–67.

Bennett, Eric. 'How Iowa Flattened Literature'. *Chronicle of Higher Education*, 10 Feb. 2014.
Bennett, Eric. *Workshops of Empire: Stegner, Engle, and American Creative Writing During the Cold War*. U of Iowa P, 2015.
Benson, Jackson J. *The True Adventures of John Steinbeck, Writer*. Viking, 1984.
Benson, Jackson J. *Wallace Stegner: His Life and Work*. Viking, 1996.
Blotner, Joseph. *Faulkner: A Biography*. UP of Mississippi, 2005.
Book Facts 2001: An Annual Compendium. Book Marketing Ltd, 2001.
Boroff, David. 'The Muses Meet in Squaresville'. *Mademoiselle*, Nov. 1961.
Bosha, Francis J. *Faulkner's Soldiers' Pay: A Bibliographic Study*. Whitston, 1982.
Bouchy, Florence. 'Devenir écrivain en huit séances'. *Le Monde*, 17 Mar. 2017.
Bourdieu, Pierre. *The Field of Cultural Production: Essays on Art and Literature*. Columbia UP, 1993.
Bourdieu, Pierre. *The Rules of Art: Genesis and Structure of the Literary Field*. Polity Press, 1996.
Bradbury, Malcolm, editor. 'Cultural Ties in the Making'. *The Guardian Journal*, 18 Oct. 1955, p. 4.
Bradbury, Malcolm, editor. 'The Rise of the Provincials'. *Antioch Review*, vol. 16, no. 4, 1956, pp. 469–77.
Bradbury, Malcolm, editor. *Stepping Westward*. Picador, 1965.
Bradbury, Malcolm, editor. 'One Man's America'. *The Author*, no. 2, Summer 1968, pp. 61–5.
Bradbury, Malcolm, editor. 'The Textuality of Sexuality'. *The Times Literary Supplement*, 14 Dec. 1979, p. 114.
Bradbury, Malcolm, editor. 'How I Invented America'. *Journal of American Studies*, vol. 14, no. 1, Apr. 1980, pp. 115–35.
Bradbury, Malcolm. 'Books of the Year'. *Observer*, 30 Nov. 1986.
Bradbury, Malcolm, editor. *My Strange Quest for Mensonge: Structuralism's Hidden Hero*. Translated by David Lodge. Andre Deutsch, 1987.
Bradbury, Malcolm, editor. 'Critical Years: Some Thoughts on Brian Cox and *CQ*'. *Critical Quarterly*, vol. 35, no. 4, 1993, pp. 31–5.
Bradbury, Malcolm, editor. *Class Work: The Best of Contemporary Short Fiction*. Sceptre, 1995.
Braun, Rebecca. 'Fetishising Intellectual Achievement: The Nobel Prize and European Literary Celebrity'. *Celebrity Studies*, vol. 2, no. 3, Nov. 2011, pp. 320–34.
Brier, Evan. *A Novel Marketplace: Mass Culture, the Book Trade, and Postwar American Fiction*. U of Pennsylvania P, 2010.
Brome, Vincent. 'Chairs for Writers'. *The Times Literary Supplement*, 14 May 1964, p. 415.
Brooks, David. *The Road to Character*. Penguin, 2015.
Brooks, David. *The Second Mountain: The Quest for a Moral Life*. Random House, 2019.
Bruccoli, Matthew J. 'Ezra Pound "Yr Letters Are Life Preservers"'. *Paris Review*, no. 163, Fall 2002.
Buckingham, Will. 'Hanif Kureishi Is Wrong about Students'. *Times Higher Education*, 13 Mar. 2014.
Byrne, Robert. *Writing Rackets*. Lyle Stuart, 1969.
Cain, Sian, et al. 'Nobel Prize in Literature 2017: Kazuo Ishiguro Wins—as It Happened'. *The Guardian*, 5 Oct. 2017.
Campbell, James. 'Obituary: Gregory Corso'. *The Guardian*, 20 Jan. 2001.
Campbell, James. 'Interview: August Kleinzahler'. *The Guardian*, 17 Apr. 2009.
Cantwell, Robert. 'Books: When the Dam Breaks'. *Time*, 23 Jan. 1939.
Carey, Peter. *Oscar and Lucinda*. Faber, 1988.

Carroll, Gordon. 'Editorial: This Matter of Marketing'. *Famous Writers Magazine*, Spring 1963, p. 5.
Carroll, Gordon. 'Editorial: When You Feel Discouraged...'. *Famous Writers Magazine*, Fall 1968, p. 5.
Casanova, Pascale. 'Consécration et Accumulation de Capital Littéraire. La Traduction Comme Échange Inégal'. *Actes de La Recherche En Sciences Sociales*, vol. 4, no. 144, 2002, pp. 7–20.
Casanova, Pascale. *The World Republic of Letters*. Translated by M. B. DeBevoise. Harvard UP, 2004.
Casanova, Pascale. 'Literature as a World'. *New Left Review*, no. 31, Feb. 2005, pp. 71–90.
Cassely, Jean-Laurent. *La Révolte des premiers de la classe: Métiers à la con, quête de sens et reconversions urbaines*. Arkhê, 2017.
Cassely, Jean-Laurent. *NO FAKE: Contre-histoire de notre quête d'authenticité*. Arkhê, 2019.
Chappell, Bill. 'Kazuo Ishiguro Wins Nobel Prize in Literature'. *NPR*, 5 Oct. 2017.
Charles, Ron. 'After the Bob Dylan Nobel Prize Backlash, Will Honoring Kazuo Ishiguro "Make the World Happy"?' *Washington Post*, 5 Oct. 2017.
Charney, Maurice. 'Schwartz, Delmore'. *American National Biography Online*, Feb. 2000.
Chasar, Mike. *Everyday Reading: Poetry and Popular Culture in Modern America*. Columbia UP, 2012.
Cheney, O. H. *Economic Survey of the Book Industry, 1930–1931, as Prepared for the National Association of Book Publishers*. New York Bowker, 1960.
Chereau, Antoine. *Le bonheur d'être auteur*. Pixel fever, 2018.
Cima, Rosie. 'The Gender Balance of The New York Times Best Seller List'. *Pudding*, June 2017, https://pudding.cool/2017/06/best-sellers/index.html. Accessed 30 Apr. 2021.
Cirves, Norma C. 'Runaway'. *Famous Writers Magazine*, Fall 1968, pp. 15–18.
Clements, Toby. 'From Beer to Books: Faber & Faber's Tale of Independence—Toby Clements Traces the Success of the Publisher as It Celebrates 80 Years in Print'. *The Daily Telegraph*, 8 Aug. 2009.
Collins, Ian. 'Active and Far from Retiring'. *Eastern Daily Press*, May 1998, pp. 6–8.
Colwell, Anne Agnes. 'Bishop, Elizabeth'. *American National Biography Online*, Feb. 2000.
Conrad, Joseph. 'Preface'. *The Nigger of the Narcissus*. Doubleday, 1914, pp. 11–16.
Cooke, Alistair. 'Education on Two Sides of the Atlantic'. *The Listener*, 29 May 1935, pp. 925–7.
Cooke, Alistair. 'American Game'. *The Listener*, 17 July 1935, p. 122.
Cowdrey, Katherine. 'Sceptre Wins Debut Suicide Club after 'Heated' Auction'. *Bookseller*, 27 June 2017.
Craig, David. 'Creative Writing at Lancaster'. *Critical Quarterly*, vol. 26, no. 4, Dec. 1984, pp. 81–5.
Craig, David. 'History of Protest at Lancaster: The Craig Affair (ii): The Bailrigg Witch Hunt'. *Subtext*, no. 9, May 2006, https://www.lancaster.ac.uk/subtext/archive/issue009.htm. Accessed 30 Apr. 2021.
Cross, Nigel. *The Common Writer: Life in Nineteenth-Century Grub Street*. Cambridge UP, 1985.
Dai, Fan. 'English-Language Creative Writing in Mainland China'. *World Englishes*, vol. 29, no. 4, Dec. 2010, pp. 546–56.
Dai, Fan. 'English-Language Creative Writing by Chinese University Students'. *English Today*, vol. 28, no. 3, Sept. 2012, pp. 21–6.
Daien, April. '"The Quality of Writing Is Wanting"'. *Women's Arizona Republic Forum*, 28 Nov. 1969.

Damrosch, David. *What Is World Literature?* Princeton UP, 2003.
Dana, Robert, editor. *A Community of Writers: Paul Engle and the Iowa Writers' Workshop.* U of Iowa P, 1999.
Darnton, Robert. 'What Is the History of Books?' *Daedalus*, vol. 111, no. 3, 1982, pp. 65–83.
Davies, Peter Ho. 'Review of Body of Work: 40 Years of Creative Writing at UEA, edited by Giles Foden'. *The Guardian*, 22 Jan. 2012.
Dempsey, David. 'Let the Would-Be Writer Beware'. *Saturday Review of Literature*, 13 July 1963, pp. 22–3.
Díaz, Junot. 'MFA vs. POC'. *The New Yorker*, 30 Apr. 2014.
Diepeveen, Leonard. *The Difficulties of Modernism*. Routledge, 2003.
Dobbs, Jeannine. *Not Another Poetess: A Study of Female Experience in Modern American Poetry*. PhD dissertation, University of New Hampshire, 1973.
Dorne, Albert. 'Letters to the Editor'. *Saturday Review of Literature*, 3 June 1961, pp. 27–8.
Dowling, David Oakey. *A Delicate Aggression: Savagery and Survival in the Iowa Writers' Workshop*. Yale UP, 2019.
Drabble, Margaret. *Angus Wilson: A Biography*. Secker & Warburg, 1995.
Du Bois, Peter C. 'Learning by Mail: Long-Range Prospects Are Bright for U.S. Correspondence Schools'. *Barron's National Business and Financial Weekly*, 3 Apr. 1961, pp. 14, 41.
Dumoulin, Sébastien. 'Écriture auteurs en verve à la fac du Havre'. *Le Monde*, 31 Jan. 2013.
Dunn, Adam. 'In the Land of Memory'. *CNN*, 27 Oct. 2000.
Dunn, Peter. 'A Premium Poet'. *The Sunday Times*, 26 Jan. 1975, p. 64.
Earle, David M. *Re-Covering Modernism: Pulps, Paperbacks, and the Prejudice of Form*. Ashgate, 2009.
Eliot, T. S. 'Mr Leacock Serious'. *New Statesman*, vol. 7, no. 173, July 1916, p. 404.
Eliot, T. S. *The Sacred Wood: Essays on Poetry and Criticism*. Methuen, 1920.
Ellis, Bret Easton. *Less than Zero*. Simon and Schuster, 1985.
Ellis, Bret Easton. *The Rules of Attraction*. Simon and Schuster, 1987.
Ellis, Bret Easton. *American Psycho*. Vintage Books, 1991.
Ellis-Petersen, Hannah, and Alison Flood. 'Kazuo Ishiguro Wins the Nobel Prize in Literature 2017'. *The Guardian*, 5 Oct. 2017.
Elman, Richard M. *Namedropping: Mostly Literary Memoirs*. State U of New York P, 1998.
Engle, Paul. 'American Poetry. Review of A Book of American Verse, edited by A. C. Ward'. *The Listener*, 21 Aug. 1935, p. 333.
Engle, Paul. 'The Writer and the Place'. *Midland: Twenty-Five Years of Fiction and Poetry Selected from the Writing Workshops of the State University of Iowa*, edited by Paul Engle. Random House, 1961, pp. 1–10.
Engle, Paul. *On Creative Writing*. Dutton, 1964.
Engle, Paul. *A Woman Unashamed, and Other Poems*. Random House, 1965.
Engle, Paul. 'Learning from Other Writers'. *Famous Writers and Writing—Book One: Famous Writers Annual*, edited by Gordon Carroll. Famous Writers School, 1970, pp. 229–34.
Engle, Paul, and Cecil Day Lewis. 'Modern Poetry—English and American'. *The Listener*, 15 May 1935, pp. 852–4.
English, James F. *The Economy of Prestige: Prizes, Awards, and the Circulation of Cultural Value*. Harvard UP, 2005.
Ennis, Stephen. 'Taking Note of the Kazuo Ishiguro Archive'. *Ransom Center Magazine*, 15 June 2016.

Etulain, Richard W., and Wallace Stegner. *Stegner: Conversations on History and Literature*. U of Nevada P, 1996.

Faber, Toby. *Faber & Faber: The Untold Story*. Faber, 2019.

Famous Writers Course—Fiction Writing, Vol. 4, Famous Writers School, 1960.

Famous Writers Course—Principles of Good Writing, Vol. 1, Famous Writers School, 1960.

Fausset, Hugh l'Anson. 'Review of American Song, by Paul Engle'. *The Times Literary Supplement*, 11 Apr. 1935, p. 240.

Fenza, David. 'A Brief History of AWP'. *Association of Writers & Writing Programs*, 2011, http://www.awpwriter.org/aboutawp/index.htm. Accessed 3 Feb. 2012.

Fisher, Ruth D. 'A Conversation with Sir Angus Wilson (13 Dec. 1980)'. *Four Quarters*, vol. 31, no. 4, 1982, pp. 3–22.

Flood, Alison. 'Nobel Judge Fears for the Future of Western Literature'. *The Guardian*, 7 Oct. 2014.

Flood, Alison. 'UK Publishes More Books per Capita than Any Other Country, Report Shows'. *The Guardian*, 22 Oct. 2014.

Flood, Alison. 'Literary Fiction in Crisis as Sales Drop Dramatically, Arts Council England Reports'. *The Guardian*, 15 Dec. 2017.

Foden, Giles. *Body of Work: 40 Years of Creative Writing at UEA*. Full Circle, 2012.

Foerster, Norman. *The American Scholar. A Study in Litterae Inhumaniores*. U of North Carolina P, 1929.

Fosdick, Raymond B. *The Story of the Rockefeller Foundation*. Harper, 1952.

Frederick, John T., editor. *Out of the Midwest: A Collection of Present-Day Writing*. McGraw-Hill, 1944.

Fredericksen, Elaine. 'Baldwin, Faith'. *American National Biography Online*, Feb. 2000.

Friedan, Betty. *The Feminine Mystique*. Norton, 1963.

Friedman, Melvin J. 'O'Connor, Flannery'. *American National Biography Online*, Feb. 2000.

Fulcher, Paul M. Review of *Writing the Short Story* and *Significant Contemporary Stories* by Edith Mirrielees. *English Journal*, vol. 19, no. 5, National Council of Teachers of English, 1930, pp. 422–3.

Gale, Robert L. 'Stegner, Wallace'. *American National Biography Online*, Feb. 2000.

Gensane, B., Menegaldo, G., and Shusterman, R.,. 'An Interview with Malcolm Bradbury, Oct. 1992'. *European English Messenger*, vol. 2, no. 1, Spring 1993, pp. 39–45.

Gildner, Judith. 'Paul Engle: Champion of His Kind'. *The Iowan*, vol. 26, no. 2, Winter 1977, pp. 34–41.

Gilliam, Harold. 'A Report on the Writing Center'. *San Francisco Chronicle*, 5 Mar. 1950.

Giroux, Robert, and Lloyd Schwartz, editors. *Elizabeth Bishop: Poems, Prose, and Letters*. Library of America, 2008.

Givner, Joan. *Katherine Anne Porter: A Life*, rev. ed. U of Georgia P, 1991.

Glass, Loren. *Authors Inc.: Literary Celebrity in the Modern United States, 1880–1980*. New York UP, 2004.

Glass, Loren. 'Middle Man: Paul Engle and the Iowa Writers' Workshop'. *Minnesota Review*, no. 71–2, Mar. 2009, pp. 256–68.

Glass, Loren. 'Getting with the Program'. *Iowa Journal of Cultural Studies*, no. 12/13, 4 Jan. 2010, pp. 151–8.

Glass, Loren, editor. *After the Program Era: The Past, Present, and Future of Creative Writing in the University*. U of Iowa P, 2017.

Glass, Loren, and Nicholas M. Kelly. *Gender Trends at the Iowa Writers' Workshop—The Program Era Project*. 9 June 2017, https://dsps.lib.uiowa.edu/programera/2017/06/09/gender-trends-at-the-iowa-writers-workshop/. Accessed 30 Apr. 2021.

Gordon, Edmund. *The Invention of Angela Carter*. Chatto & Windus, 2016.
Gordon, Richard. 'How I Became a Famous Writer'. *Punch*, 28 May 1975, pp. 930–2.
Gottlieb, Eli. 'À l'école du formatage'. *Courrier International*, no. 1063, 17 Mar. 2011, p. 53.
Graff, Gerald. *Professing Literature: An Institutional History*, 2nd ed. U of Chicago P, 2007.
Graham, Carol. *Happiness for All? Unequal Hopes and Lives in Pursuit of the American Dream*. Princeton UP, 2017.
Grimes, Tom, editor. *The Workshop: Seven Decades of the Iowa Writers' Workshop*. Hyperion, 1999.
Grimes, Tom. *Mentor: A Memoir*. Tin House Books, 2010.
Guillory, John. 'Canon, Syllabus, List: A Note on the Pedagogic Imaginary'. *Transition*, no. 52, 1991, pp. 36–54.
Gutek, Gerald Lee. *Education in the United States: An Historical Perspective*. Prentice-Hall, 1986.
Gwynn, Frederick L., and Joseph Blotner. *Faulkner in the University: Class Conferences at the University of Virginia, 1957–1958*. U of Virginia P, 1959.
Hall, John. 'Novels from the Unconscious'. *The Guardian*, 30 Apr. 1970, p. 10.
Halliwell, Martin. *American Culture in the 1950s*. Edinburgh UP, 2007.
Harper, Graeme, editor. *A Companion to Creative Writing*, 1st ed. Wiley, 2013.
Harper, Graeme. *The Future for Creative Writing*. Wiley-Blackwell, 2014.
Harper, Graeme. 'A State of Grace? Creative Writing in UK Higher Education, 1993–2003'. *TEXT*, vol. 7, no. 2, Oct. 2003, http://www.textjournal.com.au/oct03/harper.htm. Accessed 30 Apr. 2021.
Harper, Graeme, and Jeri Kroll, editors. *Creative Writing Studies*. Multilingual Matters, 2008.
Haslinger, Josef. 'Warum Creative Writing?'. *Wie werde ich ein verdammt guter Schriftsteller? Berichte aus der Werkstatt*, edited by Josef Haslinger and Hans-Ulrich Treichel. Suhrkamp, 2005, pp. 176–91.
Hebert, Hugh. 'Mr Bradbury's Finishing School'. *The Guardian*, 28 Feb. 1983, p. 11.
Heinich, Nathalie. *Être écrivain*. La Découverte, 2000.
Heng, Rachel. 'On Applying'. *The MFA Years*, 24 Oct. 2017, https://readtheworkshop.com/2017/10/24/on-applying/. Accessed 30 Apr. 2021.
Heng, Rachel. *Suicide Club*. Sceptre, 2018.
Hentea, Marius. 'Late Modernist Debuts: Publishing and Professionalizing Young Novelists in 1920s Britain'. *Book History*, vol. 14, 2011, pp. 167–86.
Hepworth, James R. 'The Art of Writing: An Interview with Wallace Stegner'. *Bloomsbury Review*, Mar.–Apr. 1990, pp. 8–10.
Herskovitz, Jon. 'Novelist Ishiguro's Notes and Works Head to Texas Library'. *Reuters*, 22 Aug. 2015.
Hickman, Lisa C. *William Faulkner and Joan Williams: The Romance of Two Writers*. McFarland, 2006.
Hicks, Granville. 'Mail-Order Creativity'. *Saturday Review of Literature*, 29 Apr. 1961, pp. 12, 35.
Hicks, Granville. 'Letters to the Editor'. *Saturday Review of Literature*, 10 June 1961, p. 29.
Hirsch, Fred. *The Social Limits to Growth*. Harvard UP, 1976.
Hoffman, Frederick J., et al. *The Little Magazine: A History and a Bibliography*, 2nd ed. Princeton UP, 1947.
Hoffman, Josef. 'Playing with Fire: Dan J. Marlowe, Al Nussbaum and Earl Drake'. *Mystery File*, Nov. 2004, http://www.mysteryfile.com/DMarlowe/Drake.html. Accessed 30 Apr. 2021.

Holeywell, Kathryn. 'The Origins of a Creative Writing Programme at the University of East Anglia, 1963–1966'. *New Writing*, vol. 6, no. 1, 2009, pp. 15–24.

Houdart-Merot, Violaine. *La Création Littéraire à l'université*. Presses Universitaires de Vincennes, 2018.

Howsam, Leslie. *Cheap Bibles: Nineteenth-Century Publishing and the British and Foreign Bible Society*. Cambridge UP, 1991.

Hunnewell, Susannah. 'Kazuo Ishiguro, The Art of Fiction No. 196'. *Paris Review*, no. 184, Spring 2008. *Paris Review*, http://www.theparisreview.org/interviews/5829/the-art-of-fiction-no-196-kazuo-ishiguro. Accessed 23 Jan. 2022.

Ishiguro, Kazuo. *A Pale View of Hills*. Faber, 1982.

Ishiguro, Kazuo. *Interview by Malcolm Bradbury*. 17 Mar. 1982, http://sounds.bl.uk/Arts-literature-and-performance/ICA-talks/024M-C0095X0015XX-0200V0. Accessed 30 Apr. 2021.

Ishiguro, Kazuo. 'I Became Profoundly Thankful for Having Been Born in Nagasaki'. *The Guardian*, 8 Aug. 1983, p. 9.

Ishiguro, Kazuo. *An Artist of the Floating World*. Faber, 1986.

Ishiguro, Kazuo. 'Introduction'. *Snow Country and Thousand Cranes*, by Yasunari Kawabata. Penguin, 1986, pp. 1–3.

Ishiguro, Kazuo. *The Remains of the Day*. Faber, 1989.

Ishiguro, Kazuo. 'How I Wrote The Remains of the Day in Four Weeks'. *The Guardian*, 6 Dec. 2014.

Ishiguro, Kazuo. *My Twentieth Century Evening—and Other Small Breakthroughs*. Stockholm, Sweden, https://www.nobelprize.org/nobel_prizes/literature/laureates/2017/ishiguro-lecture_en.html. Accessed 30 Apr. 2021.

Ishiguro, Kazuo, and Oe Kenzaburo. 'The Novelist in Today's World: A Conversation'. *Boundary 2*, vol. 18, no. 3, 1991, pp. 109–22.

Jacobson, Dan. *No Further West: California Visited*. Weidenfeld and Nicolson, 1957.

Jaillant, Lise. *Modernism, Middlebrow and the Literary Canon: The Modern Library Series, 1917–1955*. Routledge, 2014.

Jaillant, Lise. 'Subversive Middlebrow: The Campaigns to Ban Kathleen Winsor's *Forever Amber* in the US and Canada'. *International Journal of Canadian Studies*, vol. 48, no. 1, May 2014, pp. 33–52.

Jaillant, Lise. *Cheap Modernism: Expanding Markets, Publishers' Series and the Avant-Garde*. Edinburgh UP, 2017.

Jaillant, Lise. 'From Letters to Emails: Reading Ian McEwan's Correspondence'. *TLS Online*, 21 Nov. 2017, https://www.the-tls.co.uk/articles/public/ian-mcewans-emails-letters/. Accessed 30 Apr. 2021.

Jaillant, Lise. 'After the Digital Revolution: Working with Emails and Born-Digital Records in Literary and Publishers' Archives'. *Archives and Manuscripts*, vol. 47, no. 3, Sept. 2019, pp. 285–304.

Jaillant, Lise. "Invisible Poetry: Women, Ethnic Minorities and the Forgotten History of Carcanet Magazine." *Review of English Studies*, vol. 72, no. 306, 2021, pp. 756–774.

Jarvey, Natalie. 'What MasterClass Online Courses Pay to Lure Hollywood Stars as Teachers'. *Hollywood Reporter*, 14 Apr. 2017, https://www.hollywoodreporter.com/news/what-masterclass-online-courses-pay-lure-hollywood-stars-as-teachers-993159. Accessed 30 Apr. 2021.

Johnson, Simon, and Justyna Pawlak. 'Mixing Kafka with Jane Austen: Ishiguro Wins Literature Nobel'. *Reuters*, 5 Oct. 2017.

Jones, Alice, and Nick Clark. 'Hanif Kureishi: Creative Writing Courses Are a Waste of Time'. *Independent*, 3 Mar. 2014.

Jones, Malcolm. 'The Dean of Western Letters'. *Newsweek*, 26 Apr. 1993, p. 68.

Kakutani, Michiko. 'Novelists Are News Again'. *The New York Times*, 14 Aug. 1983, p. BR3.

Kaledin, Eugenia. *Mothers and More American Women in the 1950s*. Twayne Publishers, 1984.

Kam, Wei Ming. 'Janet Ellis Is the 16th CBC Student to Gain a Publishing Deal'. *Curtis Brown Creative*, 14 Apr. 2015, https://www.curtisbrowncreative.co.uk/janet-ellis-book-deal/. Accessed 30 Apr. 2021.

Keene, Ann T. 'Eberhart, Mignon G'. *American National Biography Online*, Jan. 2001.

Kennedy, Randy. 'The Draw of a Mail-Order Art School: Famous Artists School Archives Go to Norman Rockwell Museum'. *The New York Times*, 20 Mar. 2014.

Keyser, Catherine. *Playing Smart: New York Women Writers and Modern Magazine Culture*. Rutgers UP, 2010.

Kindley, Evan. 'Big Criticism'. *Critical Inquiry*, vol. 38, no. 1, 2011, pp. 71–95.

Knights, Ben. 'Intelligence and Interrogation: The Identity of the English Student'. *Arts and Humanities in Higher Education*, vol. 4, no. 1, 2005, pp. 33–52.

Lacey, Paul A. 'Blackmur, R. P'. *American National Biography Online*, Feb. 2000.

Lasden, Martin. 'Wallace Stegner on His Own Terms'. *Stanford Magazine*, Spring 1989, pp. 23–31.

Leader, Zachary. *The Life of Saul Bellow, Volume 1: To Fame and Fortune, 1915–1964*. Knopf Doubleday, 2015.

Lecherbonnier, Sylvie. 'Le Désir d'écrire Fait Éclore de Multiples Formations'. *Le Monde*, 3 Apr. 2019.

Lederman, Marsha. 'Kazuo Ishiguro: "I Apologise to Margaret Atwood"' *The Globe and Mail*, 5 Oct. 2017.

Lee, Hermione. 'The Booker Prize: Matters of Judgement'. *The Times Literary Supplement*, 30 Oct. 1981, p. 1268.

Levin, Harry. 'From Bohemia to Academia: Writers in Universities'. *Bulletin of the American Academy of Arts and Sciences*, vol. 44, no. 4, 1991, pp. 28–50.

Levy, Andrew. *The Culture and Commerce of the American Short Story*. Cambridge UP, 1993.

Lewis, Barry. *Kazuo Ishiguro*. Manchester UP, 2000.

Lewis, Philip. 'Preface'. *Folies et raisons d'une université: Paris 8: de Vincennes à Saint-Denis*, Pétra, 2015, pp. 11–18.

Lodge, David. *Nice Work*. Secker and Warburg, 1988.

Lodge, David. 'David Lodge on Malcolm Bradbury's The History Man'. *The Guardian*, 12 Jan. 2008.

Lodge, David. *Lives in Writing*. Harvill Secker, 2014.

Lodge, David. *Quite a Good Time to Be Born: A Memoir, 1935–1975*. Harvill Secker, 2015.

Long, Elizabeth. 'The Cultural Meaning of Concentration in Publishing'. *Book Research Quarterly*, vol. 1, no. 4, Dec. 1985, pp. 3–27.

Lutz, Tom. *Cosmopolitan Vistas: American Regionalism and Literary Value*. Cornell UP, 2004.

Lutz, Tom. 'The Cosmopolitan Midland'. *American Periodicals*, vol. 15, no. 1, 2005, pp. 74–85.

Lynch, Audry. 'Two Views of Stanford's Teaching Legends: Margery Bailey and Edith Mirrielees and Their Effect on John Steinbeck and Irma Hannibal'. *Steinbeck Review*, vol. 10, no. 1, 2013, pp. 63–9.

Lyon, Janet. 'Cosmopolitanism and Modernism'. *The Oxford Handbook of Global Modernisms*, edited by Mark A. Wollaeger and Matt Eatough. Oxford UP, 2012, pp. 387–412.
Macdonald, Dwight. 'A Theory of Mass Culture [1953]'. *Mass Culture: The Popular Arts in America*, edited by Bernard Rosenberg and David M. White. Free Press, 1957, pp. 59–73.
Macdonald, Dwight. *Interviews with Dwight Macdonald*. UP of Mississippi, 2003.
Macdonald, Dwight. 'Masscult and Midcult'. *Masscult and Midcult: Essays against the American Grain*, edited by John Summers. New York Review Books, 2011, pp. 3–71.
Maloney, Douglas J. 'No Poet Laureate of Women's Lib. Review of Angle of Repose, by Wallace Stegner'. *Pacific Sun*, 7–13 July 1971.
Manne, Anne. *The Life of I: The New Culture of Narcissism*. Melbourne U Pub, 2015.
Manuel, Diane. 'Tending a Legacy: Mary Page Stegner on Life and Work'. *Stanford Today Online*, Mar./Apr. 1996.
Marcus Aurelius, *Meditations: A New Translation*. Translated by Gregory Hays. Modern Library, 2002.
Matthews, Sean, and Sebastian Groes, editors. *Kazuo Ishiguro: Contemporary Critical Perspectives*. Continuum, 2009.
McCarthy, Mary. 'The Revolt of the American Authors'. *The Listener*, 26 Nov. 1953, pp. 901–2.
McCrum, Robert. 'Letters: Short Stories'. *The Times Literary Supplement*, 5 Oct. 1984, p. 1127.
McCrum, Robert. 'My Friend Kazuo Ishiguro: "An Artist without Ego, with Deeply Held Beliefs"'. *Observer*, 8 Oct. 2017.
McDonald, Gail. *Learning to Be Modern: Pound, Eliot, and the American University*. Clarendon P, 1993.
McEwan, Ian. *First Love, Last Rites*. Cape, 1975.
McEwan, Ian. 'Class Work'. *Class Work: The Best of Contemporary Short Fiction*, edited by Malcolm Bradbury. Sceptre, 1995, pp. xv–xix.
McEwan, Ian. *Sweet Tooth*. Jonathan Cape, 2012.
McEwan, Ian. 'When I Was a Monster'. *The Guardian*, 28 Aug. 2015.
McGrath, Charles. 'The Ponzi Workshop'. *The New York Times*, 14 Apr. 2009.
McGurl, Mark. *The Program Era: Postwar Fiction and the Rise of Creative Writing*. Harvard UP, 2009.
McKay, Sinclair. 'I'll Scratch Your Hardback… If You'll Scratch My Paperback'. *The Mail on Sunday*, 29 Oct. 1989, p. 9.
McKenzie, D. F. *Bibliography and the Sociology of Texts*. British Library, 1986.
McLaren, Leah. 'Learning the Write Stuff; A Prestigious British Publisher Has Founded Its Own Writing School, and It's Coming to Canada'. *The Globe and Mail*, 4 July 2010.
Meriwether, James B. 'An Introduction for *The Sound and The Fury*'. *Southern Review*, vol. 8, 1972, pp. 705–10.
Meyerowitz, June, editor. *Not June Cleaver: Women and Gender in Postwar America, 1945–1960*. Temple UP, 1994.
Milliot, Jim, and Rachel Deahl. 'What's the Matter with Fiction Sales?' *Publishers' Weekly*, 26 Oct. 2018.
Milne, John. '2nd Opinion'. *Time Out*, 5 Apr. 1984.
Mirrielees, Edith R. *Writing the Short Story*. Doubleday, Doran, 1929.
Mirrielees, Edith R. *Significant Contemporary Stories*. Doubleday, Doran, 1929.
Mirrielees, Edith R. 'Courses in Contemporary Literature'. *Newsletter of the College English Association*, vol. 2, no. 4, 1940, p. 1.
Mirrielees, Edith R. *Stanford, the Story of a University*. Putnam, 1959.

Mitford, Jessica. 'Let Us Now Appraise Famous Writers'. *Atlantic*, July 1970, pp. 45–54.
Mizener, Arthur. *The Saddest Story: A Biography of Ford Madox Ford*. World Pub. Co, 1971.
MLA Office of Research. *Report on the Survey of Earned Doctorates, 2013–14*, Dec. 2016, https://www.mla.org/content/download/57926/1844181/SED-Report-2016.pdf. Accessed 30 Apr. 2021.
Moat, John. *The Founding of Arvon*. Frances Lincoln, 2005.
Moggach, Lottie. 'Words Don't Come Easy'. *The Times*, 6 Mar. 1999, p. 15.
Mooney, Bel. 'Respectable Hype'. *The Listener*, 2 May 1985, p. 20.
Moretti, Franco. *Distant Reading*. Verso, 2013.
Morgan, David. 'Cultural Work and Friendship Work: The Case of "Bloomsbury"'. *Media, Culture & Society*, vol. 4, no. 1, 1982, pp. 19–32.
Morrison, Theodore. 'Special Instructors at Harvard'. *Newsletter of the College English Association*, vol. 2, no. 4, 1940, pp. 1–4.
Moullot, Pauline. 'Comment apprendre à devenir écrivain'. *Slate.fr*, Oct. 2012, http://www.slate.fr/culture/63903/apprendre-devenir-ecrivain-ecriture-creative. Accessed 30 Apr. 2021.
Myers, David Gershom. *The Elephants Teach: Creative Writing since 1880*, 2nd ed. U of Chicago P, 2006.
Neill, Rosemary. 'When Everyone's an Author'. *The Australian*, 9 Feb. 2008.
Nguyen, Viet Thanh. 'Viet Thanh Nguyen Reveals How Writers' Workshops Can Be Hostile'. *The New York Times*, 22 Dec. 2017.
Nichols, Lewis. 'American Notebook'. *The New York Times*, 26 May 1968, p. BR18.
Nicol, Patricia. 'Can You Teach Someone to Write a Bestseller?'. *Evening Standard*, 16 Aug. 2017.
Nicolas, Alain. 'La création littéraire ? Oui, ça s'apprend'. *L'Humanité*, 25 June 2014.
Nussbaum, Albert F. 'Letters to the Editor: Writers in Prison'. *The New York Times*, 19 Dec. 1965, p. BR16.
O'Brien, Edward J., editor. *The Best Short Stories of 1915 and the Yearbook of the American Short Story*. Small, Maynard, 1916.
Officer, Lawrence H., and Samuel H. Williamson. 'Purchasing Power of British Pounds from 1270 to Present'. *MeasuringWorth*, 2020, http://www.measuringworth.com/ppoweruk/. Accessed 30 Apr. 2021.
Oishi, Shigehiro, Selin, Kesebir, and Ed Diener. 'Income Inequality and Happiness'. *Psychological Science*, vol. 22, no. 9, Sept. 2011, pp. 1095–100.
Ong, Walter J. *Orality and Literacy: The Technologizing of the Word*. Routledge, 1982.
Onwuemezi, Natasha, and Heloise Wood. 'Ishiguro Wins the Nobel Prize in Literature'. *The Bookseller*, 5 Oct. 2017.
O'Toole, Fintan. *Late Show*. BBC, 24 Jan. 1995.
Palmer, Richard. 'You Scratch My Book: Lit Crit's Cosy Little World'. *The Sunday Times*, 17 May 1992, p. 7.
Parke, Richard H. 'Convict Leaving Jail an Artist; Practiced on His Cell Walls'. *The New York Times*, 31 Aug. 1961, p. 29.
Petersen, Kristelle. 'Let Us Now Appraise: Paul Engle, Famous Writer'. *The Daily Iowan*, 4 Nov. 1970.
Polking, Kirk. 'Creative Education'. *Writer's Digest*, Apr. 1962, pp. 17–22.
Pryce-Jones, David. 'Westward Ho'. *The Financial Times*, 5 Aug. 1965, p. 16.
Puchner, Martin. *Poetry of the Revolution Marx, Manifestos, and the Avant-Gardes*. Princeton UP, 2005.

QAA. *Subject Benchmark Statement: Creative Writing [UK Quality Code for Higher Education]*. Feb. 2016, p. 22.

Quinn, Mary Ann. 'The Rockefeller Foundation, Imaginative Writing and the Wellbeing of Mankind'. *Rockefeller Archive Centre Newsletter*, 2007, pp. 7–10.

Radford, Tim. 'Booker Goes to Ishiguro's "Beautifully Paced" Novel'. *The Guardian*, 27 Oct. 1989, p. 24.

Radway, Janice. *A Feeling for Books: The Book-of-the-Month Club, Literary Taste, and Middle-Class Desire*. U of North Carolina P, 1997.

Richardson, H. E. 'Anderson and Faulkner'. *American Literature*, vol. 36, no. 3, 1964, pp. 298–314.

Rideout, Walter B. *Sherwood Anderson: A Writer in America, Vol. 2*. U of Wisconsin P, 2006.

Riesman, David. *The Lonely Crowd: A Study of the Changing American Character*. Yale UP, [1950] 1961.

Robbins, Bruce. 'Comparative Cosmopolitanisms'. *Cosmopolitics: Thinking and Feeling beyond the Nation*, edited by Pheng Cheah and Bruce Robbins. U of Minnesota P, 1998, pp. 246–64.

Rose, Jonathan. *The Intellectual Life of the British Working Classes*. Yale UP, 2001.

Rowe, Adam. 'The £6 Billion UK Publishing Industry Sees a 3% Rise in Digital, 5% Drop in Physical Sales'. *Forbes*, 30 June 2019.

Royle, Nicholas. 'Composition and Decomposition'. *The Times Higher Education*, 28 Mar. 2013.

Rubin, Joan Shelley. *The Making of Middlebrow Culture*. U of North Carolina P, 1992.

Rushdie, Salman. *Imaginary Homelands: Essays and Criticism, 1981–1991*. Penguin, 1992.

Sage, Lorna. 'Obituary: Professor Nicholas Brooke'. *Independent*, 10 Nov. 1998.

Sanderson, Michael. *The History of the University of East Anglia, Norwich*. Hambledon and London, 2002.

Sanderson, Michael. 'Thistlethwaite, Frank (1915–2003)'. *Oxford Dictionary of National Biography*, Oxford UP, 2007, http://www.oxforddnb.com/view/article/89466. Accessed 23 Jan. 2022.

Sapiro, Gisèle. 'Je n'ai jamais appris à écrire'. *Actes de la recherche en sciences sociales*, vol. 3, no. 168, July 2007, pp. 12–33.

Schlatter, N. Elizabeth. 'Wood, Grant'. *American National Biography Online*, Feb. 2000.

Schwartz, Lawrence H. *Creating Faulkner's Reputation: The Politics of Modern Literary Criticism*. U of Tennessee P, 1988.

Séry, Macha. 'Pour écrire, il faut avoir été touché par ses lectures'. *Le Monde*, 26 Apr. 2013, p. LIV3.

Shaffer, Brian W. *Understanding Kazuo Ishiguro*. U of South Carolina P, 1998.

Shaffer, Brian W., and Cynthia F. Wong, editors. *Conversations with Kazuo Ishiguro*. UP of Mississippi, 2008.

Shelton, Richard. *Crossing the Yard: Thirty Years as a Prison Volunteer*. U of Arizona P, 2007.

Showalter, Elaine. 'Killing the Angel in the House: The Autonomy of Women Writers'. *Antioch Review*, vol. 32, no. 3, Fall 1972, pp. 339–53.

Shute, Jenefer. 'Lionel Shriver'. *BOMB*, 1 Oct. 2005, https://bombmagazine.org/articles/lionel-shriver/. Accessed 30 Apr. 2021.

Siff, Stephen. *Acid Hype: American News Media and the Psychedelic Experience*. U of Illinois P, 2015.

Siracusa, Joseph M. 'Cousins, Norman'. *Encyclopedia of the Kennedys: The People and Events That Shaped America*, vol. 1, ABC-CLIO, 2012, pp. 155–6.

Skinner, Richard. 'Kazuo Ishiguro & The Art of Narration'. *Faber Academy News & Features*, 20 Dec. 2014, https://www.faberacademy.co.uk/news/2014/12/kazuo-ishiguro-and-the-art-of-narration/. Accessed 30 Apr. 2021.
Snape, Daniel. 'A Brief History of the University of Lancaster'. *SCAN*, 1 July 2014, http://scan.lusu.co.uk/index.php/2014/07/01/a-brief-history-of-the-university-of-lancaster/. Accessed 25 July 2019.
Snelling, Steve. 'Making a Drama out of the Booker'. *Eastern Daily Press*, 23 Oct. 1998, p. 32.
So, Richard Jean. 'The Invention of the Global MFA: Taiwanese Writers at Iowa, 1964–1980'. *American Literary History*, vol. 29, no. 3, Sept. 2017, pp. 499–520.
Stegner, Wallace. 'Writers' Conference in the Rocky Mountains'. *Providence Sunday Journal*, 24 Aug. 1941.
Stegner, Wallace. 'Is the Novel Done For?' *Harper's Magazine*, 1 Dec. 1942, pp. 76–83.
Stegner, Wallace. 'Advice to a Young Writing Man'. *Pro Tem (Cambridge, Mass.)*, vol. 1, no. 3, Nov. 1943, pp. 1, 3.
Stegner, Wallace. *The Big Rock Candy Mountain*. Duell, Sloan & Pearce, 1943.
Stegner, Wallace. 'New Climates for the Writer'. *The New York Times*, 7 Mar. 1948, p. BR1.
Stegner, Wallace. 'The Anxious Generation'. *English Journal*, vol. 38, no. 1, 1949, pp. 1–6.
Stegner, Wallace. 'What Besides Talent?' *Author & Journalist*, Mar. 1956, pp. 11–13, 29.
Stegner, Wallace. *The Gathering of Zion: The Story of the Mormon Trail*. U of Nebraska P, 1964.
Stegner, Wallace. *The Twilight of Self-Reliance: Frontier Values and Contemporary America*. U of Utah, 25 Feb. 1980.
Stegner, Wallace. *Where the Bluebird Sings to the Lemonade Springs: Living and Writing in the West*. Random House, 1992.
Stegner, Wallace. *The Uneasy Chair: A Biography of Bernard DeVoto*. U of Nebraska Press, 2001.
Steinbeck, John. 'Preface'. *Story Writing, by Edith Mirrielees*. Writer, inc., 1972.
Stodghill, Dick. 'Al Nussbaum—Bank Robber, Mystery Writer'. *Stodghill Says So*, 1 June 2006, http://stodg.blogspot.com/2006/06/al-nussbaum-bank-robber-mystery-writer_01.html. Accessed 30 Apr. 2021.
Story, Jack Trevor. 'Art Attack'. *Punch*, July 1977, pp. 80–1.
Stover, Justin. 'There Is No Case for the Humanities'. *Chronicle of Higher Education*, 4 Mar. 2018.
Strychacz, Thomas F. *Modernism, Mass Culture, and Professionalism*. Cambridge UP, 1993.
Sullivan, Walter. *Allen Tate: A Recollection*. Louisiana State UP, 1988.
Sussman, Peter Y., editor. *Decca: The Letters of Jessica Mitford*. Knopf, 2006.
Svensén, Bo. *The Swedish Academy and the Nobel Prize in Literature*. Translated by Kim Loughran. Swedish Academy, 2011.
Svetvilas, Kanchalee. 'Poet Never Forgot His Iowa Roots'. *Iowa City Press Citizen*, 25 Mar. 1991, pp. 1A–2A.
Swenson, Jeffrey. 'Middling Modernism and the Midwestern Little Magazine: The Midland (1915–33) and Prairie Schooner (1927–)'. *The Oxford Critical and Cultural History of Modernist Magazines, Vol. 2*, edited by Peter Brooker and Andrew Thacker. Oxford UP, 2012, pp. 558–75.
Swift, Rebecca. 'Group Sects'. *Independent*, 4 Feb. 1996, p. 26.
Targett, Jocelyn. 'A Writer of the Floating Word'. *The Guardian*, 13 May 1989, pp. 6–7.
Tate, Allen. 'Miss Emily and the Bibliographer'. *Praising It New: The Best of the New Criticism*, edited by Garrick Davis. Swallow P/ Ohio UP, 2008, pp. 39–48.

Taylor, Ben, editor. *Saul Bellow: Letters*. Penguin, 2010.
Taylor, D. J. *A Vain Conceit: British Fiction in the 1980s*. Bloomsbury, 1989.
Taylor, D. J. 'Angus Wilson: From Darling to Dodo'. *The Guardian*, 23 Aug. 2013.
Taylor, D. J. *The Prose Factory: Literary Life in England since 1918*. Chatto & Windus, 2016.
Thomann, Xavier. 'Un cursus universitaire pour devenir écrivain'. *Bibliobs*, 6 July 2012.
Thomson, Liz. 'Are Publisher Run Courses about Creative Writing, or Accounting?' *The Times*, 11 Apr. 2013.
Thwaite, Anthony. 'Brilliant Performance'. *Observer*, 4 May 1975, p. 28.
Thwaite, Anthony. 'Ghosts in the Mirror'. *Observer*, 14 Feb. 1982, p. 33.
Tivnan, Tom. 'Kazuo Ishiguro: Interview'. *Bookseller*, 21 Jan. 2015.
Tookey, Christopher. 'Sydenham, Mon Amour'. *Books and Bookmen*, Mar. 1986, p. 33.
Toossi, Mitra. 'A Century of Change: The U.S. Labor Force, 1950-2050'. *Monthly Labor Review*, May 2002, pp. 15-28.
Tremain, Rose. 'Angus Wilson, Malcolm Bradbury and the Dead Cat'. *Punch*, 15 Apr. 1988, p. 24.
Trewin, Ion. 'Deborah Rogers Obituary'. *The Guardian*, 4 May 2014.
True, Michael. 'Allen Tate as Teacher and Poet'. *Cross Currents*, vol. 29, no. 3, 1979, pp. 324-30.
True, Michael. 'Teaching Poetry: Many Teachers Don't'. *English Journal*, vol. 69, no. 5, 1980, pp. 42-3.
Turner, E. S. 'Writers in Residence'. *Punch*, 26 Nov. 1975, p. 979.
Turner, Jenny. 'A New Kind of Being. Review of *The Invention of Angela Carter: A Biography*, by Edmund Gordon'. *London Review of Books*, vol. 38, no. 21, 3 Nov. 2016.
Underwood, Thomas A. *Allen Tate: Orphan of the South*. Princeton UP, 2000.
United States Congress Senate Committee on Post Office and Civil Service. *Adjustment of Postal Rates*. 1951.
Van Duyn, Janet. 'Why Women Want to Write'. *Writing, Revising and Editing*, edited by Gordon Carroll. Doubleday, 1969, pp. 35-41.
Wade, Dyan. 'Angus Wilson Gives Advice to Young Writers ... and Young Lovers'. *University and College Magazine*, Winter 1964-1965, pp. 28-9.
Walkowitz, Rebecca L. *Born Translated: The Contemporary Novel in an Age of World Literature*. Columbia UP, 2015.
Wallace, David Foster. *Infinite Jest*. Little, Brown and Company, 1996.
Wallace, David Foster. *This is Water: Some Thoughts, Delivered on a Significant Occasion, about Living a Compassionate Life*. Little, Brown Book Group, 2009.
Walsh, Colleen. 'Harvard's James Wood on Nobel Prize for Kazuo Ishiguro'. *Harvard Gazette*, 5 Oct. 2017.
Walsh, John. 'Still Looking for the Happy Ending'. *Independent*, 17 Mar. 2005, p. 4.
Wandor, Michelene. 'Creative Writing and Pedagogy 1: Self Expression? Whose Self and What Expression?' *New Writing*, vol. 1, no. 2, Oct. 2004, pp. 112-23.
Wandor, Michelene. *The Author Is Not Dead, Merely Somewhere Else: Creative Writing Reconceived*. Palgrave Macmillan, 2008.
Watkins, Claire Vaye. 'On Pandering'. *Tin House*, 23 Nov. 2015, https://tinhouse.com/on-pandering/. Accessed 30 Apr. 2021.
Weill, Nicolas. 'Gisèle Sapiro: "En France, les éditeurs monopolisent l'accès au métier d'écrivain"'. *Le Monde*, 23 Aug. 2017.
Weitz, Alice C. 'Edwin Ford Piper'. *Midland Schools*, vol. 42, no. 2, Oct. 1927, pp. 39-42.
Whiteside, Thomas. *The Blockbuster Complex: Conglomerates, Show Business, and Book Publishing*. Wesleyan UP, 1981.

Whyte, William H. *The Organization Man*. University of Pennsylvania Press, [1956] 2013.
Wilbers, Stephen. *The Iowa Writers' Workshop: Origins, Emergence & Growth*. U of Iowa P, 1980.
Wolfe, Tom. 'Stalking the Billion-Footed Beast'. *Harper's*, vol. 279, no. 1674, Nov. 1989, pp. 45–56.
Wong, Cynthia F. *Kazuo Ishiguro*, 3rd ed. Liverpool UP on behalf of Northcote, [2000] 2019.
Wood, Grant. 'Revolt Against the City'. *Grant Wood: A Study in American Art and Culture*, edited by James M. Dennis. U of Missouri P, 1986, pp. 229–35.
Wood, James. 'The Uses of Oblivion: Kazuo Ishiguro's Folly'. *The New Yorker*, 23 Mar. 2015.
Wood, James. 'Kazuo Ishiguro, the New Nobel Laureate, Has Supremely Done His Own Kind of Thing'. *The New Yorker*, 5 Oct. 2017.
Wroe, Nicholas. 'Living Memories: Profile, Kazuo Ishiguro'. *The Guardian*, 19 Feb. 2005.

Index

academia, *see* universities
academics, *see* literature departments
Algren, Nelson 6, 107, 125–126
Altacruise, Chris 6
Amazing magazine 164–166
American artists in Paris 34–35, 38
American Universities, number of creative writing programmes 6
American writers
 France, in 13, 233, 234–235
 Germany, in 32
 lower middle-class backgrounds 2
 marginalization of women writers 2–3, 8–9, 76–77, 95–96, 243
 Nobel laureates 55–56, 177, 187
 'Program Era,' and 7, 21
Amis, Kingsley 158, 170–171
Anderson, Elizabeth 45–46
Anderson, Sherwood 13, 27, 42–46, 49, 54–57, 233–234
Ansley, Clarke Fisher 24–25
Aristotle 29–30
Arizona, University of 243–244
Arts Council
 Compton Bequest 168
 funding by 16, 138, 143, 151, 167, 198, 200, 202, 211, 213
 Literature panel 168, 198
 maintenance grants 164
 National Portfolio Organisation 200, 203, 211
 reports by 241
 writers-in-residence programme 154, 169–174, 198
 'Writers in Schools' programme 153, 170–171
Arvon Foundation 129, 197–202, 204, 207, 211, 213, 247
Association of Writers & Writing Programs 10, 14, 144
Atwood, Margaret 149, 175, 179, 214
Austen, Jane 162, 182
Australia
 creative writing programmes 8, 130, 208
 international literary recognition 178
authors, *see* writers

Bailey, Paul 176, 186
Baldwin, Faith 106, 109, 117–120
Baldwin, James Arthur 96
Batuman, Elif 7
Beach, Sylvia 208
Becher, Johannes R. 217
Becker, Jurech 217
Beckett, Samuel 165, 176
Bellow, Saul 95–98, 99–101, 104, 141, 146, 155
Bennett, Eric 8, 21, 63, 84, 152, 156
Benson, Michael 147, 149
Berryman, John 67, 90
Bigsby, Christopher 183–184
Binns, Ron 166
Birmingham, University of 90, 135–136, 149, 167
Bishop, Elizabeth 84, 101, 103
Blackmur, Richard Palmer 85–89, 92, 94, 96
Black Paper 153, 166–167
Bloomsbury Group 4
Blumenthal, Marcia 2–3
Blunden, Edmund 22, 32, 36–37
Borthwick, Ruth 201–202, 213
Bourbon, Harris (fictional character) 158–160
Bourdieu, Pierre 16, 43, 164, 177, 185, 189, 204, 241
Bradbury, Malcolm
 context of UEA's development, within 132–137
 expansion of UEA Creative Writing Programme 142–150
 founds first British graduate creative writing programme at UEA 81–82, 125, 246
 Henfield fellowship, and 163–164, 166–167
 Ian McEwan, and 137–142
 influence and power 3–5, 16, 231, 237–240, 246–247
 Kazuo Ishiguro, and 176, 183–186, 193
 lower middle-class background 2
 'mythical' status in literary history 129–131
 Paul Engle compared 131, 134, 136, 143, 154, 231, 237, 247
 writer-in-residence, and 151–154, 158, 160, 163–164, 166–167

Braun, Rebecca 177
Bread Loaf 47, 65–69, 75, 77
British Universities
   beginning of creative writing in 16
   new universities (1960's) 5
   number of creative writing programmes 8–9
   separation of literature departments and creative writing programmes 1
   see also American Universities; United Kingdom; writer-in-residence
British writers
   conservative worldview 4
   France, in 190, 199
   lower middle-class backgrounds 2, 4
   Nobel laureates 8, 16, 175, 194
   'Program Era,' and 175
   radical politics 5
   translations from and to French 181
Brome, Vincent 161–162
Brooke, Nicholas 134–135
Brooks, Cleanth 11–13, 86, 132
Brooks, David 110, 235, 240
Brown, Dan 214
Brownjohn, Alan 152
Buckingham, Will 231–232
Burdick, Eugene 75–76
Burnham, James 98
Burns, Alan 138, 141, 163–165
Byrne, Robert 123–124

Caldwell, Erskine 47–48
Cambridge, University of 10, 134, 168
Canada 64, 82, 115, 132, 175, 208
Cape, Jonathan 139
Carey, Peter 239
Carnegie Foundation 13, 85–86
Carroll, Gordon 113
Carter, Angela 3, 16, 131, 144, 146, 172, 176, 183–186, 192–193
Carter, Charles 5
Casanova, Pascal 144, 178–179, 181
Cassely, Jean-Laurent 225–226
Cassill, R.V. 48
Cerf, Bennett 50, 67, 105, 107, 110–112, 123
Chasar, Mike 152
Cheney, O.H. 239
Ciardi, John 47, 67
Cixous, Hélène 221
Clarke, Desmond 146
Clark, Leonard 170
Commins, Saxe 243

Compton, Boyd 97
Conrad, Joseph 65
Conroy, Frank 21, 234–235
Cook, Jon 6, 140–141, 194, 205
Coren, Alan 185
Corso, Gregory 81
Cox, Brian 153–154, 164, 167–169
Craig, David 5, 129
Craig, Hardin 25, 29
'création littéraire' 8, 220, 222, 226
creative writing programmes
   American-centric scholarship on 8
   American origins 8
   author's contribution to study of 5–6, 9, 246–247
   barriers to achievement of freedom, money, and celebrity 240–241
   'book history from below' approach 9, 246
   content and structure of book 14–17
   'creative writing programme' (Iowa) model of training (Model no. 2) 229, 233, 235–236
   criticisms of 6
   enduring impact of 1
   feminization of 242
   future of European programmes 216–227
   'informal mentorship' model (Model no. 1) 229, 233–235, 246–247
   institutional location within universities 10
   Iowa University origin 238
   male dominance 2
   marginalization of women writers 2–3
   media responses 6
   modernist roots 11–14
   music departments compared 10
   nepotism 2, 3
   New Criticism and 10–11
   new universities (1960's) 5
   number of 6
   'Program Era,' and 7, 21, 220
   publishing industry change, impact of 238–242
   'radical individualism' ('literary rebel') model (Model no. 3) 230–231, 233, 236–240, 242–245
   rise of 6–10
   separation from literature departments 1, 10–14
   success 4
   universities' response to rise of 7
   within literature departments, relations with academics 1

creative writing programmes (*Continued*)
 'writer factories,' as 1, 16, 196
 see also literature departments; writers
Culpepper, James 15, 41–48, 50–59, 229, 246
Cummings, E.E. 95
Curtis Brown Creative 198, 202, 209–211, 213–214

Damrosch, David 187
Dana, Robert 235
Danius, Sara 177–178, 182
d'Arms, Edward 63, 92–94, 97
Davis, Anna 209–210
Day-Lewis, Cecil 33–34
Deleuze, Gilles 221
De Montfort University 231
de Tocqueville, Alexis 98
DeVoto, Bernard 47, 65
Dickens, Charles 6, 160, 162
Dickson, Lovat 82
DLL, *see* Institute of German Literature
Dobbs, Jeannine 120
Dobie, Frank 122–123
Dockrill, Laura 205
Doer, Anthony 242
Dorne, Albert 107–108, 112, 117, 123
Dowling, David O. 8
Driver, C. J. 171
Dunant, Sarah 203
Dunthorne, Joe 205
Dylan, Bob 175, 177–178

East Anglia, University of
 beginning of creative writing at 3, 5, 8, 16
 Faber Academy, and 208
 first British writer-in-residence 152–154, 157, 161–163, 174, 198
 'founding myth' of creative writing at 129–131
 Guardian Masterclasses 205
 Henfield Writing Fellowship 154, 163–167
 Kazuo Ishiguro, and 176–177, 183–189, 192–196
 Malcolm Bradbury's role in context 132–137, 246
 marginalization of women writers 3
 nepotism 3
 Paris 8 compared 216–217, 221
 publishing industry change, impact of 239–241
 rise of creative writing programme 142–150
 rise of 'UEA Clique' 137–142
Eberhart, Mignon G. 117–118
education, secondary, *see* schools

Eliot, T.S. 11–12, 31, 33, 67, 85–86, 90, 93, 100, 132, 177, 186–187, 207–208
Ellard, Ian 206–208, 215
Ellis, Bret Easton 238
Ellis, Janet 214
Engle, Paul 2, 9, 53, 156, 235
 career at Iowa University 22–23, 31, 125, 136
 cosmopolitan regionalist, as 31–34
 Famous Writers School, and 107, 121, 124–125
 international ambitions for Iowa University 34–40
 Iowa literary scene (1920s-early 1930s), and 31
 Kazuo Ishiguro compared 181
 leadership of Writers' Workshop reappraised 21–24
 Malcolm Bradbury compared 131, 134, 136, 143, 154, 231, 237, 247
 New Criticism, and 85, 94
 Rockefeller Foundation, and 92–94, 101
 Wallace Stegner, and 58, 60, 62–63, 67, 71–72, 84, 92–94, 201, 231, 237, 246–247
 writer-scholar gap, and 15
 see also Iowa Writers' Workshop
English, James 177
English literature departments, *see* literature departments
Ennis, Stephen 193–195
European programmes, future of 216–227

Faber Academy 188, 197–198, 202–213, 215
Fahs, Charles 71, 91–92
Fairfax, John 197–199
Falk, Josephine 171–172, 174
Famous Artists Schools 107–109
Famous Writers School (FWS) 9, 15–17, 105–107, 109–126, 198, 210, 214–215, 247
Fanthorpe, Ursula 173–174
Faulkner, Estelle 42, 46, 54
Faulkner, William 13, 14, 15, 38, 41–48, 52–58, 93, 141, 151, 153, 156, 161, 177, 237, 246
Fausset, Hugh l'Anson 32–33
Fleming, Alexander 110
Foden, Giles 130–131, 153, 161
Foerster, Norman 29–31, 37, 62, 65, 72, 94
Ford, Ford Madox 12–13
Forster, E.M. 4, 69
Fox, Genevieve 213
France
 American artists in 34–35, 38
 American writers in 13, 233, 234–235
 British writers in 190, 199

creative writing programmes 8, 176, 207, 216–217, 220–227
culture protection 190–191
'informal mentorship' model of writers' training 233
Nobel laureates 176
Paris as leading international literary centre 24, 36, 41, 49, 57–58, 133
translations from and to English 181
Francis, Richard 169
Frederick, John T. 23–29, 34
Freund, Gerald 97, 99, 101–102, 104
Frost, Robert 47, 65, 151–153, 161
Fugitives-Agrarians 13, 23

Gee, Maggie 131, 138, 147, 167
Gerber, John 27, 39
Germany
 American artists in 35
 American writers in 32
 creative writing programmes 216–220
 Nobel laureates 188
Ghiselin, Brewster 122–123
Gide, André 177
Ginzburg, Ralph 79
Glass, Loren 7–8, 21–22, 156, 189
Gordon, Richard 125–126
Gottlieb, Eli 224
Graham, Kenneth 172
Gray, Simon 167
Green, Judith E. 21
Grimes, Tom 234–236
Guardian Masterclasses 188, 204–205
Gueorguieva, Elitza 222–223

Haas, Robert 42, 44, 48, 52–55, 58–59
Halliwell, Martin 243
Hampton, Christopher 185
Harper, Graeme 9
Harris, Peter 139
Harris, Wilson 166
Harry Ransom Center (University of Texas) 5, 110, 121, 140, 178, 191–195
Harvard, University 2, 11, 31, 66–67
Haslinger, Josef 216–220
Hawkins, Paula 242
Heinich, Nathalie 225
Hemingway, Ernest 3, 23, 38, 41, 47, 69, 141, 155–156, 233–234
Henfield Writing Fellowship 136, 138–139, 153–154, 163–168
Heng, Rachel 208–209
Hicks, Granville 121–123

Hirsch, Fred 231
Hoggart, Richard 167
Holeywell, Kathryn 129, 131, 134
Hornex, Colin J. 132
Houdart-Merot, Violet 8, 225
Houellebecq, Michel 4
Hudson, Havelock 200
Hughes, Ted 185, 197–198, 200, 208
Hunter College, New York 228

Indiana, University 4, 70, 131–132, 135
Ink Academy 204, 211–215
Institute of German Literature (DLL) 216–220
Institut für Literatur 217
institutional outsider, paradox of 247
International Writing Program (IWP) 39–40, 72, 216–217, 247
Iowa, University of
 Angus Wilson papers 162
 British writers at 151
 Flannery O'Connor, and 53, 91
 Iowa literary scene (1920s–early 1930s), and 24–31
 Paul Engle's career at 22–23, 31, 125, 136
 Paul Engle's international ambitions for 15, 34–40
 'Program Era,' and 7
 Rockefeller Foundation, and 94
 studies of 7–8
 Wallace Stegner, and 63, 74
Iowa Writers' Workshop
 beginning of 1–3, 6
 Faber Academy, and 208
 Flannery O'Connor, and 53
 Frank Conroy's leadership 235
 Institute of German Literature compared 219
 length of programme 47
 marginalization of women writers 2–3, 243
 Paul Engle's international ambitions for 38–39, 41
 Paul Engle's leadership of 14–15, 85, 125, 136, 246
 Paul Engle's leadership reappraised 21–24
 Random House Fiction Fellowship, and 48–51
 separation from University literature department 1, 159
 studies of 7–8
 see also Engle, Paul
Irwin, Thomas L. 24, 27
Ishiguro, Kazuo
 Anglo-Japanese dichotomy 180–183
 archive at University of Texas 9, 191–196

266 INDEX

Ishiguro, Kazuo (*Continued*)
  Booker Prize 167, 240
  Bret Easton Ellis compared 238
  celebrity to canonical writer 188–191
  Faber Academy, and 183–188
  Ian McEwan, and 175, 181, 185, 186, 196
  Malcolm Bradbury, and 144–147
  Nobel banquet speech 179
  Nobel Prize for Literature 8, 16
  originality 180
  Paul Engle compared 181
  Robert McCrum, and 239–240
  significance of Nobel Prize award 175–178
  UEA, at 3, 131, 138, 141, 143–147, 183–188, 238, 246
IWP, *see* International Writing Program

Jacobson, Dan 76, 151–152, 154, 157–158
Jaillant, Lise 5, 168, 246–247
James, E.L. 242
Jameson, Fredric 7
Johnson, Samuel 109
Jonathan Cape 32, 187
Jones, Richard Foster 62, 71
Joyce, James 23, 38, 111 112, 118, 207, 235

Kafka, Franz 182
Kawabata, Yasunari 180
Keats, John 14
Kemp, Marina 211–213
Kennedy, Arthur G. 67, 68, 70
Kenyon College 86, 94, 99, 244
Kenyon Review 13, 15, 47, 86, 88–90, 93–94
Keyser, Catherine 156
Kingston, University 229
Kleinzahler, August 229–230, 232, 244
Knights, Ben 14
Knopf, Alfred 234
Kunitz, Stanley 97, 99
Kureishi, Hanif 229–232, 244
Kurella, Alfred 217

Lancaster, University 5, 129–131, 169, 198
Leavis, F. R. 4, 90
Lee, Harper 242
Leggett, Jack 2–3
Leipzig Institute of German Literature 216–217
Leipzig, University of 216
Lessing, Doris 180, 194
Levy, Andrew 28
Lewis, Philip 221
Lewis, Sinclair 13, 93

Lewis, Wyndham 234
Limongi, Laure 226
Literary Consultancy, *see* TLC (The Literary Consultancy)
'literary rebel' image 4, 141, 218–220, 231, 237, 245
literature departments
  decline 6
  healing of breach between writers and scholars 242–245
  institutional outsider, parodox of 247
  rejection of freedom-outside-academia idea 229
  relationship between academics and creative writers within 1
  separation by creative writing programmes from 1, 10–14
  see also creative writing programmes
Literature Institute Maxim Gorky, Moscow 217
Literature Institute [Schweizerisches Literaturinstitut] 216
Lloyd-Jones, Richard 39
Lodge, David 4, 81, 129, 131, 135–136, 140, 147, 151, 153, 166–167, 218, 240
Loest, Erich 217
Long, Elizabeth 239
Lopez, David 222–223
Louisiana State University 12–13
Lowell, Robert 13, 97–99, 103
Lowry, W. McNeil 72
Lyon, Janet 22
Lyotard, Jean-François 221

Macdonald, Dwight 155–156
MacKaye, Percy 152
Manchester, University of 153–154, 167–169, 195
Mansfield, Katherine 69
Marcus Aurelius 245
Marlowe, Dan J. 116
Marshall, John 86–89, 91–92, 94–97
Marvell, Andrew 161
Masscult and Midcult 155–156
Matthews, Sean 192
Maule, Harry 48, 51
Maurer, Georg 217
Maxwell, Baldwin 30, 37
Mayer, Peter 139
Mayer, Tom 81
McCarthy, Cormac 84, 101–102, 104
McCarthy, Mary 102, 155–156, 159
McConnell, Suzanne 3
McCrum, Robert 185–187, 239

McDonald, Gail 11
McEwan, Ian
  Amazing magazine, and 164–165
  archive at University of Texas 5, 9, 192, 193, 194, 195
  Kazuo Ishiguro, and 175, 181, 185, 186, 196
  'radical individualism model,' and 237–238
  UEA, at 3, 6, 8, 129–130, 131, 132, 137–147, 149, 205, 240, 246
McGinniss, Joe 238
McGrath, Charles 7
McGrath, Earl 37
McGurl, Mark 7–8, 21, 47, 53, 58, 152, 220
McKenzie, D.F. 43
McNeil, Helen 147
Menand, Louis 7
Mencken, H. L. 26, 28
Merlin-Kajman, Hélène 225–226
Miami University in Ohio 152
Mills, Paul 169
Mills, C. Wright 98
Mims, Edwin 11–12
Minnesota, University of 14, 67, 134
Mirrielees, Edith 68–70
Mitchell, Julian 185
Mitford, Jessica 106–107, 111, 113–115, 119–120, 124
Moat, John 197–200
modernist roots of creative writing programmes 11–14
Modiano, Patrick 176
Moggach, Lotttie 200
Mooney, Bel 187
Moretti, Franco 43
Morgan, David 139, 141
Morrison, Theodore 1, 65–67, 71, 75
Mo, Timothy 181
Mott, Frank Luther 29, 34
music departments, creative writing programmes compared 10
Myers, D. G. 7, 30, 152

Nebout, Elise 226
Newcastle University MA in Writing Poetry 204
New Criticism 10–11, 23, 73, 84, 94–95, 132, 155, 156
New Critics 10–11, 13, 15, 23, 85, 92, 94, 133
New Humanism 29
Nobel Peace Prize 39
Nobel Prize for Literature
  age range of winners 175
  American laureates 55–56, 177, 187
  British laureates 8, 16, 175, 194
  controversial awards 177–178
  diversity of winners 178–183
  European laureates 176, 177, 188
  European model of literary production, and 16, 176, 177
  marginalization of women writers 175
  women laureates 179, 194
  see also Ishiguro, Kazuo
Nobel Prize for Medicine 110
Nobel Prize for Physics 82
Nussbaum, Albert F. 115–116

O'Brien, Edward J. 26–28
O'Connor, Flannery 8–9, 15, 43, 53, 57, 91, 95
Olivet College, Michigan 13
Ong, Walter 239
Orwell, George 163
Oulipo 223
Oxford, University of 10, 32, 75, 162, 168, 174

Page, Stephen 207
Paris, *see* France
Paris 8 Vincennes Saint-Denis, University of 8, 216–217, 220–223, 225
Petersen, Kristelle 124
Piper, Edwin Ford 23, 25–26, 29, 30–31
Pittsburgh, University of 25
Plato 29–30
poet-in-residence, *see* writer-in-residence
Poetry School 203–204
Porter, Katherine Ann 13, 95–96
Pound, Ezra 11, 24, 35, 67, 100, 132, 199, 234
Princeton, University 13, 67, 92, 94
'Program Era'
  American writers and 7
  British writers and 175
  creative writing programmes and 21, 220
  women writers and 243
Proust, Marcel 23, 183
Pryce-Jones, David 160
publishing industry change, impact of 238–242

Queneau, Raymond 223
Quinn, Mary Ann 84, 97, 102

Random House 41–42, 48–51, 53, 101–102, 113, 187, 243
Ransom, Harry Huntt 192
Ransom, John Crowe 11–12, 47, 71, 86, 92, 94–95, 132
Ratcliff, J. D. 109–110
Reeves, Gareth 168
Reigelman, Milton Monroe 26–27, 34

Riesman, David 98–99
Rockefeller Foundation (RF) 15, 63, 71–72, 84–86, 88–99, 101–105, 243
Rockwell, Norman 108, 112
Rogers, Deborah 145, 185
Rose, Jonathan 9
Rosenthal, Olivia 222–223
Ross, Alan 138
Roth, Philip 84, 101–102, 235
Royle, Nicholas 10
Ruffel, Lionel 221–222
Rushdie, Salman 81, 181, 186

Sage, Lorna 134
Sage, Victor 6, 134–135, 139–141
Sandburg, Carl 13, 27
Sanderson, Michael 149
Sansom, William 170
Sapiro, Gisèle 225–226
Saxon poetry school [Sächsische Dichterschule], former East Germany 217
Schädlich, Hans-Joachim 217
Schmidt, Michael 153, 168–169, 195, 204
School of Poetry' [Schule für Dichtung] 216
schools
   comprehensive school system, expansion of 16, 153
   progressive educational ideas 16, 151, 153, 198
   writer-in-residence programmes 153, 169
Schramm, Wilbur 21, 23–24, 29, 30–31, 62, 64–66, 71–72, 77
Schwartz, Delmore 67
Schwartz, Lawrence 43, 89
Scottish Arts Council 153
Scowcroft, Richard 2, 73
Seashore, Carl 25, 30
Self, Will 241, 244
Shakespeare, William 42, 191
Shaw, Christina 147
Shaw, Harry 70–71
Shelley, Percy Bysshe 14
Shelton, Richard 243
Short, Robert Stuart 164–165
Shriver, Lionel 228–229, 231, 242
Shute, Jenefer 228–232, 242, 244
Sigmund, Jay G. 27–28, 35
Sinclair, Clive 131, 138–139, 143, 145
Smith, Lillian 48
Snelling, Steve 146
So, Richard Jean 8, 227
Sorrentino, Gilbert 62
Spender, Stephen 146

Stanford University 2, 67–72, 76–77, 80–81, 82, 151
Stanford Writing Program 75, 236, 243
Stegner, Mary 58, 75
Stegner, Wallace 9, 41, 243–244
   continuing influence 231
   Dan Jacobson, and 152
   early career 64–67
   leadership of creative writing programme 67–77
   lower middle-class background 2
   marginalization during 1960s and 70s 78–79, 247
   Paul Engle, and 92
   'radical individualism' model, and 236–238
   significance of career 60–64
   Stanford University, at 2, 58
   writer-scholar gap, and 15, 80–83
Steinbeck, John 68–69
Stein, Gertrude 13, 35, 57, 112, 233–234
'Stepford Writers' 6
Steward, John 78
St John Dizzard, Cyril 172
Stone, Robert 180
Stoppard, Tom 185
Story, Jack Trevor 16, 151, 170–172, 174
Stover, Justin 232
Strychacz, Thomas 10
Swift, Rebecca 202–, 211

Tate, Allen 11–14, 47, 67, 132
Taylor, D.J. 131, 157
Tennyson, Alfred 11, 161
Texas, University of 5, 9, 121, 140, 178, 191–196
The Midland 23–29
Thistlethwaite, Frank 134, 161
Thompson, Andrew 147
Thwaite, Anthony 139, 141, 166–167, 186
Tiempo, Edilberto 38–39
TLC (The Literary Consultancy) 202–203, 211–213
Tremain, Rose 131, 138, 142–143, 147, 149, 163, 239–240
True, Michael 14
Turner, E.S. 173

United Kingdom
   comprehensive school system, expansion of 16, 153
   progressive educational ideas 16, 151, 153, 198
   publishing industry change, impact of 238–242

school-based writer-in-residence
  programmes 153, 170
  see also Arts Council; British Universities;
  British writers; writer-in-residence
universities
  response to rise of creative writing
    programmes 7
  writers' ambivalent attitudes towards
    academia 1, 228–245
  see also American Universities; British
  Universities; creative writing programmes;
  literature departments; writer-in-residence
US Association of Writers & Writing
  Programs 10
Utah, University of 2, 64, 81, 236

Vanderbilt University 11–12
Van Duyn, Janet 120
Vienna, University for Applied Arts in 216

Walker, Michael 170
Wallace, David Foster 244
Wandor, Michelene 9, 131, 152–153
Warren, Robert Penn 11–12, 47, 92
Watson, S. J. 206
Watt, Ian 134, 160–161, 163
Weber, Max 21
White, Eric W. 170–171
Whiteside, Thomas 238
Whyte, William 98–99, 235
Wilbers, Stephen 3, 7, 23, 29, 31
Wilding, Michael 8
Williams, Joan 55
Wilson, Angus
  Alan Burns, and 164
  first British writer-in-residence 134, 136,
    153–154, 157, 160–163, 166, 170, 198
  founds first British graduate creative writing
    programme at UEA 3, 125, 129, 149
  Ian McEwan, and 137, 138–142, 149, 237
  Rose Tremain, and 239, 240
Wilson, Sloan 108
Winsor, Kathleen 239
Winters, Yvor 80–81, 238
Wisconsin, University of 64, 66, 82
Wolfe, Tom 6
women writers
  feminization of creative writing
    programmes 242
  marginalization of 2–3, 175, 179, 243
  Nobel laureates 178, 194
  'Program Era,' and 243
  publishing industry change, impact of 242

Wood, Grant 30–31, 34–38
Wood, James 176, 179–180
Woolf, Virginia 4, 69, 120, 192–193, 207
Wright, Tom 153
writer-in-residence
  advantages in funding of 152
  American model 16, 151–152, 153, 154–162,
    167–168, 174
  Arts Council funding 16, 151, 169–174
  autonomy 16, 151
  British emergence, lack of previous studies
    on 152
  definitional uncertainties 151, 161, 164
  definitions of 151
  excellence and selection model 153–154, 174
  first instance in Britain 160–163
  first instance of 152
  Henfield Fellowship (UEA) 163–167
  media responses 151, 154–155, 163–164
  Poetry Centre (Manchester Univ.) 167–169
  progressive educational model 16, 151, 153,
    154, 174
  school-based programmes 153, 170
  university-based programmes 152–153
  work of 16, 151
  writers who are or were 16, 55, 151–152, 153,
    156, 160, 163, 166–168, 172–173, 176
writers
  alternative sources of income 241
  ambivalent attitudes towards academia 1,
    228–245
  barriers to achievement of freedom, money,
    and celebrity 240–241
  'creative writing programme' (Iowa) model of
    training (Model no. 2) 229, 233, 235–236,
    238
  creative writing programmes as 'writer
    factories' 1, 16, 196
  healing of breach between writers and
    scholars 242–245
  'informal mentorship' model of training
    (Model no. 1) 229, 233–235, 246–247
  institutional outsider, paradox of 247
  'literary rebel' image 4, 141, 218, 218–220,
    231, 237, 245
  lower middle-class backgrounds 2
  models of training 229–235
  Nobel laureates 177–180, 187, 188, 194
  non-recognition by academia 1
  'radical individualism' ('literary rebel') model
    of training (Model no. 3) 230–231, 233,
    236–240, 242–245
  'writer factories,' as 1

writers (*Continued*)
  see also American writers; British writers; creative writing programmes; women writers; writer-in-residence
Wylder, Jean 25

Yale, University of 12
Yale University Press 31
Yeats, W.B. 14, 23, 38

Zola, Emile 6